Also by Steve Kluger

Fiction
Changing Pitches

Nonfiction
Lawyers Say the Darndest Things

Stage Plays
Bullpen
Cafe 50's
Pilots of the Purple Twilight

Screenplays
Almost Like Being in Love
Glory Days
Over My Dead Body

YANK
THE ARMY WEEKLY

WORLD WAR II FROM THE GUYS
WHO BROUGHT YOU VICTORY

Irwin Shaw ★ William Saroyan ★ Andy Rooney
Walter Bernstein ★ Merle Miller
The Original "Sad Sack" Cartoons of George Baker
and
Other Treasures from YANK's Soldier-Contributors

STEVE KLUGER

ST. MARTIN'S PRESS ✪ NEW YORK

Dedicated to

KILROY

—and to the 14,216,097 dogfaces, swabbies, leathernecks, airhogs, crate pushers, and Seabees who fought beside him

Editor: Jared Kieling
Design by Robert Bull Design

Library of Congress Cataloging-in-Publication Data

Kluger, Steve.
    Yank : World War II from the guys who brought you victory / by Steve Kluger.
      p.   cm.
    ISBN 0-312-04675-8
    1. World War, 1939–1945—United States. 2. United States. Army—History—World War, 1939–1945. 3. Soldiers—United States—History—20th century. I. Title.
D769.2.K58   1990
940.54'1273—dc20   90-37306
                              CIP

First Edition
10 9 8 7 6 5 4 3 2 1

★

_____

The hurdy-gurdies, the birdies,
The cop on the beat,
The candy-maker, the baker,
The man on the street,
The city charmer, the farmer,
The man in the moon,
All sing Elmer's Tune.

—Glenn Miller and
the Modernaires

Cafe Rouge
November 22, 1941

CONTENTS

★

ACKNOWLEDGMENTS

I WISH to express my deepest thanks to Col. Charles G. Cavanaugh and Normand Lussier of the Department of Defense, who said yes to everything without resorting to any red tape whatsoever; former GIs Edgar A. Rosen (U.S. Cavalry) and Loyal C. Pulley (Army Air Corps), who remembered it well; Chris and Paul at Chic-A-Boom in Hollywood, who turned up the first batch of *Yank* magazines and who also own an original "V for Victory/Deposit Scrap Metal Here" collection bin; Rose Blaz at The Bookie Joint in Encino, who managed to locate all of the British editions of *Yank* without having to make more than one telephone call; Elinor La Fontaine at The Word Shop, who downloaded software fonts faster than the material could be typed; and Patrick, Corrine, and Norman Lobo, who never so much as flinched when I said things to them like "It's just a thousand pages, and I only need twenty copies . . . Bound . . . By tomorrow." Special thanks also to Bill Mauldin, who didn't think I was being obsequious when I told him he's been a hero of mine for most of my life; to Jared Kieling at St. Martin's Press, who agreed to publish the book quicker than it takes most people to order a shrimp salad sandwich; to Frances Goldin, the most energetic agent in the world, who on her 65th birthday advised her clients that she was cutting her workweek back to sixty hours; and most of all to Sydelle Kramer, who read the original proposal and said, "I think you've got something here. Now, this is what I want you to do."

World War II was a collaborative effort. So was this book.

—Steve Kluger

AUTHOR'S NOTE

MOTION PICTURES had come of age, newspaper and magazine circulation had expanded to global proportions, and radio had established itself as the nucleus around which most families revolved. World War II was the first "media" war; its GIs packed pens, typewriters, and Brownies along with their 1903 Springfields and K-bar knives—determined, like a million khaki-clad Hemingways, that the story would unfold accurately. And with all deliberate speed. When Gen. Patton slapped an unfortunate private in Europe, he was censured in lunchrooms all across Seattle. When Allied infantry broke through the German lines at Anzio, grocers in Cleveland knew about it before the foot soldiers themselves did. And when six men raised a flag over a Pacific island on a Friday afternoon in 1945, the photographic evidence was on the front page of *The New York Times* Sunday morning. With all deliberate speed—lest we forget.

Fifty years have passed since the outbreak of the Second World War, and what we are left with is a kaleidoscope of impressions stamped upon time—in celluloid, in newsprint, and on vinyl. Some of them are outrageous, such as Madison Avenue's claim that flea powder was winning the war; some of them are self-indulgent, such as the Hollywood sergeant who always seemed to be saying things like, "There ain't no atheists in foxholes, son"; and some of them are the real McCoy, such as the corporal who fled Corregidor with Douglas MacArthur, convinced he'd never forget it as long as he lived, then realized two decades later that the thing he really remembered about 1942 was Jimmy Cagney singing "Harrigan." Even in war, nothing strains credibility like the truth. And though many of the more poignant observations contained in these pages and elsewhere were attributed by the press to anonymous sources— "one tired dogface" or "a squad of scruffy-looking Marines"—their words, like Kilroy's, remain scribbled forever on the walls of history. . . .

"Joe, yestidday ya saved my life an' I swore I'd pay ya back. Here's my last pair of dry socks."

INTRODUCTION

If our correspondent survives, we have a story. If he doesn't, we have a casualty.
—Sgt. JOE McCARTHY
Yank editor

THEY CAME from all over. From Painted Post, New York, and Scott City, Kansas, and Comanche, Texas, and Brunswick, Maine. From Spokane, Washington, and Broken Arrow, Oklahoma, and Pawtucket, Rhode Island, and Wakefield, Massachusetts. From Bel Air, California, where they'd taken their first faltering steps holding a nippled bottle in one hand and an imported French rattle in the other, to Pigeon Forge, Tennessee, where they drank Kickapoo Joy Juice and couldn't read past "A." From Fairmount, Indiana, where they baked homemade bread and attended Quaker services every sabbath, to Flatbush Avenue near Bedford and Sullivan, where they'd been weaned on Nathan's hot dogs and orange pop, and where they'd learned at a very early age that religion was looking up at the sky and saying things like "Hail Mary, full of grace, please don't let Lavagetto hit into a double play."

Together they comprised the last bunch of guys who went to war willingly, who abdicated youth for loyalty, puppy love for national pride, and home cooking for stuff that came in a tin and was indistinguishable in every way from camouflage paint. Yet they embraced it wholeheartedly and went nonetheless; by whatever means and down whatever roads would take them there, lying about their ages and memorizing eye charts in advance, the same way they'd only yesterday memorized the fundamentals of plane geometry, so that the medics wouldn't discover how nearsighted they really were. Or how undernourished. Gangly arms hung alongside Depression-stunted legs, and underdeveloped chests were incongruously flanked by biceps the size of basketballs. Nobody had to tell these guys that life was tough. They'd already figured that out.

Some of them actually knew what they were doing. The lucky ones didn't. Harlon Block had been raising hell in Weslaco, Texas, when the Japanese Zeros made their first passes over Hickam Field; lack of prescience alone left him happily unaware that, at some point during whatever future he had left, the only raising in which he was likely to participate involved a flag, five buddies, the 28th Marines, an astute photographer, and bronzed immortality on the banks of the Potomac River. Had he been blessed with such extrasensory insights, he might never have come out from under his bed. And even if he had, it is doubtful that he would have been accorded much in the way of genuine sympathy by Charles Graves, a conscientious young man of conservative sensibilities who had seen the handwriting on the wall as early as the Anschluss in 1938. Being pragmatic as well as conscientious (a thoughtful combination, especially then), Chuck joined up while he still had a choice, figuring he'd serve his hitch and get the hell out before any real trouble started. It almost worked. He was due to be discharged on December 10, 1941. If bluer prosaism was ever shot out of a purpler face, it was neither recorded for posterity nor survived by the living. Then there was 19-year-old Bill Mauldin, an aspiring artist first and a flat-broke aspiring artist second, who had enlisted in 1940 because he'd run out of pencils. Insofar as military protocol was concerned, he didn't know his ass from a barracks bag. Yet, in time, his brutally sensitive Willie and Joe cartoons would give names and faces to an entire generation of incandescent young men who didn't love war, but who fought as if they did.

In May of 1942, *Yank*, the GI weekly, was first published "by the men. . . . for the men in the service." Its rules were simple and direct—if you had dogtags and a nickel (or $2 for a year), you were in. If not? Forget it, Charley—read *Newsweek*. Initially the top brass dismissed it as another self-indulgent noncom rag catering to a bunch of homesick kids, an assessment they might have been inclined to reevaluate had they invited a psychic to analyze the bylines: Andy Rooney was still calling himself Andrew in those days; Walter Bernstein was only then beginning to fancy himself a screenwriter, two decades before *Fail Safe* and half that many before Joseph McCarthy and the House Un-American Activities Committee would try to change his mind; Irwin Shaw was recording his impressions daily, only to revive them collectively as *The Young Lions*; William Saroyan, getting as much mileage out of a title as circumstance and Hitler would allow, was doubtless convincing his foxhole buddies that this was the time of their lives; and Bill Mauldin, oblivious to the Pulitzer that would put him on the map by the age of 23, was just as blind to the fact that one day, a generation hence, the phrases "by Mauldin" and "cardiac arrest" would come to be regarded as synonymous on Capitol Hill.

Originally intended as a morale builder at a time when MacArthur was desperately attempting to salvage something akin to confidence out of the shambles of Corregidor and Bataan, *Yank*'s popularity was both instantaneous and overwhelming; possibly because it was well written, possibly because its pinups merited the Army-Navy "E" for Excellence; and probably because in its pages a private felt free to express his innermost thoughts without fear of reprisal, particularly if he called himself "Name Withheld." 'Cause boy, did they gripe. From Anzio to Biak, from Port Moresby to Algiers, from Iron Bottom Sound to the Huertgen Forest, the enlisted men finally had a chance to tell *their* side of the story, just the way it was happening. With humor. With honesty. With integrity. And whether Patton liked it or not. Perhaps their manners left something to be desired —the world, after all, was a vastly different place then, and words like "Nip," "dago," and "kraut" were not without their considerable rhetoric. That is, until they pulled cleanup on Tarawa and found

out that a dead American body smells just as bad as a dead Japanese one. Or until they watched a German soldier of eighteen lose most of his face without uttering a sound, and it hit them all of a sudden that everybody bleeds the same. Only they weren't likely to tell things like that to the chaplain. They told them instead to *Yank*.

They had their heroes, sure. Bobby Feller was one of them, Joltin' Joe another. The rest fluctuated along with their moods: Gary Cooper when they first got their guns, John Wayne when they learned how to work the triggers, Betty Grable and Lana Turner when they were feeling sexy (which wasn't as often as you'd think—it's difficult to maintain passion when you're staring down a Krupp 88 or dodging a Mitsubishi), President Roosevelt when they were scared, and Eleanor when they were lonely or maybe a little homesick and just needed to be tucked in. But mostly their heroes were themselves. As Bill Mauldin observed:

"Just gimme a coupla aspirin. I awready got a Purple Heart."

"This damn tree leaks."

"Beautiful view. Is there one for the enlisted men?"

"I wish I could stand up and get some sleep."

They knew enough to be cynical, but enough not to quit.

In the end, it all came down to the unforgettable prose of Ernie Pyle, who always suspected his luck would give out before Axis ammunition did; and who, when that happened, on an unjustly unremarkable little island called Ie Shima, became his own last column. Pyle had long since warned his readers, "This is *your* war"—and in so doing had inadvertently evoked the words of Alexander Hamilton a century and a half earlier. Hamilton, at the Constitutional Convention, had presaged America's role as a future world power when he stated, with less equanimity perhaps than blind faith, "It belongs to us to vindicate the honor of the human race."

Well, these were the men who pulled it off.

—S. K.

1941

PERFIDIA

WE WERE A COUNTRY preoccupied with enjoying ourselves—the Depression was over, Whirlaway had won the Triple Crown, Alexander Fleming had found something called penicillin growing in a petri dish, and Glenn Miller's orchestra was playing for a whole month at the Glen Island Casino, just outside New York City. Steaks at the Pig 'n' Whistle still cost only $1.65, Bogey and Peter Lorre haggled over a Maltese falcon, and jukeboxes favored "Bewitched, Bothered and Bewildered" over that recent God-blessing-America nonsense by Irving Berlin, who clearly had hit bottom in search of another "Blue Skies." Some even preferred "The White Cliffs of Dover," but that, of course, was a war song that belonged over there.

The United States, for the first time since 1865, found itself a nation divided. There were those, like an unusually outspoken Charles Lindbergh, who thought that we should mind our own business and keep our noses out of foreign affairs. These were called America Firsters, isolationists, and Mothers Against the Draft (MAD). There were others who believed just as vehemently that the blitz on London was the same thing as a blitz on Washington, and likewise demanded a full retaliatory response. These were called interventionists and New Dealers. Roosevelt, however, had his hands tied by a conservative Congress that would not grant him the power to wage war, and so he was able to do no more than bait Hitler, by degrees—for Roosevelt, like so many others, knew that hostilities were inevitable. Thus, Executive Order No. 1776, also known as the Lend-Lease Act, became the first step in a minuet calculated to provoke the erratic German chancellor into making the first move. When that failed, FDR pledged unrestricted naval protection to all British ships in neutral territorial waters. An enterprising reporter inquired, "Sir, does that extend to the Rhine?" The president replied, "If necessary." The undeclared war in the Atlantic was on.

Unfortunately for Roosevelt, Hitler chose that particular moment to behave rationally. Adhering, for once, to the advice of Herman Göring and his other advisors, all of whom implored him not to antagonize the United States, the little house painter from Austria held his tongue, at least for the moment. Vengeance could always be exacted later, he knew—and he already suspected that such retribution would be carrying a Rising Sun on its wings.

Roosevelt did not. To all outward appearances, the war in Europe was the only war. What he still lacked was an event that would galvanize the people of his country into taking some kind of a unified stand. But without Hitler's cooperation, without some new and significant atrocity from the Third Reich to spark it all, it would require a calamity of such deliberately treacherous proportions that the possibility was not even worth considering.

MAJOR BATTLES:
Dodgers vs. Giants, Dodgers vs. Yanks, "Fibber McGee and Molly" vs. "The Burns and Allen Show"

HOLLYWOOD'S BEST:
Citizen Kane (Orson Welles)

HOLLYWOOD'S WORST:
Lady Scarface (Judith Anderson)

HOLLYWOOD'S SILLIEST TITLE:
You're in the Army Now

MOST POPULAR WAR SONG:
"What war?"

MOST POPULAR SONG—GENERAL:
"When You Wish Upon a Star"

LEAST POPULAR SONG—GENERAL:
"God Bless America"

MOST READ BOOK:
The G-String Murders, by Gypsy Rose Lee

LEAST HEEDED AMERICAN PROPHET:
Woody Guthrie: "Did you have a friend on the good Reuben James?"

MOST FATHOMABLE CRAZE:
Signing up with "America First"

LEAST FATHOMABLE CRAZE:
Signing up with the U.S. Navy

WHAT YOU SAID TO AN AMERICAN OF JAPANESE DESCENT:
"Two pounds of oranges and four tomatoes, please."

WHAT YOU CALLED A BLACK CORPORAL WITH THREE PURPLE HEARTS:
Fiction

BEST VALUE FOR YOUR DOLLAR:
Jitterbug records

BEST ANNIVERSARY PRESENT FOR MOM AND POP:
A General Electric toaster

WHAT YOU GOT WHEN YOU TRADED TWO STEELIES AND AN AGGIE:
Disappointed. *Every*body had two steelies and an aggie.

MOST ADMIRED AMERICAN FEMALE:
Veronica Lake

MOST ADMIRED AMERICAN MALE:
Lou Gehrig

MOST UNFORTUNATE ACRONYM:
Commander-in-chief, U.S. Pacific Fleet— CINCUS

THE DATE YOU FINALLY GOT TO SIT ON THE FIFTY FOR A REDSKINS GAME:
Sunday, December 7

WHAT THE SCORE LOOKED LIKE BY THE FOURTH QUARTER:
A long haul. . . .

Port of embarkation (POE) was a brief stopover between boot camp and the real thing; a place where you left all of your nonessentials behind, including—regrettably—your youth.

STAGING AREA

—Pvt. ALAN SURGAL
Sketches by Sgt. Howard J. Brodie
June 9, 1944

A T A Port of Embarkation Staging Camp—It is 0700. You hitch your field bag forward where it cuts into your shoulders and stumble stiffly out of the curtained coach, still wiping the hot, dusty sleep from your eyes.

You stare at the vast cindered expanse, and a squadron of butterflies spills into a soft-shoe power dive in your stomach.

You stand nervously waiting for directions, and they're not long in coming.

"Troops will form at the rear of the train in a column of threes," booms a bodyless voice through an invisible amplifier.

You scramble to obey, and the butterflies level off a little.

You look at your buddy, Florida, and he grins back at you. You start to say something, but the voice without a body breaks in again.

"You are now at a classified address," it explains. "You will send no letters or telegrams, and you will not be permitted to telephone until you have specific instructions."

Censorship! You've heard about it, and now it's here. You feel a momentary exhilaration and then a sudden isolation. You think of a dozen messages that suddenly seem desperately urgent, but you can't send them. Not for the duration and six you can't.

Even Florida is quiet.

Then for the first time you notice your officers, especially your platoon commander. Dressed in regulation GIs, scuffing his unpolished combat shoes on the cindered siding, he looks inches smaller than in his tailored pinks. And a lot more nervous. You're suddenly liking him better than you ever have before.

He steps back, bawls "Battery atten-tion!" and you stiffen into position.

"Forward march!"

The morning echoes abruptly with the cadenced crunch of GI shoes on cinder. Somewhere in the rear a band strikes up, and you're off to your last camp in the States.

It is 0900.

You're in your barracks now, and you're snatching a little bunk fatigue. You've captured yourself a lower and Florida is on top.

At first you both waited uneasily for someone to bark you out into some detail or formation, but no one has and it doesn't look as if anybody intends

to. So you've settled yourself comfortably, and you're quietly thinking.

"Wonder where we're going from here, Florida?" you ask idly.

"Wonder if they give any passes?" he says, completely ignoring your question.

You notice a name carved on the board above your head.

"Pfc. C. E. Hollis," you read aloud.

"I wonder what Pfc. Hollis is doing right now," you add meditatively.

"Don't get corny," Florida replies.

You settle back again with your thoughts, but after a moment they're sharply interrupted by the staccato bark of your platoon sergeant.

"Okay, boys! Off and on! Hit the deck!"

"What is it this time?" you ask, propping yourself on your elbow.

"Show-down inspection."

"*Show-down* inspection?" you repeat incredulously. "Why, we had 12 of those at the other camp!"

"See the chaplain," snaps the sergeant.

You pause, transfixed, staring vacantly past him.

"Funny," you think to yourself. "That's not a bad idea—now."

It is 1300.

You've had your clothing inspection, and you're on your way back from chow.

By now you've looked over the camp, and you're impressed most by its impermanence. Not the buildings so much, though even they seem less stable than the ones at the other camps. Mostly it's the people.

Ever since you knew for certain that you were going overseas, you've somehow resented the cadre at the other processing camps. Jaunty noncoms with colorful shoulder insignia preparing you for something they may never undergo themselves.

But here it's different. Here everybody seems to be going. Everybody's a transient. Here, literally, everybody is in the same boat. And somehow it makes you feel a lot better.

It is 1500.

"Christ, Florida, did you ever see so many GIs in one place before?"

You're gathered in a huge commons for what they call a general orientation meeting. A saltwater bull session. All the GIs in the world seem to be here.

You listen politely through the speeches of the Army Emergency Relief officer and the Red Cross man, and you're impressed when the chaplain tells you to buddy up with God now and not to wait until you get foxhole religion.

But you're eagerly attentive when the Military Intelligence officer steps forward and starts to talk about "the boat."

The boat! It's been only a stabbing little flanking thought until now, but now it's ripped through to the front-center of your consciousness.

The MI officer is a breezy, good-humored fellow with a slight Bronx inflection, and you like him

immediately. He starts out by telling a few GI yarns right out of *Private Hargrove*, but you don't mind because he tells them well.

And when he begins to talk in earnest about the boat, you get the secure feeling that he's not reading from any prepared script. You listen closely, and you learn plenty.

You learn, for example, that you will mess only twice a day aboard ship; that water is scarce; that fire and panic are more dangerous than submarines. And, above all, you learn that the greatest menace to your safety is *you*. You and your big fat mouth.

You can see everybody's impressed.

You turn to Florida, who's looking unnaturally solemn.

"What's on your mind?" you ask sympathetically.

"Chow," he snaps without hesitation. "I'm hungry."

It is 2300.

"Lights out," and you're lying quietly in bed, thinking.

It's been a full evening, and you've written your first censored letter and made your first restricted telephone call. You've sneaked off for a lonesome walk in the nearby fields, drinking in your last few glimpses of American landscape, your last few draughts of American air. You've idled back to the barracks and continued guessing with the boys, trying to decide on your overseas destination. You've dropped a fast deuce in a friendly crap game, and before you know it, the evening's spent.

Now it's "lights out," and you're lying quietly in bed, thinking.

1942

MAKE-BELIEVE BALLROOM TIME

"**T**HEY STARTED IT, we'll finish it" became the most popular rallying cry since "Remember the Alamo." Yet, by mid-1942, it appeared to be a motto based less on fact than on feeble hope. The fleet had been wiped out at Honolulu, the United States had been caught completely off guard, and the Japanese—with deadly accuracy—had swept through the Philippines, Singapore, New Guinea, and Guam, establishing impenetrable barriers around every key Pacific base.

At home, the nation was off to a slow start. While the Pearl Harbor attack had effectively eliminated all talk of isolationism, America was nonetheless entirely unprepared for the exigencies of war. Typically, it was Tin Pan Alley that schooled the public in what had to be done. "We'll Knock the Japs Right into the Laps of the Nazis," "Put the Heat on Hitler, Muss Up Mussolini, and Tie a Can to Japan," "Let's Put the Axe to the Axis," and "You're a Sap, Mister Jap" were some of the earliest object lessons—not that anything was necessarily done with them. Hollywood, too, was learning how to get in its own two cents' worth: *To the Shores of Tripoli, Flying Fortress*, and *Wake Island* were among its better contributions; *Nazi Agent, Bombs Over Burma*, and *Little Tokyo USA* were not.

While Hitler was imprisoning most of the Jews in his Reich, something similar was occurring stateside. For reasons best known to a xenophobic Earl Warren and his California constituents, Roosevelt was advised that the nation's West Coast issei and nisei—first- and second-generation Japanese-Americans—posed a serious threat to the country's security ("Caps on Japanese Tomato Plants Point Toward Airbase!" announced the *Los Angeles Times* in early 1942). Either Roosevelt was too easily led or he simply was too preoccupied (he had, after all, only recently approved a top-secret defense appropriation to investigate the fissionable propensities of the uranium atom)—for on February 19 he signed into action Executive Order No. 9066, authorizing "military areas" from which "any and all persons" might be excluded, by order of the U.S. government. All major West Coast cities immediately were declared military areas from which any and all persons, coincidentally of Japanese descent, were indeed excluded. Their property and bank accounts were seized (rarely to be returned), and their families were separated. Most were sent to "relocation camps" in remote desert areas—principally Manzanar and Tule Lake, both in California—where they would remain for as long as three years. Not that the issei and nisei were the only victims of a heightened national racism: at certain Army camps across the country, white soldiers had adopted the practice of drinking to inebriation— generally on Saturday nights—then appropriating the communal Jeep, driving down to the "colored PX," and shooting any black soldier who happened to be in the vicinity. Prompted by Mrs. Roosevelt, the chief executive likewise found it necessary to implement the Fair Employment Practices Act to forbid discrimination in the hiring of blacks. Even with a war on they had been locked out of factories sorely in need of additional manpower.

   The first sunbeam in the military sky came in June of 1942, when the Nipponese forces at Midway were turned back by the U.S. Navy. Though at best the match was a tie, Adm. Isoroku Yamamoto— Japan's military genius—knew then that the war was over. Despite the fact that he himself had orchestrated the attack on Pearl Harbor, he had done so under duress, warning his warlords that the United States was a sleeping giant that should not be awakened at any cost. The Allied victory at Midway, coming so soon after the wholesale destruction of its Pacific Fleet, was Yamamoto's vindication. And he was the only one who had suspected it. Certainly the American people hadn't. For many the war was still a novelty, not to be taken seriously outside of ration stamps and nylon shortages. Awareness ultimately came in the form of a little island called Guadalcanal, site of the first U.S. offensive in the Pacific theater. Initially, the August 7 invasion seemed to be a repeat of Corregidor; the Marines were clearly outnumbered, and flight—once again—appeared to be the only viable alternative. But these guys just wouldn't give up. Even President Roosevelt was impressed, although there was precious little he could do to assist them; committed as he was to an Atlantic-first battle plan, his few available troops were already in Europe, bombing Rouen, invading Dieppe, and attempting to establish a toehold in North Africa. And so the Marines on Guadalcanal had to do it by themselves, while the home front watched. And waited.

MAJOR BATTLES:
Bataan, Corregidor, Midway, Guadalcanal, Oran, El Alamein, Tobruk

HOLLYWOOD'S BEST:
Casablanca ("Here's looking at you, kid.")

HOLLYWOOD'S WORST:
The Devil with Hitler ("Mein Führer—there is a man here who says he is Satan.")

MOST POPULAR WAR SONG (nonracist):
"We Did It Before and We Can Do It Again"

MOST POPULAR WAR SONG (racist):
"Goodbye, Mama (I'm Off to Yokohama)"

MOST POPULAR SONG—GENERAL:
"God Bless America"

LEAST POPULAR SONG—GENERAL:
"Rockabye My Baby, There Ain't Gonna Be No War"

MOST READ BOOK:
See Here, Private Hargrove, by Sgt. Marion Hargrove

LEAST READ BROCHURE:
Germany for Tourists

MOST VALUABLE ITEM RATIONED:
Scrap rubber

LEAST VALUABLE ITEM RATIONED:
Lobster forks

MOST OVERRATED QUESTION:
"Don't you know there's a war on?"

LEAST OVERRATED QUESTION:
"Hey, soldier—buy you a drink?"

MOST FAMOUS THIRTY SECONDS:
Jimmy Doolittle's, over Tokyo

WHAT MADISON AVENUE SAID WAS SINKING U-BOATS IN THE ATLANTIC:
Westinghouse air conditioners

WHAT MADISON AVENUE SAID GENERAL ELECTRIC COULD MAKE BOMB INDICATOR LAMPS WITH:
A paring knife

WHERE MADISON AVENUE SAID FIGHTER PLANES CAME FROM:
Owens-Corning fiberglass kitchen ranges

MOST FATHOMABLE CRAZE:
Victory gardens

LEAST FATHOMABLE CRAZE:
Getting all the words right to "Flat-Foot Floogie With a Floy-Floy"

WHAT YOU SAID TO A GUY (EVEN IF YOU WERE ANOTHER GUY):
"What's cookin', good lookin'?"

WHAT YOU SAID TO A GAL:
"I do."

WHAT YOU SAID TO AN AMERICAN OF JAPANESE DESCENT:
Probably nothing, because he was locked up in a so-called relocation center along with the rest of his family

WHAT YOU CALLED A BLACK CORPORAL WITH THREE PURPLE HEARTS:
"One of Eleanor Roosevelt's niggers"

MOST PATRIOTIC WINDOW SIGN:
Lem Ah Toy Chinese Laundry, Seattle: GO TO WAR. CLOSED DURATION. WILL CLEAN SHIRTS AFTER CLEAN AXIS. THANK YOU.

BEST VALUE FOR YOUR DOLLAR:
War bonds

BEST ANNIVERSARY PRESENT FOR MOM AND POP:
War bonds

WHAT YOU GOT WHEN YOU TRADED TWO STEELIES AND AN AGGIE:
War bonds

MOST CREATIVE USE OF DER FUHRER'S NAME:
"When you ride alone, you ride with Hitler! Join a car-sharing club today!"

MOST FAMOUS GRIPE:
"Situation normal—all fucked up."

MOST FAMOUS RETORT:
"Tell it to the chaplain."

MOST ADMIRED AMERICAN FEMALE:
Eleanor Roosevelt

MOST ADMIRED AMERICAN MALE:
The GI

NPM 1516
2ØF2 183Ø ØF3 ØF4 Ø2FØ O
FROM: CINCPAC
ACTION: CINCLANT CINCAF OPNAV
AIR RAID PEARL HARBOR THIS IS NOT A DRILL

The Great Debate ends in flames at Pearl Harbor.

⭐

In December of 1937, the Japanese Navy "mistakenly" sunk the U.S. gunboat Panay. Though appropriate apologies were tendered, the American military nonetheless began arming itself for what many felt was inevitable.

HOW WAR CAME

—Sgt. JONATHAN KILBOURN
Various Editions, 1942

THE SOLDIERS, circling the days on the calendar, waiting for the year of training to end, made bunks, scrubbed floors, policed up cigarette butts, learned to say "sir," marched, read in the newspapers of civilians getting rich, sometimes shot guns, more often shot craps, learned much of soldiering and a little of war. They didn't have a lot of equipment. They told a story about a soldier on maneuvers who pointed a wooden gun at another soldier on a wooden cart and said: "Surrender." And the tanker in the wooden cart replied: "Surrender, hell! You're dead—you're standing on a spot marked 'mine.' "

For a long time Americans had been arguing: Should we aid the democracies, and if so, how much? Some people said we should mind our own business. Then Hitler sent his tanks into the Low Countries and across France, piling the British into the sea on a beat-up piece of beach named Dunkirk. It was all over in six weeks. France was licked, and Hitler stood at the English Channel. Americans kept on arguing: Would England fall? Could Hitler cross the ocean? Was America's frontier on the Rhine, at the channel, or on a creek outside Poughkeepsie?

England stood; Hitler wheeled and attacked Russia. In China the Japs tightened their grip, gobbled more land. Americans geared, gabbed, and waited.

The Great Debate got hotter. There was a lot of name-calling. Men and women argued whether this was or wasn't our war, and quite a few people seemed to think the decision was up to them.

Newspaper reporters toured the sprawling new Army camps, ate officers' chow, drank officers' whiskey, rode in officers' station wagons, wrote that the morale of the enlisted trainees was bad.

Congress decided that selectees more than 28 years old were no longer needed in the Army.

On Sunday, Dec. 7, 1941, at Camp Jackson, South Carolina, in the barracks of I Company, 13th Infantry, 8th Division, Sgt. James McBride huddled over a table, writing a letter advising friends that he was to be discharged the next day because he was over 28.

A radio on the corner of the table was broadcasting dance music. The music stopped and an announcer came on the air. Pearl Harbor, he said, had been attacked by the Japs.

Sgt. McBride tore up his letter.

"I'm screwed," he said. And he added softly, "I'm screwed."

Three thousand three hundred and three Americans died at Pearl Harbor. The Great Debate had ended. The United States was in the war. People cried, prayed, made war jokes, bought war bonds, ate less butter, became air raid wardens. In Chicago someone wrote a note and pasted it on a slot

14

machine in a saloon: "In case of an air raid stand next to this machine because no one has ever hit it."

The Great Debate had ended, but the talk went on. People sat in cocktail lounges and well-stuffed clubrooms with heat coming out of radiators, drew tablecloth diagrams, and talked about where the United States should attack and on what front and in what formation, as if war were a football game.

People didn't talk about how a soldier's feet sometimes rot in the jungle or how to get rid of lice or how a dead man stinks in the desert sun. A lot of people seemed to think that soldiers were killers itching for a fight, not scared kids or scared fathers with kids of their own back home.

For the United States, war meant the beginning of a long retreat.

Finally at Corregidor there was only a little crowd of American soldiers and Filipino soldiers and American nurses at the beaches, with nothing at their backs but the waters of the Pacific, and the flag came down. Bataan and Corregidor became symbols, like Valley Forge.

It was a time of dedication, and some people wept. Some people put REMEMBER BATAAN posters on their cars and drove up to filling stations to buy black-market gas.

Burma fell. We were taking a beating. But we gained a breathing space by shellacking the Japanese Navy in the battles of the Coral Sea and Midway.

At home, the people's army was taking shape.

And then in the gray light of Aug. 7, 1942, Americans landed on a matted chunk of jungle 80 miles long and 25 miles wide. They fought there for a long time, and the rats got fat on American blood.

The United States had started the long march back at a place called Guadalcanal.

Bataan became a symbol, like Valley Forge.

MAIL CALL

Dear *Yank*:

Can anything be done about where they put us poor men on boats? I mean about sleeping on the way over and who you get above you and below you, to say nothing of on each side of you. It was bad enough in the barracks back in camp where I had two guys on each side of me snoring so that I thought someone was ripping branches off the trees all night long. But on the transport not only am I trying to sleep with even better snorers in the same clink, but they are seasick as well. Up and down, up and down. I can't even shut my own eyes, two lucky bimbos are snoring away like hell, and the rest of the mob is seasick all over the joint. What I want to know is, why can't they classify the snorers and the non-snorers, the guys who get seasick and the guys who don't?

We'll win this damn war, but I can't face that trip back.

—Pvt. Sam Shapiro
Ireland

Don't kick, Sam. You're lucky you had a berth to sleep in. But you have a fine point and we'll try to get to the undersecretary on sleeping conditions when our next messenger goes to Washington.

Dear *Yank*:

I wish you would do a story on what goes on in those G.I. laundries. Last week I sent two pairs of drawers, white cotton, to be washed. Yesterday I got back what looked like a parachute.

—Pvt. Joe Gazione
Somewhere in Ireland

Don't complain, brother. You never know when a parachute might come in a damned sight handier than two pairs of white drawers.

Dear *Yank*:

Before I went in the Army I had a girl in the Bronx, but now that I am in Hawaii I have a girl here, too. Lesser men might be stumped by this problem, but I fixed everything up fine. I wrote to my girl in the Bronx and said that though my girl in Hawaii is my War Girl, she is my Peace Girl. She thinks it's a fine idea, as she is a very self-sacrificing sort. I recommend this treatment to any other soldiers faced with the same problem.

—Cpl. Joe Grogan
Hawaii

Dear *Yank*:

Will you let me know in some future issue those three or four reasons why they call soldiers "dog-faces"? As I recall they were pretty good reasons—at least more adequate than the reason for referring to those of us in naval aviation as "airedales."

—ARM 2/c T. N. Aiken
U.S. Navy

We wear dog tags, sleep in pup tents, are chow hounds if heavy eaters, and come on the run when whistled at.

Dear *Yank*:

If *Yank* is going to be another of those corny Army papers with cartoons about rookies peeling potatoes and jokes about supply sergeants and top-kicks, you can cancel my subscription before I even subscribe. Before we left the United States it looked like all we ever saw about the Army was that sort of thing. And I for one do not want to be chased all over Northern Ireland by the same damned thing. What do you say about giving us a break?

—Sgt. Anthony J. Lavagetto
Somewhere in Ireland

We promise to do our best to keep the corn out. To us, the potato peeler and the supply sergeant have grown a little thin and none of our readers are rookies. We will step heavily on those antique stories and cartoons. Brother, you are among friends.

Dear *Yank*:
I wonder if you would consider printing a little something for a beat-up corporal in this one-sided war (which is being won by the Allies) that would probably bring results that writing has not done for me in the past eight years. You see, *Yank*, this guy was one of the best pals a guy could ever hope for, and to think that I may never see him again is worse than being in front of the Jap and German Air Force in a link trainer. I am enclosing a snapshot of myself and would like to have it put in the above mentioned column so that he might recognize it and decide to write to me. I also am sending my address along just in case.

The guy's name is Ted Byrley whose home is in High Point, N.C., and I met him going to Jamestown High School, N.C. By the way, my name is W. Morris Caudle which is of no importance.

Well, boys, I have got to git on that ole ball, so I will close. You are doing a grand job and keep it up while Hitler's mustache is being trimmed.
—Another *Yank*,
Bill
APO 825
New Orleans, Louisiana

Dear *Yank*:
There isn't anything down here but lizards. What I mean is that there isn't anything extra to listen to. We have a short wave that's pretty good, but there isn't enough of it. So we figured that you'd be willing to write Crosby and Allen, and maybe Benny, and tell them to talk louder or more often or something.
—Very truly yours,
T/Sgt. Mander Lunk
Somewhere in Australia

Don't worry. You'll be getting more broadcasts.

Dear *Yank*:
Never mind how a sailor got a copy of your first issue, which I didn't like much, except for the cartoon on page 15. What I want to know is: I read the editorial and one sentence in it got me. The man who wrote it says "When there is poetry it will reflect our poetry." Now what the hell does that mean? I'm not dumb, just cagey.
—Signalman T. S. Endicott
A Caribbean Base

Poets are queer guys. You have to appeal to them in language only they can understand. Our editorial writer is a poet, so he knows the lingo.

Dear *Yank*:
Do you fellows know whether it's okay to paste your girl's picture inside your foot locker cover, or can you get gigged for it?
—Pvt. John Fannoli
A Reception Center

Depends on what she looks like . . . and the officer who's inspecting.

Dear *Yank*:
Why don't they let the men at West Point grow mustaches?
—Pvt. Dutch Guinan
Aruba

You know what Hitler looks like.

Dear *Yank*:
In the "Mail Call" (*Yank* Aug. 12) Cpl. Tony Maccio states that a man in his outfit can drink 21 warm beers at one setting.

If he thinks that is a record listen to this. Two men from my outfit can drink one gallon of torpedo juice at one setting and still move around. Now if there is anyone who can compare with this let's hear about it through the "Mail Call."
—Pvt. K. F. Pitman
Somewhere in Alaska

The GIs never even had a chance. Coming only weeks after Pearl Harbor, it was too soon for reinforcements and too late for MacArthur, who bailed out (by presidential order) on March 11. His men held on until May 6 before yielding to the Japanese, a surrender they might have reconsidered had they suspected that their captors intended to march them to death.

We're the Battling Bastards of Bataan,
No mama, no papa, no Uncle Sam.
No aunts, no uncles, no nephews, no nieces,
No pills, no planes, no artillery pieces,
And nobody gives a damn.

Bataan was where many learned for the first time that war was ugly stuff.
Even a glamorous one.

HOMAGE TO BATAAN

July 8, 1942

Here is a Story of Courage that becomes more beautifully American with each telling. It's a story that Americans hold sacred, and ever will. To the memory of those who died in the flaming maelstrom of Bataan, these pages are dedicated.

THERE WAS an island called Luzon, and on this island there was a peninsula called Bataan.

It was a small peninsula, and it was hot. On the west were foothills choked with tropical growth, on the east steaming swamps and burning lagoons.

Only in the center of Bataan was there open ground, made up of jungles and rice fields, sunbaked and burning.

It was a hot and bloody place. The Japs came down from Aparri in the north and Lingayen Gulf in the northwest. They came by thousands, like an army of ants, and there were not enough defenders to stop them.

It was like a knife through cheese, the Japs thought. Easier than China.

Then Bataan got up and hit the Japs in the face, with the old one-two, the uppercut, the right

Basic Training didn't prepare them for the secrets of the Pacific jungle.

cross, the hook. The Japs got a GI kick in the teeth and a GI boot in the behind and a GI slap in the puss.

That was Bataan.

That was the first sector. . . .

The Yanks dug in at Hermosa. It was a strong line and they held it, for three bloody months, from January to April. They held it till they were the wonder of the world.

They weren't even very special. They were just guys. They came from ordinary places, like Kentucky, Michigan, and New Mexico. They were guys who drank Cokes at the corner drugstore, who dated your kid sister, who tipped their hats to a girl they met on the street. You played baseball with them, and wrestled with them on the vacant lot, and talked with them about Benny Goodman and the new suit you were going to buy.

19

But they held that line.

The Colonel and the Sergeant were caught in a bombardment and jumped into a hole. It was intense bombardment, and the Colonel started to pray out loud. He heard the Sergeant praying, too. When the bombardment was over the Colonel said, "Sergeant, I noticed you were praying."

"There are no atheists in foxholes, Colonel," the Sergeant said.

It was the sweetest line you ever saw.

When the Japs tried to crack it they hit the riflemen first. The riflemen were Filipinos, and they were neat on the trigger and they liked yellow meat.

Behind the riflemen were Yank regulars and a mess of barbed wire. Machine guns were trained down every trail. Land mines waited in the hot, damp earth and every foxhole held a sharpshooter.

The Yanks fought like Indians, from behind trees and on their bellies. They moved like ghosts in the night. They stuck thousands of bamboo stakes in the ground, stakes that were fire-hardened and sharpened and could pierce the sole of the thickest shoe. There would be a cry from someone who stepped on a stake and a sharpshooter finished the job.

The Yanks began to remember things that had been forgotten since Daniel Boone moved into Kentucky. The Japs tried to fight like Indians, but they were up against guys who had a copyright on the process. They got their ears pinned back and a bayonet in their gut: They were hurt, and they didn't like it.

They sent bombers over by fifties and by hundreds, but the bombers couldn't see accurately. The jungle hid the defenders and the bombers dropped their loads at random.

The kid from the Quartermaster Corps picked himself up after a bombing. He was mad. "Wait till I see my old lady," he said. "When I was enlisting she told me to get in the QMC so I'd be safe."

Bataan was hot as the middle of Hell. A man couldn't see to shoot sometimes because sweat ran into his eyes. But sometimes the Japs came on in such numbers a man didn't have to aim. Japanese bodies piled higher and higher in front of the line and still the yellow men came on. They came on by hundreds and thousands. It was ten to one. The barrels of the Yank rifles were red hot and then it was nine to one. Yank machine guns bit into the hordes on the jungle trails and it was eight to one. Yank artillery sent shells screaming over the line and it was seven to one.

But Jap replacements swarmed from transports down into Bataan. The bores of Yank rifles wore out and the ammunition diminished, a little more each day. The defenders turned their eyes to the sea, searching for the battlewagons, looking for the relief that might race across the horizon, hoping for just a few more planes, a few more shells, a few more cases of ball ammunition. But in their hearts the defenders knew that they would never come.

"Where the hell's the fleet?" the gunner wanted to know.

"That's easy," the other gunner said. "The last letter I got from a girlfriend of mine was postmarked St. Louis. She never lets the fleet get more'n ten miles away from her, so it's up the Mississippi."

You could count the remaining Yank planes on the fingers of your hands, and the defenders joked about them. They were the "Bamboo Fleet" and the "Baling-Wire-and-Glue Transport Line." The pilots got them up, though, and when they were told they were too tired to fight, they disobeyed orders and knocked down a couple of Zeros. The planes were P-40s patched up so often with wire that they looked like pianos, but they had slugs in their guns and the pilots said, "What the hell. . . ." One guy went up in a flying piano with a shotgun across his knees and a bolo around his waist. The shotgun was for aerial combat and the bolo was to cut himself from his harness if he had to bail out.

He never bailed out.

The pilots took off many times a day, week after week. They'd talk big over the radio, and if three planes went up they'd say, "Well, let's get these 70 planes off the ground," and the Japs were scared to go up after them.

When the Japs did go up they toted bombs and kept above the range of the flak. Sometimes the gunners cried at their guns because the Japs flew so high. But sometimes they connected and then it was exit, Tojo, and the gunners felt better.

The Coast Artillery private stood up on the parapet of his gun pit and rolled out the thunderous phrase from the Koran: "The heavens and the earth and all that is between them, think ye we have created them in jest?"

There was a silence, and then a Tennessee drawl from below answered: "If you can do that well on a cup of yesterday's coffee, what couldn't you do on a bottle of cold beer?"

The food ran low, and at last there was not enough to go around. Day by day the defenders weakened. The QMC set up bakeries behind the lines and for a while there was plenty of bread, but at last even the bread ran out.

The slaughterhouses butchered the horses, the mules, the wild pigs and the carabao, but it wasn't enough. And the defenders laughed and accused the QMC of killing pythons and crocodiles and issuing them as food.

The rice ran out early and a little inter-island steamer sneaked through the Jap blockade with rice and bananas and eggs. But that was the last boat. That was in January. Even that early the defenders went on half-rations.

The canned goods went bad, the sugar gave out, the salt was made from sea water. The coffee was so weak that guys asked for a whiff instead of a cup of the stuff.

There was no fruit, no vegetables, no milk.

While the meat lasted they made the most of it. It was tough, but so were the guys who were eating it, and at least when it went down it stayed.

The carabao wasn't so bad. It made good sandwiches. The men called the sandwiches "caraburgers." They were something you couldn't buy at Coney Island in a million years.

The old artillery sergeant looked dubiously at the forkful of mule meat he held in his hand. "Well," he said, "I beat hell out of these critters for twenty years—they're sure getting back at me now."

The Jap hurled himself at the line continually, and he didn't give a damn about losses. Some places the earth was soaked with blood, and the roots of jungle plants drank up the life of men. The field hospitals were packed with wounded. Nurses threw away their white uniforms and wore khaki shirts and slacks.

The hands of the nurses were covered with blood, and when one of them wiped sweat from her forehead her face would be bloody, too. Almost everyone had at least one wound, and if it was only one no attention was paid to it. The wounded men went back into the line and gritted their teeth and kept firing.

An infantry colonel returned to action with his third wound unhealed, a great, yawning hole in his arm that was sprinkled with sulfanilamide and covered with a dressing. As the battles went on, the faces of the men grew tense and tight and drawn. Their eyes sank into their heads and the shape of their skulls appeared in sharp relief through drawn cheeks.

Three privates were cut off and out of ammunition. A general grabbed a browning machine gun and, taking a sergeant with him, crossed the Jap lines and brought the privates back. "You boys ought to be more careful," the general said.

While there was ammunition and while there were planes the artillery had a circus. They knew where the Japs were and they knocked them off by the hundreds. The ammunition ran low and there were no more planes. The guys from the Air Force went into the line and those who didn't know the weapons available were taught how to use them.

The Japs got cagey, painted themselves and their rifles green, and fought from behind trees. They would wait behind a tree for hours, never moving, until something crossed their sights.

The time for Bataan was running out, and the Japs knew it.

They waited while the defenders grew weak from hunger and wounds and disease, waited behind their lines, eating some of the best food they had been given for a long while, drinking sake and biding time. Jap officers spent long evenings caressing their huge swords. They would wait. Their time was coming.

The dirty engineer private spat on the bole of the tree. "One thing I know," he said. "There won't be any purgatory for us. After Bataan we'll go right on through without any local stops."

At last the clocks on Bataan stopped. It was April, and at home the spring was swinging up through Georgia toward the Great Lakes. In the cities robins were hopping in the parks, and in the country thrushes were singing on the pasture fences.

The line was still there, but something had gone out of the men who held it, something that hunger and death and disease had dragged out of them. They were game, but they hadn't the strength.

The Japs cracked the line and cracked it hard. It split down one end. The yellow men poured through the hole and it was almost over but the shouting. Even then the Yanks tried a counter-attack, but it was too late. They stumbled forward,

hardly able to see, hardly able to think, and the fresh thousands of Japs caught them.

Blood ran out on the ground, blood from a lot of game guys who didn't know when they were licked, who stuck when it was hopeless. They went down fighting, and when the ammunition was gone they used their bare hands and their teeth, and they almost threw the attack back on sheer nerve.

But it wasn't in the cards.

The Japs swept over Bataan and death came with them. One by one the defenders fell, and at last there was only a little crowd left at the beaches, with nothing at their back but the waters of the Pacific.

They made a last stand on the beaches and died there one by one. Across the bay unsullied Corregidor stood grim and game, waiting for the fate that it knew must come. Finally all was quiet on Bataan and the cold-eyed gunners of Corregidor waited for the death that would soon come to them from every side of a lost island. . . .

That was the island called Luzon—the peninsula called Bataan.

Americans fought a bloody fight there in the Year of Our Lord 1942, in the Year of the American Republic 166.

Many of them will not be coming home again. They lie where they fell. They will never again see an American sun shining on an American meadow, or step a sedan up to ninety, or grab some pie and coffee at a corner diner.

They were clerks and truck drivers, insurance salesmen and short-order cooks. They were little guys, but they went out big.

We'll be coming back to Luzon one day, coming back hard and tough, with plenty of planes, plenty of guns, plenty of everything. We owe these guys a debt, and we've got to pay it.

We'll pay it with interest.

★

On April 18, 1942, 16 medium-range B-25 Mitchell bombers and 80 Army airmen, led by Lt. Col. James H. Doolittle, took off from the decks of the aircraft carrier Hornet *and conducted the first strike against the allegedly unassailable Japanese homeland—bombing key targets in Tokyo, Yokohama, Osaka, Kobe, and Nagoya. The damage inflicted by the Doolittle raid was negligible, but its effect on the morale of the two nations was electrifying.*

—Sgt. EDWARD J. SAYLOR
Engineer-Gunner,
U.S. Army Air Force
July 8, 1942

Sgt. Edward J. Saylor is only 23, but he has seen what few men alive have seen. He's looked down on Japan at war, and when he finished looking there was a little less of Japan down there to make war. Saylor was one of General Doolittle's men on that raid, and we don't have to tell you what raid.

About Sgt. Saylor, he's a native of Brussett, Montana. He calls it just a little "crossroads post office," but after a few more raids on Japan like the one he went on, he may be able to describe Tokyo in the same manner.

Saylor finished high school at Jordan, Montana, in 1937 and spent the next two years working in western states as a logger, farm hand, and cow puncher. He enlisted in the Air Corps in 1939. Eglin Field, Florida, was his last American base before he was engaged in active duty over Japan.

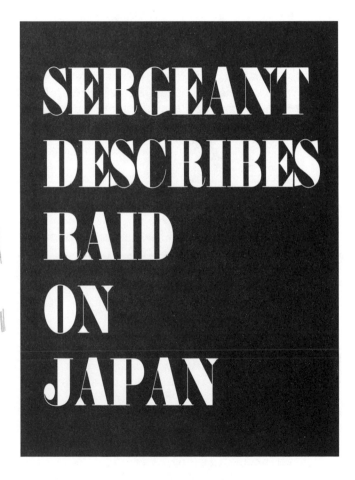

OVER KOBE, JAPAN [Delayed]—Hirohito, the Yanks are coming, pal!

They're coming with a rush and a roar and some hell to be splattered over this little island empire.

I can hardly wait, bub. We're over Japan now.

It's 1:40 p.m., and a clear day. Below me the country is rugged, but through the valleys the land is streaked with green, with trees and terraces.

Maybe I got a little bit of a catch in my throat, but I don't notice it much. We're just 15 minutes away from our target, and we're sailing along at 4,000 feet. We're flying B-25s, and they're very new and fast.

The skies are empty and clear. We've left the other planes in our squadron, and here we are all alone, sitting over several million Japs.

Yes, I have got a catch in my throat, because thinking of all those Japs down there somehow makes me think of Bataan peninsula, and to think of Bataan peninsula makes me sore.

That gives you a strange feeling to be sore when the ground below looks so peaceful and when you see the farmland down below and it looks so damned impersonal.

I used to live out west, and I've never been to Japan before, thank God, but I've heard stories about how they plant stuff on these terraced hillsides in the Far East, and I keep wondering how they work it, having been a farmer once myself.

I am also keeping a sharp watch out for cherry trees. I have been meaning to go to Washington for years to see them, but I have never seen them and I understand they are out of fashion right now.

These are just random thoughts, and all these thoughts probably come and go in a fraction of a second, because I am looking for enemy planes eight to the dozen every second, and there are no more enemy planes than there are cherry trees.

The skies are empty.

I have been sitting here just feeling the throb and roar of the big B-25. They're beautiful ships,

wonderful ships. I think of the other boys off over Tokyo and Yokohama, Osaka, and Nagoya now. We're headed for Kobe, to hit the big wharves there, and then over to an aircraft factory where they make Yakashimas. I promise I will get a few of those babies which I understand are being used to strafe our troops. After I pour some lead into those babies, those planes will look like St. Valentine's Day in Chicago has come to the aircraft industry of Japan.

The skies are still empty and vacant, and very clear. It's 1:43 now, and we're all at battle stations.

Our pilot is Lt. Donald G. Smith of San Antonio, Texas, and he knows his business. He can throw this little old ship around like I once saw a guy throw an old Jenny around at a fair back in Montana, and he could do more things with that Jenny than a monkey can do with a coconut. Smith is sure good, all right. When we started coming into Japan, he skimmed the waves so close I could almost taste the salt water from the spray in my mouth, no kidding.

Our navigator-bomber is a guy named Lt. Howard A. Sessler. He's from Boston, and he's ready to go to work with his bombsight.

Hirohito, you better watch out for guys named Sessler and guys from Boston.

Now this will give you birds a laugh. Here we are sitting up over Japan in a few hundred thousand bucks' worth of airplanes, and what kind of bombsight you think we got?

The damned thing cost 20 cents, no kidding. Doolittle—*General* Doolittle—he was afraid that in case any one of us got shot down, we didn't want the Japs to get hold of those Norden bombsights. So we rigged up a sight that cost 20 cents.

But, brother, that sight is going to cost Emperor Hirohito and what they call the elder statesmen several million bucks worth of stuff in a few minutes.

Few minutes! Right now, I mean. We just sighted the outskirts of Kobe. The skies are still vacant, and that scares you a little. It's 1:52 and we're over the edge of the city. We're coming in

D.F.C. for All in Raiding Crews

WASHINGTON—While Brig. Gen. Jimmy Doolittle watched with a proud grin, the twenty officers and three enlisted men who helped him bomb Tokyo and other Japanese cities on April 18 received their share of honor here at Bolling Field.

They lined up at attention before a row of bombing planes and Lt. Gen. Hap Arnold, chief of the Air Corps, pinned the Distinguished Flying Cross on each one of their khaki tunics.

The Doolittle Raid opened the door to regular air assaults on Japan herself.

at 2,000 feet. Lt. Sessler is talking over the interphone in his Boston accent which always gives me a hell of a boot, it sounds so English:

"That's our baby," the looie is saying. "I see the target."

We roar across the city, raising such an almighty racket the noise kind of bounces back, it seems like, and the Japs down there are running back and forth in the streets like so many ants in an ant hill. Buses are running back and forth, but the Japs don't seem to catch on to the fact that the Stars and Stripes Forever are right up there over their heads, equipped with plenty of horsepower and plenty of bombs and that darned old 20-cent bombsight.

There's our target.

She's an aircraft factory, a mess of buildings down there, scattered over a block or better. There are the docks.

All we got to do now is let go.

Hirohito, the Yanks are coming, sprinkling it along the course.

"Let 'er go. Sess," Smith yells to the bombardier.

I felt her go when she went. The bombs, I mean. Sweet as you please, that B-25 takes a sudden uplift, a little bit of a lurch, and the minute I feel it I know:

Hirohito, the Yanks have arrived.

I can't see where the bombs land, but I know that we're square on the target with the whole works. We're rolling along at 240 m.p.h. now, and that ain't any cadence count, either. We're well away from that factory before the hell starts breaking loose and the fires start.

The Japs are waking up, though. They start a mild epidemic—that's what the lieutenant called it—a mild epidemic of anti-aircraft fire.

The stuff comes up like powder puffs, but we're hightailing it away from the barrage. The Japs can't estimate our speed, and they never catch up with us. We don't give them a chance, either. We drop right down almost to water level and haul out of there in a hurry, and there I get salt spray, it seems like, in my mouth again.

I wish I could have stuck around to see the look on Hirohito's face when they brought him the messages that night.

CAMP SHELBY, MISS.—S/Sgt. Barone of Company C, 259th Infantry, tells about a private who was detailed as a range guard while his buddies fired a combat problem. Among the spectators were several generals and other high-ranking officers. One brigadier general said to the private: "There's a lot of brass around here today, son. Do you know what you're going to do?" The private answered: "Yes, sir. Pick it up."

CAMP GRUBER, OKLA.—Pvt. Dick Ashmore of Company F, 232d Infantry, was hard at work digging a latrine on bivouac when Pfc. Paul B. Crane handed him a letter from his college. "They never forget a guy," said Ashmore after he opened his letter and read:

"We want to let you know how much we appreciate your contribution to the war effort. We hope you will soon be back to give us, in exacting details, the colorful story of your interesting work. . . ."

NAVY NOTES—When a detachment of Seabees arrived at Pearl Harbor recently, the censors allowed no mention of the location in letters home. But they gave it away to one Seabee's wife. He started his letter, "Dear Pearl" (that *was* her name), and the "Pearl" was neatly clipped out.

Bombs with Teeth

Cpl. Bernie Abrahams, of the Royal Regiment of Toronto, tells of an air-raid warden trying to hustle an English woman out of her home into a shelter during a bombing.

"Wait till I find my teeth," said the woman.

"What do you think they're dropping, lady, sandwiches?"

DOGFACE DICTIONARY

Bunk—the only thing in camp that can afford to be tight before inspection.

Buttons—clothing accessories much treasured by a worker in the Quartermaster Laundry, who removes them from shirts and takes them home for his kids to play with.

Canteen—a hardware water bottle or a GI refreshment stand, neither of which is worth much if it's dry.

Clerk, Company—the spelling demon in the orderly room who has no trouble with "Dziordzynki" but always puts a spare "e" on "Brown."

Furlough—a week or 10 days when a soldier can rest his nerves after the ordeal of sweating out a furlough for three days.

GI—Galvanized iron.

Haircut, GI—a tonsorial operation, too close for a haircut, too long for a shave.

Latrine orderly—a fireman: the only man in the barracks who keeps cooler than the water in the showers.

Mail call—an interlude in which you can stand around resting while you listen to the music of other men's names.

Master sergeant—an elderly gentleman who knows three times as much as you do about any given civilian subject because he's been in the Army for 29 years.

Metal sergeant—a noncommissioned officer identified by the silver in his hair, the gold in his teeth, and the lead in his backside.

Old army—a large group of first-three-graders who spent the prewar years thinking up sentences beginning with, "By God, it wasn't like this in the———."

Rank (*rangk*) [Anglo-Saxon, *ranc*: strong, proud] offensively gross or course, indecent; strongly scented.

Recreation officer—the company officer who solves the problem of your spare time by detailing you to put up basketball goals.

Recruit—a man who has been in the service at least two days less than you have.

Sick call—a morning social hour for the leisure classes of the regiment.

Supply sergeant—the fellow who won't lend you a cigarette unless you give him a memorandum receipt.

Through channels—from San Francisco to Los Angeles by way of Washington, D.C.

—Cpl. Marion Hargrove

Mechanical-minded Gob

A sailor in Chicago was being interviewed on a local radio program. The question was: "While you are in Chicago, what type of girl would you like to meet?"

The gob looked down at his white uniform. Then he delivered his answer.

"If it's all the same to you," he said, "I'd like to meet a girl who has a washing machine."

We'll Take the Hi Wave . . .

Last week, the Navy came out with a new slogan for its enlistment campaign, which read as follows:

"Join the Navy, and give the Japs their half of the ocean.

". . . The *bottom* half!"

ARMY JOKES

These are the best Army jokes that have come to Yank's big ears. Know any better ones? Send them in.

Captain: "Why didn't you salute me yesterday?"
Private: "I didn't see you, sir."
Captain: "Good, I was afraid you were mad at me."

Private: "I feel like punching that sergeant in the nose again."
Pfc: "Again?"
Private: "Yes, I felt like it yesterday, too."

Soldier: Hello."
Girl:
Soldier: "Oh, well."

Sweet young thing (leaning out the window): "Hey, soldier, have you the time?"
Eager private: "Sure, lady, where'll I park the jeep?"

The officer of the day approached the post. The rookie executed the guard routine perfectly and the OD looked pleased. With precision the rookie rattled off the general and special orders. His uniform was smartly pressed, his rifle oiled, his shoes shined.
"I guess," the OD said, "everything is in order."
"And not only that," replied the rookie, winking, "but I've got a wonderful bottle of Scotch on me. Want a drink?"
"Corporal of the guard," yelled the infuriated and astounded OD.
"Shhhhh," shushed the rookie. "There won't be enough for the three of us."

Lady: "Oh you poor soldier—do you always march with a full pack?"
Smoker: "No ma'am, I have to bum them once in a while."

Private: "How long was your last top kick with you?"
Corporal: "He was never with us. He was against us."

Two dogfaces are walking along and pass a major. Instead of saluting, one of the doggies hauls off and lets the major have it on the chin. It is a terrific wallop.
The major staggers to his feet, and just as he straightens his shoulders the other doggie lets go. Whammo! Down goes the major again.
As quick as a furlough can be cancelled, the two soldiers find themselves in the guardhouse. Then they're brought before the major.

"Why did you hit me?" the major asks.
"Well," the first doggie says, "when you passed me you stepped on my bunion. I saw red. I forgot who you were. I swatted you."
The major nods understandingly.
"I see what you mean." he says. "I have a bunion myself and I appreciate your feelings."
The major turns to the other soldier.
"And why did *you* hit me?" he asks.
"Gee," says the second one, "when I saw what my buddy did, I thought the war was over."

Private: "Are you going to try to get a commission?"
Second private: "No, I just want a straight salary."

It was a French class and the instructor was quizzing soldiers on the meaning of certain French idioms. "Translate *femmes de guerre*," he asked one private.
"Women of war," the soldier aptly replied.
Professor: "That's literally correct, but really that phrase is an idiom and means 'camp followers,' or women of easy virtue."
Soldier: "I thought that was '*hors de combat*.'"

In the cozy cottage of a kind old lady came two billeted soldiers. She greeted them with a friendly smile, showed them to their room, and watched them dump their belongings—tin helmets, gas masks, packs, etc. Then a worried look came into her eyes as she asked:
"Young men, are you sure you came by all those things honestly?"

Soldier: "I'd like to marry you or something."
Girl: "You'll marry me or nothing!"

A second lieutenant on his honeymoon wired his CO the following message: "It's wonderful here. Please extend furlough several more days."
The CO wired back: "It's wonderful anywhere. Come back."

It was like crossing the River Styx in a Higgins boat and finding out that Hell had beaches. On August 7, 1942, the first Allied offensive of the Pacific war commenced in the Solomon Islands with simultaneous attacks on Guadalcanal and Tulagi. Some had anticipated a milk run; in fact, Guadalcanal alone would not be secured until February 9, 1943.

SAGA OF THE SOLOMONS

September 9, 1942

For many it was the first real landing, and for many it was the last. They waded to shore in good order, and then spread out. They caught the Jap flat-footed, with his pants down, and they hunted him through the jungle and into the caves. They dropped him out of the trees and off of the cliffs, and they didn't take enough prisoners to fill a subway car. And when it was all over they said "Thank you very much for this nice equipment" and settled down to stay for a while. That was the Marines in the Solomon Islands in August 1942.

THE MARINES were going to work. They sprawled on the decks of great transports and watched the dim shore of the South Pacific port fade behind them. Around their transports hulking cruisers and destroyers like whippets sent their smoke pouring out in the blue air of a clear August day, by their mere presence giving a feeling of security to the tough men who were oiling their rifles and polishing their bayonets. The Marines knew that they were the largest force ever assembled to engage in a landing operation, and the amount of scuttlebutt—Marine

for "latrine rumor"—about where they were going reverberated from the transports' decks. Guesses ranged from the geisha houses of Yokohama to the Admiral Byrd Mountains of Little America. Wherever they went, the Marines were glad they were going.

The convoy had been out three days when the call came to take to battle stations. Three planes had appeared, and as they came out of the horizon the Marines waited tensely, trying to identify them. They turned out to be friendly craft—the eyes of approaching reinforcements. Later that day smoke appeared on all points of the horizon, and as time passed, a Marine could see, fore and aft and port and starboard, big aircraft carriers, heavy cruisers, and enormous transports moving along with him.

Where they were going was still the big question. During the next two days the skies were dark, overcast. Great cloud banks sank down against the water. This was good, though; no enemy plane could spot them in weather like that. Occasionally, through fog, they could make out a few friendly islands.

It was not until these islands had been passed that unit commanders called their men together and told them where they were going. Their objective was the Solomon Islands, a Japanese-held group 200 miles south of the equator in mid-Pacific. The Solomons were the Japs' southernmost conquest. More important, these were the islands that were being developed by the enemy into a base from which U.S. shipping routes to New Zealand and Australia could be attacked.

Now that the Marines knew where they were going, they were ready. The talk and the guesswork subsided. Each man busied himself with his equipment. When a man is going to do a lot of gun using, he wants his gun to be right.

On the night of August 6–7, all hands turned out at 2 a.m. The ships continued to slip through calm waters as the Marines lined up below decks for a breakfast of steak, scrambled eggs, fried potatoes, toast, jam, and coffee. They knew that for days to come they would be on iron field rations; no man was going to miss this opportunity for good chow.

Outside, the weather had cleared. The mist and low clouds had disappeared and there were bright stars and strange constellations in the southern sky. To the right the faint outline of an island could be detected. That was Guadalcanal. Slowly another island loomed into being on the left. That was Florida. The huge convoy was making its way slowly, silently, stealthily through the passage between Guadalcanal and Florida Island to the very heart of the Solomons 15 miles north—to the harbor at Tulagi. And not one peep was yet to be heard from the enemy-held shore.

Dawn comes much later this time of year in the tropics than it does in the U.S. Not until 5:25 a.m. did the ship's crew take to battle stations. Not until 6:05 a.m. was the order given to "stand by to lower boats." And it was not until 6:17 a.m. that the big cruisers' guns began to boom. As they opened up the big Navy bombers and the smaller dive-bombers went to work on shore installations and batteries. Jap camps were bombed and strafed. Jap ships were sunk in the harbor. Most important of all, nine Zeros equipped with floats, five big patrol seaplanes, and one four-engine bomber were put out of action before they could get out of the water. That left the Japs in the Solomons with not one plane to fly.

Bothered and Bewildered Japs

All up and down the 15-mile stretch of water hell was breaking loose, to the obvious consternation of a bewildered Jap garrison. So effective was this preliminary bombardment that not one Jap shore battery was able to reply. Here and there, sporadic machine-gun fire; nothing else.

Boats swung out on davits and were lowered as Marine combat groups made ready to strike for shore. Around the big transports hundreds of smaller craft were swarming—landing barges, tank lighters, amphibious tanks that the Marines call "alligators," amphibious tractors to serve as machine shops on shore. The landing barges all flew small U.S. flags.

"H" hour—the hour for attack—differed up and down the line, but generally it was set at 0800. A company of Marines under Capt. E. J. Crane landed first, the spot chosen being a promontory on Florida Island which overlooked Tulagi. Not a Jap was in sight. Not a Jap shot was heard.

Thirty minutes later a Marine raider battalion under Col. Merritt Edson landed on a beach at the northwest end of Tulagi. Again not a Jap was seen, and only one Jap shot was fired; that by a lone sniper.

An amber flare from the shore of Guadalcanal announced that Combat Group A, under Lt. Col. L. P. Hunt, had made a third landing. Again there were no Japs, no shots.

The lack of defense was eerie, but no Marine believed for a minute that it was going to be this easy all the way. In fact, they would soon discover that the Japs had simply been surprised out of their wits by this early bombardment and had fled in haste to what they thought were safe positions in dugouts, caves, and caverns far back in the hills. There they would fight until dead.

On the two biggest Solomons, little *did* happen on that first day. The Marines made no attempt to push inland on Florida. On Guadalcanal they

Guadalcanal: the men move in after days of heavy shelling.

spread out through the coconut groves and tall grass at the same time that tanks and tractors were landed and a headquarters was set up on the beach. The day was steaming hot and toward night a heavy tropical rain set in. The Guadalcanal Marines bivouacked that night under palm trees, sleeping for the most part in mud puddles. They were uncomfortable, but undisturbed.

The picture was different in the Tulagi area. After landing there, the raiders, their heavy packs on their backs, climbed the steep cliffs, dragged machine guns up behind them, and, after splitting into two separate parties, headed cautiously southeast toward the chief settlement of the Solomon Islands—the town of Tulagi.

This was a hilly, heavily wooded section and it

took one party of the raiders two and a half hours to cover a mile and a half of this terrain. At the end of that time they ran into their first serious trouble—a series of machine-gun nests hidden in limestone caves dug into the hillside. To wipe out these nests, men crawled up the hill under fire and then slipped down a cliff to throw grenades into the mouths of the caves. This was the first indication of the kind of desperate opposition that the U.S. Marines were to face on the Solomon Islands.

Cricket Field Fighting

The other party of raiders worked their way on the other side of Tulagi's chief ridge into the town. They took the hill on which stood the old British residency, symbol of happier days, and captured the cricket field just below it. Jap snipers seemed to be behind every rock, in every tree, and in every building in the area. The raiders, however, ran into something more formidable—a ravine, the other side of which was literally studded with a labyrinth of pillboxes and dugouts from which poured withering fire. This was the Japs' main line of defense on Tulagi Island. Capt. Harold T. A. Richmond, commanding this detachment, decided to bide his time and hold a purely defensive position until reinforcements arrived.

The small islands of Gavutu and Tanambogo, connected with each other by a concrete causeway, lie just off Tulagi. Gavutu, about a mile long, the site of the seaplane base destroyed in the early bombing, was ordered attacked at noon on that first day by Marines under Maj. Robert H. Williams. Major Williams was badly wounded as he landed under fire on the wharf, and the command fell to Capt. George Stallings.

Gavutu was perhaps the best fortified of the islands. Rising abruptly in the center of the island is a hill 148 feet high which was honeycombed with scores of spacious limestone caves. Tunnels connected many of these underground chambers, most of which also were equipped with radios. They were ideal for defense, and the Japs made the most of them. Landing under a rain of fire, the Marines knew that the only way to get the Japs off this island was to blast in the caves.

Torgeson and TNT

It was Capt. Harry L. Torgeson who showed the way to conquer Gavutu. He crept slowly up the hill, covered by the fire of only four men. Into the mouth of one cave he hurled charges of TNT tied to boards with short fuses. The blast was deafening. The hillside seemed almost to fall in. The Japs inside were either blown up or buried alive. Captain Torgeson proceeded to pay calls on other caves for hours, using up 20 cases of TNT. Once he ran out of matches and had to call for more. He broke a wristwatch; his pants were blasted off. But he also blew up 50 caves and killed unknown numbers of Japs.

To mention all the heroes of Gavutu would mean going through the roster of the men who fought there. Cpl. Ralph W. Fordice mopped up seven dugouts, each harboring at least six Japs. Out of one cave alone he dragged eight dead enemies. Cpl. George F. Brady killed two Japs with his submachine gun, and when his gun jammed used the butt to kill a third. After that he took his knife and disposed of two more.

Cpl. John Blackan cleaned out five dugouts single-handed. Sgt. Max Keplow killed three Japs playing dead on a beach, then blasted out two dugouts. Platoon Sgt. Harry M. Tully operated as a sniper hunter for 48 hours, picking off Japs one by one. One night he lay on a beach and watched a Jap swim ashore behind a log flat. He waited patiently without stirring for 18 minutes until the Jap raised his head. Then Tully got his man.

On that afternoon of August 7, the Marines planted the Stars and Stripes on the Gavutu hilltop, the bugles blew, and the Marines stopped fighting for a split second to cheer. The Rising Sun still floated above Tanambogo, 500 yards away, but Marine sharpshooters shot it away.

At dusk that evening, the first attack on Tanambogo took place. The connecting causeway was covered by Jap fire; an advance across it would have been suicide. Another boat-landing operation was thus called for. The Marines here were to be guided by an Australian flight lieutenant who knew every inch of the islands.

Destroyers laid down a five-minute barrage as

the boats came to shore. The last naval shell fired hit a fuel dump which lit up the landing dock so brilliantly that the Marines were exposed to the full view of the Jap machine gunners; the attack had to be called off for that night, to be resumed the following morning. Two tanks were sent over to Tanambogo in advance of the landing party. One tank had made its way inland about 100 feet when Japs began to swarm over it. They thrust iron rods into its treads. They poured gasoline over it and set it afire. At that moment the Marine lieutenant operating the tank opened the turret top, turned his gun on the Japs, and killed 23 of them before he himself was knifed to death. Within an hour this lieutenant's life was avenged when Tanambogo was subjected to the tried-and-true methods that had conquered Gavutu.

Jap Attack Balked

At 2230 on August 7, with a tropical rain coming down in sheets, the Japs pulled a surprise night attack on Tulagi. They came out of their caves with knives, rifles, and grenades. They almost captured one Marine lieutenant colonel, who vacated his post only two minutes before the enemy arrived. For a time they even surrounded one company of Marines. Lt. John B. Doyle, Jr., and eight men held an observation post on a high cliff and spent their time pushing Japs off the precipice. A reserve Marine company was soon brought up to settle matters, and the Japs went back to their caves.

As August 8 dawned, the Marines held all of Gavutu and most of Tulagi and had toeholds on Florida and Guadalcanal. After taking Tanambogo, the next order of the day was cleaning out the Tulagi ravine. By early morning this ravine was covered by fire from three sides. By 3 p.m., every last Jap in every cave had been killed.

One unnamed sergeant tried to blow out a dugout with grenades, only to find that as fast as he tossed them in, the Japs tossed them back out. He tried dynamite next, and that came back too. Then he charged inside and trained his machine gun on four Japs. He found eight others lying dead there.

There was no silencing of any Jap dugout until

There's always another island ahead . . .

every one in it had been killed. As soon as one Jap machine gunner was killed, another would take his place. One lone Jap held out in a cave for two days without food or water, surrounded by the corpses of eight fellow soldiers killed by a grenade. He, too, finally met his death. In another cave, three Japs fought until they had just three bullets left. One of these Japs killed his two buddies with two of the bullets and used the third for himself.

On that second day of fighting, the Marines on Guadalcanal moved inland to capture, virtually without opposition, an 85 percent completed airfield with a 1,400-foot runway. They ran into the enemy later, although he offered here no such resistance as the Marines had experienced on Tulagi. The Japs worked mostly from isolated machine-gun nests.

Platoon Sgt. Frank L. Few, a part Indian from

Arizona, had a brief encounter with three Japs on Guadalcanal, killed all three in hand-to-hand combat, and then was obliged to swim four-and-a-half miles to safety.

Total Surprise for Nips

It was obvious as time went on that the Japs had been overwhelmed by the suddenness of the attack. They left breakfast tables covered with bowls of rice half eaten and with chopsticks handy nearby. Jap soldiers' pants hung on wash lines at one field; A Jap officer's outdoor bath was filled; he obviously had left hurriedly and dripping.

Large stores of food were captured, including such luxuries as beer, champagne, soda pop, soap, and clothing. But there were also ammunition dumps intact, pom-poms, all sorts of fuel, radios that still were operating, trucks, cars, refrigerators, even an electric light plant. One shore battery was found loaded and ready to fire. The machinery for finishing the magnificent airport—roller and all—was there for Americans to use.

Robbed of aerial resistance in the Solomons themselves, Jap airmen on nearby islands were sent to the rescue. At 1526 on the first day of the attack, 25 heavy Jap bombers came over, skimming the trees. They hit nothing, but ran into heavy ack-ack fire; many went down in flames. Others met their fate out over the open sea, where Navy fighters were waiting. At 4 p.m. that day, 10 dive-bombers came over and did hit one U.S. destroyer. At noon the next day, 40 torpedo planes attacked. They hit an unloaded transport and another destroyer, but 12 of these were shot down by ships' anti-aircraft fire and another two by U.S. shore batteries. It was a suicidal raid. In those first two days, the Japs lost at least 47 planes. In days to come, the score went up to above 100.

On the night of August 8, Jap warships moved to the attack but never got within range of either transports or cargo ships. On the 9th, Japs landed some 700 well-equipped men on Tulagi's beaches. Morning came and 670 of these were killed, 30 taken prisoners. Meanwhile, all transports and cargo ships were unloaded, and by nightfall of August 9 the merchantmen departed for safer berths. After that the Jap Navy made several stabs in the direction of the Solomons, and each time were turned back. Lately Jap planes have been coming over, always at noon. Every once in a while a Jap submarine will pop up in the harbor and pepper a beach or so but do little harm.

By noon of August 10 it could be said that all major resistance on five islands had been overcome and that for all intents and purposes the Solomons were ours. Exactly how many Japs were buried alive or killed in this two-and-a-half-day battle only Tokyo would know, and Tokyo was not talking about this affair.

On Tulagi there had been at least 600 Japs—and not a one surrendered.

On Gavutu there had been a good 1,200—and they were all killed.

Results That Count

On Tanambogo and Guadalcanal there were several hundred more apiece, and virtually none of them was captured. In fact, the only Japs captured during the first two days of fighting were seven from a labor battalion and three who suffered from malaria and were left behind in the camps. There was no shrinking from the fact that we, too, had had casualties, but they amounted to not one fraction of those suffered by the enemy and, in the words of Maj. Gen. A. A. Vandegrift, who commanded the Marines in this action, were "by no means disproportionate to the results achieved." Summed up the general in congratulating the men in his command: "God favors the bold and the strong of heart."

⭐

HOT SATURDAY OVER THE SOLOMONS

September 16, 1942

All the fighting in the Solomons wasn't done by fleet units and ground forces. Once the islands were taken, the Japs sent over bombers in the hope of ousting the Yanks. Marine pilots had a lot to do, and sometimes they had a hot time doing it. This is what happened to a Marine fighter pilot on Saturday, August 8, 1942, a beautiful day above Guadalcanal, though a very noisy one.

THEY RAN into the Japanese bombers at 12,000 feet. There were 27 of them, two-motored jobs, out to get the warships that lay off Guadalcanal. Lt. James J. Southerland, leading a flight of Marine fighters, saw them coming out of the sun, in three divisions of nine each, their wings gleaming in the air.

"Too many of 'em," Southerland said over the radio. "Time's short. Make three attacks on one run."

The Marine flight went screaming down on its target. Southerland let go at the first division, then cut in on the second. He went up under one plane, and as he did he saw the bomb bay explode. He fired at a plane in the third division, and smoke began to stream from one of its motors. As he pulled away he noticed that his baggage compartment was itself filled with smoke. "Been hit," he said aloud.

Four Zeros had come up behind him. They had been high up, riding herd on the bombers, waiting for just this opportunity. Southerland saw them too late. He looked around, and there they were —weaving through the sky, letting him have it, one at a time.

They Even Smashed His Goggles

Southerland crouched low in his seat and tried to watch behind him. He could tell when a Jap was going to open fire by the way he jockeyed his Zero, and by turning when the moment came he avoided getting full bursts. But the Japs were slugging them in, just the same. Southerland took a wound in his left arm, another in his right foot, and another in his right leg. His eyebrow was grazed and his goggles shot off. He had pieces of shrapnel in his leg and the back of his head.

When Southerland crossed over the northeastern end of Guadalcanal, at 4,000 feet, his plane resembled a sieve. The instrument panel was shot out; the whole upper surface of the left wing was torn away. And then the plane caught fire.

Flames came up into the cockpit. Southerland's wrists began to blister. It was time, he decided, to go away from there. Behind him the Zeros waited. He started to climb out of the cockpit, shielding his face from the wind-fanned tongues of flame, only to discover that something was holding him back. It was his pistol. Fastened in a holster on his belt, it had caught in the torn fuselage.

Southerland doesn't know how he did it, but he ripped the heavy web belt apart with his bare, burned hands. When he went over the side he was only 300 feet above the ground.

His ripcord came away in his hand. "My God," he thought, "the chute isn't going to open."

This Sock Came in Handy

He fumbled clumsily with the cord. Then, at 200 feet, his shoulders were jerked back convulsively and a great white billow of silk spread over his head. The Japs still circled above him. He spilled the air out of the chute to hasten his fall. He expected the Japs to strafe him. They didn't. He came down fast, and just before he hit the ground he saw his plane go into a wing-over and crash. The Japs still circled, like vultures. He crawled into the jungle to hide.

He had lost a good deal of blood. His right leg was the worst, with a great hole in it. There was no bandage, so he took off his sock and stuffed it into the wound. It was a clean sock; he had washed it himself the night before. Then he tied his shoe very tight to stop the bleeding.

Resting only a few minutes, Southerland took off on foot through the jungle. He was weak; the jungle was thick and tough. Vines caught him and roots tripped him. He didn't know where he was going. Several times he fell. It became harder each time to get up again.

After two hours he reached a clearing and saw a Jap flag in the distance. There was no turning back, so he ripped a branch from a tree and limped toward the flag. There was no one home; the Japs had taken off. He searched the camp for food or bandages and found an old searchlight with batteries. He took out the reflector to use as a semaphore. The sun was still high, so he rested and signalled with the reflector.

He Opens Coconuts with His Bare Hands

All afternoon he sat with his back against a tree, desperately trying to attract help. Once a plane saw the flash and came down and waggled its wings. Southerland waited all night, not daring to sleep, but no help came. The next morning he started out again.

During the night he had washed out his wounds with salt water, but the right leg was a dead weight. He went on painfully, slower and slower. He found a native canoe, cut a palm frond for a paddle, and started off, but the canoe was rotten. It took in water faster than he could bail it out with his shoe. He beached it and continued on foot—*one* foot.

He had not eaten for more than a day. About noon he found a coconut and broke it open with his hands, with the same desperate strength he had used to rip his web belt. Later he stumbled on a clear stream and fell on his face before it, drinking and plunging his head into the cool water. Then he found oranges and ate them. His wounds were no better, although most of the bleeding had stopped. The wounds were crusted and stiff and painful. He had blisters on his hands from the burns.

He was almost gone when two natives saw him. He was staggering from tree to tree then, head up, fighting to keep his body on the move. The natives came forward to help. Through a mist he heard them say they were Catholics. He was too weak to do anything but smile.

He Gets Chicken à la Solomon

They took him to a native village, where they washed his wounds and got him clean clothes. They gave him a little food and the next day cooked him a chicken and some hard-boiled eggs.

As soon as he was able to talk, Southerland tried to get the natives to take him back to camp, but the sound of gunfire frightened them. Later he saw an American ship touch the beach several miles away. He begged the natives to take him to the boat, assuring them that the American ship wouldn't be there if the battle weren't won. He was too weak to argue much; he could only point and repeat a few words.

At last the natives put him in a canoe and paddled toward the ship. On the way they passed another Jap camp where the flags were flying, although the Japs had fled. The flimsy canoe finally landed where some Marines, dirty and battle stained, were dug in. The Marines carried Southerland back to a field hospital.

He still had the sock he had stuffed in his leg.

How to Take Care of YOUR Replacement

By Sgt. RALPH STEIN

Greet him with gusto. (This is easy.)

Screen him from reality.

Feed him well and regularly.

Protect him from heat . . .

. . . and from cold.

And don't let him get away!

"It's our Hugo, home for Christmas!"
—Sgt. Irwin Caplan

"Must be going back to the States."
—Pfc. Tom Creem

When Java fell to the Japanese in early 1942, Allied evacuation was both advisable and immediate. That is, for the most part.

FLIGHT TO GLORY

—Sgt. J. DENTON SCOTT
Yank Staff Writer
July 15, 1942

TEN ZEROS dived, peeled off, and faded away to specks in the sky. Below, on the island of Java, 18 American citizens rose slowly to their feet. They had been lying on their stomachs while the Japs machine gunned the ground.

In the rush of abandoning Java, the 18 Americans had been left behind. Now, huddled near a deserted and bomb-scarred airfield, they were looking desperately around for guidance. The only uniform in the place belonged to MSgt. Harry Hayes. The only man among the 18 who could fly was a young volunteer pilot named Cherry Mission.

The airfield was a mess. Scattered about its tarmac were four crippled planes, one B-18, and three Flying Fortresses. Mission, a small man, pointed to the B-18. "It's a wreck," he said, "but it's the only one I can fly. I'm pursuit, and that's all."

"I'm not even pursuit," Sgt. Hayes said. He glanced at the sky. "But we've got to get out of here. Fast."

Mission climbed into the B-18. No good. The motor was as dead as a Jap's honor. His face grim, Mission got out of the plane. "It won't work," he said.

Sgt. Hayes didn't say anything. He went to the plane, looked at the motor, took off his shirt, and went to work.

He worked on the motor for two full days. His daily nourishment was three sandwiches and a little water. And on the third day the motor was repaired. The B-18 would fly.

But on the third day the Zeros came again. Concentrated machine-gun fire reduced Sgt. Hayes handiwork into rag-doll scraps. The 18 Americans, including Mission's young wife, were worse off than they had been before.

Sgt. Hayes still kept his mouth shut. He sized up the three Flying Fortresses on the field. Once brilliant giants of the air, they were now useless hulks. When the Japs came again, Hayes knew, they wouldn't waste bullets on ruined planes. Their slugs would be for the "American intruders."

Sgt. Hayes left the little group on the airfield. The 18 puzzled Americans waited for his return. They didn't have long to wait. In 15 minutes Hayes was back, with 60 Dutchmen. He showed them the planes, spoke to them quietly.

The 60 Dutchmen went willingly to work to help the desperate Americans. They stripped two of the Flying Fortresses, taking everything of use and transferring it to the third plane, the least damaged of the three.

In 72 hours the motors of the Flying Fortress were working. There was still plenty to do, though. The wings of the plane were in tatters. The tail was shot away. There weren't any wing flaps at all.

"I don't think we can get her off the ground," Mission said.

"We've got to," was all Hayes replied.

In four days the big plane was repaired. It looked like a jig-saw puzzle imperfectly put together, but it looked as though it might fly. Everything in the interior had been stripped out. Parachutes, seats, everything.

"We need the space," Hayes said. "Eighteen people take up a lot of room."

Sgt. Hayes called the group before him. "I want you to know," he said, "that you are putting your lives in my hands. I have never flown a plane before. I don't know how long this plane will stay together. I can't even promise you that she'll get off the ground, or that I can get her off. If the Japs attack us while we're in the air, we won't have a chance. If anyone thinks he or she will be safer here, he is quite free to stay."

No one wanted to stay.

Quietly, tensely, the 18 filed into the plane.

They sat down on the bare floors. Sgt. Hayes and Mission took over the seats of pilot and copilot. Hayes started the motors, and one by one they coughed and burst into noisy life. As they warmed, Hayes studied the unfamiliar controls.

Unheard above the roar of the Fortress's four motors, seven Zeros dropped from the sky. Machine-gun bullets slapped the side of the plane and cut through the thin metal. The 18 Americans huddled against the floor.

Sgt. Hayes's hand moved toward the throttle. Mission stopped him. "For God's sake, Hayes," he said. "Don't take off now. They'll shoot us down like an October duck."

Hayes waited. For ten minutes death hovered over the plane as the Zeros spat bullets at it. And then the Zeros, satisfied that they had done their job, disappeared toward the horizon. Sgt. Hayes and Mission surveyed the damage. It was negligible, and no one had been killed. But a bullet might have done something to the plane that wouldn't show up until it tried to take off. No time to think of that now, though. The chance had to be taken.

Sgt. Hayes's hand moved forward on the throttle. The great ship moved down the runway, gathering speed. It wobbled slightly as it moved, but it held together.

Faster and faster went the Fortress. Then Mission's face went white. "Hayes," he shouted in the pilot's ear, "even an empty Fortress needs a 3,000-foot runway to lift. This one isn't more than 2,800, and we're filled. Move that stick gently, boy. Move it gently."

Sgt. Hayes moved it gently. The Fortress lifted off the ground, came down, bounced. Not yet, he thought.

Mission watched the manifold pressure climb from 46 to 50, four points above danger. Once more Hayes's hands pulled the controls back. This time the Fortress lifted. Her engines wheezing, her once-smooth lines wobbling like a wounded bird, she went into the air. Crouched in the fuselage, the 18 Americans saw trees flash by underneath them. Minutes passed, and they were over the Sea of Timor.

The sea was a black, foreboding face beneath them, and the sky was a darkness from which Zeros might swoop at any moment. The motors coughed unsteadily. Mission, his eyes on the horizon, offered navigation advice from time to time. His wife acted as observer.

Without maps, without instruments, and at the controls a man who had never flown a plane before, the Flying Fortress moved over the sea toward Australia. Hours passed, and then Mission pointed ahead. "Land," he said.

The northern coast of Australia hove into view. But things weren't finished yet. The toughest job of all—setting the plane down—remained to be done. For all they knew, they might be landing in Japanese-held territory.

"There's a clearing near that beach," Mission said. "Maybe you can set her down easy and run up the beach."

Hayes nodded, and the nose of the Fortress pointed down. This was the worst moment of all.

The Fortress hit the beach hard, staggered, jounced, and leveled off. Nineteen people stepped out on the free earth of Australia. The man who had never flown a plane before had made it.

Sgt. Hayes looked back at the sky through which they had come. "I'd like to be a real pilot someday," he said.

★

HOW DOES IT FEEL TO BOMB EUROPE?

—Sgt. Robert Moora
Yank's London Bureau
October 7, 1942

Just a routine raid—a brisk little hop across the channel to lay a few eggs where they'll do the most good. But these 40 minutes of action, as seen through the eyes of a waist gunner, prove that even a routine raid over Nazi-occupied Europe can pack more kick than a whole battalion of those well-known Army mules.

SOMEWHERE IN England—The left waist gunner of the Flying Fortress, Sgt. Bob Knight, of Schenectady, New York, is lying in his barracks bunk, his mind half on the bacon and eggs he's just finished and half on the weather outside. Good flying weather today—good bombing weather at the 'drome and probably the same on the other side of the channel.

It's no surprise, then, when the voice comes over the loudspeaker: "Stand by for announcement. All combat flying personnel will report to the briefing room at once."

Knight glances over in the corner where Smitty is snoozing peacefully, probably dreaming of the sunny skies over Winter Haven, Florida, his hometown. A brisk poke in the midriff reminds Smitty to step on it. Can't leave the top turret man behind.

In the briefing room, he joins the assembled crews. When they've quieted down, the old man begins. He points out on a map where the planes are going and what they're going to do.

Now Knight learns what's ahead. It's to be a routine raid over Rotterdam, Abbeville, Rouen, or any of the enemy-occupied cities that have felt the weight of bombs from Uncle Sam's Flying Fortresses. He listens attentively as the old man talks calmly, slipping in a wisecrack now and then. When the old man comes to the bombing run—the objective of the raid—he goes into great detail and repeats a lot. Watching the old man, Knight's reminded of Pop Burns giving a lecture in the dressing room before a football game.

His spine tingles anew when the old man goes into a few other details, such as where the Spits will pick up the bombers and where the Jerries will be encountered. It's an open secret that the old man is astonishingly accurate in his predictions.

"Right here," the old man illustrates, pointing to the map, "is where we'll run into heavy flak—four AA batteries. We'll give them as wide a berth as possible, but it will be hot for a few minutes."

Scared Now; Calm in the Air

Knight notices about this time that his hands are cold and clammy. It's funny. The only time he's really scared in the whole operation is when he's sitting there listening to that calm voice telling what lies ahead.

That feeling is gone, he later notices, when he's in the air. Then he's calm—calmer than on that red-letter day he trotted onto the field for the old Thanksgiving game. Sure he sweats, even though it's 40 below zero at 24,000 feet. He sweats even in fatigues, without an electrically heated flying suit. But he's not scared. Any Flying Fortress man can swear to that. However, when he sees Jerry coming in at 400 miles an hour with his guns belching smoke and flame, and maybe a shell rips his pant leg and cuts the interphone wire, or when he has to level off for 40 seconds of smooth flying to get the bombs away and the Focke-Wulfs are buzzing around like hornets—brother, he sweats. . . .

Finally the briefing is over. Knight hops on his bike and pedals over to the dispersal point where their plane—*Flaming Mayme*, perhaps—is standing, pretty as a picture against the green fields and trees beyond. For just a second, as the low beams of the morning sun catch her wingtips, she actually does seem to flame, and he wonders what Mayme, the red-headed girl she's named for— Lt. J. O. Wikle's girl back in Madison, Alabama —really looks like.

The ground crew is lolling on the grass, like a bunch of country boys after a swim. They haven't been idle, though. They've been fussing and fuming around Mayme ever since the last run, and Knight knows the engines and the guns are in perfect condition.

In a few minutes, everybody is ready for the takeoff—oxygen masks adjusted, engines turning over. They taxi across the field as the lead plane goes up, and a few minutes later the ship is in a tight formation upstairs, heading for the coast.

Over the interphone comes a query from Lt. R. A. Birk, of Burlingame, California "Navigator to tail gunner: How's it look back there?" Knight hears the answer from T/Sgt. Johnny Burger, who used to help his old man on the farm back in Jefferson, New York:

"They're getting into position okay."

Conversation Across the Channel

He settles down then for the ride over. It will be a while before anything starts popping. Down below, a crazy quilt of fields—neat little English farms—floats by. Charley Nease, at the right waist gun, comes in with his Savannah drawl, something like: "You'd think those farms'd raise some good fryin' chickens, wouldn't you?" And maybe Charley Hooks, of Platteville, Wisconsin, curled up in the ball turret down below, answers, "Yeah, but they don't. I'm through orderin' chicken in English restaurants. They must feed 'em sawdust, they're so scrawny."

That's the way the conversation runs on the way over. Smitty, up in the turret, may kid one of the boys about the little blonde in town. Somebody asks how the Dodgers did yesterday. Or Burger might muse, back in the tail, that it's corn time in the States, and how'd it be to have a half dozen ears just dripping with butter. That's the talk on the way to the fight. . . . Yes, even sex rears its pretty head once in a while.

Then Lt. Balaban—James A. Balaban, from North Dakota, who used to be a tech sergeant in coast artillery until he switched to the Air Force —cuts in: "Here comes the Spits, boys."

They're a pretty sight. Long and slim and simple. Coming from all directions. Knight is damned glad to see them. A Fortress has a formidable pack of guns sticking out of it, but it can't do the tricks a Spit can do.

Across the Channel and Here Comes Jerry

The channel is down below now, and a few minutes later the continent. The conversation on the interphone has died down. Knight is looking all over the sky for Jerry and wondering whether that's a Spit or a ME190 over there at 1 o'clock.

"Here he comes—10 o'clock about 15,000."

It comes over the interphone and he swings his guns toward 10 o'clock. While he's doing it he thinks of Sven Hansen, another California boy who's on radio. He feels a little sorry for Sven. He's facing the tail and can't see 10 o'clock. It's no fun to be there and wonder how close Jerry is and when the bullets might start plowing through at the rear.

There they are—three Messerschmitts—coming up fast on the left. Too far away yet—

Then the flak begins. Much too far away to do

any damage; doesn't even rock the ship. But it makes him look and that's what it's thrown up for—to divert his attention. Then he hears someone on the interphone say that more MEs are in sight, this time about 2 o'clock at 20,000. And then more. The boys all over the ship sound them off, one by one, as they come in. They speak quietly, almost monotonously, as if they are reading off stock quotations, and after each sentence they pause to give the next guy a chance. It sounds like this:

"There are a couple at 4 o'clock; watch 'em. . . . See that one at 11 o'clock, Hooks? Coming up from about 15,000. . . . Let them have it, boys . . ."

Knight thinks of his buddies in the ships to the right and left. The same thing is going on over there, only instead of using 4 o'clock and 11 o'clock and so on, they might be saying "10,000 feet on the green beam" or "Get 'im, Alec, high in front of the red beam," and they know which way to look because there's a green line painted along the right wing and a red one along the left. Or maybe they're using plain old port and starboard. His gang, though, sticks to the o'clock system, as on the rifle range, because it seems easiest to follow. And quickest, which is important.

They're coming in now, plenty of them and fast. They've got yellow bellies. Göring's prize squadron, eh? Pick of the Luftwaffe, out to get the Fortresses. Okay, let them come; they'll find out.

It's not smooth riding now. Old Mayme is weaving from side to side and rolling up and down as if she were hedge hopping. Knight's guns are leading the three Jerries closing in from 10 o'clock. Two thousand yards . . . 1,500 . . . 1,000. He lets go with a burst and watches the tracers fade off. He wishes to hell the tracers would carry just a little farther. The MEs peel off as two Spits dive in. A wisp of smoke curls from one Jerry's engine; a second later the whole plane is enveloped in smoke, and he's falling, fast.

Almost to the target now. He hasn't thought about it, but he can hear the navigator talking to the pilot and the bombardier—almost as if they were discussing a business deal.

Then maybe this happens:
"Pilot to bombardier: Watch your 4 o'clock."

When the Target Is Reached

Bombardier—that's Lt. Blair. A. D. Blair, an Alabama kid. In a second or two he hears Blair's guns open up. Blair loves his machine guns—practically fondles them—and now he's working them for all he's worth. A Messerschmitt is coming in from below, his guns chattering. No hit yet, on either side. Jerry peels off and circles for another try.

Then comes the warning. "Navigator to bombardier: Target coming up."

Time to sweat now. Jerry on their right, Jerry on their left, ready for the kill—and they've got to level off and fly as straight as a commercial airliner long enough to dump the bomb load.

The ME has circled and is coming in again—400 m.p.h. or better. Blair, he knows, is busy with the bombsight. He has a pretty good idea what is going through Blair's mind. He can see himself in the same spot: two good machine guns in front of him with belts of .50-calibre bullets just aching to get going, and Jerry coming up with his guns spitting at the plane—and he's got to ignore him and get those bombs away. Rivers of sweat roll down his body.

Thirty to 40 seconds for the bombing run . . . 30 to 40 seconds of the roughest smooth flying he's ever put in . . . 30 to 40 seconds of pure sweat.

Blair sings out: "Bombs away!" Knight can picture them floating downward toward the target. He hears Blair's verdict: "Direct hit, smack on the railroad tracks."

But he's not thinking of Blair any more. Now he's thinking of Eddie Smith up in the top turret. He's just heard over the interphone: "Here he comes, Smitty—in high at 11 o'clock."

Smitty swings the turret to 11 o'clock. Jerry's about 1,000 yards away, and he can't tell whether he's aiming at him or the ship to the left, but his guns are blazing so furiously he looks as if he's on fire.

A thousand yards is a long distance, but Smitty

lets Jerry have a burst anyway. He's scored a hit. Smoke trails from Jerry's engine. Still Jerry comes on. His whole ship is afire, and still the guns blaze away. The smoke gets thicker and thicker. It's suicide.

The ship to the left shudders and the wing makes a sickly dip. Jerry's bullets have clipped an engine. Knight sees it out of the corner of his eye as he keeps pouring bullets into Jerry. Then Jerry's broken through the fire. His nose goes down and he starts to spin, leaving a trail of smoke. He's out of vision.

The interphone is talking again.

"Tail gunner: Watch the red beam. He's circling around, Johnny, watch him."

Johnny Burger, astride his bicycle seat in the tail, knees planted firmly on the floor, mutters an unintelligible answer. Now Jerry snaps out of his bank and comes in fast at 4:30 o'clock.

Jerry is the grim counterpart of a hummingbird, poised at a flower and suddenly darting away. That's how he looks—so fast he can hardly be seen.

There's a flash of flaming wings—that's his guns —and the flare of sunlight on his propellers. Then he's gone.

Burger is just as quick this time, though. Burger's guns begin to chatter as Jerry comes out of his bank. It's over almost before it started. Smoke curls up from Jerry's cowling. He snaps upward, and then down, and he's through.

Forty Minutes and It's All Over

It's quiet momentarily, and Knight looks down. To his surprise, the channel is looming up ahead. The coast already? He's hardly noticed that the plane had swung around. He looks at his watch. Forty minutes since he first saw the formation of MEs off there at 10 o'clock. Now he looks around and there isn't a sign of Jerry. He's retired for today.

Knight starts singing into the interphone. The others join in. It's the song they always harmonize on the way back.

"Tangarine. She is all they claim. . . ."

Good harmony number, too.

Mary's Lamb

Mary had a little lamb,
Its fleece was khaki brown,
But everywhere that Mary went
Her lamb could not be found.
For Mary's lamb was kinda stuck.
He couldn't get a pass;
He spent his time in writing notes
To his adoring lass.
And this went on for weeks and weeks,
Till Mary got quite fed;
She wrote a note to her sweet lamb
And this is what she said:
"Oh, Mary had a little lamb
Whose heart she so preferred;
But she couldn't wait and quickly wed
A wolf who'd been deferred."

—Pvt. K. P. Anon

To the Fighting Man

I want to walk by the side of the man who has
    suffered and seen and knows,
Who has measured his place on the battle line, and
    given and taken blows.
Who has never whined when the scheme went
    wrong nor scoffed at the failing plan,
But taken his dose with a heart of trust and the
    faith of a gentleman.
Who has parried and struck and sought and given
    and scarred with a thousand spears,
Can lift his head to the stars of heaven and isn't
    ashamed of his tears.
I want to grasp the hand of the man who has been
    through it all and seen,
Who has walked in the night with an unseen dread
    and stuck to the world machine.
Who has beaten his breast to the winds of dawn
    and thirsted and starved and felt
The sting and the bite of the bitter blasts that the
    mouths of the foul have dealt.
Who was tempted and fell and rose again, and has
    gone on trusty and true
With God supreme in his heart and courage burn-
    ing anew.

—Pfc. Charles W. Bodley
Alaska

Ode to the Medics

They give me shots for tetanus;
For typhoid, I get three.
The yellow fever is excuse
For one more hole in me.

They stick the needle in me dry;
They stick it in me wet.
They punch me full of holes, it seems,
At ev'ry chance they get.

Typhus, measles, housemaid's knee,
There's shots for ev'ry thing;
Fallen arches, leprosy:
Boy, those shots do sting.

Sometimes those vampires stick me good
Right in a vein on me,
And then they take a pint of blood
And smile with fiendish glee.

Oh, I haven't been in battle, yet;
In war I haven't starred.
But if you saw the holes in me.
You'd swear I'm battle scarred.

—Cpl. John Readey
Camp Stoneman, California

Dogface Calendar

A better June brought out the brides,
But now this month means halftrack rides
All up and down the choking sand
Of Caroline maneuver lands.
July is bright with bursting crackers,
And picnic snacks and ball-club backers.
In Trinidad we celebrate
By just continuing to . . . wait.
With August comes a hint of autumn,
The falling leaves in Foggy Bottom.
But in the Irish Base Command
It's just a month of guard to stand.
September was a month of schools
With students breaking all the rules.
Outside of Melbourne we, perforce,
Attend a heavy weapons course.
Six months have turned October fruity
But Hallowe'en's a tour of duty,
And any punkin head that's lit
Gets three weeks' Guard house. That's tough . . .
    luck.
November brings the same Thanksgiving
Our fathers used in thanks for living.
Like them we eat a timely turkey
But canned and tanned, and moist and murky.
December, when it comes this year
Would throw us deep in Christmas cheer.
If, in our stocking, we could find
"An Allied Victory—Peace is Signed."

—Pvt. Al Hine

G.I. Soap

Oh, G.I. soap, of thee I sing,
You're chemically an awesome thing:
Concerning you my thoughts are rife,
You dominate my G.I. life.

You take the grime from barracks floors.
You shrink my long, gray woolen drawers.
You peel the grease from pots and pans.
And chew the skin right off my hands.

You eat holes in my cotton jeans,
You sanitize G.I. latrines,
You're in my hair, my clothes, and now,
I even taste you in the chow.

Your powers of destruction seem
The answer to a chemist's dream.
You look as though you're meant to be
Just soap. Inside, you're TNT.

The War Department isn't wise
To waste time on inventive guys.
All G.I. soldiers have the dope.
Our secret weapon's G.I. soap!

—S/Sgt. S. E. Whitman
Fort Devens, Massachusetts

Pledge from the Solomons

'Twas the seventh day of August
When we landed on the Isles,
And though our hearts were revengeful
Our faces were lit with smiles.

We knew what we were entering
When we landed on that beach-head;
We knew that some of us would not return
For some of us would be dead.

Nature, too, was against us
With diseases, storms and all;
And before the fight was over
She caused many to fall.

So to those brave, courageous fellows
Who died, but not in vain,
I pledge that ere this war is over
Those dirty———

Will plead, beg and bellow
For mercy and for peace,
Which we really shouldn't give them
Since they've caused us so much pain;
But we will, since unlike them,
We are, at least, humane.

So rest in peace, you comrades true;
We'll win this war for America,
What it means,
And you.

—Pvt. G. B. McDonough
Marine Corps
Solomon Islands

Fairy Tale

Little Miss Muffet decided to rough it
In a cabin both old and medieval;
A soldier espied her,
And plied her with cider,
And now she's the forest's prime evil.

—The Shermanic
Sherman Field, Kansas

The Night Life Gets Me Down

A young Marine was trudging
Upon a night patrol,
No moon was there to guide him
Around the swampy hole.
The briars tore his clothing,
His feet slipped on the clay
And as he fell into the mud,
His buddies heard him say:
"It's not the fleas and blood-ticks
I mind when on the trail,
The heat and rain may pelt me
And yet I shall not fail.
The hardships of the boondocks,
My weary, aching feet,
The thirsty, dreary, endless miles,
Have never made me bleat.
For rugged, ragged, rock-strewn hills
And canyons, sere and brown
Are easy in the day time. It's
The night-life gets me down."

—Marine

The Sergeant

I do not like the Sergeant's face,
I do not like his chatter.
And what I think about his brain
Is censorable matter.

He sits in a tent
At the end of the street
And clutters the desk
With his oversized feet.

I do not like the Sergeant's nose;
It would look better broken.
I do not like his tone of voice
When drill commands are spoken.

He walks in the rear
When we're out on the march
And never relaxes
To "Route Step, Harrch!"

I do not like the Sergeant's views
On Army Life and such,
But what I think about the Sarge
Don't seem to matter much.

He can still pull his rank
When I enter my pleas,
And I find myself stuck
With the chronic K.P.'s.

—Pvt. Joe Sims

Genealogical Reflection

To know one thing I've often yearned,
One fact I would discover:
I'll never rest until I have learned
Do MPs have a mother?

—Pfc. Dan Laurence
Australia

Subtle Differences

The sergeant flays his cringing brood,
With curses lurid, crisp and crude.
The colonel's equally emphatic,
But uses swear words more grammatic.

—Armored Castle
Fort Benning

Mother Goose, 1942

Rock-a-bye Troopship
On the wave's top.
When the surf rolls
The Troopship will rock;
When the surf breaks
The Troopship will fall,
And up will come breakfast,
Dinner, and all.

—Pfc. Dan Laurence
Australia

"I keep him here for slamming down the telephone."—Pfc. ALDO

★

———————————————

The guys used to say that the entertainment up there was swell—they got to watch the ice melt. Yet securing the Aleutian Islands quickly became one of Roosevelt's more constant concerns. Steppingstones to the North American continent, their capture by the Japanese at any time would have rendered air raids on the United States a certainty.

KISKA JAPS GOOD-BYE

—Sgt. GEORG MEYERS
October 21, 1942

SOMEWHERE IN Alaska—Two hundred one years ago a dogged old sea dog, Vitus Bering, discovered Alaska.

But it took a ferret-fanged Oriental with horn-rim circles under his eyes to unveil to most Americans this land where the Danish skipper ran aground one foggy July morning.

Then it was too late. Alaska had become one of Uncle Sam's prickliest military secrets.

But it's no secret to the sourdoughboys of the Alaska Defense Command that Bering had bashed his barkentine, or the Russian equivalent thereof, smack against the most astonishing piece of real estate now under the Stars and Stripes.

Like old Vitus himself, the men who man the guns under the midnight sun are in on a big discovery.

They've discovered, for instance, that blubber is not the staple diet of either sourdough or Eskimo. And that a dog team in the paved main streets of any of the territory's four major cities would draw almost as big a throng of curbstone gawkers as the same string of malemutes would

attract at Hollywood and Vine. And maybe even bigger, considering some of the sights that pass Hollywood and Vine.

In short, the lads who had the notion they were about to sojourn for the duration in America's last frontier have discovered that the frontier is streamlined.

Except where it isn't.

But that's a story that will be better told over the tomb of the potentate who pitiably confused the Land of the Rising Sun with the Land of the Midnight Sun.

The fact is, every second soldier you meet in Alaska is disappointed because the frozen north is so much like home. And every first is earnestly proposing that everything north of Mount Olympia should be given back to the Russians.

There are even a few yardbirds in every camp who permit themselves to be quoted that as far as they are concerned, the Japs would have been welcome to their cold cuts off the Aleutian sparerib —if they had only had the decency to say "please."

First in the hearts of all George Washington's countrymen-in-olive drab has ever been the subject of food. Except in a handful of camps that are within easy access of the territory's larger centers of population, fresh fruits and vegetables have be-

*He carries eighty-five pounds on his back—
but it's tough to break a sweat in Alaska.*

come the second-most-popular tent-time topic of conversation. Milk, save in pulverized form, is but a lily-white memory, and even the hens in Alaska lay powder.

In fact, there is one favorite recipe for GI flap-jacks in an Alaska mess sergeant's jotbook that calls for one gallon of pancake flour, one gallon of powdered milk, and two cups of powdered eggs. Add water.

Everyone in camp wonders how he makes any-thing come out of it except concrete mix. So does he.

Fresh meat, beyond an occasional camouflaged flank of reindeer, caribou, or moose, is a delicacy. But to date, none of the kitchens have been re-duced to lading out that delight of the Eskimo from Bethel to Barrow—muktuk. Muktuk, not to be confused with the fur boot called mukluk, is a tal-lowy morsel sliced from the underhide of an Arctic whale.

For entertainment, troops stationed within hik-ing or bus-ride distance of cities lack little that their buddies at home enjoy. Movies, bowling, skating, dancing, and bars in abundance that purvey (between 6 p.m. and 10 p.m. only) all the standard mixes and numerous startling concoc-tions of local formula—all these are available.

The USO has made inroads. Joe E. Brown, Al Jolson, and the Bob Hope–Jerry Colonna–Frances Langford triolet have bobbed about to the military establishments within the confines of Alaska's 586,400 square miles. Hope even volunteered to give a special performance on Attu Island as a possibility for ridding the Aleutians of the only winged pests in the world larger than Alaska mos-quitoes. Hope said all he wanted to do was Kiska Japs good-bye.

Girls there are in Alaska—one of the pleasant shocks that greet new overseas assignees. They come in all the traditional sizes, shapes, and de-grees of romantic susceptibility. Indian and Es-kimo lasses included, the crop is miles from adequate, and competition is razor-edge keen.

Commercial radio broadcasting stations in Fair-banks, Anchorage, Juneau, and Ketchikan keep those interested informed on world news received via the same news services that operate in the States, and the disciples of jive are always hep to the latest swing, transcribed.

Short-wave reception is erratic but mostly lis-tenable. Radios among the soldiers, however, are only slightly more prevalent than penguins in the pantry, and since the Quiz Kids, everyone knows the habitat of penguins is the South Pole.

By one of those devices that make Uncle Sam's Army ofttimes the wonder and despair of foreign strategists, many of the Alaska-based troops hail from the deep South. To them, the 20 hours of daylight throughout the quickie summer season is a blessing out of Dixie. But they are now counting that blessing on one finger as the long dark of winter begins to black out the Northland, leaving shortly less than a fistful of hours when artificial illumination will not be necessary for anybody who wants to see.

Soldiers like to say that Alaska has only two seasons—winter and July. Sourdoughs of the more frigid stretches go them one better. They designate seasons as "winter and poor sledding."

There are many definitions of what constitutes a sourdough. The basic requisite in almost all of them is that you must have seen the ice come and go in the Yukon or one of its tributaries. From there on, definitions vary.

But all that is one corner of the Alaska portrait: the corner labeled "theater of operations." Those areas dubbed "combat zones" have another tale to tell—stories of long hours of fatigue with no relief details in what the U.S. Weather Bureau proudly calls the "world's worst weather."

Alaskans of the Aleutian chain won't take the blame for the sleety downpour that batters the archipelago on the bias. They claim "it rains in Siberia, and the wind just blows it over here."

Right now they're on the brink of the season of better sledding. Within a few weeks the barrack-room spiders will begin spinning their webs in thermometer tubes at the zero mark.

That's when you'll hear the boys from Dixie begin hollering, "Give it back to the Russians."

Not one of them yet has entertained the sug-gestion of giving it to the Japs.

WHAT'S YOUR PROBLEM?

Changing Names

Dear *Yank*:

The name. Just look at it! Can I change it, *Yank*? Can I?

—Pvt. Wolwoff Zylbercweigz
Hawaii

Sure. But you'll have to see your legal assistance officer, because authority to change your name is granted by the individual states, and state laws vary. Generally the court requires a good reason—for example, "it is too long" or "people can't pronounce it" or "for business." To get your new name on the Army records, you must show your CO a certified copy of the court order. See WD Cir. 254 (1943), Sec. II.

GI "Minors"

Dear *Yank*:

I enlisted in the Army while I was under age; I lied to the recruiting officer and served two years before I was discovered. The Army gave me an honorable discharge, however. Since then I have been drafted and am now nearing the end of my first "drafted" year. This, added to my earlier service, gives me three full years in the Army, but I have been told that I cannot wear a hash mark for that three-year hitch because I enlisted under false colors. I don't think that's fair. After all, I've done nothing I should be ashamed of.

—Pfc. James N. Heller
Iran

According to regulations, service stripes can be worn by those "who have served honorably," whether continuously or not, and the fact that you were discharged because you were under age does not bar you from wearing a service stripe. Your discharge is an honorable one, and that's what counts. Refer doubters to AR 615-360 (39) and AR 600-40 (46-e).

Shave and Haircut

Dear *Yank*:

I have a very serious problem that I would like your advice on. We are allowed to go to town in fatigues, mixed uniforms, and practically anything we want. But can we grow a beard? Hell, no. I have started one four different times. They vary in length from five to 15 days. About that time a shave tail that isn't old enough to grow a beard pipes up: "Soldier, I will give you 30 minutes to get that beard shaved off." What we would like to know is, do soldiers overseas have the right to grow beards?

—Cpl. Glen Carlsen
India

That's a tough one. AR 40-205, Paragraph 7, says the soldier will keep ". . . the beard neatly trimmed." Looks to us as if you'll just have to hide in the jungle until your struggling whiskers get to where they can stand trimming. Even then it's our guess that most COs will insist that a "neatly trimmed" beard is simply a smooth shave.

Drilling Square Holes

Dear *Yank*:

Ever since I came into the Army, I've been plagued by doubting Thomases when I told them what I did in civilian life, and I know I've lost out on some good deals because resentful officers thought I was pulling their legs when they interviewed me for various jobs. So *Yank*, if you will please put into print that fellows *can* make a living out of drilling square holes (and that this has no connection with left-handed monkey wrenches or sky hooks), I will carry your clipping around as official protection against Army wise guys.

—Pvt. Nicholas Komito
Australia

Glad to help. As a matter of fact, there is a tool firm in Pennsylvania that drills square holes. A special drill has three lips, with the heel of each "land" rocking the drill so that it turns a corner as its lip finishes a side cut. The motion of the chuck enables the drill to move in alternate cycloid curves whose cords————. But, say, this can go on for a long time. Suppose we just say you're right. Okay?

SGT. GEORGE BAKER

52

The Kokoda Trail was 58 miles of mud and trenchfoot, cutting a swath across the Owen Stanley Mountains in Port Moresby. Nevertheless, if Australia was to be protected by an Allied Pacific base to the north, New Guinea had to be taken. And that meant taming the Kokoda.

NO GLAMOR HERE

—Sgt. E. J. KAHN, JR.
Yank Field Correspondent
December 16, 1942

AN ADVANCED Base in New Guinea [By wireless]—American ground forces, who often don't know one day from another, have ceaselessly pressed on through inhospitable terrain along which the Japs have had months to construct heavy defense fortifications.

Old General Mud has long been accepted as a formidable obstacle to the progress of a military machine, but to spend a day in mud only knee-deep would seem a comparative lark to some of America's jungle fighters who have waded into action with only their heads and arms out of water, pushing on grimly toward concrete pillboxes embedded by the enemy in the thick, concealing undergrowth. In this kind of fighting, where large masses of men can't be deployed according to venerable military theories, and where a column of twos is frequently much too wide a marching for-

mation for the only available trail, it takes a lot of individual initiative and a lot of collective guts to crack open an enemy position.

Riflemen edging cautiously through the jungle sometimes don't actually see a Jap from morning to night, though they have good reason to believe that the little men are crawling in hollows, popping unexpectedly out of holes like land crabs, and clinging to clusters of coconuts in the tops of palm trees.

One Yank, back from the front lines after five wet and weary days up there, was asked if he had shot any Japs.

"Well, I don't know for certain," he said, "but I sure nailed a lot of coconuts."

To spend a week or so in constant jungle fighting, never dry, never knowing where the next meal is coming from but aware that it probably won't be very hot or very tasty, bothered incessantly by mosquitoes and other insects, wearing tattered uniforms and shoes sucked to shreds by the stinking tropical mud, bombed and strafed from the air and endlessly harried from the ground—to go through that would be a tough test for the most hardened professional soldier.

Green American troops are doing it now, doing it moreover, after having in many cases marched through the jungle for several weeks to get to their battle positions. It takes nerve to stand up under the gruelling treatment our infantry has been taking, and no better evidence of the presence in large quantities of the nerve required exists than the example—just one of many—of Pfc. George Warfield of Glenwood, Minnesota, number-one gunner of a machine-gun squad in a heavy weapons company.

A Jap bullet ripped into his foot down by his heel, went clean through the ankle, and came to rest protruding from his legging. Warfield, knocked down, got up a moment later and pulled the bullet out of his legging. He put it in his pocket and walked down the trail to the nearest field hos-

pital, to the wonder of several doctors who regarded his hike as little short of miraculous.

"I just got hit here with this," he said, holding out the bullet and extending a foot whose shoe had two holes in it.

Somebody asked him how he had ever managed to get down the trail on his wounded foot. "Oh, it wasn't too bad," he said. "It loosened up while I was moving and when I stopped once it got a little stiff, so I didn't stop again."

There are some Yanks, as there must be in all wars, who won't walk back or come back at all, and since evacuating the wounded is a difficult enough problem without bothering about the dead, they are being buried with full military honors, in crude graves dug out of this lush wilderness.

Soldiers don't cry much, but one first sergeant, as merciless a man as ever penned a KP roster, made no attempt to hide his tears last week when they laid a soldier to rest high on a hill covered with tall, wavy grass.

"Did you know him?" he was asked.

"Yeah," said the topkick. "He was one of my boys."

1943

IN
THE
MOOD

EARLY IN THE WAR, an earnest broadcaster for the BBC began opening his program with the introduction to Beethoven's Fifth Symphony—*dit-dit-dit-dah*. In Morse code, it was a *V*. For Victory. And within less time than it takes to bomb a munitions dump, it had become the most popular worldwide symbol since the crucifix: people greeted one another with two raised fingers; newborn infants were named Victor or Vickie or Vincent; and Tiffany's immediately sold out of its diamond V brooches, priced at only $5,000. All of this for good reason.

Nineteen forty-three was the year many GIs remember with something almost akin to fondness. The war was still new enough that they weren't entirely bone weary, and by February it had become increasingly evident to both Hitler and Hirohito that the Axis powers might, after all, be waist-deep in dangerous waters and sinking slowly. This is not to imply that the balance of war had tipped in favor of the Allies—yet—but merely that they finally had found a toehold from which they would not be dislodged, no matter how long it took them to reach the next rung. Guadalcanal, the impossible dream, fell to them on February 9, six months after they'd first stepped upon its beaches; the rout at Kasserine Pass was redeemed at Tunis and later on at Sicily, after the Reich's Afrika Korps had surrendered unconditionally; and Tarawa, representing the costliest operation in U.S. military history, was littered with the pierced bodies of wounded Marines who nonetheless were tended to beneath the shadow of a red, white, and blue flag. Indeed, the headlines themselves offered consummate proof that, by 1943, we finally were getting into the swing of things.

Meanwhile, back in Hollywood, Daffy Duck was evading the draft, as a legion of mice rebelled against a suspiciously Oriental-looking feline by building a Liberty Bulldog and chanting "We Did It Before and We Can Do It Again." Some of the motion picture industry's more adult fare? "I don't want any dead heroes in this outfit," "My legs! Where are my legs?" "Now go, darling, and don't look back," and "It's Ramirez! What's left of him" were typical examples of what screenwriters were handing the American public. The tunesmiths were no better. "You Can't Say No to a Soldier" was a training manual for the companion arts of promiscuity and infidelity; "I'm Doin' it for Defense" was doubtless written in a courtroom during one of the ensuing divorce proceedings; "As Mabel Goes, So Goes the Navy" was practically a rallying cry for organized prostitution; and "Bell Bottom Trousers" wasn't even allowed on the radio until 1945, and then only after it had been entirely rewritten.

Madison Avenue, too, was coming of age. If the previous year had seen a number of products attempting to cash in—obliquely—on war fever, 1943 was the blitz revisited. Many think it began when Lucky Strike was forced to pull the color green from its cigarette packaging, as green ink had a metallic base that was clearly more essential to airplane production than to smoker's hack. Nothing unusual there— such shortages were common. But then some mysterious brain trust at American Tobacco decided to turn adversity 180 degrees by proclaiming: "Lucky Strike Green Has Gone to War!" After that, *everybody* wanted in on the act. Macaroni was bombing Bougainville, electric toasters were falling on Berlin, and the skies over Tokyo were allegedly dotted by various toiletries. Hard-pressed to explain what *they* were dumping on the Axis, laxative manufacturers contented themselves with putting the smiles on aviators' faces.

Elsewhere on the home front, families were planting victory gardens ("Backyard radishes can hasten the homecoming"), saving kitchen fats ("for the kid in Upper Four"), and trying to figure out ration books. It always seemed that the day you finally got your hands on some butter, there was a sudden shortage of bread to spread it on; and when—at long last—they sold you that pack of Camels, there wasn't a match to be found for love nor A coupons. But few complained—after all, most had seen the pictures of London after the buzz bombs. Instead they went to the movies and bought war bonds from celebrities like Carole Lombard (ultimately killed in a plane crash on her way to another rally), they listened to the radio and kept it tuned to the news instead of Edgar Bergen and Charlie McCarthy, and they learned to do without. Because, judging by the reports from Tarawa, it suddenly seemed that sacrifice led to bigger things; and by the end of 1943, at long last, all of America was speaking the same language.

MAJOR BATTLES:
   Kasserine Pass, Bismarck Sea, Sicily, Salerno, Empress Augusta Bay, Tarawa
HOLLYWOOD'S BEST:
   This Is the Army (Irving Berlin and Ronald Reagan)
HOLLYWOOD'S WORST:
   They Came to Blow Up America (George Sanders and Poldy Dur)
MOST POPULAR WAR SONG (Nonracist):
   "They're Either Too Young or Too Old"
MOST POPULAR WAR SONG (Racist):
   "Since He Traded His Zoot Suit for a Uniform"
MOST POPULAR SONG—GENERAL:
   "Mairzy Doats"
MOST READ BOOK:
   One World, by Wendell Willkie
RUNNER-UP:
   The Bible
WHAT MADISON AVENUE SAID GENERAL ELECTRIC COULD MAKE AIRPLANE LANDING LIGHTS WITH:
   A glass pie plate
HOW MADISON AVENUE SAID FIGHTERS ON THE PRODUCTION FRONT GOT THEIR ENERGY:
   By relaxing at the Hotel New Yorker
WHAT MADISON AVENUE SAID JIMMY WAS GIVING HIS LIFE FOR:
   Monroe adding machines
THE ONLY PRODUCT THAT DIDN'T CLAIM TO BE WINNING THE WAR:
   Kreml hair tonic (but it sure made soldiers look slick)
THE NUMBER OF TIMES JUDY GOT MICKEY AT THE END:
   All of them
FAVORITE PLACE TO LEAVE YOUR HEART:
   The Stage Door Canteen
WHAT SOLDIERS WERE, AFTER A FIFTH OF RYE:
   "Knee-walkin' tight"

WHAT OTHER PEOPLE WERE, AFTER A FIFTH OF RYE:
   Unconscious
MOST FATHOMABLE CRAZE:
   Reflective ankle bracelets that dimmed out in case of an air raid
LEAST FATHOMABLE CRAZE:
   Frank Sinatra
WALTER WINCHELL ON RATIONING:
   "Roses are red, violets are blue, Sugar is sweet—remember?"
FAVORITE MEMORY OF GROWING UP:
   Giving your bike to the scrap drive, even if it meant all you had left were some marbles and an old football
LEAST FAVORITE MEMORY OF GROWING UP:
   When Billy Pincus next door came home from Tarawa—trying not to stare at his legs, because he didn't have them anymore
WHAT YOU SAID TO AN AMERICAN OF JAPANESE DESCENT:
   "Shut up and get back in line."
WHAT YOU CALLED A BLACK CORPORAL WITH THREE PURPLE HEARTS:
   "Hey, you."
MOST MEMORABLE LINE FROM THE ETO:
   "Th'hell this ain't the most important hole in the world. I'm *in* it!"
MOST MEMORABLE LINE FROM THE PACIFIC:
   "Banzai this, you son-of-a-bitch!"
BIGGEST CHUMPS:
   The Army censors—especially when you wrote home asking for India nuts and they cut out the India part because that's where you were stationed, so Aunt Dubby wound up looking in the atlas to see if there was a place called Macadamia
MOST EFFECTIVE REMEDY:
   Captain Eddie Rosen, who phrased the second sentences of his V-mail to his Uncle Lou so that the first letters of each word spelled out where he was: "Gee, usually all doctors are lucky—camps and nurses and leaves."

BEST VALUE FOR YOUR DOLLAR:
   War bonds
BEST ANNIVERSARY PRESENT FOR MOM AND POP:
   Shoes
WHAT YOU GOT WHEN YOU TRADED TWO STEELIES AND AN AGGIE:
   Butter
MOST CREATIVE USE OF DER FÜHRER'S FACE:
   Donald Duck thumbing his nose at it
HOW YOU KNEW YOU WERE A REAL SOLDIER:
   When you called the replacement depot a repple-depple just like everyone else, and nobody thought you were trying to show off

HOW YOU KNEW YOU HAD A LOT LEFT TO LEARN:
   When you told that big bruiser from Fargo that if he wanted sympathy, he should look in the dictionary between *shit* and *syphilis*, and he broke one of your front teeth
MOST ADMIRED AMERICAN FEMALE (Limbs Only):
   Rita Hayworth
MOST ADMIRED AMERICAN FEMALE (the Whole Package):
   Rosie the Riveter
MOST ADMIRED AMERICAN MALE:
   The GI

A DOGFACE ANSWERS A COLLECTION AGENCY

March 19, 1943

New Guinea
Jan. 26, 1943

Dear sirs:
Your letter of 11/19/42 was duly rec'd today and after reading the contents therein I am pleased to note that I will be summoned to appear in court to make payment due you of $14.80 plus interest and costs.

Gentlemen, the opportunities your letter presents are beyond my wildest dreams.

I believe by law the court is required to send a process server to deliver the summons in person. In that case I will inform you of certain essentials he will require for jungle travel.

The first item advisable is a self-inflating life raft, as ships even in convoys are sometimes sunk. The raft will also be useful later in crossing rivers and swamps in New Guinea. He should also bring the following items: mosquito bars, head net, pith helmet, quinine, salt tablets, vitamin pills, mosquito and sunburn lotions, medical supplies for tropical infections, poisonous snakes, and spiders, steel helmet, gas mask, waterproof tent, heavy-caliber rifle for shooting Japs, crocodiles, and other game, machete, chlorine capsules, flashlight, and soap.

In choosing this process server, make sure that he is not an alcoholic, as there isn't a drink to be found on the whole island. Furthermore, he must not be allergic to mosquitoes, heat rash, malaria, dengue fever, snakes, spiders, lizards, flies, crocodiles, and tall grass with a few head hunters in it. These are trivial matters, and he may never come in contact with any of them, especially if his convoy is attacked by the enemy's battle fleet.

I am telling you all this as I am much concerned over his safe arrival. If he reaches this location our meeting will be much more impressive than Stanley and Livingstone's. I will see that the best possible care is taken of him on arrival. As soon as he has recovered from his jungle trip we will be on our way back to civilization and the law court. I trust he is already on his way, and I am packing my barracks bags to avoid any waste of time.

Here's hoping that this letter finds you in the best of health.

—Respectfully yours,
Pvt. Oris Turner

"CAN" RATIONS

—Robert L. Schwartz Y3c
Yank Staff Writer
January 6, 1943

Destroyer men tell boudoir stories, but 18 days at sea change the scuttlebutt to adventures without a heroine.

A FTER EVENING chow on the destroyer, the men sit on the fantail and tell tall stories. Most of the crew come to these bull sessions, and in the two hours before dark they tell tale after tale of boudoir experience.

But one night was different. We had been out for 18 days. Maybe the men were tired of bedroom stories or maybe it was the weather, which had turned sharp and cold, but anyway, they stopped talking after a few stories had fallen flat.

One of the sailors sitting on a row of depth charges sighed and said, "It's too damned quiet these days."

The other men nodded. "Two thousand miles this trip," another said, "and we didn't even hear a sub on the sound gear. That's what comes from cleaning a place out too good."

They were quiet for a while longer and then a yeoman said, "It wasn't like this the first few times we came out here." He laughed and the other men laughed with him, and then he went on talking.

The Yeoman's Story

Do you remember the time we spotted the first sub? I was on the bridge as a "talker" that night.

It was warm and very dark; you couldn't see your hand in front of your face. I was nervous. It was my first trip to sea.

Besides listening over the phone, I would take the captain's commands and call them out over the phones for the men on the guns and in the lookout posts. The job wasn't hard, but I was new at it— and all of a sudden the port lookout calls in that he spotted a periscope dead ahead on the surface.

I was so damned scared I didn't know what to do. Only the captain was calm. I never saw anyone so calm in all my life. My hands were sweating like I'd dipped them in water, and he was just standing there whistling softly through his teeth.

The captain asked me for the phone set and I gave it to him. He talked in it to all the gun crews. "Fill your loading lines and load your guns," he said quietly. "The chief signalman will turn on the main searchlight when the sub is within range. Do not fire when the searchlight goes on. You will be given the preliminary command 'stand by' and then the command 'fire.' I repeat: do not fire when the searchlight goes on. You will be given the command 'stand by' and then the command 'fire.' "

He gave me back the phone set and I hung it around my neck again. The captain went back to his low whistling. It was a thing called "Lady Be Good."

The port lookout shouted, "They're loading their deck gun, sir." The searchlight came on. Out

Destroyer, transport, or cruiser—it's always a tight fit.

on the water was a vague gray object, low in the waves.

The captain stopped whistling. He pointed to me and the phone set, motioning for me to repeat his command: "Shoot it," he said. "Shoot it! Shoot it!"

The men shook their heads when the yeoman finished, each remembering his part in the engagement. The radioman came away from the rail where he had been standing and joined the circle. He was blond, thin, about 23. He had left Massachusetts to join the Navy three years earlier. Before the war, he had spent his shore leaves visiting museums and going to concerts.

The Radioman's Story

That reminds me of a trip we took with a lot of new recruits. They were good guys and good to talk to, probably nervous, but they never showed it much, and they spent most of their time in small groups up on the fo'c'sle watching the bow cut through the water, like all new sailors seem to do.

I was up gassing with them one day when suddenly a big column of smoke shot into the air up ahead on the horizon. A tanker had just been torpedoed. We shot up to full speed and depth-bombed the whole area. Some smaller ships came up and picked up the survivors and we went back to join them after we finished.

All the freighter men thrown in the water had life jackets on, but most of them were dead and their jackets had slipped down around their waists. They just floated around with their heads under water and their butts sticking up.

When I finished my work I went back up to the fo'c'sle to see how the new guys were taking it. I walked clear up to them before I noticed they were all crying. Their fists were clenched so tight you could see their veins standing out.

The bosun's mate cleared his throat and spat into the sea. He was a regular navy man of many hitches. Before joining the Navy he had shipped as helmsman in the Merchant Marine.

The Bosun's Mate's Story

I remember that rescue. There was a small raft with a little pole on it floating around in the wreckage. Two guys were on the raft and the damned thing was burning like a son of a gun. We launched a boat and went to take them off. Just before we got to them one of the guys jumped off. He sank before we could get to him.

I was helmsman of the boat and I didn't want to steer too close to the raft because it was burning pretty high now. I pulled up near the thing and told the other guy to jump off and swim over. He wouldn't move. The raft was burning, the guy's clothes were smoking, and the little mast he was hanging onto was all on fire. But the damned fool

wouldn't let go. We could see his hands getting burned and he just stood there and stared at us. Finally our ensign jumped overboard as I edged in close, grabbed the guy, and threw him aboard our boat. Two hours later, back here on the destroyer, the guy was perfectly all right except for the burns on his hands.

"That's the way it goes," the yeoman said. "They go right out of their head sometimes."

"Yeah," a seaman said, "I remember once—"

"You remember," the gunner's mate said scornfully. "You ain't old enough to remember anything." The gunner's mate was another old navy man: he was short, Irish, and bald. He had served in the last war and loved to tell stories. Now he packed his pipe down and settled back to enjoy the respectful silence he always got.

The Gunner's Mate's Story

Our strangest rescue, if you can call it that, was one day up around Newfoundland. It was a dark, gray day, like they always are up there, when we suddenly heard a plane up above. It was one of our planes and it signalled that there was a raft floatin' around with someone on it, just like you told about, and it was about 10 miles back of us. So we turned around and headed back for it through an ocean that looked like one of them new cocktails—full of slush and chipped ice.

It was snowing by then, and we had a hard time findin' the raft. When we finally made it out, there didn't seem to be no one on it. There were footprints in the snow on the raft, but not a soul aboard. The new snow hadn't even covered the footprints up yet.

We sank it with our machine guns.

"Sometimes you get a queer one," the torpedoman said. He was a short, dark Italian who had once fought in the Golden Gloves.

The Torpedoman's Story

We were out with some other ships and an American sub, just practicing. The sub would go under and we would listen for it with our sound machines. When we found it, we'd blow our whistle and then the sub would move off somewhere else and we'd do it all over again. There were five of us there: three PC boats, a Canadian corvette, and us on the destroyer.

Finally, after we'd found it a few times, the sub starts to surface. Our starboard lookout says, "Periscope at oh-four-five, sir." About two seconds later the port lookout says, "Periscope at two-six-oh, sir." Nobody knew what to make of it. We weren't sure which sub was ours, and nobody believed a Nazi sub would come right up among five of our ships. We waited and waited, not knowing what the hell to do, and finally the port sub came clear out of the water and we saw it was ours.

Well, we started after the other one, but as soon as it saw where it was, it pulled down its periscope and disappeared.

The American sub came up, saw what was happening, and ran like hell.

You won't believe this, but with five antisubmarine ships against one lousy sub, we never got the guy. We had to be careful not to sink our own sub.

The men all shook their heads at this and some of them laughed.

"I remember—" the seaman started to say.

"My God!" said the gunner's mate. "There he goes again."

"I remember—" the seaman repeated, but the gunner's mate reached over and put his hand over the seaman's mouth.

"Hush now," the gunner's mate said gently. "Hush now before poppa spank."

The Fire Controlman's Story

You know that nothing scares you so much as sitting still in the water when you know there are subs around. Sometimes we lower a boat when we have to rescue people and keep the destroyer circling around so they can't line us up for a tin fish. We did that once up north when we picked up three guys from a raft. That was one of those peculiar experiences—not the circling around, but those men on the raft. One of them was a British professor who was going to America to teach in some college. Both of his legs were frozen when we picked him up, and they had to be cut off. One of the other men lost one of his legs, too. But the third man, a merchant seaman, had just walked back and forth on this little raft for two days, and he was perfectly okay.

I still wonder about that sometimes. It seems funny that this dumb seaman knew enough to walk back and forth while the professor just sat there and froze.

There was little talking after this story until the silence began to work on the coxswain, a kid of 20. He was staring at the deck and finally looked up.

The Coxswain's Story

You know, I had a good friend once on a destroyer. He was a fireman and we were in boot camp together. He was on duty in the fireroom during a sub patrol. Another fireman, who was off duty, came down to get a cup of coffee. Usually there's a coffee pot in the fireroom, but this time they had run out of grounds for making more. My friend and this other guy flipped to see who'd go up and get some more from the galley. It was good and cold out, and none of them wanted to go, but my friend won and the other had to go up. My friend stayed down on duty.

While this other guy was up in the galley, a torpedo hit right smack in the number-one fireroom.

Nobody got out.

"Flying the Hump" was crate pusher slang for crossing the Himalayas by air, and if you happened to be a bomber crew stationed in the CBI (China-Burma-India theater), duty carried its own unique hazards. These nine men played peek-a-boo with death over Rangoon—and lived to tell the tale.

JINX FLIGHT

—Sgt. ED CUNNINGHAM
January 20, 1943

A T A U.S. Bomber Base, India—There are nine Yank airmen at this U.S. base who will give you odds that they can make any nine-lived cat turn green with envy. They're members of a combat crew that played tag with borrowed time so often on a recent bombing mission that the law of averages is in grave danger of being repealed.

Here are the names of these nine guys with the charmed lives. Don't put a wooden anna on the line against them until you've read their story.

FIRST LT. WILLIAM R. BERKELEY, 25, pilot,
  Cleveland, Ohio.
SECOND LT. THOMAS L. MURPHY, 22, copilot,
  Shreveport, Louisiana.
FIRST LT. FRANCIS N. THOMPSON, 25,
  navigator.
M/SGT. HOWARD C. DARBY, 32, bombardier,
  Plattsburg, New York.
T/SGT. WILLIAM O. FROST, 25, engineer,
  Jaffrey, New Hampshire.
S/SGT. JOHN E. CRAIGIE, 25, radio operator,
  West Haven, Connecticut.
S/SGT. BERNARD L. BENNETT, 23, tail gunner,
  Peru, Indiana.
S/SGT. ADOLPH R. SCOLAVINO, 22, belly
  gunner, Providence, Rhode Island.
SGT. EDWARD M. SALLEY, 22, waist gunner,
  Houston, Texas.

This tale starts at Rangoon, where the boys were headed recently to drop a few explosive calling cards on the Japs. Fifteen minutes from the target area, a fire broke out down in the nose of the plane. A parachute placed too near the electric heater had caught fire, flooding the plane with smoke. Lt. Thompson's fire extinguisher quickly drenched the blaze and averted the first threat of disaster.

Then, right over the target, all four motors cut out. The plane dipped down toward the spitting Jap ack-ack guns, while Berkeley feverishly twisted the controls, trying to get the motors back. He succeeded momentarily, only to have them conk off again. For seconds that seemed hours, the B-24 started losing altitude. Then the motors came on again and Berkeley leveled off.

After Darby had dropped his load of thousand pounders, the B-24 headed for home. Berkeley and his crew stopped sweating then, bolstered up by the fact that they had weathered three threatened disasters. Other than a few frayed nerves, the only damage was the burned parachute. But what the hell, there was an extra chute anyway. A ground crewman had left one back in the cabin by mistake. It was the first time the B-24 had ever carried more than the usual nine chutes.

But the headaches were just beginning. The B-24 was still 100 miles at sea when its electrical system went out. So did the auxiliary. Shortly after, the batteries went, too. The ship had no electrical power at all. That meant no electric governor for the propellers, which were fast approaching the red danger line on the RPM gauge. No means of putting out distress signals or radio identification. No landing lights.

Everything was dead except the vacumatic instruments. Only the flight indicator and the gyro compass were working. Murphy's flashlight, trained on the instrument panel, was the only light available for the pilot to watch his course.

Frost, the engineer, worked frantically trying to get the power back. But no soap. Only a tight-rope walker standing against a 170-m.p.h. gale out on the wingtip could get at the source of the trouble. The electrical system was unrepairable in the air.

They were over land by now but still without landing lights. Circling over a city, they were looking for an airfield when a British Hurricane fighter made a pass at them in the darkness. Unable to radio their identification, they had been spotted as an enemy bomber. Fortunately, the Hurricane pilot must have recognized the B-24 twin-tailed design. He didn't open fire on them.

The number-three engine was running away now. The finger on the RPM gauge was up to 3,300, far beyond the danger point and way too far beyond the normal 2,700 revolutions per minute. That number-three engine might fall off at any minute.

When it started to splinter, Berkeley gave the order to bail out. He cut off the main switches, to prevent explosions, then followed his crew into the night. His was the spare parachute.

The nine parachutes floated earthward through 7,000 feet of darkness. Seven of them swayed crazily, their riser lines unguided by the seven unconscious men strapped to their rubber seats. Only Darby and Scolavino saw the B-24, with its number-three engine falling to pieces, plunge past them. The others had been knocked out by the flailing buckles of their chest straps just seconds after they had pulled their ripcords. They hadn't had time to adjust them properly before jumping.

When they hit the cool layer of air about 5,000 feet up, they came to.

Only the wind lapping against the billows of their flying canopies broke the silence of the night. They could control their riser lines now, but that didn't prevent the wind from carrying them apart. It would be every man for himself when they hit the ground.

Darby was better prepared than the rest; he had his .45 with him. Frost had jumped ready for action, too, carrying a tommy gun, 125 rounds of ammunition, a camera, and a musette bag. But he hadn't figured on that strap buckle. When he recovered at 5,000 feet, he had nothing left in his hands but his flight cap. That had been on his head when he bailed out.

Darby, uninjured and armed, took his delayed descent in stride. He pulled a pack of cigarettes out of his pocket, lit up, and settled back to enjoy his trip down to earth.

The others weren't so comfortable. Salley, with a gaping lip wound where two teeth had been driven through by the strap buckle, landed in a tree. Fortunately, he managed to shake his chute loose and fall to the ground without injury. Craigie, bleeding profusely from a broken cartilage in his nose, landed in a lake. He had to swim and wade through mud for nine hours before being rescued by an Indian boatman. Frost barely missed a tree, landing by pulling his legs up under him and tugging on the riser lines.

Some of the crew landed in rice paddies, others in swamps. All but Murphy, Darby, and Craigie spent the night where they landed, sleeping on the ground with their parachutes as pillows. The copilot and bombardier reached Indian villages after walking several hours, and spent the night there. Craigie swam and walked until dawn. Ironically, he was the only one who heard the yells of any of his crewmates. He heard Bennett calling soon after they landed but couldn't call back because of his wound.

Some of them had to do a little improvising before being rescued. Lt. Berkeley lost a shoe coming down. He made a substitute by cutting off a piece of canvas from the back of his parachute and sewing it into slipper form with a fish hook and fishing line from his jungle kit. Berkeley managed to wet his parched lips during the night by collecting a little dew on a waxed candy paper. Murphy went native and draped himself in a silk shawl while the villagers were drying his uniform.

When the sun came up, all nine of the crew started for a nearby Indian city by different routes. Some of them met along the line. Craigie and Salley ran into each other in a native village and boarded a train together. At the next station, Bennett got on. Scolavino and Lt. Thompson had caught an earlier train, at different stations, but the conductor put them in the same coach.

Frost met Darby along the river and got a boat to take them to the city. Lt. Berkeley also was making his way by boat when he was hailed by Lt. Murphy from a village along the riverbank. He picked up his copilot, and they, too, caught a train that took them to the city.

The entire crew met that night at a hotel in the city. And that's where their luck ran out, according to Salley.

"We stayed at that hotel eight days waiting for travel orders back to our base. But do you think we drew expenses? Like hell! We all had to pay our own hotel bills!"

MAIL CALL

Dear *Yank*:
My plane was in Los Angeles at the height of the so-called zoot-suit riots. I saw several of them and was ashamed of the servicemen involved. It must be understood, and no amount of fancy newspaper baloney can hide it, that the zoot-suit riots were really race riots, directed mainly against the Mexican, and to some degree, the Negro citizens of Los Angeles. It's about time a certain element in the armed forces be told that a man can be a good American and a damn good citizen, regardless of the color of his skin, and has all the rights of a citizen. To those servicemen who took part in the riots I'd like to ask a question: What the hell uniform do you think you're wearing, American or Nazi?

—Crew Chief
Patterson Field, Ohio

Dear *Yank*:
I am not a lover of dogs, but the short story "The Sweetheart of Company D" [in the First Anniversary edition of *Yank*] was to me a very interesting story. I would like to see it made into a book-length novel by some good writer who was caught in the draft and now longs to have something to write about during his time off. I'm not a critic but a lover of good stories.

—Sgt. George Saunders
England

We'll pass the word on to the author of "The Sweetheart of Company D," Pvt. William Saroyan. Other works by the same writer: "The Human Comedy," "The Time of Your Life."

Dear *Yank*:
If the war is over before my subscription runs out, I hope you will just forget about it, for I know I will.

—Cpl. Jule C. La Perkis
Alaska

Dear *Yank*:
We hadn't been over here in England very long till three of us guys bought a phonograph, the three being Sgt. Willis B. Zumwalt from California, Cpl. Leo H. Fellmar from Chicago and myself.

A few days later we wrote Bing Crosby for a few of his latest recordings, then completely forgot about it till one day at mail call we received a large package containing one dozen brand new records from the Decca Record Co. of New York. We think Bing is a swell guy.

—Cpl. Morris W. Wood
England

No War Songs in America

Dear *Yank*:

Why are there no war songs in America? The way I see it, the trouble is due to commercial song writers who have no feeling nor understanding why people are fighting fascism. They doctor up sweet, sugary stuff to try to take our minds off reality when at this crucial time we need a stimulant like music to give us guts. I think musicians have missed the boat. The current war songs are an insult to America's dignity. Perhaps it reflects healthy nostalgia to sing "Johnny Doughboy Found a Rose in Ireland." I feel it would be better if we had a song called "Johnny Doughboy Found a Second Front in Europe."

—Cpl. George Kauffman
Australia

Pinups

Dear *Yank*:

I don't know who started this idea of pinups, but they say that it is supposed to help keep up the morale of the servicemen, or something like that. Here is my idea of the help it is. In the first place, I would say that 24 out of 25 of the men in the service are either married or have a girl at home whom they respect and intend to marry as soon as this war is over. . . . How many of you GIs would like to go home and find the room of your wife or girlfriend covered with pictures of a guy stepping out of a bathtub, draped only in a skimpy little towel, or see the walls covered with the pictures of a shorts advertisement or such pictures? None of you would. Then why keep a lot of junk

hanging around and kid yourself about keeping up morale? . . .

I would much rather wake up in the morning and see a picture of a P-51 or 39 hanging above my bed or over the picture of my wife, whom I think is the best-looking girl in the world, than of some dame who has been kidded into or highly paid for posing for these pictures.

—Pfc. Joseph H. Saling
Myrtle Beach AAF, South Carolina

Dear *Yank*:

We boys do not approve of your very indecent portrayal of the spicy-looking female in a recent edition of our much-loved and eagerly read *Yank*. It seems the intelligent-looking Irene Manning would never pose for such a suggestive-looking picture. We may seem old-fashioned, but sending *Yank* home to wives and sweethearts with such a seductive-looking picture, we feel compelled to make an apology for this issue.

Is this the much publicized "Pinup Girl" that the Yankee soldiers so crave? We have our doubts! Miss Manning is well dressed, but the pose—phew! (Hays office please take note.)

Believe it or not, our average age is 23

—Sgt. E. W. O'Hara*
Britain

Also signed by Cpl. P. Pistocco, Jr., and D. E. Clark.

Dear *Yank*:

. . . Maybe if some of those panty-waists had to be stuck out some place where there were no white women and few native women for a year and a half, as we were, they would appreciate even a picture of our gals back home. The good sergeant [and the other two signers of his letter] alibi that perhaps they are old-fashioned and go so far as to apologize for the mag [when sending it home]. . . . They must be dead from the neck up—and down. They can take their apology and jam it and cram it. And Pfc. Joseph H. Saling—isn't he just too

too? We suggest that when the next issue of *Yank* hits the PX these little boys refrain from buying it, as it is too rugged a mag for them to be reading. Perhaps later, when they grow up. We nasty old Engineers still appreciate *Yank with* its pinups.

—T-5 Chet Straight*
Alaska

Also signed by T-5s F. A. Wallbaum and Cooper Dunn and Pfcs. Robert Ross, Lloyd W. Finley, and Elom Calden.

Dear *Yank*:
Why we GIs over here in the Pacific have to read your tripe and drivel about the WACs beats me. Who in the hell cares about these dimpled GIs who are supposed to be soldiers? All I have ever heard of them doing is peeling spuds, clerking in the office, driving a truck or tractor or puttering around in a photo lab. Yet all the stories written about our dears tell how overworked they are. I correspond regularly with a close relative of mine who is a WAC, and all she writes about is the dances, picnics, swimming parties and bars she has attended. Are these janes in the Army for the same reasons we are, or just to see how many dates they can get? We would like them a hell of a lot better, and respect them more, if they did their part in some defense plant or at home, where they belong. So please let up on the cock and bull and feminine propaganda. It's sickening to read about some doll who has made the supreme sacrifice of giving up her lace-trimmed undies for ODs.

—Sgt. Bob Bowie
New Hebrides

Dear *Yank*:
I was disgusted when I opened the pages of a recent *Yank* and saw some silly female in GI clothes. I detest the WACs very thoroughly and I hope I never meet one. That is also the opinion of all my buddies.

—Pvt. William J. Robinson
New Zealand

WACs Hit Back

Dear *Yank*:
After reading the letters of Sgt. Bob Bowie and Pvt. William Robinson [in a February issue] I think it is about time the WACs had their say. Their stubborn, prejudiced attitude makes many of us wonder if it is really worth it all. . . . There are many heartbreaking stories behind many of our enlistees, stories that have not been published and will never be known, and there is a wealth of patriotism and sincere motives to be found in these girls.

—Pvt. Carol J. Swan
Fort Crook, Nebraska

Dear *Yank*:
. . . After reading Sgt. Bowie's disgusting opinion of the WACs I must say that I think he's one hell of an American.

—Pvt. Helen London
Indiantown Gap, Pennsylvania

Dear *Yank*:
Hell hath no fury like a WAC criticized. . . . Many of these frilly females Sgt. Bowie blows his top about are a lot closer to action than a smug soldier who apparently has enough time to sit at his desk in the New Hebrides and write letters critical of the WACs.

—Pfc. Mildred McGlamery
Fort Sheridan, Illinois

Dear *Yank*:
. . . We have *not* given up lace-trimmed undies; most of us still wear civilian underwear. And, incidentally, I'll bet two months' pay that Sgt. Bowie was drafted. At least we all know we did not have to be forced to serve our country. We volunteered.

—WAC Private
Selman Field, Louisiana

Dear *Yank*:
About five months ago—while winding up three-and-a-half years in the Pacific—I wrote to your magazine an article about how much I detested

the WACs. But now I realize what a first-class heel I was. . . . My narrow-minded opinion has changed entirely, and I am very proud of those gallant American women. . . . What this country needs is more of those wonderful girls. . . . Please print this, as I got quite a few letters from WACs after they read my last article, and every one of them wrote such nice letters and wished my buddies and me the best of luck. I felt more ashamed than I have ever been before.

—Pvt. Wm. J. Robinson
Letterman General Hospital, California

Japanese GIs

Dear *Yank*:

In a recent issue some GI made a few cracks about the new Oriental-immigration bill. At this school we have several native Japanese, citizens of the Empire, doing a man-sized job trying to insinuate knowledge of their tongue into GI skulls. If they were to be transported to Tokyo they could expect short shrift. As they are very talented, intelligent gentlemen I see no reason why American citizens should try to exclude them from sharing in our citizenship.

Though most of their parents are in relocation centers or concentration camps, and though occasionally they get pushed around by white trash, they have no bitterness. In closing, I'd like to ask that guy who wanted to exclude the Japanese if he ever saw a Jap or is he like most Americans— calling the Chinese wonderful and the Japs terrible, and not knowing one from the other?

—Cpl. Robert L. Hill
SCSU, Harvard, Cambridge, Massachusetts

"Wally O'Connell, what are you doing here?"
—CPL. ERNEST MAXWELL

"About your running down to the native village all the time, Mitchell—" —CPL. FRANK R. ROBINSON

"Miss the flight deck again, Higgins?"
—STAN FINE, S1c

★

―――――――――――――

They sang about Dirty Gertie from Bizerte as they overran Hill 609 and snapped the last line of Axis retreat on the Cape Bon Peninsula. Undaunted by the earlier setback at Kasserine Pass, the British and French, under Montgomery, and the Americans, under Eisenhower, all but concluded Operation Torch at Tunis, and so left the North African campaign to history and to Hollywood. Here's looking at you, kid.

TUNIS: *COMMUNIQUÉ—ALLIED HQ.* ONLY ROUTINE PATROL ACTIVITY

—Yank's North African Bureau
January 27, 1943

ON THE Tunisian Front [By radio]— "There was only routine patrol activity," the communiqué said. But communiqués never say much; an eyewitness account does.

What our CO told us that moonless, brooding night while we stood impatiently beside our two jeeps was more like it.

"Your mission," he said, spreading out his map, "is to discover whether the enemy has occupied this point; if so, with what type of guns. You will attempt to secure this information by observation. If that's impossible—and it probably will be—you will draw his fire and observe the number of guns, their location, and their type. You will keep one jeep well to the rear for your getaway, so we'll be certain to get the report. Any questions?"

There were no questions. When you're staring night in the face, with the enemy somewhere out in that night, you understand your orders well

enough. The questions you're thinking, you don't ask. Nobody could answer them anyway.

Ten men were picked for this particular job, one that had been made possible by the hard, intelligent inland fighting of Col. Edson D. Raff and his paratroops.

Commander a Very Cool Guy

We were under the command of Lt. James A. Root, of Middlebury, Vermont, a graduate of Middlebury College and a veteran of Camps Devens, Blanding, and Benning. He's a very cool guy in a tight spot.

There were Sgt. George P. Nestor of Atlantic City; Cpl. Bernard Sabin of Philadelphia, and Cpl. Lawrence Thompson of London, England, who were in charge of a little side project involving TNT; Pfc. Harold Wilburn of Vox, Kentucky, and Pfc. Elmer J. Graw of Copake, New York, who

70

*It turns out to be a hell of a fight: infantrymen of
the 1st Armored Division enter Maknassy in Tunisia.*

drove one of the jeeps; Pfc. Earl Barber of
Oneonta, New York, Pvt. Lloyd Kissick of Dover,
Illinois, Pvt. Joseph Prendick of New York City,
and Pvt. Francis Scooner of Bryn Mawr, Pennsylvania.

We crowded into the two jeeps, giving our drivers as much room as possible. Lt. Root rode in the
first jeep. In the second, in addition to our two-
man getaway party, were the demolition experts,
who were to sneak around the enemy position and
blow up a few telephone poles and other installations. Their objective was five miles away. They
were to leave the jeep, plant their stuff, and return. If they didn't get back in time, they were to
hide out until the next night.

Our little expedition crept past the French
guard stations until finally we reached our last
outpost. There was only a lookout station left
ahead of us, some two miles down the road.

You've no idea how much noise a jeep can make
running along at five or six miles an hour in the
utter silence of the African night.

As we approached the point where our lookout
should have been, the lieutenant stopped the cars
and went forward with Sgt. Nestor to scout. They
came to a roadblock without any guard, and
couldn't tell whether it was our own or one of the
enemy's we hadn't heard about.

Thinking black thoughts about ambushes, we
went on about a quarter of a mile, when a shot
rang out and a bullet sang over our heads.

We were all in the ditch beside the road in nothing flat, with our guns ready. If this was our own
lookout post, it certainly wasn't where the map
said it should have been. While we waited, a second shot kicked up the dust. The lieutenant yelled
out, "Who the hell are you?" as the third shot came
over.

To our great relief and profane disgust the lieutenant was answered in unmistakable Yank dialect. Our lookout had challenged us before, and we hadn't heard him. The language we used in telling him how to get the lead out of his mouth would have done credit to the toughest topkick in this man's army.

Demolition Project Abandoned

In the meantime, our lieutenant sent the getaway jeep a half mile down the road to await the outcome of our little expedition. Surrounded by darkness, the jeep ran off the road into the ditch; then it ran over Cpl. Sabin's foot. At the same time, we discovered that we had lost our explosives, so Sabin's little demolition project had to be abandoned.

We went forward again, with the stars giving off just enough light to enable the drivers to stay on the road. We kept our guns ready, and the lieutenant manned the mounted machine gun, swinging it on every suspicious shadow cast by the bushes.

As we crept along, we stopped every half mile or so, and Lt. Root went ahead to scout. We had seven miles of this, with nothing but the curious high-pitched singing of the telephone wires and the metallic chorus of insects breaking the stillness of the night.

We finally reached a spot where the road dipped between rising slopes of ground. This was where the enemy position was supposed to be. The jeeps stopped and turned around, the getaway car about 200 yards behind ours. Driver Graw stayed with it.

Desired Information Obtained

The rest of us started out on foot, up the rising ground to the right. There wasn't a bush in sight, only stones about the size of your two fists. We crossed what appeared in the darkness to be a new road. By feeling the ground we detected tracks that seemed to have been made by large vehicles, possibly tanks.

We went on up to the top of the ridge, spreading out 20 yards apart.

Suddenly we heard voices speaking Italian. A shot rang out, followed by the staccato chatter of two machine guns. With dust and stone chips flying about us, we lay flat on our faces, guns ready but not firing. Our position was well enough known as it was. We lay still until the message came down the line from Lt. Root informing us that the Italians were closing in on our right and ordering us to work our way back toward the road.

About this time, another pair of machine guns opened up from a position on the opposite side of the road. We were caught in a cross-fire.

Sliding on our bellies as quietly as possible, now and then getting up into a crouch for a short run, we worked our way back and flopped into a ditch by the side of the road.

The getaway jeep had long since roared off.

Machine-gun fire followed us down the hill, but miraculously, no one was hit. Then the enemy opened fire at our ditch with mortars. This was what we wanted to know. All we had to do now was escape with our information from this little private war.

The lieutenant sent back word to watch him. When we got to our feet, we were all to make a dash for the jeep.

This we did.

The motor roared, and so did the enemy's machine guns, mortars, and hand grenades, but we were on our way. Driver Graw suddenly had acquired the best case of night vision in North Africa. Unerringly, he stuck to the road, roaring along at 50 m.p.h. until the firing died away in the distance.

Nobody was hurt. Headquarters would get its information.

When one of the boys said, "I bet that'll scare the Wop army clear back to Italy," everybody roared.

The next day the communiqué said, "There was only routine patrol activity on the Tunisian front."

Routine, hell!

Londoners used to say, "The trouble with Yanks is that they're overpaid, oversexed, and over here." But the Tommies in the field were another story entirely.

WHAT DO WE THINK OF THE BRITISH?

—Sgt. Burgess Scott
July 30, 1943

CAIRO—The medium-sized figure of this story is the average buck private I've met in the British Desert Army—British in this case meaning the United Kingdom and Northern Ireland. He's got a sun-browned face and hands, and he comes from England, Scotland, Ireland, or Wales.

His speech is naturally the first thing that strikes you, but after a few weeks or a month you're able to place him, like you'd place a man from Georgia or Maine. You can walk up and say, "You're from the Midlands" or "from Scotland." You can't guarantee to be 100 percent right, but it gives you a kick when you are.

You're just about used to his speech when you realize that he doesn't speak much. He's a quiet man. When he says, "I'll lay on a lorry," he doesn't mean he's going for a nap. That's his way of saying, "I'll go rustle up a truck." He's pretty good at verbal shortcuts.

After you talk a while you find that, although he's pretty well up on his British Isles and has a speaking acquaintance with the rest of the Empire, he knows less than a Brooklynite about the outside world. He's not quite certain whether Alaska is one of the 48 states of the Union or whether the Grand Canyon is the title of a Hollywood film. And he wants to know if all our girls are like movie stars.

You try to learn something about his country and soon find he hasn't the average American's yen for politics. He's just not interested in the doings of his or anybody else's statesmen.

He wants to get on with his job. But he'll open up on the subject of football or his hometown or his neighborhood beer joint.

He's a good cook. He can take some tin cans, a pile of sand, and a pint of gas and do swell things to a can of bully or M & V. And he is a wow at brewing tea, which he can prepare and drink while you think that there isn't time.

He's kindhearted. He shows that in his dealings with the inhabitants of any country in which war places him. In the desert he'll take time to give biscuits and bully to a needy Arab, and he'll take in any pie-dog that hangs around his bivvy.

He won't take "bastard" from you, not even if you smile. It's just not done in his Army. But you can call him a "bugger" and he'll give you no more than a chuck in the ribs or an American "goose" he's learned to administer.

He's not worried about sex to the extent of letting it get him down; rather, he's marking time for better days. Given the chance, he's handy with his nights off.

For a man who hails from a verdant land, he takes to the desert uncommonly well. A quart of water will, if necessary, last him for two days. But even when water is plentiful, you never see him take a drink of it straight, no matter how much you watch him. His tea and his beer—when he can get them—evidently provide enough liquid for his system. He can go for hours without sleep and not show it. When he does get a chance for some shut-eye, he doesn't appear really to relish it. He just disappears into his bivvy and emerges several hours later looking no better—or worse—for his rest.

Watching him soak up his arid hardship, you get an impression that nothing ruffles his military calm.

Which is correct so long as you don't try to chisel him out of his rights. But try to put anything over on him, and you have a righteous uproar on your hands. In the desert, for example, a man's bivvy is his castle and shall not be invaded. You can't turn him out of it, but he'll step outside any night of the week and give you his bed if you're in a jam.

He writes reams of bad poetry on two subjects, home and the desert, which he promptly mails to his service paper.

The poems about Britain are noble and nostalgic; the poems about the desert are not usually complimentary to that section of the earth. Both types carry on in a rather bumpy meter guaranteed to leave his editor with a headache. When not writing a poem, he's writing a letter to find out why his last one wasn't used.

He's brave under fire. He doesn't dash to the top of the rise among the bullets to wave a Union Jack in Jerry's face. His is a calm valor, as displayed by the member of the Durham Light Infantry who stayed by his gun with one arm blown off and fired on till he fell dead.

He's brave with a bullet in his guts or a leg left behind. If the pain gets too great, he breaks down like any man will, but you have to lean close to hear it. Recently a hospital orderly picked up a letter to mail for a wounded man. It read: "Dear Dad: I'm knocked about a bit, but I'll be all right. Don't worry." That guy had an arm off and an eye out. Tommy's like that.

ZEROS AMPLE

—Sgt. Don Harrison
Yank Staff Correspondent
February 10, 1943

How 10 men in a Flying Fortress fought a sky full of Jap planes, sank a Tojo ship, and got away.

SOMEWHERE IN New Guinea—"Zeros ample, ack-ack limited."

When ribbed for his austerelike report of an ensuing Flying Fortress attack on a Japanese naval convoy, Cpl. Dick Hemphill, first radio operator, a former printer from Greer, South Carolina, explained with a grin, "At the time, I was kind of busy to do much sparkin' with headquarters."

In the last tottering days of the Buna-Gona butchering, Cpl. Hemphill and his nine mates took the lead in an attack on six Jap destroyers attempting to land reinforcements in New Guinea.

The weather was soupy, the ceiling low. Visibility at best ranged to 7,000 feet. It was a poor day for bombers, an ideal day to expect Zeros. And the Nips lived up to expectations.

The "Red Moose" squadron spotted their targets 50 miles off Rabaul. Battle stations were readied, bomb bays opened; Hemphill's bombardier plotted the course, calculated his sights for the opening attack.

All Hell Broke Loose

"Zeros! Ten o'clock above." The power turret gunner's voice vibrated through the headsets, shattering the tenseness of the moment, yet adding to its intensity. The multiple guns of the upper turret sent a brief shudder through the ship. Then—the vibration ceased.

"My guns are jammed! They've knocked out my guns!" yelled gunner Bartlett as "Made in Japan" hail began rattling on the plane's exterior.

Kicking the rudder hard, the pilot dipped the right wing and brought the guns of the side well and ball turret within range of the oncoming attackers. The din of gunfire that followed could be heard above the throb of the four motors.

"Look at 'em come," exclaimed Texas-born Cpl. Roy Schooley, manning his side-well guns.

Five at a time, 20 Zeros and two other unidentified aircraft kept up the relentless attack, droning like bees around a huge hive, their gunfire resembling blood-soaked stingers. And they did draw blood as more and more holes appeared like dry, festering sores on the metal hide of the tormented flying monster.

Hemphill had just logged his message when Pvt. Jimmie Wilson dragged a trail of blood through the small door leading aft to the tail gunner's pit. His face was marred with pain. He tried to speak, but his voice was muffled by the racket. Instead of words, only blood flowed past his lips.

Turret Gunner Is Blinded

Leaping from the radio controls, Cpl. Hemphill broke open the first-aid kit and stripped the red-stained shirt from Wilson's body. Two holes stared like sightless eyes from the wounded man's breast where two bullets had gone through his body, puncturing one lung. A third bullet lodged in his shoulder.

Having administered what medical aid he could, Hemphill sat with Wilson's head eased in his lap and wiped away the red foam oozing through the gunner's clenched teeth.

Suddenly, an almost unrecognizable head appeared coming up from the ball turret. It had to be Cpl. Swanson, although his face was so covered with blood that it appeared as a solid red blot. His eyes stared wildly and he pawed the air with red-stained hands. Shattering glass from the gun turret had multilated his face, robbed him of his sight.

"Dick, take care of Swanson," pleaded Wilson. "He's hurt bad."

Schooley, seeing Hemphill burdened with two casualties, dropped his guns to lend assistance.

As he bent over Wilson, the injured gunner shouted in his ear, "Get back to your station. We have only four guns working now."

Schooley returned to his guns—with a vengeance.

Still the Zeros attacked, getting more daring as they found resistance dwindling. As one came screaming down on the nose of the still-defiant Fortress, the copilot voiced the warning, "Zero at one o'clock. Zero at one o'clock above. Get 'em, Ritenour."

The flight engineer yelled back into his mike, "Dammit, I can't. My guns are out. They're . . ." His voice went dead as round after round of slugs tore into the ship, shattering the observation bay and scattering glass all around the bombardier's compartment. One burst exploded two oxygen tanks, between which Bill Ritenour sat frantically working to free his clogged machine guns. Another blast from the nearing Zero punctured a water canteen between his feet. A third severed the cord of his neck mike, silencing his prayers and curses.

As the Jap fighter pulled off, Ritenour thanked God he was still alive, wondered why he wasn't dead, and hoped that he might still see Virginia again. But his hopes seemed futile. Tracer bullets had hit a box of ammunition and set it ablaze.

Living, Fighting on Borrowed Time

"Head for the ceiling. We're on fire!" thundered the bombardier through his mike as he helped fight the blazing box that threatened to explode and blow men and ship to pieces.

The plane climbed steeply and entered a protective layer of clouds. The engineer and bombardier heaved the burning gun powder through the shattered bay of the pungent, smoke-laden compartment. With a sickly grin, Ritenour went back to work on his disabled guns, and the bombardier again plotted the run over the target. Neither

showed outward signs of nervousness, but both knew they were living on borrowed time. Both wondered just when the interest would fall due.

Following the bombardier's instructions, the pilot again nosed his plane down through the clouds and leveled off at 3,500 feet.

"Circle wide and come in at six o'clock."

The plane banked, leveled off, and approached the fantail of one of the scattering destroyers. No heed was paid to the bursting shrapnel that threatened men and machine.

Brakes or No Brakes, He Landed Her

"Steady-y-y. Hold 'er. Bombs gone! Let's get movin' the hell out of here," shouted the bombardier. The pilot needed no further encouragement, and he pulled the wheel into his middle, jazzed the motors, and started aloft.

But before the huge plane could puncture the clouds overhead, two Zeros roared in from behind and below, fishtailing to get greater coverage as they sprayed the metal belly above them. It was their last bid for revenge for Tojo and the destroyer listing in a sea of its own burning oil.

"Hot lead whistled through our compartment like buckshot," related Cpl. Hemphill, "and reminded me of the time I got caught in a melon patch back home. One burst completely shattered the hydraulic system, and hydraulic fluid temporarily blinded the navigator and bombardier. I was instructed to radio the 'drome and tell them to get the basket ready. We were limping home with four men injured, four control cables shot away, the left aileron damaged, and the hydraulic system completely gone.

"Our pilot said he intended to land her on the crash runway, brakes or no brakes—and I prayed to heaven that if he couldn't have mechanical brakes at least give 'im a spiritual break.

"He got it and landed her intact, right side up.

"As we staggered out of the plane the CO said something about Silver Stars. But frankly," drawled the 29-year-old Southerner, "I was too damn busy thankin' my lucky stars to worry much about wearin' one."

The POETS CORNERED

To Future Inductees

Do not with your noncoms try to
reason,
For in the Army they call that
treason.
> —Pvt. William Carpenter Good
> Jefferson Barracks, Missouri

All Aboard!

If you live in the East, they will send you
West;
If you live in the North, they will send you
South.
What the hell does it matter? The Army knows
best,
So grab your luggage and shut your mouth.
> —S/Sgt. A. L. Crouch
> Camp Shelby, Mississippi

You Told

You kissed and told
But that's all right;
The guy you told
Called up last night.
> —T/S Horace L. Woodward
> Army War College
> Washington, D.C.

Praise the Silk

As I sat in the plane with my chute
on my back
I was as frightened as could be.
The jumpmaster was ready in the
door—
I knew, for I could see.
The boys on the ground looked like
bugs from afar,
The ground it looked so black.
"Stand up, and hook up!" the jump-
master cried,
And I found myself on my back.

When I stood on my feet like a leaf
did I shake
As my knees were beating a tune,
But bravely I said, "Move over men,
Move over and give me room."
I stood in that door with a prayer
on my lips,
Wondering why I was there,
When I saw the jumpmaster leave
the plane
And sail out into the air.

Then out I went into the blue
With my face as white as could be;
I tried to count and check my feet,
But God, why couldn't I see?
I opened my eyes and my chute
finally opened,
My knees, they even stopped knocking;
I looked up above and saw my true
love,
Made from—400 *silk stockings*.
> —Pvt. Irving E. Taffel
> Fort Benning, Georgia

To the Sergeants and Generals

Feel not your oats too much,
Proud wheel horses of Mars;
A zebra has more stripes than you,
The sky has still more stars.
> —Cpl. Clyde Kenneth Hyder
> Australia

Beer and Sex

The soldiers in the Army.
All the he-men and the wrecks.
They do a lot of talking
About beer and also sex.

Now, it's my observation,
In spite of all they boast of,
That between beer and women,
Beer is what they get the most of.
—Sgt. Irving Caress
New England

A Dogface Is No Sea Dog

In the garrison we were happy
    But now they've got our goat,
'Cause they've got us bag and
        baggage
    On a damn banana boat.
On the desert, in the mountains,
    We were as happy as could be
But we're having lots of trouble
    Since they sent us out to sea . . .

Where the left side is the port side
    And the toilet is the head,
Where you bang your skull in the
        hatchways
    Till you wish that you were dead,
Where a chow line ain't a line at all
    But just a milling bunch,
And you finish up with breakfast
    Just in time to start with lunch.

And you hit the hay in layers
    Like a pre-war layer cake
With bunks four high, that touch
        the sky;
    Oh, what a chance you take.
Each time you wish to turn and toss
    Amid your fitful slumber,
You have to warn the other guys
    And do it by the numbers.

The drinking water's salty,
    And if you should need a shave,
Your buddies sadly wish you luck
    And bid you to be brave.

You'll know exactly what I mean
    If you've been on a boat,
For the chances are 50-50,
    When you shave you cut your
        throat.

When the weather's nice and sunny
    They keep you down below,
But you'll guard guns upon the deck
    If it should rain or snow.
We've heard that on the bounding
        main
    All things are pretty swell,
So let the Navy have their boats,
    And let them go to hell.
—Author Unknown
Submitted by Cpl. Ray E. Thomas,
Fort Ord, California

Pills

The Army doctors have a cure
    They use for all your ills:
No matter what the case may be
    They always give you pills.

A man can well be dying,
    Still, no matter how you fret,
They throw a flock of pills at you,
    And soldier, you're all set.

I've taken pills for everything
    From broken legs to gout;
I've even put them in my shoes
    To keep the water out.

One time we were in battle,
    And we ran plumb out of lead:
We needed ammunition, so—
    We used those pills instead.

Well, sir, you won't believe me,
    But a lie I never tell:
The enemy couldn't take those pills—
    They're all as dead as hell.
—Cpl. George Hindberg
Camp Adair, Oregon

Thoughts of an Aerial Gunner

I'm just a lad who got fighting mad
When the Axis got treating folks mean;
So I figured I'm one
To be handling a gun
From the tail of a B-17.

Oh, it's a far cry from the earth to
   the sky,
Where the blue of the sea looks
   serene;
And I sometimes wish
I were starting to fish
From the tail of my B-17.

But it doesn't take long to prove I
   was wrong
For having such thoughts in my
   bean;
For I'm soon spitting lead
At a Jap Zero's head
From the tail of my B-17.

Now I've heard it said that a gunner
   is dead
In a minute or somewhere between;
But the only death rattle
I've heard is the battle
In the tail of my B-17.

And if it's my place to fall out of
   the race
And fade somewhere back of the
   scene:
I'd rather expire
In the heavens or higher
In the tail of my B-17.

—Cpl. Fred R. Charlton
AAFTTS, Goldsboro, North Carolina

To an Unknown Soldier, Killed in Action

He takes his last look at the stars
   tonight,
Alone, here, on the outskirts of the
   earth.
He thinks now of the mystery of
   birth,
Of the tangent between shadow and
   light,
Of how to struggle is not to fight,
Of how in darkness there is little
   mirth,
Of how in effort there is little worth,
And yet he knows there is a wrong
   and right.
He takes his last look and prepares
   to die.
Death will come silent when he does
   not know,
When his fingers burn and his head
   is high;
A wind will blow through him like
   driven snow.
He will say no prayer, he will ask
   not why,
Yet he will smile when it is time
   to go.

—Pvt. Robert W. Taylor
Fort Monmouth, New Jersey

For nearly two years they fought, surviving not only combat but jungle rot, dengue fever, and malaria as well. The New Guinea campaign never really ended—it sort of fizzled out when the crumbling Japanese defenses further north in the Pacific required the War Ministry's more immediate attention.

NO FRONT LINE IN NEW GUINEA

—Sgt. DAVE RICHARDSON
March 12, 1943

ANY SCHOOL kid can tell you that the equator is an imaginary line running around the center of the earth, but all the brains in the world couldn't locate the front line in New Guinea. There just isn't any such thing.

One newcomer, creeping up through the mud to a grimy, sweating Yank in a foxhole, asked the veteran where the front line was.

"We don't fight that way, buddy," was the answer. "There are Japs up ahead but there also may be Japs behind me, and I'm sure as hell there's a couple of them a few yards over to the side. We can't be bothered with technicalities like front lines. We just keep looking for Japs, killing them, and pushing ahead."

Jungle fighting is all very informal. There are no elaborate sandbagged trenches, no dugout living quarters, and no fields of barbed wire as there were in France back in 1918. The climate is too blazing hot for soldiers to go to the trouble of build-ing much more than shallow slit trenches and fox-holes. The daily rains would fill up deep trenches. Barbed wire is too heavy; the only way things can be carried here is on your back.

When Americans, Australians, and Japs clash, no more than a few dozen men on either side are involved. There's none of that dramatic "over the top" stuff here. Patrols go out every day to feel out the Jap pillboxes and strong points. Then stronger forces come in to knock them out, supported by mortar and light artillery fire.

When the pillboxes and machine-gun nests are gone, more Yanks and Aussies come in to mop up the snipers and occupy the area.

The Yanks, most of them from Wisconsin's thickly wooded country, are beating the Japs with tactics borrowed from America's original fighting men—the Indians. These tactics involve swift, silent movement, sudden thrusts out of jungles. The rifle is the basic weapon.

Wet from blood and rain, weary of jungle and war . . .

The machine gun has been tried in New Guinea but to little advantage. A handful of light tanks was used by the Aussies in the bitter fight for the Buna airstrip, some of the relatively open dry ground in the Buna-Gona area. But generally the undergrowth is too thick and the mud too deep for tanks to be used in many other places.

Few Americans ever went into action with as little equipment as these soldiers carry. Battle dress seldom consists of more than a helmet, jungle-green uniform, socks, shoes, rifle belt, extra bandoliers of bullets, pockets full of grenades, and a rifle or a Tommy gun. Packs are brought up only after an area is occupied.

During these wet, wearying months of jungle warfare, the Yanks have developed a healthy respect for the craftiness of the Japs they seek to kill. The Americans know the Japs as past masters of jungle fighting, as experts at camouflage, fanatics in their courage, and magicians at pulling disconcerting tricks in battle. Several nights during the battle for Buna Mission, the Japs played a machine-gun record on a phonograph to draw American fire. Other times they threw rocks at

American outposts after dark or shouted, "What's the password?"

If they succeeded in drawing American fire, they spotted the rifle or machine-gun flashes and picked off the men who fired.

For signaling each other, the Japs often use bird calls. When a lot of bird calls start filling the jungle air, Yanks usually cheep in with a few more just to confuse the issue. On one occasion, this caused a Jap to growl in good English, "Shut up, you American bastards."

On patrol an American soldier ducked behind two bushes when Jap bullets whined close to him. Suddenly the bushes started to move. They were Jap observers covered with brush.

Grinning at his good luck, the Yank casually took a grenade from his pocket and tossed it into the bushes as they slowly moved away. In a second the bushes became two very dead Japs.

Pfc. William H. Ford of Port Royal, Kentucky, had even better luck outwitting the Japs. An Army driver, he wasn't permitted to go with his buddies when they went out to attack the Japs, and was left behind to guard the CP.

About dusk he saw someone walk out of the jungle toward the CP humming "One Dozen Roses" and wearing a brand-new American uniform. The clean uniform puzzled Ford, because the swamp and jungle living had ruined every shirt and pair of pants in his outfit.

It was too dark to see the stranger's face under his helmet, but Ford got a good look at his feet in the moonlight. Instead of American shoes, they were tiny, split-toe, tree-climbing sneakers which only the Japs wear.

" 'One Dozen Roses,' eh?" Ford yelled. "Well, here's three of 'em for you!"

"Don't shoot, American!" the stranger begged, but he had hardly got the words out when Ford pumped three MI slugs into him.

Now Pfc. William H. Ford, former truck driver, is fighting right up front.

Buna Beach, New Guinea—August 1943. This photograph inspired more verse than any other picture taken during the war.

BUNA BEACH

—Pfc. KEITH B. CAMPBELL
AAFTAC, Orlando, Florida

Perhaps they struggled with geography
When they were boys, lisping the sinewy names
Of far-off lands they never hoped to see,
With thoughts intent upon their outdoor games;
The wild halloos and shouts of after-school,
A rag-tailed kite against a gray March sky,
And boyish laughter ringing "April Fool!"
When someone took their bait.

Well, here they lie,
Three lads on Buna Beach, grotesquely laid
In the informal pose of sudden death;
While we, who live secure because they paid
In currency compounded of their breath,
Would hesitate and ponder on a scheme
To bargain interest to preserve their dream.

THOUGHTS WHILE GOLDBRICKING

—Pvt. WILLIAM SAROYAN
October 8, 1943

"I SUPPOSE," PVT. Push Delaney said to his pal, Pvt. Brick Stumblefeather, "the way to win a war is to go right in there and put a stop to it."

"Correct," Pvt. Stumblefeather said. "Correct you are," he said softly.

The two men were stretched out on their backs on the far side of a new latrine pit coming up in Fort Oglethorpe, Georgia. The sweet weather of Southern autumn had swooned down almost as if the place weren't a camp at all but a lot of lazy land lying around for worms, bugs, and butterflies to fool around in—which they were doing.

The only other thing that was fooling around nearby was a human being, a corporal.

He was in the pit with a shovel, digging.

His name was Orville Swoop. He wore glasses, kept abreast of the times by reading the latrine walls, and believed in reincarnation. Even though he was in charge of the detail, he was in the pit fooling around with a shovel and the two privates were lying in the grass, listening to the butterflies and continuing their nine-month-old Socratic dialogue.

This memorable conversation regarding man's role in nature and art had begun when Push Delaney, running to chow, misjudged his direction, ran into chapel, and pushed his mess kit in front of Brick Stumblefeather, who was on his hands and knees with GI soap, a brush, and a bucket of water.

Brick dipped the mess kit into the bucket of water and handed it back to Push, a total stranger. Push surveyed the situation and saw the mistake.

"Religion," he said.

He poured the contents of his mess kit back into the bucket, whereupon Brick said the second word of the now-famous Delaney-Stumblefeather dialogues.

"Methodist?"

"Episcopalian," Push replied, "but *reformed* Episcopalian."

In this manner the two thinkers of Fort Oglethorpe began their friendship. Nine months had ripened the friendship to the consistency of camembert cheese.

In the pit, doing his duty (as he liked to say), Cpl. Swoop felt that all was right in the world. As the smallest of the three men, he had been convinced by the other two that *his* place was in the hole with the shovel and theirs outside under the sky. Cpl. Swoop had been digging the hole for 11 days and the two men themselves, extremely critical of such things, had said it was a pretty hole, getting prettier every day.

"I notice," Pvt. Push Delaney had told the corporal only three days before, "you've gone to work and pushed the hole southward, so to speak, rather than northward. That is the sign of a superior man—a leader of men, a man doomed to be a candidate for OCS. The South is God's own region, and all things push toward it."

"Correct," Pvt. Stumblefeather had said. "By God, if I ever heard a correct thing spoken, that southward stuff was it."

Cpl. Swoop was a fighting 127 pounds in weight, wearing away to a cool hundred, while Pvts. Delaney and Stumblefeather were each past the 200 mark, going on 210, and no kidney trouble. One of them, if settled into the pit, could work along with a shovel very nicely, but Pvt. Delaney demonstrated to the satisfaction of Cpl. Swoop that if it came to swift, effective action—the free use of the arms and feet—it wouldn't quite do. Here Push stretched his arms out and touched the walls of the pit, then kicked them.

"The responsibility here," he said, "is plainly the privilege of the smaller type of man. It is a responsibility to cherish and thank God for."

"Correct," Brick said, "and the sooner the better." Whereupon Brick lifted the little man and gently lowered him into the hole, while Push got out of the way, saying, "After you, corporal."

The butterflies got noisy along in the afternoon and woke Push out of a dream of Betty Grable.

"And I suppose, further," he said, "the way to win a girl, or as the boys from Brooklyn say, *goil*, is to go right in—"

"Correct," Brick said.

"Go right in," Push continued, "and ask her what seems to be the trouble. Girls have a heap of trouble men don't know about, and the only way to find out what's bothering them is to ask them."

"Correct," Brick said. "I ask them every time. I don't leave it to chance. Correct you are," he said softly.

The thinkers looked at the sky and went on with their thinking, the worms fooled around here and there, the corporal dug the pit. In this manner another day wore on pleasantly, as correct as correct can be.

"He's not much good, but he rattles the other pitcher."
—SGT. CHARLES PEARSON

The SAD SACK

"Change of Climate"

SGT. GEORGE BAKER

★

_____

"The Slot" was the nickname given by the Marines to the channel that cut through the Solomon Islands. "The Tokyo Express" was a similar colloquialism representing the Japanese task force. On November 14, 1942, the latter once again made its way down the former. One of the results was this story, originally titled "Fifty Minutes of Hell."

THE BIG BASTARD

—ROBERT L. SCHWARTZ Y2c
April 16, 1943

The Big Bastard, a U.S. battleship, got her nickname when she first arrived in the South Pacific to protect American carriers from aerial attack.

She did her job so well that a carrier admiral radioed his planes, "Stay away from that big bastard. When she gets through shooting down Japs, she'll use you for target practice." Now, throughout the Pacific, she's known as the *Big Bastard*, and her men wouldn't swap her nickname for a general citation.

This is the story of the *Big Bastard*'s first surface action, pieced together from the accounts of the men of her complement. The action—the Battle of Savo Island—began at dusk, 24 hours after the *Boise* and the *San Francisco* steamed between two columns of Jap ships and smashed them apart. It formed a part of what's known in naval annals as the Fifth Battle of the Solomons.

On the afternoon of Nov. 14, 1942, a task force of the *Big Bastard* and several other battleships

and destroyers cut away from its carrier for a little show of its own. And at Savo Island, just north of Guadalcanal, it found a nest of hiding Jap ships and got mixed up in one of the roughest night surface engagements ever fought anywhere.

When general quarters sounded at 9:30 p.m., no one aboard the *Big Bastard* knew the size or strength of the enemy. But at midnight, someone on the bridge sighted three enemy ships in the channel ahead and reported the formation to the admiral's flagship nearby. Fifteen minutes later, the admiral's ship fired a nine-gun salvo that set afire the leading Jap battleship. From that moment on, the *Big Bastard* and the rest of the U.S. task force saw plenty of action.

Her range finders set on the enemy fire, *Big B* swung her heavies into play, sank her first target, and blew up her second. Meanwhile, Jap guns exploded three U.S. destroyers.

87

Big B's third target was a Kongo-class battle-ship that passed her starboard beam and was cut in half by a salvo from her number-three turret aft. Her secondary batteries continued to pour fire into eight Jap destroyers hiding in a cove.

There was a lull then. *Big B* steamed alone in a circle of burning ships. The admiral's battleship had disappeared in the darkness. Into the narrowest part of the cove came four more enemy ships. The second one threw searchlights on *Big B* and she opened fire. From her rear came supporting salvos, indicating that the admiral's ship was still in the fight.

The assistance was welcome, for *Big B* was being pounded heavily by the guns of three hard-punching Jap warships. Six- and eight-inch shells ripped through the top of her superstructure, then cut into her secondaries. Her deck was riddled with shrapnel. Fire broke out in the tattered superstructure. Her own wreckage lay everywhere.

But *Big B* kept right on rolling. She opened her main battery on the enemy line. Her secondaries chattered continuously, and soon a tongue of fire poked up at the sky from each of the enemy ships. Then the *Big Bastard* knew she had won.

During the night, the *Big Bastard* and the other U.S. ships ran completely around the island and wiped out an enemy fleet in less than 50 minutes. Most of the men said later that they thought they had been running the channel at least half the night.

SOMEWHERE IN the South Pacific [Passed by Navy censor]—Hodgen Othello Patrick Y1c, talker on the *Big Bastard*'s sky patrol, highest lookout post where the ship took its first hit during the Battle of Savo Island, came as reasonably close to being killed as can be expected of any man.

Patrick remembers squaring for battle and from his high perch seeing the Jap ships come up. He saw the first salvo leave the flagship up ahead. His next recollection is of being thrown against a bulkhead and finding somebody's arm, without a body,

across his face. A dead weight lay across his chest, pinning him.

"I'm dead," he thought, and the remembrance of it is still clear in his mind. "Here I am dead. This is what it's like to be dead." But the earthy touch of shrapnel in his knee and his hip convinced him that he was still alive. He looked around. The two officers lay dead. Seven enlisted men were still. Four wounded looked at Patrick, not knowing what to do next.

Patrick pressed the button on his headset. "Sick bay," he called, "send help." He doesn't know why he took command. There was another petty officer who not only rated him but was able to struggle to his feet and walk around. The sound of firing roared up from his own ship. He heard hits coming aboard. But no help came.

Patrick ordered the two least wounded to go below and then put tourniquets on the other two, using their own belts. He applied the same treatment to his own leg above the bleeding knee, then remembered to loosen all three every 15 minutes throughout the night. He hunted a long time for morphine before he found it and divided it with the others. As he was about to take his share of the sedative he noticed that several of the men he had thought dead were stirring. Without a moment's hesitation he divided his share among them. He didn't feel heroic about it. He didn't even think about it.

Despite his injuries, Patrick found that he could get to his feet. He saw that he could report better while standing and remained that way until the end of the battle. Afterward, he fell again to the deck, but he never stopped his regular reports until he was relieved the next morning.

Patrick was the only enlisted man of the crew who was recommended for the Navy Cross.

When general quarters sounded on the *Big Bastard*, Rufus Mathewson Y2c took his post as a talker in the conning tower.

"It'll be a pushover," he heard someone say. "Just a bunch of armed transports. We'll knock 'em off like sitting ducks."

Mathewson said to himself, "I wish I was

A U.S. cruiser framed in a U.S. gunsight during the ongoing battle for the South Pacific.

home." The thought kept running through his head as he watched the captain and the navigator walk calmly back and forth in the narrow steel-walled compartment.

Hours ticked by. Shortly after midnight, the loudspeaker carried a cold, steady voice from plot room. "Target 20,000 yards, bearing 240 degrees . . . target 19,800 yards, bearing 241 degrees . . ." Slowly the target drew closer.

There was a terrific explosion up ahead. Mathewson dashed to one of the slits and felt his stomach drop as he saw a battleship ahead, silhouetted by flame. "Lord, let me out and I'll change my ways," he said aloud. A direct hit had dissolved one of the destroyers.

The captain called for a stadimeter reading to determine the distance to the battleship ahead. A lieutenant on the bridge tried unsuccessfully to take a reading through the narrow slot in the armor. It would have been difficult in the daytime and was virtually impossible at night.

"What kind of a crew have I got when I can't get a stadimeter reading?" the captain asked.

Mathewson felt sorry for the lieutenant. Over the lookout's phone came a voice, "Destroyer sinking on our starboard bow." The captain ordered left rudder, and the helmsman swung the wheel. They skirted the destroyer, then came back on their course. From over the phone came the admiral's voice: "Fire when ready."

The men on the bridge looked at one another. For a full minute, no word came over the amplifier from plot room, then a voice gave the range and bearing. The captain looked at Mathewson. "Tell them they can fire now." Mathewson relayed the command. He could hear compressed air being blown through the 16-inch barrels as the gun crews cleared them before loading. Thirty seconds later, shells screamed out. The captain and the navigator were jarred away from their positions at the scopes, but voices came in over the phone.

"Right on!"

"The damn thing has dissolved!"

"Looked like a cruiser."

"That was a battleship!"

In rapid succession, Mathewson heard a loud crash, a rolling explosion, and then the searing rattle of metal fragments as they crashed into cables, guns, and superstructure. The ship shrugged, leaned back into a volley of six- and eight-inch shells that raked through the sky control tower, topmost position on the ship.

Quickly Mathewson called sky control on the battle phone. "Patrick, you there?"

"Here, but our officers are dead, and all of us are wounded."

Mathewson asked for permission to go relieve Patrick, but his request was denied. Mathewson and Patrick were close friends, and now the thought of Patrick lying wounded on sky control beyond the help of anyone because of fires burning below him almost brought tears to his eyes.

Methodically *Big B* went on firing.

"Torpedo off the port bow."

"Hard starboard rudder."

The tremendous craft swung over. Everyone strained, bracing for another explosion above the crashing shells and shrapnel. The torpedo missed, but in the confusion following the battleship's evasion tactics, she became separated from the other ships and lost her own course.

"If you swing to port you can go back out the way you came in," chart house advised, "but the water's shallow off that way. If you turn to starboard you have to go around the island."

"Starboard," said the captain. And then, as a pleasant afterthought, "Full speed ahead."

Six- and eight-inch shell fire peppered the bridge with steel fragments. It was almost impossible for shrapnel to penetrate the armor of the bridge, but the men inside heard one shell smack through the gun director just aft the bridge and then explode against the chart house. Directions for course and bearing stopped coming in.

Over the amplifier from chart house came a voice, "My God, this man's bleeding to death. Send help. Hurry. Please hurry."

Melvin McSpadden, the engine control talker, was first to answer. "Sick bay is on this circuit and they'll send a doctor. Give us some bearings."

"This poor guy's bleeding to death. Have you got any bandages? I can't leave him like this."

McSpadden tore down a blackout curtain hanging over one of the slots, stuffed it through the aperture, and shouted to a seaman on the catwalk outside, "Take this to the chart house, quick."

Another torpedo was sighted and the ship swung sharply to starboard. From all over the ship came the excited voices of talkers, "We're heading for the beach!"

"Why did we make that turn to starboard?" The query came in over McSpadden's phone and he recognized it as that of Batt II, which he had thought abandoned.

He quickly reassured them: "The captain is conning the ship!" That stopped the queries, the torpedo failed to materialize, and the captain swung again to port. The huge ship churned up a massive letter *S* in the white-topped water. Some of the waves in the wake astern were 20 feet high.

Batt II, which is the auxiliary control room situated inside the superstructure below the sky control tower, was the hardest-hit portion of the ship. One of the talkers in Batt II was Tom Page S1c of Greensburg, Pennsylvania.

Page remembers it was a beautiful night. There was a big moon and it was very warm and quiet. The smell of gardenias was strong from off Florida Island. The association of the gardenias with the action that followed caused Page to lose all desire to smell a gardenia again.

Over the amplifier came a voice, "Guadalcanal on our starboard hand." Big, vivid flashes lit the sky—some of it gunfire in the distance, some of it lightning. Everybody in Batt II was tense. Not until the *Big Bastard*'s guns went off did everyone's confidence return. Page went to one of the slots and watched the shells fly through the air like three red dots slowly converging into one, then landing off in the distance. He saw Japs running back and forth on the beach with flashlights.

Page sat in a corner on an overturned bucket, feeling comfortable now that the big guns were booming. He noticed that the commander, usually a very nervous man, was very calm. Then he was

knocked off his bucket by a shell hit. The molten metal from the shell ran across the floor like lava and he stepped out of the way. Steam pipes were broken, electrical fires sputtered. Noise and heat from the steam were unbearable. He screamed over the phone to engine control to shut off the auxiliary steam line that went through the compartment to the whistle. Somebody on the bridge answered, "They heard you, Page," and in a moment added, "Secure and get out if there's nothing else you can do."

Several men who had walked out on the catwalk reported that flames were climbing up the tower. Robertson, a quartermaster third class, came through the opening from the catwalk and said, "I've lost my shoe; help me find my shoe." He stood there holding one bare foot off the hot deck, groping in the dark. Everyone helped him, even two commanders. The shoe was not found until next morning—under a body on the catwalk.

No direct hits had been scored on Batt II, but flames, explosions, and escaping steam threw the place into disorder. Bernard Wenke S1c, the auxiliary helmsman, had been thrown from behind the wheel and lodged in between the bulkhead and the deck. He stayed there, keeping one hand stretched out to hold the bottom of the wheel. Not until flames from below made the deck almost red hot and set his pants afire did he move.

The executive officer pushed aside one of the men to look out the slot and drew back his hand covered with blood. For the first time, he realized that men had been wounded. He called for a talker to relay the information to the bridge but got no answer. He felt in the darkness until he found a talker with phones on and dragged him to a standing position. Shaking him vigorously, he gave him the message to relay. The talker repeated the message over the phone, and the commander walked away. The talker slumped back to the deck.

Another officer came into the compartment. He walked to the quartermaster and said in a strained voice, "Feel my arm. It's been hit and I can't tell if it's still there. Go ahead, tell me." The quartermaster, still standing without his shoe, timidly reached for the officer's shoulder but then decided to find out the other way. He groped his way up the officer's leg until he came to his hip, then reached out for his hand. Finding it still there, he ran his hand up the officer's arm until he came to a gaping shrapnel wound in his shoulder. He reported what he had found, and the officer said "thanks" and walked out.

During the entire action, one of the lookouts standing by a slot kept repeating in a low voice: "Lord, I'm scared. Nobody has any idea how scared I am. How could anyone be this scared? My God, I'm scared." He said that over and over for about 10 minutes. Nobody thought it strange.

Men began crawling to their feet. Above the noise of the steam and the fire there rose excited voices. Men asked one another who was hurt, where was the ship damaged, how high were the flames. They speculated on their own chances of getting out. Occasionally they shot glances at the executive officer looking for help. He noticed but didn't know what to say. Finally he blurted out, "Shut up! I'll do all the talking in here!"

The talking stopped. Only the noise of the steam escaping could be heard above the gunfire below. Then the gunfire ceased and within a minute the steam went off. A new noise could be heard now —the moans of the injured and the dying. Pharmacist's mates went among them, injecting shots of morphine. From below came the noise of damage-control parties, fighting their way through with hoses and extinguishers. Page grabbed the end of a hose that was passed up to him and pulled on it, but it was too heavy. As someone walked past him into Batt II he called out, "Lend a hand, you fool!"

"Shut up, Page," said a voice. "That's Comm. Gorton!"

"That's all right," said the commander, "I'm just one of the boys."

Working with the hose, they extinguished the flames, then settled back in the darkness to await further action. The steel under their feet was still so hot that they were compelled to keep moving.

Outside on the catwalk, Page noticed a life jacket on one of the bodies periodically smoulder and burst into flame. Using steel helmets, the men scooped water from the compartment deck and poured it on the life jacket.

Damage-control parties are formed when general quarters sounds. They go to their posts and wait for calls. When there is damage in their area, they run to the spot with equipment that includes everything from fire extinguishers to monkey wrenches.

John Hagenbuch was a nozzle man on a hose party. While he was directing the stream on a fire in the shadow of the number-three turret, Chief Turret Capt. Bowman came out from inside and passed the word for the group to move along. He was ready to fire a salvo, and the concussion would be tremendous.

Everybody evacuated the area but Hagenbuch. Standing at the head of the line, he had been forgotten when the word was passed. The guns lowered directly over his head and went off with a blinding flash.

Hagenbuch was thrown to the deck so hard he almost bounced. Slowly he staggered to his feet, temporarily blinded and deafened by the explosion. It had been so powerful that two planes were blown out of their catapults and into the sea.

As Hagenbuch groped his way back and forth, the guns went off with another mighty roar, and again he was thrown to the deck. One of Hagenbuch's hose men saw the whole action and rushed out, lifted him to his feet, and dragged him away from the turret as a third salvo thundered.

Thirty minutes later he was back on his feet, volunteering to climb to the top of a smokestack to put out a fire there.

When John P. Buck left Athens, Ohio, and enlisted in the Navy, he went in as an apprentice seaman. Several months later, while cruising the Pacific, the chaplain found that Buck could type. He got him a rating and had him placed on the muster roll as chaplain's yeoman.

Buck's duty at general quarters was after-battery lookout. Technically speaking, his post was in the surface, horizon, and lower sky lookout station, situated just below the after-main-battery direction finder.

Buck leaned against the open door to the compartment and felt the warmth and silence of the night. Early in the channel run, he had noticed the smell of the gardenias and had started to put on his gas mask before a talker on the bridge told him the smell was really just gardenias. About 65 feet aft from where he stood, Buck could see the big 16-inch barrels poked out over the starboard rail. He was lazily watching them when they suddenly fired a salvo with a deafening roar. Buck was picked up bodily and thrown inside the compartment. He heard his helmet fly off and strike a bulkhead 30 feet away, then roll around the floor. The explosion blinded him for about 15 minutes, during which time he groped on the floor and found his helmet. When he took it off the next morning he found it wasn't his. Whose it was and where it came from, he never learned.

Regaining his sight and finding that there was a lull in the battle, Buck offered to aid the pharmacist's mates in caring for the wounded. Before he could leave, however, the after battery once again opened fire, so Buck stayed where he was.

Over five miles away, a 14-inch shell came screaming out of the muzzle of a gun on a Jap battleship. Buck first saw it when it was about two miles away from him, looming larger and larger as a red dot in the sky. He knew it was going to hit and knelt down in the compartment.

The shell came through at exactly deck level. It tore through a slight coaming where the deck joins the hull, made two neat holes through a rim around a hatch leading below, and then crashed against the barbette of the after turret. There was a blinding flash and roar, and shrapnel rained down like cinders. Buck mentally marked turret number three off his list. But when he went out to look, he found that the turret was still there; beside it was a yawning hole in the deck.

Looking over the starboard rail, he saw a Jap ship racing up. He reported it but worriedly wondered how they were ever going to hit it, with the after turret almost certainly out of action. Then he heard the secondaries open fire with a staccato *bang-bang-bang*, finally reaching the ear-splitting regularity of machine-gun firing, though in each of the little turrets, men were flinging in shells by hand.

The after turret, meanwhile, turned slowly toward the approaching ship, now so close that the elevation on the barrels was almost nil.

Nobody was more amazed than Buck when the after turret fired. He had no idea it was still in action. Then he saw that the Jap ship had been hit almost point-blank by all three shells. There was a big flash where the ship had been and then smoking, bubbling water. In the few seconds before the Jap went under, Buck had seen one of its turrets fly high into the air and the ship start to split in the middle. But it sank before it had a chance to fall apart.

The firing stopped and Buck left to help in the care of the wounded. At sick bay he found men stretched out on every available table, with doctors and pharmacist's mates working over them while standing in four inches of blood and water on the deck.

He was sent with a doctor to the top of the superstructure to help the wounded men who had been cut off there. Only Patrick was still there. The doctor stayed with Patrick, giving Buck Syrettes of morphine to administer inside the superstructure on the way down.

Descending on the inside of the tower, Buck found a man lying on one of the upper levels with one leg shot off. He took out his knife and walked over to a dangling electrical wire, cut it loose, and wrapped it around the injured man's leg. He wrenched loose the shattered rung of a ladder and used it to twist through the wire, making a tourniquet.

On the next level down, he felt his feet get tangled in something in the water on the deck. An officer came along with a flashlight and they dis-

covered that his legs were entwined by someone's insides floating on the water.

He kicked himself loose and went down to the main deck, where he saw a man sitting wearily against a bulkhead.

"Hey, Mac, are you okay?" asked Buck.

No answer came, so Buck asked him again. When he got no answer this time, Buck reached down to feel his pulse. The man was already cold. Buck left and went back to his post.

Up above decks, the wounded Patrick was giving out morphine. Page was trying hard to keep breathing above the escaping steam, and Buck was trying to recover his sight after being dazed by shell fire. Below decks, in the engine control room, was Chief Yeoman Cheek reading an old issue of the *Reader's Digest*.

The huge panel of gauges in front of him was functioning perfectly. The engine was at top speed, the boilers were maintaining a magnificent head of steam, and the blowers were keeping the room quite cool and comfortable. When a command came through, Cheek carried it out, then returned to his reading.

There was nothing else to do.

The noise of the battle was distant and removed. Around him the men stood talking quietly or merely looking at the gauges. In a vague sort of way, they all worried about the 600 pounds of steam coursing through the pipes all around them. Engineers always worry about steam. But they had faith in the armor, faith in the engine, faith in one another.

So Cheek kept on reading the *Reader's Digest*.

Some reports of injuries could be heard over the phone, but not much. The men down in engine control couldn't tell the difference between hits and the noise of their own guns.

It was morning when Cheek walked up onto the deck and saw the destruction. Then he realized, for the first time, how many shells had ripped into the ship during the night.

After he saw the damage, he couldn't sleep for three days.

Every troop transport, every battleship, and every destroyer had at least one puppy smuggled aboard by the men. Here, Pvt. William Saroyan takes time out to talk about his own favorite canine.

THE SWEETHEART OF COMPANY D

—Pvt. WILLIAM SAROYAN
June 25, 1943

THERE IS something in the heart of street dogs that draws them close to men, and there is probably no camp or post of the Army that does not have at least one dog, whether the post is in a Far Western desolation or in a suburb of New York, as my post is.

Our Company D has one of these dogs. He is called Shorty by some of the men, Short End by others and Short Arm by still others. Shorty is small, lazy, and given to a bitter attitude toward civilians, including children. Somewhere in Shorty's family is a dachshund, as Shorty has the lines of such a dog, but not the hair.

The theory of the men of Company D is that Shorty spends the greater part of his time dreaming of women—or at any rate, women dogs. He doesn't come across such creatures very often; he doesn't come across any kind of dog very often. Whenever he does, male or female, Shorty goes to work and gives the matter a stab, so to speak. It is a halfhearted stab, with Shorty more bored than fascinated and not the least bit sure of what he is trying to do, or whether or not he isn't making a fool of himself.

Now and then Shorty will be discovered in the middle of the street, dreaming of love or whatever it is, while two or three trucks stand by discreetly waiting for him to make up his mind. Shorty may have come into the world thoughtlessly, but it is not likely that he will leave any children standing around. He is either too tired, too troubled, or too old, even though he is probably not more than two.

I have observed that Shorty makes himself available to any man in uniform, bar none, and while our post is made up mostly of men of talent, Shorty is not above giving himself over to the affections of a man of practically no talent at all, such as our top sergeant, who was not in civilian life the famous man he is now. Our top sergeant may be a genius, the same as all the rest of us: Two-Teeth Gonzalez, Bicycle Wilkinson, Henry the One Hundred and Fifty-first Million, and all the others. He probably deserves a story all to himself, but somebody else will have to write that story, as I want to write sonnets. (That is, if I ever learn to spell.)

My hero is Shorty, not our first sergeant. The sergeant is his mother's hero, I suppose, and I wish to God she'd never let him out of the house. If he thinks getting me to do KP is the way we are going to bring the war to a satisfactory conclusion, I believe his education has been neglected. That is not the way to do it. Give me a map of the world, a pointer, and a good-sized audience and I believe I can figure the whole thing out in not more than an afternoon. The idea that generals are the only kind of Army personnel capable of figuring out ways and means and all that stuff is unsound. For every general there ought to be one private on the ground floor. As it is, half the time I don't know what is being done, what the idea is, or anything else. The result is that I must go out into the yard and whistle for Shorty, who, instead of leaping to his feet and running to me, opens his eyes and waits for me to run to him.

Shorty knows me all right, but what kind of planning can you do with a dog, and a sleepy one at that—a daydreamer, an escapist, a lover of peace, an enemy of children in sailor suits? I don't know who the chaplain of Company D is, but for my money he can pack up and go to some other post, because Shorty is doing the same work and sending in no reports to anybody. He is a quiet creature, he is patient, he will listen to reason or anything else, and he will get up after a half hour of heart-to-heart talk and slowly wag his tail. He will wag thoughtfully, with effort, and unless you are blind, you will know what advice he is giving you after carefully considering your case.

Now, there was the celebrated case of Warty Walter, the Genius from Jersey, who had a secret weapon all worked out in his head that he believed could finish the war in two weeks. Warty mentioned this weapon to our top sergeant, only to hear the man say, "You do what I say, Warty, or you're going to hear otherwise."

Warty went out into the yard to Shorty and unburdened his heart, whereupon Shorty got to his feet, stretched his body until it hurt, wagged his tail three times, kissed Warty on the hand, turned, and began wending his way across the street where a girl of six in a sailor suit was looking at a movie billboard. That was the end of Warty's secret weapon. The following day he got his orders

to go to Louisiana, took Shorty in his arms to say good-bye, and the war is still going on—a good three months after Warty got his idea for the secret weapon. Our top sergeant said, "If it's a secret, what the hell are you coming to me about it for? Keep it a secret."

Not every man at our post is as brilliant or as sincere as Warty, but I can think of no man who is not as devoted to Shorty. No girl of the USO has done Army morale as much good as Shorty. He may not be a dancing dog, but he's got eyes, and many a man's seen a lot of understanding in those brooding eyes—many and many a man.

As for the little girl in the sailor suit, she turned and ran, so that Shorty, not knowing what else to do, went up to a second lieutenant and bit him. The following day there was a notice on the bulletin board saying: "Yesterday an enlisted man was bitten by a dog who might or might not have had rabies. Therefore, in the future, any man caught without his dog tags will be given extra duty." This, of course, was a subtle way of saying that Shorty had rabies, a lie if I ever heard one.

The basic failing of Shorty, if he must be given a failing, is his love of comfort, his passion for food, and his devotion to sleep or The Dream. Shorty probably does not know this is 1943. I doubt very much if he knows there is a war going on, and I am convinced he does not know that the men of Company D are soldiers. I believe he has some vague notion that we are orphans.

Shorty eats too much and never does calisthenics. He has seen a lot of men come and go. He has loved them all, and they have all loved him. I have seen big men with barracks bags over their shoulders bend down to whisper good-bye to the sweetheart of Company D, get up with misty eyes, swing up into the truck, and wave to the little fellow standing there in a stupor. And I have heard them, as the truck has bounced out of the yard on its way to the war, holler out—not to me or to our top sergeant, but to Shorty: "So long, pal! See you after the war!"

I don't think they will see Shorty after the war. I think he will lie down and die of a broken heart once the boys take off their uniforms. Shorty lives to watch them stand reveille and retreat. All that stuff will stop after the war, and Shorty will be out in the cold, just another dog of the streets, without honor, without importance—lonely, unfed, despised, and unwanted.

That is why I have written this tribute to him.

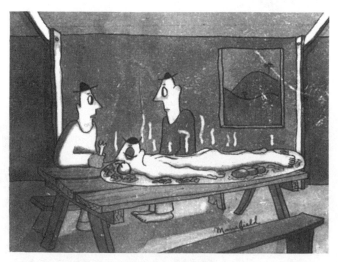

"I understand he and the mess sergeant had a little spat."—Pvt. Walter Mansfield

★

─────────────────────

They talked about girls, they talked about beer, they talked about everything under the sun—except the job they were about to do. Irwin Shaw was one of them.

PREPARATION FOR INVASION

—Pvt. IRWIN SHAW
September 10, 1943

IT WAS at a bar. In Cairo, the heaviest military concentrations are at bars. From the bars of Cairo, these days, men fan out and conquer the world. The city has a good central location for conquering purposes, the natives are friendly, and the climate is endurable on gin and beer.

Two of our brave boys far from home were enduring the climate in front of a pile of sliced limes that the bartender had thoughtfully prepared for the midday concentration.

This was a farewell meeting. One was leaving for India, the other for Sicily.

"Sicily," said the man who was going to India, staring moodily into his glass. "Why, you ought to have to pay the Army to be allowed in."

"There's no sense," said the man who was on his way to Sicily, "in going to extremes."

"In another week," said the man who was going to India, "you'll be in Italy. What a place to invade!" He closed his eyes in quiet ecstasy. Then he opened them bitterly. "And where'll I get to invade? China, Burma, Japan, tropical islands full of head hunters and malignant bacteria."

"The Burmese girls," protested the man who was going to Sicily. "You could do worse."

"Yeah," said the man on his way to India. "Figures not bad. Breasts, model 1943, angle of deflection 45 degrees. I admit that. But the faces— " He scowled at the limes. "Mediocre. You would have to develop the taste. But Italy— " He shook his head reverently. "All those pear-shaped Italian women, irritated at the Italians, full of gratitude at being delivered from *Il Duce* and *Der Führer*. Do you know any Italian?"

"A little," said the man who was heading west. "I patronized an Italian restaurant in Greenwich Village for seven years. Lobster, Neapolitan style, with garlic sauce."

"Can you say, 'What are you doing tonight, Signorina?' "

"Yes."

"Roses, roses all the way," sighed the man with China on his mind. "A rich agricultural country with a climate like California's, full of sound little local wines. The Army should charge admission."

"I wish you'd stop saying that," complained the man on his way to Rome. "Some finance officer is liable to hear you and before you know it, you'll have to buy tickets two weeks in advance to get onto a transport."

"The sky is blue," murmured the connoisseur of Burman beauty, "the rivers are broad, the art of 2,500 years is scattered from one end of the land to the other. Michaelangelo, Da Vinci, Raphael,

Titian, the palaces of the Doges on the Grand Canal. And you will no doubt arrive in time for the opening of the opera season at La Scala. You will be a cultured man when you arrive in America. You will be in demand by hostesses for their parties from Park Avenue to Nob Hill. And I—." He laughed mirthlessly. "I will get to the romantic East in time for the opening of the monsoon season. I will be there for the mud-and-jungle meeting of the Jap-and-Snakebite Sporting Club. I will be in great demand by specialists in obscure tropical diseases when I return to America." He waved bitterly to the bartender to signify that he was ready to endure some more climate. "There is no justice in a war," he said.

"Perhaps you're right," said the man who was going to be at La Scala when the curtain went up. He also waved at the bartender, but not bitterly.

"It is going to be one of the great marches of all military history," said the man facing the Himalayas. "A long, narrow, green country full of handsome people who have been enslaved for 20 years and are now being liberated, and know it. You will be greeted like water in the desert, like a circus on the Fourth of July, like Clark Gable at Vassar. The Chianti will flow like water. And can you imagine," he speculated, narrowing his eyes dreamily, "what it will be like to be an American lieutenant of Italian descent?"

"I can imagine," said the other in a low, pensive voice. "He would never reach Florence. He would be worn to the bone with hospitality, and would have to be invalided back to the States."

"Aaah," they both sighed.

"And after that, France," said the man on his way to Tokyo. He shook his head. "I can't bear it," he said as he paid the check. "The Army should really charge admission." And he went to the supply room to draw a mosquito net.

"All right! Let's dress up this damn line!"
—PVT. THOMAS FLANNERY

They called it Operation Husky and put it into play on July 10, 1943. By the end of the next day, 80,000 troops and 8,000 vehicles had massed along five beaches in southern Sicily. The long road to Rome had been staked.

INVASION OF SICILY

—Sgt. RALPH G. MARTIN
August 13, 1943

First Day

THURSDAY, JULY 9, 1943, ON A U.S. WARSHIP SOMEWHERE IN THE MEDITERRANEAN—We know we are headed somewhere, for something big. We know we are headed for trouble, but except for the shortage of women and deck chairs, this has been like a peacetime Mediterranean cruise, at least until a few days ago. Then things changed, and today's latrine rumor says we're finally shoving off tomorrow. The captain put teeth in the rumor when he announced we couldn't use the ship's radio to monitor the news any more.

Second Day

FRIDAY, SOMEWHERE IN THE MEDITERRANEAN —This morning, as far as we could see in whatever direction we looked, the Mediterranean was covered with ships of every kind. The smallest were LCIs (troop-landing barges), looking like submarines every time they hit a big wave. All of us kept hoping the sea would calm down; nobody can fight on a seasick stomach.

Our much-talked-about air umbrella seemed to have boiled down to an occasional group of Spitfires. Somebody wisecracked that it was like the naked emperor's new clothes: "Only the good people can see them." But an officer explained that it was not a matter of air cover but of air control. And the truth is, we haven't seen a Jerry plane yet. The biggest morale-builder imaginable is the sight of 100 Allied bombers and fighters heading out on a bombing mission above us.

At a naval rendezvous this afternoon, our fat convoy swelled even fatter, with a strong skirt of sub chasers and destroyers and an outer fringe of cruisers and battleships. The boys have quit worrying about torpedoes.

We were briefed today, told where we were going and what we could expect to find lined up against us. That spiked the flood of rumors that had us heading practically everywhere from Havana to Yankee Stadium.

Third Day

SATURDAY, OFF THE COAST OF SICILY—H-hour came at 2:45 a.m., and shortly afterward we saw the first flashes from the big coastal guns. Five bombs thudded a hundred yards from our ship just before dawn today. They were dropped by a single plane flying high, a plane that came and went in a hurry before anyone could spot it. Our ship is cruising up and down several miles off the Gela beaches, where American troops are being landed. We can't get too close because the enemy's artillery has been splattering shells in the sea all around us.

The town of Gela itself is ringed around with thick smoke, hiding the area where all the fighting is going on. We've had some air raids, but they have been mostly sneak stuff. Our warships, nice big babies, have been parading up and down the Sicilian coastline, letting loose eight-inch shells

Sicily was hot—and the Germans offered little opportunity to cool off.

with a terrific *whoom!* They've been focusing their attention on the enemy batteries several miles from the beaches.

All day long we've been hearing war noises. Some of the boys are getting a little supersensitive, confusing the sounds of the ships and the sea with the noise of guns and planes. Everybody sleeps in his clothes now. You never know when to expect the long, shrill ring that means "general alarm." It is a nerve-jangling thing, that alarm, even to guys who spent months in the Tunisian fighting.

Everyone agrees with Pvt. John Griggs of New-ark, New Jersey, who said, "The main reason I get jittery on these ships is they make me feel like a duck in a Coney Island shooting gallery."

Fourth Day

SUNDAY, OFF THE COAST OF SICILY—Enemy planes are flying in a crisscross pattern around us, and six bombs have landed right off starboard. We are in the Axis backyard now, and they've been throwing all kinds of planes at us all day long. They come in small formations, but they come often and from all sides.

Thus far we haven't captured many Sicilian air-fields, so most of our fighter-plane cover has to come all the way from Africa. On the other hand, the Messerschmitts and Macchis have to fly only a few minutes from their bases to reach us.

One of the favorite Axis tricks, something they've done a dozen times today, is to send a single plane tearing out from inland to sweep across the beaches where our men are landing, in a fast strafing job. Another favorite dodge is to send a couple of dive-bombers barely skimming above our docked ships.

Sometimes when the Spits are around we can watch a movie-thriller kind of chase. Twice we have seen concentrated black puffs of flak crunch into their targets, and both times the MEs crashed.

After enough action of this kind, your raw nerves become dulled and you don't get excited the way you did at first. But when a flock of 50 Jerry bombers passes right overhead, not too high, in a tight formation, and there is light enough for them to see you very plainly, it is tough for anyone to appear disinterested.

I have never seen so much flak freckling the sky as I did when those bombers came. Every ship in the harbor threw up everything it had, but the Jerries didn't seem interested in us. They were bound for somewhere else.

Fifth Day

MONDAY, SOMEWHERE IN SICILY—Shortly after midnight our time came, and we loaded our ve-hicles and troops onto barges and landed in Sicily.

Just before dawn we started for Gela, with our necks craned upward looking for Jerry. This time we saw a perfect cover of Spitfires all over the place. It was really beautiful.

Gela itself looked like a slightly overgrown Gafsa, minus the Arabs. Some of its streets were even narrower than those in the Medina "off lim-its" native quarter of Casablanca.

A jetty had been blown up in the middle and the wires were down, but only a few of Gela's houses were damaged heavily by bombs or shells. Everywhere the people looked at us as we moved in, but there was no cheering, no *Viva Gli Stati Uniti!* These people have relatives and friends fighting our soldiers only a few miles from here.

Still, some were glad to see us. "We've starved too much," one man said. On all sides you could see Yanks handing out their rations and cigarettes to the poorly dressed people with their skinny lit-tle kids.

Long lines of prisoners marched through the town all day. Dark, wiry men, they looked small beside our huge MPs. The prisoners walked past buildings on which were posted encouraging mes-sages signed by their Duce. Some women on the sidelines were bawling, but one of them, recog-nizing an Italian prisoner, yelled, "You're all right now, you're all right now!"

I hitched a ride with the provost marshal, Maj. Thomas Lancer, for 14 years a member of the New York State Police. Lancer is the officer charged with keeping order in Gela. "We didn't have any trouble with these people," he said, "after they learned we were too many for them. They knew when they were licked."

His biggest job was the evacuation of prisoners. Thousands of them streamed from all sections of the front. There was no sniping. "These Italians don't go in for that," the major said.

We met some of the Rangers who had just come from the fighting in the nearby hilly country, where a heavy concentration of enemy infantry poured in on them. The two hills captured by the Rangers looked like two little knobs placed close together, but they were important because they commanded the nearby roads.

It wasn't like the *djebel* country of the Tunis-Bizerte sector, but still, there were lots of hills. Most of the fields around the town were littered with Axis tanks, blasted by Yank cannon in the same artillery duel that had burned down so many nearby wheat fields.

Everywhere we went, we saw the all-purpose two-and-a-half-ton "duck" trucks that will go anywhere and carry anything. They are the only vehicles not even slightly bothered by sand—and what mud is to Oran, sand is to Sicily.

Sixth Day

TUESDAY, SOMEWHERE IN SICILY—Random jottings picked up here and there in the American zone:

Aboard ship, all of the Yanks promised themselves that the first thing they'd get when they landed in Sicily was a nice spaghetti dinner. One of the really lucky GIs was S/Sgt. Louis Caronilla of Sacramento, California. Whether it was his fluent Italian or his friendly face, or the combination of both, he was irresistible to one Sicilian family, and they fed him spaghetti with a magnificent Italian sauce, tomato-and-onion salad, and a bottle of 20-year-old wine.

There were 24 MPs who spent just five minutes on Sicilian soil before returning to North Africa. They were assigned to guard prisoners captured in the initial fighting and had to accompany them on an LCI back to a larger vessel and then to Africa.

At Vittoria, about 15 miles southeast of Gela, a Sicilian approached Pfc. David Simon of the Bronx, New York, pulled out his American citizenship papers, and gave Simon a snappy salute. Besides being a U.S. citizen, this particular Sicilian had fought with the American Army during the last war and later was stationed at Fort Jay, New York, the original home of one of the First Division components in the invasion force. After being demobilized, he returned to his hometown in Sicily.

An artillery observation post in Sicily attracts a fan.

Two Junkers 88s landed at Comiso Airfield just after the Yanks captured the place. As the flyers climbed out of the JUs—one crew was German, the other Italian—they waxed highly indignant. "We were told our forces still held this field," they said.

Capt. Robert Hermann of Jacksonville, Florida, told about two GIs who saw a nice-looking Italian gun resting peacefully on a table. As a test, one of them gently attached a long string to the gun and went all the way back to a nearby foxhole. Jumping in, he pulled the string. Nothing happened to the gun, but the foxhole blew up. There was a mine in it. The other GI, watching the whole thing from the distance, now has the gun. It's a good gun.

Sicilian parents keep bringing their children to Army headquarters, asking officers when the Americans will open schools and teach English to the kids so they can go to the United States.

The first Sicilian wounded while fighting for the American cause was Gios Connero, who voluntarily acted as water boy and litter bearer for the first American paratroopers to land. He worked hard for us until he was stopped by a shell fragment in his head. The Americans evacuated him with their own wounded. Gios had lived for 14 years in New York City.

Sicilian women are now returning from their hiding places on outlying farms, to which they fled when Nazi soldiers quartered in the towns picked out the women they liked, commandeered the houses, kicked everybody else out, and then raped the women. If a woman had somebody with her, and that somebody protested, he was shot.

"When I get off this boat," said seasick Cpl. L. L. Williams of Dallas, Texas, before landing, "I'm going to walk and walk and walk." And he did. The Signal Corps put him to work laying 20 miles of wire.

Seventh Day

WEDNESDAY, SOMEWHERE IN SICILY—Things were finally settling down today into a highly schemed order of things. Italian-speaking Yanks, and there seemed to be a lot of them, went around

Lying in wait was often the most brutal part of it.

telling the people we were there to help and not hurt them.

S/Sgt. Frank Sclafani of the Bronx, New York, has spent most of his free time among the Sicilians quoting Tom Paine in Italian, something about "we fight not to enslave but to set the country free and make room upon earth for honest men to live in."

It's been a long week—a long week during which we fought our way into Sicily and established our first foothold on Europe. Now we are giving the people of Sicily candy and cigarettes and Tom Paine.

Olga, the Vital Cog

Nominated for this week's grand prize—a box of ginger cookies and a one-way ticket to Moosejaw, Saskatchewan—is little Miss Olga McCleery who works at the quartermaster laundry.

Miss McCleery is a vital cog in the war effort.

She is the lady who punches all the holes in the tops of soldiers' socks. Her assistant ties the socks together with heavy cord in knots that cannot be cut, neither can they be untied. If she is a good assistant and devises better and harder knots, she may some day be promoted and permitted to punch the holes.

But we are not talking of the assistant. We are talking of Miss McCleery herself.

Miss McCleery's work is hard. Sometimes a sock comes back to the laundry so many times that there are dozens and dozens of holes punched in it. Miss McCleery has to look and look to find a place to punch another hole. These holes are necessary for tying the socks together.

Miss McCleery is a cheery and a conscientious worker. She likes to punch holes. Before she started working for the quartermaster laundry she was a vital cog in the telephone exchange in town. She was the lady whose voice came over the wire saying, "I'm sorry; your three minutes are up."

Let us praise the work of Miss McCleery. If she continues to do the work she is doing now, the quartermaster laundry will give her a promotion.

They will give her a white collar job.

She will be in charge of the Element of Surprise Department. All she will have to do all day long is to take drab white undershirts from people's laundry and substitute cotton polo shirts that say "U.S. Army—Fort Leonard Wood" on the front.

After the war, she can go back to the telephone exchange and tell customers their three minutes are up.

—Cpl. Marion Hargrove

Shipping Overseas, Yank Finds Brother's Name Carved on the Rail

SOMEWHERE ON THE ATLANTIC—Cpl. D. V. Norman of Waco, Texas, stood in the chow line stretching along the ship's rail. Looking at the water and feeling the sway of the ship, he wondered where and when he'd land.

The chow line moved a little, and suddenly there on the rail was his brother's name, carved unmistakably under the initials of a guy from New York: "Pvt. Woodrow Norman, Waco, Texas."

The last time the corporal heard from Woodrow he was in the MPs back in the States. Now, he figures, Woodrow must be in Sicily or Italy: that was where the transport was headed on the trip before this one.

—Sgt. Newton Fulbright
Yank Field Correspondent

Give Him Time

CAMP CLAIBORNE, LOUISIANA—First Sgt. Jules Mechelle has heard them all, but it remained for T-4 Pang Wong, cook with the 1878th Unit, EMD, to come up with the tops for all furlough requests.

Wong, quite seriously, asked for a 65-day furlough. He explained that he wanted 30 days to go to China, 30 days to return and the authorized 5 days to spend at home.

I Love You, I Love You

AUSTRALIA—A sailor walked into a post office and put down $65 to pay for a cable to his girl back in the United States. He wrote his message, pouring out his love in endearing, four-shilling phrases, handed it across the counter and started out.

"Your change, sir," the clerk reminded him.

"Change?" asked the sailor. "If there's any change just use it up saying 'I love you.' "

Obliging post-office authorities reaffirmed his love 28 times.

Hitchhike Regulations

CAMP SIBERT, ALABAMA—After local civilians had complained about soldiers thumbing rides outside the camp, an official notice was posted on the bulletin board of the Seventh Provisional Barracks here. Excerpts from the notice.

"Thumbing rides from motorists is expressly forbidden. Soldiers may, however, stand by the side of the road and rotate eyeballs at passing cars. . . . The practice of throwing the body under the wheels of passing cars is also frowned upon . . . as there have been many complaints of injuries to tires."

Imagine This Guy's Surprise! His Buddy Turned Out to Be a Jap

SAN FRANCISCO, CALIFORNIA—Woodrow Webb, 22-year-old Marine from Wildwood, New Jersey, thinks this Solomon Island adventure is funny.

He decided to evacuate his machine-gun post in a hurry when a Jap mortar found the range. He and another guy, who rose up out of the inky jungle night, ran side by side and dropped simultaneously into a fox hole while the shells exploded around them. The young Gyrene was comforted by the presence of a buddy, but he was too breathless to say anything—which was very fortunate.

During a lull in the shelling, Webb's companion spoke—in Japanese! Webb nodded his head but didn't answer. Stealthily, he reached for a grenade, slipped the pin out and cautiously slid it under the Jap's pack.

"Then," Webb said with a grin, "I got the hell out of there!"

—Sgt. Robert N. Blum
U.S. Marine Corps Reserves

You Can't Fool with the FBI; When They Wantcha, They Getcha

SOMEWHERE IN THE MIDDLE EAST—Recently, Benton Harbor (Michigan) draft authorities sent T/5 Orville A. Wolfram of Fort Atkinson, Wisconsin, a notice to drop in and talk over his selective service status. Then he received notice to appear in New York City for physical examination. Neither of these notifications, sent to him through his APO, gave him much worry. But now he's studying a letter from the FBI, telling him to let them know of his whereabouts immediately or things will happen with a G-man escort.

Having already served 21 months in the U.S. armed forces and being here in the Middle East some thousands of miles overseas, he's a little mixed up.

—Cpl. John R. Evans
Yank Field Correspondent

Wake Island Defenders Get Help From a Totally Unexpected Quarter

SOMEWHERE IN LIBYA—"Playing tonight. 'Wake Island,' with Brian Donlevy and Robert Preston. Bring your own tin hat."

That sign might look funny on the marquee of the old neighborhood movie house, but it wouldn't have been out of place recently at the rec hall of this U.S. bomber base.

Officers and men who packed the hall to see the thrilling movie epic of the Marines at Wake Island were on the edge of their petrol cans when the sound effects suddenly seemed to go haywire at the most exciting moment.

As a formation of Jap planes swooped down on the tiny Pacific garrison whose ammunition supply had been exhausted, heavy antiaircraft fire was heard. It took a second volley and then a third before the GI patrons realized that the ack-ack wasn't Cecil B. De Mille stuff.

Dashing outside, Pfc. George Henry of Philadelphia, Pennsylvania, looked up at the sky and saw a barrage from British batteries making little puffs in the sky. "It's an air raid all right," Henry told a buddy, "but hell, the war inside's got it beat a mile."

—Sgt. Jim Swarts, Jr.
Yank Field Correspondent

The Good Earth

PANAMA—There's a little piece of ground here that T/Sgt. David Green of the Bronx, New York, will always consider as hallowed.

He wrote to his girl friend, Miss Florence Barrasch, to send him some of Uncle Sam's good solid Bronx earth to stand on, and she obliged by sending a chunk of Pelham Bay Park.

Green spread the soil out under his feet and reverently stood in the same spot for 15 minutes. He has invoked squatter's rights for the duration.
—*Yank* Staff Correspondent

Author, Author

FORT GEORGE WRIGHT, WASHINGTON—For those GIs who can't resist writing on latrine walls, the latrine orderly in the main PX here supplies a large guest book. Set on a light, easily moved pulpit of convenient height, it offers an outlet for latrine poetry and such and—saves the walls.

"I'm just not happy here."—PFC. FRANK DORSAY

It was an unsettling experience—an opportunity to see how the other half lived that made you realize at the same time how lucky you were to be an American.

PALESTINE EXPRESS

—Pvt. Irwin Shaw
October 15, 1943

TEL AVIV, Palestine—The train for Palestine pulled out of Cairo station slowly, to the accompaniment of wailing shrieks from the platform peddlers selling lemonade, cold coffee, pornographic literature, grapes, old copies of *Life*, and flat Arab bread.

The train was long and crowded, and it had seen better days. It had been standing in the wild Egyptian sun all morning and part of the afternoon, and it had a very interesting smell.

It carried Englishmen, Scots, Welshmen, Palestinians, Indians, New Zealanders, South Africans, Australians, Americans, French, Senussi, Bantus, Senegalese; it carried Egyptian civilians, Arab civilians, Palestinian civilians; it carried generals, colonels, lieutenants, sergeants, and privates—and it carried bugs. The generals and lieutenants it carried first class. The sergeants it carried second class. The privates it carried third class. The bugs it carried all classes.

It didn't travel fast. A good, strong man in the prime of life who did not smoke too much could have jumped out and trotted beside it without too much trouble from Cairo to Lydda. It stopped as often as a woman in a bargain basement. It stopped for coal, it stopped for water, it stopped

every time a barge appeared somewhere on one of the hundreds of canals we crossed, it stopped every time the tracks ran near two palm trees growing within 50 yards of each other, for that constitutes a settlement in this part of the world.

When it stopped, hundreds of Egyptians of all ages would spring up, selling pale round watermelons, dirty bunches of grapes, hard-boiled eggs, tomatoes, and warm lemon soda right out of the Nile. The merchandising was carried on in hurried, shrill yells, like a girls' dormitory after lights out, and your salesman was likely to disappear suddenly in mid-purchase as the local policeman came into view, snapping a long bullwhip over slow calves and buttocks.

The third-class cars were built by firm believers in the Spartan life for the common man. They spurned straw, spurned springs, spurned leather. Everything was made out of good, solid wood, at stern right angles with more good, solid wood. Every seat was taken, and there were packs, rifles, musette bags, and piles of canned apricots all over the aisles.

Native women squatted alongside the tracks doing their washing in canal water that had been there since St. Paul; brown boys splashed and waved at us; water buffaloes, blinded by straw hats tied over their eyes, went round and round endlessly, drawing water up to the field.

In my end of the car, there was a general confusion of British Tank Corps men, returning to their units from the hospital in Cairo, and six Indians who made themselves very much at home, setting up camp in all available space and preparing and eating their native dishes from 3 p.m. until bedtime. Across the aisle were two very tanned South Africans in shorts, who looked disapprovingly on the whole thing and conversed coldly in Afrikaans as we chugged past Suez.

By nightfall, despite the immense quantities of watermelon and lemon soda that had been consumed, there was an air of deep hunger hanging over the car, and when the word was passed around that at the next station there was a NAAFI (British Post Exchange) where we would be fed, there was a determined rush to get out Dixies and tin cups. The British soldier would no more think of going any place without his Dixie and tin cup than he would think of appearing without pants in Piccadilly Circus.

I had neither mess tin nor cup and was mournfully admiring British foresight when a little middle-aged Tommy on my right, who had spent the whole afternoon silently and religiously reading a magazine called *Gen*, perusing advertisements and fiction page by page without partiality, quietly offered me a mess tin.

There was a great combing of hair in the tradition that the Briton dresses for dinner no matter where the meal finds him, and thousands of us started leaping off the train before it had fully stopped. We lined up and were served sandwiches, cakes, and good, hot, strong tea by Egyptians in elegant white cotton gloves.

"There's beer at the other end of the station," reported a British sailor. "Ruppert's. Half a crown a can." There was no movement toward the other end of the station.

On the train was a party of sailors who had just come back from Sicily and were feeling good about it. They had manned the landing barges in the invasion and said it hadn't been bad. "We only had

two boat rides," they said. "Boat rides" meant bringing in troops under fire. "It was just like the movies," one of them said. "They kept firing at us and the water kept shooting up all around, but they never hit us."

One of them had been at the Brooklyn Navy Yard for six months during the war while the ship he was on was being repaired. "Oh, it's a lovely city, Brooklyn," he sighed. "And I had a lovely girl in Jamaica. It took me an hour in the subway each way, but it was worth it. A lovely city, but I couldn't live there. The pace is too fast for me. I'd be worn out in a year."

While everybody settled down for the night, I foolishly sat on the open platform, smoking and watching the desert roll by in the starlight. When I went in to go to sleep, I discovered that the Indians had spread a little more, and there was no place to sit, stand or lie inside. Everyone else seemed to be asleep and the car was full of snores and the rich smell of many soldiers who had traveled far in a hot climate with no water available. Only the two South Africans remained awake, staring coldly out through the closed windows at the desert.

I went into the next car. Luckily one of the sailors had rolled off the bench on a turn and remained where he was on the floor, too lazy to move. So I curled myself among the arms, legs, snores, and sleepy cries of love and battle in the crowded car and tried to sleep.

When I awoke at 4 a.m. we were in Palestine. As I sat there watching the first orange streaks over the little, dark, tree-crested hills, the two South Africans came out. We began to talk. They had just come from near Tripoli after two and a half years in the desert, fighting most of the time. This was their first leave, 21 days, and they had flown down to Cairo and were on their way to Tel Aviv.

One of them had suggested getting a truck ride up to Tel Aviv, but the other had said: "No. We are on a holiday. Let's spend some money and be comfortable. Let's take the train." They chuckled sourly as they told me.

"Third class," one of them said. "Why, in South

Africa we wouldn't send cows to market in these trains. How about in America?"

I told him that I guessed we wouldn't send cows to market in America in these trains, either.

"Third class," the other said. "Why, before the war, any place I went I would only stay in the best hotel in town."

"And in Cairo," the first one said, "any restaurant with a tablecloth is out of bounds to other ranks. I've had it. I've had this war. I volunteered and I fought for two and a half years and we were among the first to get into Tripoli. I've heard a lot of bullets go by. I've been dive-bombed and I've gone without water and I was perfectly satisfied. But this train ride finishes me. I've had this war, and they can have it back any time they want."

And he went inside to think about the pretty girls on the beach at Tel Aviv.

I sat on the platform and watched the morning sun break over the hills and light the orange groves and vineyards.

A little later the train stopped and we got off to take the bus to Tel Aviv. On the bus I met a lieutenant, a friend of mine, who had also come down by train. He looked very tired.

"What's the matter?" I asked.

"That damned first class," he said. "No room to lie down. You sit up all night. Next time I take this blasted ride, I'm taking my bars off and traveling third."

Behind me I heard a wild, snorting sound. It was the South Africans, laughing.

WHAT SHOULD YOU BRING OVERSEAS?

—Pvt. Bill Steele
Yank Field Correspondent
March 26, 1943

Take the advice of a guy in the South Pacific and slip these extra items into your baggage.

SOMEWHERE IN the South Pacific—As soon as they land down here, nine out of ten GIs say, "I wish to hell I could get back to the States—long enough to buy a knife."

Nor is it only knives we need—every Johnny Jeep among us could make out a long list of items he wishes he had thought to remember to slip into his barracks bag when he left that port of embarkation.

The moral is: Whatever you're going to need, you'd better bring with you.

Chances are that down here there won't be any civilian outlets where you can get a shaving mirror or a flashlight. And though the PXs—if you are lucky enough to be near one—try hard to supply such items, they're usually just out when *you* get there.

The foreign-bound soldier should not load himself with patented work savers and fancy gadgets. Your GI equipment, usually the best, is sufficient. But extra items have proved practical and useful. They'll add to your pleasures and do away with some of the woes of soldiering overseas.

Probably the handiest item to bring along is a hunting knife. One with a good, stout blade. You'll use it in a dozen ways just while converting your pyramidal into a place you can call home, cutting branches to hang as a clothes rack in the peak of the tent, and cutting out brush roots for a floor. The ideal possession would be a miniature kit containing a saw, pliers, hammer, and knife—but they're difficult to obtain in kits even in the States.

When you embark, you'll be completely outfitted with proper clothing—but you are probably well stocked with extra socks, shorts, and handkerchiefs. Okay, stick them in your barracks bag. Never too many pairs of clean socks.

Swim trunks—don't forget 'em! It's awkward to want a swim at a convenient seashore and not be able to for fear some nurse with a lieutenant's commission or a local maid might make a visit to the beach. You'll wear the trunks en route, too—for a sunbath on deck.

There isn't much need for military oxfords over here. Far better types of footwear to bring are rubber-soled sneaks or moccasin slippers. Something to wear when you're boxing, playing baseball, or just hitting the sack for a few minutes' rest before chow. Something you can slip on for hurry-up nocturnal trips, too.

Before you leave, get a small mirror. This mirror will henceforth lead a very rugged life, so it had better be a metal one. Bring plenty of razor blades, too. They don't take up much space, and you never know when you won't be able to buy any.

Flashlights are swell to have and impossible to

buy around here. So it's a good idea to bring one. You'll have to surrender it while aboard ship, but it's worth the trouble.

There's many a man who'd hock his Pfc. stripe for a bottle of antimosquito dope. The numerous mosquitoes here are active little fellows. They'll drain a fellow of his last corpuscles at night and appear at the Red Cross station as blood donors the next morning. Oil of citronella is effective in repelling them.

Make sure that you or somebody else brings a washboard—one of the small ones that you can buy at a five-and-ten. You'll be doing most of your laundry yourself, and fatigues can be cleaned much more easily with a washboard.

The same tip goes for a camera. Film is difficult to get, and exposures are developed GI, a very slow proposition. Nevertheless, the few cameras we have here are kept very busy indeed taking snapshots of old buddies and new scenery.

Oldtimers (anyone who has been here more than

a month is an oldtimer) will undoubtedly try to buy some of your "luxury" items, such as watches, cigarette lighters, fountain pens, and pencil sets. Sometimes local civilian shops carry them, but at fantastic prices. Since the opportunities for spending cash are limited, only too often dogfaces will part with the good green for a fancy bauble. You'll be better off, though, to hang onto your fountain pen and wristwatch than to sell them, even at black market prices.

Speaking of watches—the waterproof, shockproof timepiece is easily best if you want to invest a sizeable amount of money. But an inexpensive Mickey Mouse type wristwatch will do almost as well.

Here's a final tip to act on when the time comes for you to trade your mainland address for an APO in the Pacific. Have plenty of pictures of the girl back home with you. You'll understand the reason the first day after you arrive.

"All right, who turned off the hot water?"—SGT. TOM ZIBELLI

In spite of repeated Allied attempts to knock them out of commission, the Japanese air and naval bases at Rabaul and Kavieng remained entirely operational throughout the war. But that didn't stop the airhogs from trying.

A B-24 LOOKS FOR TROUBLE

—Sgt. DAVE RICHARDSON
Yank Staff Correspondent
October 29, 1943

IN A B-24 over the Solomon Sea—I've wound up in plenty of strange places after beer parties back home, but none half so strange as the spot I'm in this afternoon, after my first New Guinea beer party last night.

It all started when Sgt. Buell Rolens of Murphysboro, Illinois, public relations man for a U.S. heavy-bombardment outfit in New Guinea, asked me to the opening of his outfit's EM club.

At the party, first time most of us had tasted anything stronger than chlorinated water during our several months in New Guinea, the talk turned inevitably to bomber missions. Someone asked why I had never gone on a mission for a *Yank* story. "Every correspondent from Cairo to the Aleutians seems to have written eyewitness bomber-mission stories," I replied. "I want to do something different."

"If it's action you want," Rolens suggested, "why not go out on an armed reconnaissance? Fly in a bomber that goes deep into Jap territory all by itself, just looking for trouble. There's one tomorrow if you want to go."

After another beer, I said I would. "And if you don't come back," said Rolens, "can I have your typewriter?"

So now I'm on that reconnaissance in a B-24 droning over the Solomon Sea toward New Britain, New Ireland, and points east. We reach the coast of New Britain and skirt it for about an hour, meanwhile downing a lunch of oranges, canned tomato juice, cheese, and dog biscuits. As we swing over St. George's Channel near Rabaul, we spot a tiny dot in the water off the Cape.

Lt. F. E. Haag, our pilot, a former Rutgers University student from Pelham, New York, changes course and descends to identify the vessel. It's a 4,500-ton Jap freighter transport heading north. Now Lt. William H. Spencer, Jr., ex-telephone man from Roanoke, Virginia, takes over command of the bomber from his bombardier's perch. We make a bomb run at medium altitude.

Two bright yellow demolition bombs tumble out of the bomb racks. Beside me S/Sgt. Mike Nesevitch, former coal operator from Olyphant, Pennsylvania, keeps his aerial camera clicking. The bombs describe a graceful, lazy curve as the ship below swerves sharply to the right.

The bombs hit the water about 100 yards from the freighter. Lt. Spencer had figured the ship would turn the other way.

"Let's try it again," Lt. Spencer hollers over the interphone. We wheel over the cape lighthouse to make another run. Only now do we notice white puffs of ack-ack blossoming all around us. And only now do we spot another freighter, just as big, going south in the channel. Up from the second ship come two floatplanes, a biplane, and a Zero with pontons.

A hand grabs my shoulder. I turn to find S/Sgt. R. D. Brown, former cleaner and presser from Rusk, Texas, our assistant radioman, pointing out the left waist window. There, slightly below and to our left, are eight Jap planes with flaming red circles on their dirty tan wings. Four of them are Zeros, the others twin-engined bombers. Evidently they are returning from a bombing mission in the Solomons.

Lt. Haag guns the four motors on our big plane and banks it southward, toward a far-off cloud bank. The bombers and floatplanes disappear. But the Zeros climb toward us. Everyone clambers to his machine guns.

Back in the rear turret, S/Sgt. A. F. Weisberger, ex-sawmill worker from Rio Linda, California, gets in the opening burst. Soon most of the guns on our big bomber are chattering away. The Zeros split up and close in from two sides. They dart as swiftly and effortlessly as flies.

Nesevitch yells at me above the din, motioning me to his side at the right waist window. His cartridge belt has jumped its guide, silencing the gun. He yells for me to pull the end of the belt through the receiver slot as he works the belt entirely clear of the guide.

There's a Zero riding alongside us—ready to wing over and make a pass. If the Zero makes its stab right now, Sgt. Rolens will be the new owner of my battered Remington portable. But we fix the gun. Nesevitch blazes away at the Jap, who noses up to escape the tracers.

Then the Zero rolls over and curves in toward our nose. It races toward our bomber at 12 o'clock—a head-on pass. Pfc. Don Bellmore, former factory worker from Clinton, Michigan, draws a bead from his nose turret and squeezes his trigger for a long burst. At the same time, T/Sgt. Edgar F. Dow, ex-rayon maker from Lumberton, North Carolina, draws a bead from the top turret.

Tracers from their guns converge on the hurtling Zero. It falters a split second, then dives under our right wing to vanish in clouds below.

Now there's one Zero to the right of us, just beyond range, and two to the left. They ride along beside us for several minutes, eyeing us like three hungry hawks ready to pounce on a plump chicken. Short bursts of our guns keep them at a safe distance.

"Don't waste bullets, fellas," drawls Lt. D. P. Johnston, the copilot, over the interphone. He used to be an ornamental-iron designer in Memphis, Tennessee. "This heah looks like it's gonna be a long fight."

Suddenly tracer bullets streak by from in front of our plane. A second Zero is making a one-o'clock pass—coming in from almost dead ahead. Dow and Bellmore in the top and nose turrets blaze away. The Zero rolls off to the right of our plane, exposing its belly as it stands on its right wing in a sharp turn. The tracers from our top and nose turrets seem to go right through the Japs during this maneuver. The plane dives out of range, wriggling queerly. Before we can see whether it ever comes out of that dive, the Zero passes into a fleecy cloud. We score a probable.

"Look out—10 o'clock pass!" yells Lt. Haag over the interphone. A third Zero flicks in with smoking guns from slightly below and in front of us. None of our guns can follow its lightning-quick course. But the Zero never reaches our level, diving away instead. I pull the belly gun triggers. It zips right through the tracers.

The last Zero flips up in a tight Immelman turn and leaves us without attempting a pass. Now everything is silent except for the roar of our four engines. We are at last alone in the sunny, cloud-flecked sky. The running fight has lasted 12 minutes.

Over the interphone comes Lt. Johnston's Memphis drawl: "Anybody hurt?" Nobody is. "I think we took a few bullets in the nose," he says. We light up cigarettes, grin at one another, and trade comments on the fight.

Ah, I think, now back to New Guinea. I was shivering under my fleece-lined jacket before the fight, but now I'm sweating. I get all the action a guy could ask for and am still alive to write in *Yank* about it. But wait a minute, Lt. Haag's voice comes over the interphone. "We'll use up our other bombs on Salamaua," he says. My heart sinks. Migawd, hasn't he had enough for one day? Rolens will get my typewriter yet.

We fly 500 miles down to the Huon Gulf. There is a sunken freighter seaward of Lae's airstrip and Salamaua lies bomb-pocked along the narrow neck of a fat peninsula. We come in for a bombing run as the bomb-bay doors grind open. Black puffs of ack-ack surround us, and some of the stuff hits. It sounds like pebbles being thrown against a tin roof. The plane lurches and reels. Our last yellow bombs angle down toward some buildings near Salamaua's ruined airstrip.

We plunge into big storm clouds and thread our way through the towering Owen Stanley peaks. It is dusk as we set down gently on our home field. In the nine hours we've been away, we've covered more than 1,500 miles. Now the crew admits that this was the first time they've been jumped by the Japs in their 11 bombing missions.

"We had a feelin' we'd get jumped when you came along with us," says Lt. Clyde W. Vickery, ex-banker from Atlanta, Georgia, our navigator. "They say women are bad luck to have on ships. Well, correspondents always seem to bring plenty of action when they go on missions."

T/Sgt. Roy I. Nilsson, former insurance underwriter from Chicago, our radioman, tells us surprising news. "Operations has been sweating us out," he grins. "They thought we were missing after I radioed we were being jumped and then we took so long getting back."

At this point I head for the nearest telephone. I want to tell Rolens that he'll have to wait until I go on another mission before he can have my Remington portable.

Approaching Japanese positions in New Georgia . . .

. . . *and finding them.*

*First GI: Hey, you guys! I got a box of cookies for Christmas
from my girl!*
Second GI: Which girl?
Third GI: Hell with that. Which Christmas?

NOMENCLATURE OF THE PACKAGE, APO

—Cpl. JAMES O'NEILL
July 2, 1943

SOMEWHERE IN the Persian Gulf—Now that the Army Postal Service has restored the soldier's privilege of getting packages from home, we would like to commend the APS for putting in the clause that says the soldier must ask for a package to get it.

This requirement that soldiers must ask for packages is not, as some believe, an effort to limit the number of packages. It springs from the demands of soldiers that they be protected against the parcel post system. Reports might show that the first AEF in Ireland as long as a year ago was actually sabotaging incoming box-laden boats by purposely *not* claiming title to the merchandise at time of delivery.

This practice spread, until thousands of boxes lay purposely unclaimed on wharves all over the combatant world, and the Army Postal Service probably conducted an investigation to discover why. The APS no doubt discovered the reason: No soldier would claim a package because (a) he knew what was in it, (b) he had had enough of what was in it, or (c) even his worst enemy and first sergeant had had enough of what was in it.

From now on we get an even break with the

people who make up packages. We get to tell them what to put in.

Up to this time there have been only four variations of the box-sending theme.

Let us discuss them, now that they are a thing of the past:

Type A—The Goodie Box
Invariably consisted of one of two items—candy or homemade cookies. There were two choices open to the unfortunate recipient of homemade cookies. He could, if still in love and his sweetheart sent them, try to eat the cookies. This lovelorn

type cabled home the next day for a new upper plate and a stomach pump. If the guy wasn't in love or just didn't give a damn, he took the sensible course of donating love's handiwork to the engineers for road markers or dummy land mines.

Type B—Gooey-Yum-Yum Kandy Kit

En route the kit was placed by considerate stevedores between the engine-room boilers and a shipment of Grant tanks. When the soldier received it, he could use the mashed-up goo for pasting French postcards or *Yank* pinups on his barracks wall. Or, if he had a little goat's blood in him, he might start right in eating Gooey-Yum-Yum's wrappings, partitions, string, APO number, and all.

Suppose the sender was the thoughtful type and sent hard candy that stayed hard. Tell me who in hell is going to sacrifice his native-likker-weakened molars on a job a couple of Grant tanks couldn't do? The ingenious AAF is said to be using these dextrose blockbusters over Berlin, the only practical use so far discovered.

Type C—The Knit-One-and-Purl-One Box

The sort of box that caused the recent high female death rate by accidental self-stabbing. It contained The Knitted Glove or The Knitted Pullover Sweater. Already enough has been said on this gruesome subject in newspaper editorials, syndicated columns, joke books, and returned packages marked "Wrong Address."

Type D—The Odds-and-Ends Box

This always fell into one of the following subdivisions:

1. The Sewing Kit. This was the 1,442d one the helpless GI received. Despite all the Boy Scout and Sewing Kit Concession propaganda, the average GI doesn't know how to sew. Even if he did, Whistler's Mother couldn't darn the craters he plows through a sock. Upon receipt of the sewing kit, the soldier carefully took out the needles to pin up that picture of Jane Russell and threw the rest away.

2. The Compact Shaving Kit. This monster was delivered by a detail of 10 and, when opened, resembled a surgeon's operating room, complete with X-ray equipment. It so scared the dogface, he refused to shave with anything for a month.

3. The Cigarette Lighter. It didn't work, but there was plenty of fluid at the PX. It did work, but there was not a drop of fluid at the PX. Or no PX.

4. The Photograph. Usually sent by that much-maligned creature, The Girl Back Home, who, un-

less she was straight out of *Vogue*, included an original little note, "Put this in the mess hall to scare the rats away." It could do the job very well. If the girl was a looker, she had had the picture taken with one of the boys back home, "just to make you feel a teeny-weeny bit jealous." The guy looked like Cary Grant and was either sporting a pair of oak leaves or clutching a $1,000 war-industry check in one hand.

5. *The Canned Tidbit.* Usually tied in a maze of fancy ribbon, this was something the dogface hopefully ripped open with anxious hands, only to discover a can of Spam. (Last week the mess ser-

geant was clubbed to death with empty cans that had contained this ersatz chicken.)

Now that we soldiers overseas are allowed to select the contents of our packages from home, here are four types of gift boxes that we would like to receive:

A—One Lana Turner and one case of Scotch.
B—One Dinah Shore and one case of Scotch.
C—One Rita Hayworth and one case of Scotch.
D—One Scotch and one case of Jane Russells.

⭐

THE SINKING OF THE LISCOME BAY

—Robert L. Schwartz Y2c
Yank Navy Correspondent
June 11, 1944

The story of 23 terrible minutes on a baby flat-top after it was torn to pieces by a torpedo from a Japanese submarine and before it sank with the second-largest Navy casualty list of this war.

THE BABY flat-top *Liscome Bay* was sunk by a torpedo from an enemy submarine on the day before Thanksgiving of 1943. The *Liscome Bay* was on her first battle assignment, covering the occupation of Makin in the Gilberts.

The submarine attack was a complete surprise. It was the *Liscome Bay*'s third day of the invasion, and her crew had lost the tenseness that goes with the beginning of a landing operation. By this time they were relaxed, and only their standard occupational alertness remained. The scuttlebutt reported that the nearest enemy ships were two days away.

The torpedo struck a half hour before dawn, and it was still dark when the *Liscome Bay* sank.

General quarters had sounded at 0505, in keeping with the strict custom of sending men to their battle stations at dawn and dusk in combat zones. Five minutes later, a lookout shouted: "Christ, here comes a torpedo!"

It struck near the stern on the port side, and the havoc was instant and complete. The whole after section broke quickly into flames, and most of the crew stationed there died instantly.

The casualty list for the *Liscome Bay* was the second-largest of any Navy vessel in the war. The complement for baby flat-tops has never been revealed, but they probably carry about half the 2,000 men allotted to big aircraft carriers. Only 260 were saved.

Ironically, many of those men who died in the after end of the *Liscome Bay* might have been saved if they hadn't been called to battle stations before the torpedo struck. They would have been asleep in the crews' quarters forward.

Robert Joseph Charters Y1c had been in the Navy for six years. He had hoped to marry his girl before leaving San Diego, but in the hurried days before sailing, he never found the time.

The weather was hot in the Makin area, and when Charters hit the sack at midnight on the *Liscome Bay*, he simply lay down naked. He arose when GQ sounded at 0505 and put on his dungarees and the comfortable Marine shoes he had bought

Captain Crommelin had just stepped from the shower when the torpedo struck. Still without clothes, he walked out on deck and directed abandoning in his area.

before leaving San Diego. Then he left for the office, where he stood duty watches and general quarters.

It was the small office of Lt. Comm. W. W. Carroll, who served the ship as first lieutenant, a detail involving the berthing of the crew and the care of all loose equipment. During battle Mr. Carroll became damage-control officer, and it was

through this post that all damage-control parties were directed. At these times, Charters served as a talker, wearing the usual headset. The three men stationed in the office during the day—Mr. Carroll; his assistant, a jg, and Charters—were joined during battle alerts by a seaman named Galliano. He manned battle phones connected to the bridge circuit.

The others were already in the office when Charters arrived at 0508, five minutes before the torpedoing. He noted with amusement that Mr. Carroll was reading *The Virginian*. Mr. Carroll was very fond of the book. He always read it at morning general quarters but never during the day. He had almost finished reading the book when it was torn from his hand by the explosion at 0513.

The hit was farther aft and on the opposite side of the ship, but the blast was so great that it tore off Charters' life jacket, dungaree shirt, battle phones, and even his marine shoes. The lights went out. He remained in his stocking feet the rest of his time aboard the *Liscome Bay*.

The first voice was that of the jg. He said to Charters: "Are you all right?" Charters answered yes and then said to Mr. Carroll: "Are you all right?" There was no answer. He asked again. There was a pause, and then the commander said: "I'm all right." Galliano said "I'm okay" without being asked.

Flames from the hangar deck were visible overhead. Mr. Carroll felt for the doorway. "We've got to get up pressure to fight the fires," he said.

They groped outside to the passage but could not get up pressure on the hose. Charters looked at Mr. Carroll and said: "There's an awful gassy smell down here." The officer, struggling desperately with the valves to get up pressure, paid no attention. Finally Charters said: "This is no place for us. We better get out." Mr. Carroll turned away reluctantly from the valves and followed Charters without saying a word.

Three or four more men joined them and they went forward, losing one another once and finally collecting together again far forward at the base of the burning elevator shaft. There they found a warrant bosun named Hunt on his hands and knees, emptying a portable CO_2 extinguisher on the flames. Beside him lay three other extinguishers that he had already emptied.

Mr. Carroll said to Hunt: "Come on. Boats. Get the hell outta here." Without moving, Hunt motioned them to go. The other men glanced at Mr. Carroll to see if he was going to order Hunt out. It was then that they noticed for the first time that Mr. Carroll was covered with blood. He had been hit badly across the face and chest during the first explosion. The doctor was in the group, and he offered to dress Mr. Carroll's wounds, but Mr. Carroll refused.

They all went topside, coming out on the walkaway around the flight deck. Looking back, they could see that the after section of the ship was almost totally destroyed. All around them, 20mm and 40mm shells were exploding.

Mr. Carroll told them to jump. Charters walked to the side and leaped off, completely unafraid of the great height and anxious only to get away from the bursting ammunition. In the water he looked back and saw that everybody had jumped except Mr. Carroll. He was walking up and down the flight deck, ordering others to jump and helping some men over the side.

Back inside the ship, Bosun Hunt finally gave up at the fire extinguishers and came on deck. He met Mr. Carroll again. But this time, instead of Mr. Carroll urging Hunt to go, Hunt urged Mr. Carroll to leave the ship.

"Come on," the bosun said. "Let's go."

"No," Mr. Carroll replied. "You go. I'm going to stay."

"I'm not going without you. I'll get you a life preserver."

"No," Mr. Carroll said. "Go home to your wife and kids."

"If you're not going, I'm not." Hunt said. He walked across the flight deck toward the exploding ammunition, looking for an extra life jacket.

"Come on back," shouted Mr. Carroll. "Don't go back there—I'll jump with you."

The doctor came up and joined them, and together the three of them cleared the side of the ship. Mr. Carroll's condition was getting worse. The doctor held him up while Hunt swam off to retrieve a life raft. When Hunt came back, he asked how Mr. Carroll was, and the doctor looked down at the man in his arms.

"He's dead," he said.

Charters was a survivor of the *Liscome Bay*. He came back to the mainland and married his girl on Christmas Eve. They are living in San Diego now, where he has landed a job as a chief yeoman at the Naval Air Station.

A rear admiral and two captains were on the *Liscome Bay*. The rear admiral was Henry M. Mullinix, and he was in charge of the air group operating from the *Liscome Bay* and two sister carriers in the area. One of the two captains was John G. Crommelin, Jr., who served as chief of staff to the admiral. The other was Irving D. Wiltsie, and he was captain of the *Liscome Bay*.

Rear Adm. Mullinix, a kind, friendly man, was in air plot when the explosion came, and he was badly injured. Several people saw him there with his head on his folded arms, but others reported seeing him later swimming in the flame-swept waters. He did not survive.

Capt. Crommelin, one of five famous brothers who are all Navy officers, had just stepped from the shower when the torpedo hit. Naked and wet, he was badly burned. Still without clothes, he walked out onto the flight deck and directed the abandoning in his area. Later he jumped overboard himself, then swam for an hour and 20 minutes before a destroyer picked him up.

Capt. Wiltsie survived the original explosion. Concerned by the damage aft and the men who were stationed there, he walked toward the stern on the flight deck to inspect the area. Several officers called to him to come back, but he walked into the exploding ammunition and smoke. He was not seen again.

Clovis (C. M.) Roach was a storekeeper first class on the *Liscome Bay*, but, like Yeoman Charters, he has since been promoted to chief. He is a Texan, is slight and wispy in appearance, and has thinning blond hair. He looks like Ernie Pyle must have looked when he was 26.

Some months before, Roach had been a member of the crew of the *USS San Francisco* during her famous battle off Guadalcanal. Standing far below decks, passing ammunition while shells tore into the ship, he learned that battle is a serious business and fear a very real thing.

The *San Francisco* was a heavy cruiser, and he liked the security of her thick-skinned sturdiness. The *Liscome Bay*'s light metal construction scared him. He decided that he would go below decks only when he had to.

So at 2100 the night before the torpedoing, Roach went to sleep on a cot on the fantail, as usual. Reveille next morning awakened him 20 minutes before general quarters and 28 minutes before the torpedo struck.

Roach went down to the galley and bake shop, where he talked with his buddies among the cooks and bakers. He munched a coffee ring, drank a cup of coffee, and shot the breeze about who was on duty the night before. Several of the men were bitching about the lack of action. "I've seen it calm like this before," said Roach. "Something'll happen. It always does when it's calm." Then GQ sounded, and he headed forward to his battle station. He was wearing dungarees, a hat, and regular Navy oxfords and carrying his life preserver under his arm.

Roach's battle station was in the forward issue room, and it was his duty to hand out emergency issues of flight and engine gear during battle. But the forward issue room was two decks down, and because of his aversion to being below decks, he didn't go there. He went instead to sick bay, two decks above the issue room but astride the sole passage leading below. It had become his habit to stay there during GQ unless he spotted someone heading below with a request. Then he would accompany the man below, issue the requested material, and come back up to sick bay. Roach's statement on the subject is very succinct: "As long as it's necessary to stay below, I'll stay there, but if it's not necessary, I won't."

Five men had battle stations in sick bay: the ship's doctor, a chief pharmacist's mate, and three other pharmacist's mates. They were there when Roach arrived, and everyone exchanged morning greetings. With a second-class pharmacist's mate Roach went into the treatment room. He sat on the table, and the mate sat on a chair against a bulkhead. While they were talking about their mission against Makin and speculating on the success of the joint operation against Tarawa farther south, the torpedo struck.

The bulkhead behind the treatment table blew inward, striking Roach on the back and knocking him 10 feet through the door. He got up and yelled: "There may be another one." Then he hit the deck again. Another explosion followed, somewhat less violent than the first, and Roach got to his feet. So did the others, and in a general melee of voices, they all established that they were still alive. Roach groped his way back into the treatment room, searching for his life jacket. He found it in the dust and rubble on the deck, 15 feet from where he had laid it beside him on the treatment table.

Almost involuntarily, the men looked down the passages leading from sick bay. One was on the port side and one was on the starboard, but both were blocked by debris and flames from the hangar deck. As a matter of personal interest, Roach also looked down the hatch leading to the forward issue room. It was utterly impassable. He went back and tried the port and starboard passages again, without success.

The list of the ship, the smoke and flames, and the lack of communication made it obvious to everyone that it was time to get out if a way could be found. Roach spoke up. "I'm going to try working my way forward along the port passageway to the first-division compartment," he said. "Anybody want to come?" Without waiting for an answer, he started forward. He could hear others following him, but he didn't look back to see who or how many there were.

All the bulkheads were blown in. He climbed and crawled around them. He squirmed through a hole so small that he scraped off a shoe. Finally there was only one man left behind him. Together they made it through to the first-division compartment. They found it slightly damaged and empty and knew there must be a way out. To Roach it was the first clear sign that he was likely to be a survivor. Following a trail of fresh air, he climbed two ladders and came out on the high (starboard) side.

He paused and took a few deep breaths. Flames and smoke were curling up the flight deck and he knew he couldn't abandon there. He went down to the port side. By the light of the flames, he

could see heads bobbing in the water. No rafts were visible, but someone behind him said: "There are three rafts and a floater net way out there."

Roach was a lone operator. He left the others on the deck and walked forward to the anchor chain. Tightening his life jacket around his chest, he crawled over the gunwale and lowered himself slowly down the chain. He had descended about 10 feet when another man, with the same intentions but more speed, climbed down onto his shoulders. Looking up, Roach saw that the man had on a life jacket, grabbed him by the feet, and threw him into the water.

Then Roach proceeded down the chain to the anchor and dropped six feet into the water. He took off his remaining shoe and started to swim, but his life jacket held him back as flames whipped around the bow. Only a change in the wind saved him from burns. He swam out to the floater net and climbed on with about 40 others. Someone shouted: "There she goes." He looked back to see the flames perish as the ship slid beneath the waves. He felt no regret at her passing.

There was one man on the *Liscome Bay* who abandoned ship twice. Gunner's Mate Hubert Bassett crawled down a Jacob's ladder forward on the port side, near where Storekeeper Roach went in via the anchor chain. The wind was unkind to Bassett, and he soon found himself ringed by flame. He swam back to the Jacob's ladder and reboarded the ship. The oil gradually burned off the surface, and Bassett climbed down again and swam away.

When Robert H. Carley was a junior at Occidental College in Los Angeles, he found YMCA work so interesting that he decided to enter the ministry. He stayed one more year at Occidental, made the All-Southern Cal basketball team, and then went to Princeton Theological Seminary. After graduating from there, he went directly into the Navy. Young, blond, and handsome, he looked like a recruiting-poster officer.

Lt. (jg) Carley was the *Liscome Bay*'s chaplain. He was in the head when the explosion came. By the time he raised himself from among the broken

*Looking up, Roach saw that
the man had on a life jacket,
grabbed him by the feet,
and threw him in the water.
Then he proceeded down.*

sinks, toilets, and urinals, he decided that his first
job was to find his life jacket and kit of personal
belongings. The search was hopeless, and he had
to leave the gear under the porcelain dust and
broken pipes.

As he stepped outside into the passageway,
someone brushed past him. It was one of the two
patients who were confined to sick bay recovering
from appendectomies. The one who passed him
was a pilot who had been operated on five days
before. Although not a good swimmer, he rushed
up to the flight deck, jumped over the side, and
swam several hundred yards to a raft. He was a
survivor. The other patient had been brought over
from a destroyer two days before to have his operation. He survived the original explosion and
was able to walk out of sick bay, but he was not
seen again. He was not a survivor.

The next person on the scene was Dr. Rowe.
"We've got to get the patients out of sick bay," he
said, but the chaplain told him they were gone.
Mr. Carroll, still searching for a way to put out
the fires, came up with several others. There was
a little talk. In the back of everyone's mind was
the thought of the 180,000 gallons of high-octane,
gasoline stored directly beneath them. Smoke and
a strong smell of gasoline filled the area. Some of
the men started to get sick and groped their way
forward and topside.

As Chaplain Carley went through the aero-
grapher's office, he stumbled. Something in his
mind said "life jacket," and he stooped down, identified it, and put it on. Then he went out onto the
high side walkaway.

Looking forward, he saw that three officers—
Dr. Rowe, Mr. Carroll, and the nude Capt.
Crommelin—had the situation under control, so

he headed aft. All around the chaplain, 20mm and 40mm shells were exploding, but he was so glad to be out from below that they didn't faze him.

He came upon three men huddled around a machine gun and went up to them. They were dead. Farther aft he found three other men dazedly standing by another gun, and he told them to abandon. They went down a rope, and he followed them into the water.

Later, as he was being hauled onto a destroyer, he heard someone addressing him.

"Well, Padre," said the voice, "I see religion paid off."

Most of the men in the stewards' branch of the Navy are Negroes. They wait on the tables, serve as orderlies, and work in the officers' galleys.

There was an unusual messman on the *Liscome Bay*. The son of an impoverished farmer near Waco, Texas, he had joined the Navy to help his family earn a living.

It was on the ill-fated *Arizona* that he became famous. During the Pearl Harbor attack, he rushed to the bridge and manned a machine gun, firing it through the explosions and devastation around him.

For this action Dorie Miller won the Navy Cross.

In the Negro world, Dorie Miller became an idol. There were fan clubs organized for him and songs written about him. His mother was brought up from Waco for a big rally in Harlem. She spoke to the people there.

"I just got a letter from Dorie," she said. "He don't write much. But he said he thought he'd be home around 1945. . . ."

Dorie Miller was in the after section of the *Liscome Bay* and was not a survivor.

"He sort of corresponds to our chaplains."
—SGT. CHARLES PEARSON

"Supplies, supplies, always supplies. Don't you ever bring in any women?"—CPL. ERNEST MAXWELL

Faithless Wife

Dear *Yank:*

I am enclosing the exact wording of a letter sent me by wife and will be ever grateful for any possible solution, for I have tried everything I know, even prayer. Still TS. Question: Can wife get allotment without consent of me when I have this letter of bad faith? Here are her words:

Dear Ahmed—The time has come to clear things between us. You will have realized, before now, that our marriage was a mistake. I beg of you to put an end to this mistake and get a divorce. I left your house this morning, because I didn't want to saddle you with the role of a betrayed husband. As a matter of fact, I have never been yours, but now I belong to someone else, and this finishes things between us.

I have grown distrustful of what is generally known as "love," for the feelings that have alienated me from you are drawn elsewhere, and I've got to obey the secret promptings of my nerves. I want to thank you and wish you well. I am going away. It makes me unhappy to hurt you, but you are so strong. I am still your friend, and perhaps the time will come when you can be my friend, too. I am taking everything except your clothes and the typewriter, and am having my friend type this for me, for you know I write poorly.—Elaine.

—Pfc. Ahmed S.
Iran

Yours is simply a classic version of a common problem. All the proof in the world that a soldier's wife is faithless does not change the fact that a family allowance is given to her regularly as long as she remains legally married to the soldier. If you are interested in initiating divorce proceedings you should consult your Legal Assistance Officer, who can give you information about the divorce laws in your state.

"Don't be silly, darling; they'll adore you!"
—Pfc. Joe Kramer

Craps and Conscience

Dear *Yank:*

I come from the backwoods of North Dakota. I had never seen a crap game until I entered the service. When I saw my first game back in the States I joined in, just for the fun of it. It came my turn to shoot the dice. I shot $5 and made an "11." One of the boys told me this was an easy point to make, so I rolled again. The boys all offered to bet me I wouldn't make "11" again. The sergeant bet me $10 I couldn't make "11" on the next roll. I accepted all bets on this "11" and made it—breaking all my buddies, including the sergeant. After reading the gambling articles in *Yank*, I now realize that "11" was no point to roll for and that I should have won my $5 on the first roll. I also realize that making an "11" on one roll is a 17-1 bet. So here is my problem. Shall I return the money to my buddies, who I now see were trying to take advantage of me, or shall I keep it? Oh yes, I forgot to mention that I can throw an "11" any time I desire. I learned to do it while playing parchesi back home in Ellenville, N. Dak.

—Pvt. J. H. R.
Iran

Why write to "What's Your Problem?" Any guy who shoots an "11" anytime he wants to can't possibly have any problems.

"And what else did they teach you in the engineers back at Fort Belvoir?"—SGT. DOUGLAS BORGSTEDT

"I think the M1 will do for that shot."
—SGT. ROGER COWAN

Mexican Muddle

Dear *Yank:*

I'll start from the very beginning. I'm 27 years old and I entered the Army in '41. While I was at Fort Sam Houston, Tex., I became infatuated with a girl and went to Mexico and was told by a priest (or monk) there that we were married by him. I lived with her only one night. There were no papers of the marriage, and I did not sign any such papers in Mexico. I paid her no allotment till June 1942 when, unknown to me, she applied for allotment. OK. In June 1943 I again went to Mexico and got a divorce (so I was told), but not one paper was signed by me or anyone else, for it was granted by this monk (or priest, or whatever he was) in Mexico.

I went to my first sergeant in my last camp to find out about getting the allotment to stop but failed. You see, this 70- or 80-year-old monk (or whatever he was) told me I'd have to pay her alimony. But me going to all the trouble I did, and with no one who could (or would) tell me anything, I went ahead and got married to another girl. Now I can't get an allotment for my second wife because of this other mess. I was told the first girl was married again and living in Mexico—where I do not know. I don't even know what happened to her, but they have been taking pay out of my $50 every month. Now, if my divorce was not legal how can the marriage be legal? Also where and how and when did she get papers asking for the allotment? Please can you help me as I'm in enough trouble as it is and do not want to lose the one girl I will really ever love. Several people here are calling me a bigamist, and I don't think I am.

—Pvt. J. C. H.
Panama

Wow! Well, here goes. In the first place, as far as the allowance is concerned, that first girl was pretty smart, because she obviously submitted a marriage certificate of some kind to prove that she was your wife; otherwise the Office of Dependency Benefits would not have approved her application for a family allowance. In the second place, many foreign divorces are looked upon with deep suspicion by the ODB, and where there is not even documentary proof of the divorce (as in your case) the ODB would probably have to continue payments to the girl in Mexico. The ODB suggests you send full details of your case to its

"Something smells terribly good. I wonder what it could be."—Pvt. THOMAS FLANNERY

office at 213 Washington Street, Newark, New Jersey. Don't forget to include your ASN. As for the legal, social and moral aspects of your problem, see your Legal Assistance Officer. See your CO. See your personal affairs officer. See your chaplain. Quick.

All they remembered afterward were things like the candy bars just before takeoff and trying to light a Camel when they got back.

THE BIRTH OF A MISSION

—Sgt. WALTER PETERS
January 7, 1944

A HEAVY BOMBER Station, Britain—Two second lieutenants, recent arrivals from the States, walked to the Officers' Club bar and ordered whiskies.

"Make it a double," said one of them.

"Sorry, sir, no whisky is sold during alerts," said the bartender, Cpl. James Mohafdahl of Dayton, Ohio.

"Oh, I see," the other lieutenant mused. "When'd the alert come through?"

"About fifteen minutes ago, sir. Right, Dan?" The corporal turned to the other bartender, Pvt. Daniel Costanzo, an ex-cowboy and saloon owner from San Antonio, Texas.

"Yeah, about that long," Costanzo agreed.

The lieutenants smiled. "Well, we may as well get some sleep then," one said. They walked out.

"It's funny," the corporal said, "but I can practically always tell when there's going to be an alert and, better yet, whether the raid'll go through. It's just instinct. That's all. Just instinct. Ask Tiny. He'll tell you."

Tiny was a 6-foot, 260-pound former foundry worker, Pvt. Frederick Tard of Everett, Washington. He was also assigned to the club staff, but that night he was on pass.

"They're a swell lot of boys here," the corporal said. "There's no rank pulling. I've seen lots of them come in fresh from the States, and I've seen lots of them go on their first mission and never come back. There used to be one fellow, a lieutenant. He always used to come in and order a drink and never talk to anybody but me. He'd rather talk to me than to a lot of majors around. He went down on a raid. He always said: 'Corporal, you take care of me. And believe me, I always did."

Another lieutenant walked in and asked for a whisky. Costanzo explained again that no hard liquor was sold during alerts. Beer was okay, though. The lieutenant bought a beer.

The corporal took up where he'd left off. "I don't know whether the lieutenant is a prisoner of war or not. But I'd sure like to meet him again. He was a nice guy. One thing, all these fellows know where to come when they want something. They see me, Jimmy. If it can be gotten, I get it."

A sign on the wall behind the bar read: MEMBERS OF THE WORLD'S BEST AIR FORCE ARE SERVED AT THIS BAR.

Costanzo looked our way, paused for a moment, and said: "We don't sell whisky the night before a raid."

Officers and the Field Order

Beyond a one-lane winding road from the Officers' Club, deep inside a single-story building, was the intelligence room. Large maps of the fighting fronts adorned the walls, and colored markings indicated important enemy targets and other information about them.

Except for the maps, the intelligence room might have passed for a board of directors' office. In the center was a long, well-polished table surrounded by eight comfortable leather chairs. In the corner was a radio playing soft, slow music transmitted by a British Broadcasting Corporation station. An S-2 first lieutenant relaxed in one of the chairs, his legs slung over its arm. A staff sergeant walked in and out of the room incessantly, always looking very serious, always carrying what appeared to be important documents.

The sergeant walked out of the room, then returned. "The FO is in, sir," he said.

"Okay," replied the lieutenant, "call the colonel."

Three other members of the S-2 staff walked in—Maj. F. J. Donohue, chief of the group's intelligence section, a former Washington (D.C.) lawyer; Capt. Wayne Fitzgerald of Kalamazoo, Michigan, the group bombardier; and Capt. Ellis B. Scripture of Greensburg, Indiana, the group navigator.

The three men sat down and watched as the sergeant tracked a narrow red tape from the spot on the map that represented the base in Britain to the enemy target that was to be bombed the next morning. The tape followed the exact course as directed by the field order.

Presently a tall middle-aged man walked in. He was a good-looking guy with a friendly smile. This was Col. John Gerhardt of Chicago, commander of the group. With him was Lt. Col. David T. McKnight of New York, the air executive officer of the group. McKnight was short and had a personality that makes friends quickly.

Each colonel was eating a bar of candy, and they offered a bite to everyone in the room. Col. Gerhardt stood before the map and studied it. Then

he asked for a copy of the field order. A cat strolled by lazily. Lt. Col. McKnight stroked her back until she lifted her tail and purred. When the field order was brought in, the officers began to study it.

Superstition and Fate

The base theater, which also houses the chaplain's office and serves as a church on Sundays, was filled to capacity that night, as it usually is. The sergeant gunners and officers apparently liked the film, because they laughed a lot and occasionally somebody whistled. The picture was *Duke of West Point*, featuring Louis Hayward and Joan Fontaine.

Inside the Aero Club, run by the Red Cross, enlisted men were reading hometown newspapers, playing billiards, or standing in line by a long counter for an evening snack. A round-faced sergeant with a neat black mustache, Vincent Barbella of Brooklyn, New York, was drinking a Coca-Cola and doing a lot of talking. With him was T/Sgt. Harry D. Cooper, a radio gunner from Dayton, Ohio, and T/Sgt. Robert E. Bellora, a top-turret gunner from Ellwood City, Pennsylvania.

"Tomorrow's my 12-B," Barbella said, then laughed. "To hell with it. I won't call it 12-B. I'm not superstitious. I'll call it straight number 13. I certainly hope we go tomorrow, though," Barbella said. "That will make it about the sixth time I've been trying to make my 13th."

Cooper smiled. "You'll make it tomorrow. I'll bet anything on that. The night is clear and the odds are that it'll stay that way until morning."

"It's not the raids that bother me," Barbella said. "It's these damned abortions. People don't realize how much there is to making a raid. They figure all you do is jump in a Fort and up you go. They don't figure that weather out here can change within a half hour, or that after a guy is up there for a couple of hours, something can go shebang with an engine or the oxygen system, and then you have to turn back."

At an adjoining table, a sergeant was reading a newspaper. Barbella turned and read the headlines. "Berlin," he said. "Boy, is the RAF giving them the works now. Boy, would I like to go there. It'd be nice to say I'd been over Berlin."

Bellora spoke up. "For all you know, you may get the chance. You never can tell. That's where they may send us tomorrow, but I doubt it. Tomorrow will make me 21 missions. Hell, it doesn't matter where you go. If it's going to get you, it'll get you over Bremen or over Emden or over Kiel or anywhere. It's all up to fate, I think. But I'm not taking any chances. I think my two .50s have a helluva lot to do with this fate racket."

Enlisted men from the theater filed into the Aero Club when the movie was over. A short, frail sergeant stopped and whispered something in Barbella's ear. Apparently it was some sort of a private joke. Barbella laughed so enthusiastically that he had to stand up.

"What the hell's eating you, man?" Cooper asked in a friendly tone.

"Oh, nothing. Nothing," Barbella replied. "But I'm going to eat somebody's stuff out if we don't go out tomorrow." He laughed again.

Disappointment and Hunger

Tall, bespectacled First Lt. David B. Henderson, in charge of the base photographic section, walked into the laboratory looking very sad.

"He wouldn't let me go. Said maybe it'd be okay next mission," Henderson said. He had just returned from the S-2 room, where he'd asked Maj. Donohue if he could go on the next morning's mission. In civilian life, Henderson worked for the Ashland Refining Company in Ashland, Kentucky. His job on the base was an important one, but you got the impression that he'd be happier as a sergeant gunner.

There was an aroma of fried onions in the laboratory. It came from a room where a couple of staff sergeants were packing film into the combat cameras.

Sgt. David B. Wells of Trona, California, walked into the room with a loaf of bread.

"No, sir. It's nothing like this back in the States. If we're hungry, we just scrounge some grub and prepare it right in here. Wish I had a nice piece of steak to go with those onions. A guy gets hungry at this time of night. I always get hungry before missions."

"You ain't kidding, bub," said T/Sgt. Berton Briley of Wilson, Oklahoma. Briley was a musician in civilian life. Now he is a combat photographer.

Lt. Henderson walked into the room and poured some coffee into a large tin cup. "There's nothing like a good hot cup of coffee at night. Too bad I can't go out in the morning."

Combat and Comradeship

There was no electric power that night in one of the squadron areas, so a group of lieutenants sat around inside their flat-roofed quarters and chatted by candlelight.

Four of them—Lt. Robert Sheets of Tacoma, Washington; Lt. Jack Watson of Indianapolis, Indiana; Lt. Elmer W. Yong of Roachdale, Indiana; and Lt. Joseph C. Wheeler of Fresno, California—had joined the squadron only that week. They had been in the Fortress that buzzed the Yankee Stadium in New York during a World Series game in September. Mayor La Guardia raised an awful stink when that happened. The boys were hauled over the coals for it by their CO when they reported to their field in Maine.

"All of that looks funny now that we're going into actual combat," said one. "It's the first mission that counts. Once I get over the hump on that one, I'll gain my bearings. I'm just itching to get that first one in."

A first lieutenant called Hapner, who kept talking about his hometown, Hamilton, Ohio, stopped cleaning a carbine.

"I know just how you feel," Hapner said. "You change a lot after about the first five missions. I don't know how to put my finger on it, but you sort of become more human. You become more appreciative of the men you fight with and the men you live with. It's particularly bad when you lose some of the men on your crew, or if one guy finishes his ops ahead of you and then leaves the crew.

"My pilot just finished his ops and he's off combat now. He was a swell guy. He always said that as long as I was doing the navigating and he was holding the stick, we had nothing to worry about. That guy should have gotten the Congressional Medal if anyone ever should.

"Kit Carson went through more hell than anyone I know of, but he never complained. He was a very religious guy and talked about his mother an awful lot. He never talked about himself, though. Except for the way he talked, you'd never get it from him that he was from Texas.

"Kit lost his original crew. They went off without him once and never returned. He was really shook up by it. But would he complain?" Hapner turned as if expecting somebody to say something, then answered his own question. "No, Kit never complained."

"They assigned him as copilot on the *Brass Rail*. That's how we got on the same crew. The pilot at that time was Lt. John Johnson. Johnson was married and had a helluva pretty wife in East St. Louis, Illinois. On a raid over Kiel, a 20mm exploded against Johnson's side and killed him. The *Brass Rail* nose-dived about 4,000 feet and everybody in it thought sure they were goners. Ammo boxes and everything else were flying all over the plane. By some miracle, Kit was able to level the ship off. Except for Kit, the whole crew would have been goners. He got the DFC for that. I really miss that guy."

The new lieutenants listened carefully. They had met Kit just before he left the squadron, but up to now they hadn't realized what he'd been through. One of the lieutenants said: "He certainly didn't toot his own horn, did he?"

"Well, neither will you after a while," Hapner said. "Combat does something to a man. You'll see."

Hapner began to undress. "Well, guess I'll turn in. It may be a long one tomorrow."

Armament and the Men

It was 2230, and the weather was still holding up. A long single file of men, almost all of them with torches in their hands, walked out of a Nissen hut.

They were the armament men. They talked, but in low tones. Most of the officers and gunners had turned in, and armament men respect sleeping men of the combat crews.

An armament man said: "Maybe we won't have to unload again for a change. It looks too good out tonight, even for English weather."

Two sergeants stopped playing blackjack for a minute and talked about the armament men. Almost everybody else in the hut was in his bunk. The two sergeants were sitting on the lower section of a double bunk. A spotlight hung from the spring of the upper bunk, throwing just enough light on the cards.

"I suppose we ought to turn in," said one. "It may be a tough one tomorrow. When it comes right down to it, these armament guys really have the toughest racket. It must be hell on them to load up and then have to go out and unload when a mission is scrubbed. I hope it isn't scrubbed tomorrow."

From the corner of the room came a loud protesting voice. It was a Southern voice. "Damn that fire. Who the hell wants a fire on at night? It only goes out before you get up, and then we're cold as hell."

"Aw, shut up, you rebel," another voice answered.

The Southern boy complained again. "Well, I don't want to be going on any missions with a cold. Somebody ought to throw water on the fire."

The sergeants who were playing cards stopped the game. One of them spoke up. "You're liable to blow the place up if you throw water into that stove now, boy."

"I don't give a damn," said the Southerner.

Dogs and the AAF

It was 0400 and all the combat men were sound asleep. An excited voice bellowed out of the PA system: "*Attention all combat crews! Attention all combat crews! Breakfast until 0445. Breakfast until 0445. Briefing at 0500. Briefing at 0500.*"

In the kitchen of the combat mess, two cooks were standing by a stove with pans in their hands.

They were frying eggs for the men scheduled to fly that morning.

"I don't know why it is," the short cook said, "but about every dog in England seems to have found a home on this base."

"You'll find the same thing on all the bases," the other cook said. "Even the RAF has its share of dogs. Some of them have seen more combat than a lot of guys."

"You know, I was thinking," said the short one, "almost every new crew brings in a dog from the States. Now, if some smart apple of a German spy wanted to figure the Air Force strength in Britain, all he'd have to do is figure how many dogs there are on the bases and then multiply it by 10."

The other cook gave the short one a disgusted look.

"You're as crazy a guy as I've ever met. Who the hell's going to chase all over Britain counting

Superfortress gunner

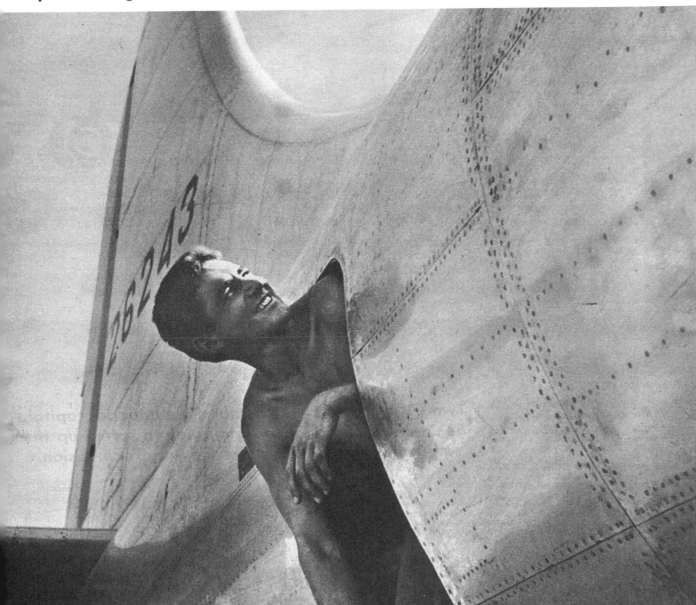

dogs? Besides, you've got to figure how many of these dogs get in the family way as soon as they land here. Trouble with you is, you read too many detective stories."

The short cook grinned. "Aw, I was only thinking," he said and went on frying eggs.

Number 25 and Herky Jerky

Briefing was over. A half-ton truck was rolling along the runway. It was about 0600, but still very dark. The truck turned into a narrow road and stopped at a small shed. Then about six men jumped out and went inside.

About 25 sergeants were cleaning caliber .50s on long benches. Above them were signs reading:

WITHOUT ARMAMENT THERE IS NO NEED
FOR AN AIR FORCE
LORD TRENCHARD, MARSHAL OF THE RAF

Sgt. Barbella was cleaning his guns alongside the top-turret gunner on his crew, Dean Hall, a tall, slim boy from New Jersey. Hall and three others from the crew of the *Herky Jerky* were making their 25th mission that morning.

The sergeants carefully enclosed their guns in burlap bags and headed for the hardstand.

A Baby and a Mission

It was five minutes before stations. Capt. Rodney E. Snow, Jr., of High Point, North Carolina, walked over by the tail of the plane and stood there for a moment. It was a ritual with him, just as it is with a lot of other men who are flying in this war.

Snow's bombardier, Lt. George Lindley of Seattle, Washington, was smoking a cigarette and telling the left waist gunner about his baby son. The baby was born on Oct. 16, and Lindley was sweating out a picture that was supposed to be on the way over. The mission didn't seem to bother him, but the absence of the baby's picture did.

"I think I'll stay in tonight and write letters."
—SGT. ARNOLD THURM

In the ground crew's tent, a little off the hardstand, two other men from the *Herky Jerky* were debating whether they'd even get off the ground that morning.

"Number seven was always my lucky number, and I think this is the seventh time we're trying for this mission. So I guess we'll make it," said the copilot. He was a big, strapping fellow, Lt. John Merriman of Spokane, Washington. Everybody on the crew razzed him about his large belly and somebody kidded him about being pregnant.

"No, that's what I got for being a chow hound, I guess," Merriman answered, taking it seriously.

Snow called on all the men to get into the plane. Then number one engine was started. Number two followed, and three and four began to roar next. The plane taxied up to the edge of the runway, and in a few minutes it was airborne. And that was the beginning of the mission.

Following the Battle of Bougainville, Admiral Nimitz's next objective in the Pacific plan was Kwajalein, up in the Marshalls, which ultimately would provide a key air base pointing directly toward Japan. But in order to get there, the Gilberts had to be taken first.

Tarawa was actually an atoll—a tiny lagoon rimmed by 38 even tinier islands, the southwesternmost of these going by the name of Betio. Less than half the size of Central Park, Betio was where the Marine Corps eventually located the Japanese airstrip—and a few other things as well.

DEATH BATTLE AT TARAWA

—Sgt. JOHN BUSHEMI
Yank Staff Correspondent
December 24, 1943

BETIO, TARAWA, Gilbert Islands—Even the dead Marines were determined to reach Tarawa's shore.

As one Higgins landing boat roared toward the dry sand, you could see a hand clutching its side. It was the hand of a Marine, frozen in the grip of death.

The Second Marine Division took this island because its men were willing to die. They kept on coming in the face of a heavy Jap defense, and though they paid the stiffest price in human life per square yard that was ever paid in the history of the Marine Corps, they won this main Jap base in the Gilbert Islands in 76 hours.

Out of two battalions—2,000 to 3,000 men—thrown onto the beach in the first assault at 0830, only a few hundred men escaped death or injury. Officer casualties were heavy. And still the Ma-

rines kept coming. The Leathernecks died with one thought—to get there.

Before dawn of the first day of the invasion, the Navy opened up with a tremendous bombardment. Carrier planes dropped 800 tons of bombs while battleships, cruisers, and destroyers hurled 2,000 tons of shells on an area two and a quarter miles long and at no point more than 800 yards wide. This was Betio, the fortified airstrip that is the main island of 26 comprising the Tarawa atoll.

The Marines were to hit the sandy beach immediately after these softening-up operations ceased, and everybody on the boats was happy because it seemed like very effective fire, the kind of intense blasting that would make the Japs "bomb happy." But that wasn't the way it worked out.

The Japs were too well dug in. Their blockhouses were of concrete five feet thick, with palm tree trunks 18 inches in diameter superimposed on the concrete. And superimposed on the trees were angle irons made of railroad steel. On top of these were 10 to 12 feet of sand and coral rock. Only a direct hit by a 2,000-pound bomb would cave in or destroy such blockhouses.

The Jap pillboxes were built out of sand-filled oil drums, buttressed by heavy coconut logs and then sandbags. Air-raid shelters were constructed from coconut tree trunks, piled high in two walls, with coral sand filling the space in between. Our heavy machine guns and 75s couldn't penetrate these emplacements or knock out the enemy eight-inch shore batteries and machine guns that were awaiting our assault waves.

Daylight had been chosen for the assault because it permitted naval gunfire and aviation as support, and because a night attack might have caused the boats to miss the beaches. But there was another important reason:

It was flood tide. At low tide, the coral shelf that forms Betio and the rest of Tarawa atoll is practically dry; at high tide there is four and a half feet of water at the shore line, and it gets deeper farther out. The assault was timed to take advantage of the flood tide.

Then the unexpected happened. A sudden shift of wind swept the water back from the beaches. Many of the Higgins boats piled up on a treacherous table reef of coral, barely submerged in the water. The Marines were forced to debark and wade in the rest of the way—some 500 to 800 yards—in the face of murderous Japanese fire with no protection.

Those few hundred yards seemed like a million miles. Even before the boats went aground on the reef, the Japs opened up with rifles, machine guns, heavy mortars, 75mm and 90mm guns. But the Marines kept coming on, across the corpses of other Marines whose lifeless heads were bobbing in the water.

The assault was made against three designated beaches by three battalion landing teams. One of the teams was so powerfully opposed that only two companies could land. Many casualties were the result of a Jap trick. Snipers, hidden in the hulk of a wrecked Jap sailing vessel on the reef, let the Marines move in beyond the hulk and then shot them down from behind.

Just after noon, a reinforcing wave of Higgins boats was sent in. Five-inch automatic Jap weapons on the flank blew two of the boats out of the water. Several companies were shifted against the Jap flanking position to protect the passage of new reinforcements.

Then the Hellcat fighters, TBFs, and dive-bombers worked over the area for about an hour, from 1430 to 1530, flying sometimes only 60 feet off the water. No point on Betio was much more than 10 feet above sea level except where the Japs had built up their emplacements.

After the planes, two U.S. minesweepers went in and tried to trade punches with the shore batteries. Then two destroyers pushed into the lagoon and fired at close range, 700 to 900 yards. Then more planes. We had absolute aerial supremacy; the greatest number of Jap planes seen at Betio at any one time was six.

Meanwhile, the blood-and-guts landing operation was continuing. Ten or 15 feet from the high-tide mark on Betio's narrow beaches, the Japs had constructed walls of coconut logs as a barrier to tanks. Marines rushed the beaches and scaled the chin-high walls in the face of Jap machine guns.

Behind the barricade, the island was ringed with about 500 pillboxes, so arranged that when you fought your way past one of the pillboxes, you were moving into the cross-fire of two inner pill-boxes.

In the shallows, on the beaches and before the Jap emplacements, Marines died by squads. In less than 100 yards on the beach and within 20 yards of machine-gun emplacements, 105 Marines were killed. But others kept advancing, until at last they took the emplacements and wiped out the Jap gunners.

By the end of the first day, the three battalion landing teams and reinforcements had secured lit-

Front line, Pacific

tle more than a toehold—three small beachheads from 70 to 150 yards in depth. The men dug in and held on there through the night. They established all-around security with orders to shoot anything that moved. There were local efforts at counterattacking. During the night, some artillery was brought ashore.

The second day, the Marines began widening their beachheads and improving their positions. The center battalion pushed ahead until it was stymied by pillboxes and blockhouses. This same day, reinforcements, including some light and medium tanks, were landed on the comparatively lightly defended west end of the island, and they pushed east down the airstrip, which forms a diagonal line across the island, to the point where the advanced Marines were being held up by the pillboxes. The Hellcats were called in again to strafe the area while the battleships and cruisers pounded from offshore. Then Marine infantry and tanks advanced.

After the second day, the battalion was able to penetrate to the opposite shore of Betio, bypassing or destroying the stubborn pillboxes and blockhouses, and by this time, the critical period was past. But the fighting was not "officially" over until 76 hours had passed from the time of the assault, and even then there was still a handful of Jap snipers in trees and dugouts that had to be picked off.

In all, an enemy force of about 4,500 defenders was wiped out, including about 3,500 Imperial Marines and 1,000 laborers. Fewer than 200 of the defenders surrendered, most of them laborers. Tarawa was taken by less than a division of U.S. Marines. We suffered the loss of 1,026 men killed and 2,557 wounded.

Within four days, the Tarawa airfield had been put into working condition by Seabees, who followed the first waves of Marines while fighting still was in progress. American planes are now operating from Tarawa as an advanced base.

A sergeant from the 165th Infantry—New York's "Fighting 69th" of First World War fame—tells about the Gilbert invasion.

"MAKIN TAKEN"

—Sgt. Merle Miller
Yank Staff Correspondent
December 24, 1943

A CENTRAL PACIFIC Base—As his landing boat edged toward the white sand and coral beach of Makin Island in the Gilberts, Sgt. Walter Schliessman fingered the right breast pocket of his two-piece herringbone fatigues. Inside the pocket were two pictures, one of his baby daughter, Mary, whom he's never seen, the other of his wife, whom he last saw in October 1941 on a 15-day furlough at his West Bayside home on Long Island, New York.

Up ahead of the landing boat, Navy planes flew low over the island, strafing Jap machine-gun positions and pillboxes. The sky was bright with the fires of burning Jap warehouses, shacks, and barracks. An oil dump exploded. There were occasional brief bursts of ack-ack. Jap machine-gun slugs sizzled overhead, piercing the top of the barge.

But as Schliessman remembers it now, the whole thing didn't seem much different from amphibious operations in training—except for the Japs. "I'd been getting ready for a fight for three years and a month," he said later, "and there it was, and I wasn't excited. I was scared, of course. I'm no hero—and no liar, either."

Ever since Oct. 15, 1940, Schliessman and most of the rest of the 165th Infantry of the 27th Division had been training for the battle of Makin—

15 months at Fort McClelland, Alabama, and in the Pacific since April 1942. They'd trained so long that they'd come to think they weren't going to do any fighting. "We walked for almost three years," Schliessman said. "I mean, that's about all we seemed to do—train like hell and walk. I figure if we'd kept going straight, we'd have circled the globe twice at the equator. We're probably the walkingest outfit in the Army."

The 165th Infantry is the old "Fighting 69th" of First World War fame, under a new name, and until just before they left for the Gilbert Islands, the men were calling their outfit "the Non-Fighting 69th." Almost all of the original members were National Guardsmen from Manhattan and Brooklyn and Long Island, New York. A lot of them were Irish. And all of them knew the legends of Father Francis Duffy, the 69th's chaplain in the last war, who got the DSC and the DSM; of Col. William J. (Wild Bill) Donovan, who won the Congressional Medal; of Joyce Kilmer, the soldier-poet of the 69th, who died in the battle of the Marne. They all knew the 69th hadn't missed fighting in a war since the Revolution, and they were disappointed because it looked as if this one would be an exception.

"I'd never have been able to go back to Long Island if I hadn't got at least one Jap," Schliessman says. He got seven confirmed and several probables in the Makin action.

Jap machine guns opened up when the boats were still 500 yards offshore. About 325 yards farther in, Schliessman's boat ran aground on a ridge of coral. The ramp was lowered and the men started toward the beach. The water was up to their chests, and at least two of the men of Schliessman's boat lost their rifles. A couple were hit, gasped once or twice, and died.

Schliessman carried his Garand with bayonet fixed, K rations for two days, a pouch of high-explosive and fragmentation grenades, a cartridge belt, a first-aid kit, a trench knife, and an extra bandolier. He didn't run, the way they do in the movies. A slow walk was the best anyone could manage.

In his hip pocket the sergeant had a map of the entire island, one he had drawn himself, showing the sandy beaches, occasional clusters of coconut palms, the chief Jap installations, and the particular objective his own and two other platoons were heading for. This was a Jap tank trap, spotted and remembered by Carlson's Raiders in August 1942. Lt. Col. Jimmy Roosevelt, USMC, who was second in command on that Makin raid, was along this time as an observer and "playing coach" with the 27th Division.

"Since our fourth day on the transport," Schliessman said, "we'd gone over every detail of the assault in a series of daily meetings in the officers' ward room. Not just the officers and noncoms—everybody. Every private knew as much about the overall picture as his company commander. That's the way it was and that's the way it should be."

When Schliessman's squad reached the sandy strip of the beach at Makin Island, everybody sought cover—Pvt. Leslie Westberry of Odum, Georgia, the first scout; Pvt. Damon Heath of Magnolia, Kentucky, rifleman; Pvt. Clarence Winkler of Hazel Crest, Illinois, assistant BAR man; Cpl. Guido Persiani of Chicago Heights, Illinois, assistant squad leader; Pvt. William Page of Holden, Missouri, second scout; Pvt. William

Henry of Michigan and Pvt. Donald Wright of Eureka, California, riflemen; and Pvt. Otis O'Neal of Bethany, Missouri, assistant BAR man. Schliessman ducked behind what must have been a Jap storehouse. There were sacks of cement outside its frame, or what was left of it. Now it was only a smoldering ruin.

It took maybe 30 seconds to get themselves organized. Then they started the slow trek across Makin. Their plan was to bisect the coral island, then make a sharp turn to the right, advance about 300 yards, and take the tank trap.

If Schliessman had learned anything at all during his three years of training—during the weeks spent on the assault course, on the combat firing course, on the combat-in-cities course and on the jungle-training course—it was to keep his men spread apart and to hit the ground low and hit it fast when machine guns started firing.

Each man in the squad was about 10 paces from any other man. They walked slowly, once in a while crawling on their bellies, occasionally stooping a little, usually standing erect. The machine-gun fire had stopped as soon as they hit the beach, and what few Japs they saw were withdrawing fast. None was close enough to be killed.

It took perhaps a half hour to cross the island. It was a quiet, almost unopposed crossing. Then they made their right turn and almost immediately ran into a Jap. As they approached a small wooden shack, the Jap, smartly dressed in an OD shirt and expensive-looking trousers, ran outside screaming. He seemed to be hysterical, and though he carried a rifle, he made no attempt to fire it.

Schliessman hit the Jap with a slug in the right leg and the Jap dropped. Then Westberry fired and hit him in the head. Altogether Schliessman and Westberry put five slugs in the Jap. When they looked the body over, they found a wristwatch that looked new but had been shattered by one of the slugs. Westberry grabbed the Jap's rifle; it, too, was new.

Their next engagement was outside of what looked like a bomb shelter—a dugout covered with coconut logs and rising about four feet above the ground, with circular, rough-hewn entrances at each end. Schliessman threw a grenade inside. There was the sound of a dull explosion, and maybe 10 seconds later an unarmed Jap emerged. As he came out, Page, who was on the roof of the shelter, made a slight noise. The Jap whirled around and Schliessman instantly killed him with a quick shot in the back, shouting: "The hell with you, the hell with you, you dirty son-of-a-bitch." Page gave the Jap another slug in the forehead but the first shot had been enough. He was a very dead Jap.

Then Schliessman lobbed another grenade into the shelter. Inside he could hear a tense, excited jabber of Japanese. A second man came out, this one in dark, apparently civilian, clothes. "Westberry and I shot the hell out of him. We fired about seven or eight slugs apiece. He fell a few feet from the other Jap."

Page tossed another grenade in the shelter and Winkler sprayed the entrance with BAR fire. After that there wasn't any more jabbering. No one bothered to go inside and find out how many Japs had been killed. By this time, the sun was bright and sweat poured down everyone's face. "It isn't the heat," cracked Page, "it's the humidity."

When they reached the tank trap, the men in Schliessman's squad threw themselves into zigzag trenches on both sides, into abandoned shellholes and shallow foxholes. Two other squads in the platoon, led by Second Lt. Charles Yarborough, a slow-talking Texan, shared the trenches and holes with Schliessman's men and the men of two other platoons. There were no Japs anywhere in sight, although nobody could be sure about the coconut palms. Any one of them might have contained snipers.

"We built our defenses under brush," Schliessman said, "and Lt. Yarborough threw a smoke bomb to let the others know we were there. Then we began to wait. We stayed there all the rest of the day and all night, just holding and waiting.

"Maybe some guys slept. I didn't. I didn't eat, either. I just chewed two sticks of gum from my rations. My mouth felt dry, and I kept hearing Jap rifle and machine-gun fire. For some reason it has a high pitch—sort of soprano.

"At 0330, the moon came out, and we kept firing at the slightest sound. Our orders were to fire at any noise at all, not to ask any questions, just fire. About 0430, I heard noise in the undergrowth nearby and I tossed a grenade at the spot, warning everybody to dig deep. I don't know whether I got a Jap there or not.

"About 0530 somebody spotted four lonely figures coming down the trail toward the tank trap. They looked silly as hell, half-covered with coconut fronds and trying to camouflage themselves. Two other men and I fired, and all four Japs fell, one by one. I fired 13 rounds at them."

The battle began all over again at daybreak, and with increased intensity. Not far offshore were the small rusting hulks of two aging Jap boats, and sometime during the night a few Japs must have swum to them with machine guns—or perhaps the machine guns were already there.

When it began getting light, the Japs opened up on the tank trap and everybody was pinned to the ground for almost an hour, helpless. Then a Navy plane came over and bombed and strafed the hulks for a few minutes. It was quiet after that.

Schliessman got his last Jap in a coconut palm about 25 yards from his shellhole. Picking off the sniper was simple. Later in the morning, scouts went out in patrols of two and three, spraying every tree with fire. That was the only way. The Japs were tied in the trees, sitting on burlap bags just above the lowest branches, and even after they were dead, they didn't fall out but simply hung there ludicrously.

By late afternoon, the battle was over, except for killing a few stray snipers, and Makin belonged to the men of the 27th Division. Maj. Gen. Ralph Smith, who commanded the division, messaged Rear Adm. Richmond Turner, commanding all amphibious operations in the Gilberts: "Makin taken."

MAIL CALL

Deep in the Heart

Dear *Yank:*

Recently I was a dinner guest of the president of the Texas Christian Federation of Women's Clubs in Brownwood, Tex. The hostess told me she had tried to get her club to invite soldiers to members' homes, and I thought GIs would like to see the reply she got from one of the members. Unfortunately it is representative of what the "better class" of moguls really think. Here's the letter:

Dear Mrs. President. When you propose that we ask soldiers to our homes we feel as though you have failed us in the most critical situation which has ever arisen to face us. To ask the women of Texas to place their daughters on the altar of sacrifice to the evil that will come from the program which you presented is asking too much. I know our boys are lonely, but unless they have manhood enough to deny themselves some things for a few short months I do not believe they are courageous enough to sustain our democratic government.

Let us just look at the situation. If the social contacts at the camps were the end of those meetings quite another outlook could be seen, but you know those boys will go out on the weekends and contact our girls again. This time they will not be chaperoned, and for the virtue of how many girls who have thus lost their purity will we be held accountable? We just can't do this. Do not let us sell our daughters in such a racket. Maybe a few would meet life companions, but think of the sorrow and misery and sin we would be leading the numberless ones into! Men and women of the convention were hurt by your proposal. The decision almost wholly was that we mothers and fathers will not stand for this. We feel that the class of boys

whom the girls would meet under your plan are the ones who deliberately want to meet strange girls and they are not the best class of selectees. Many are filled with uncontrolled passion and lust, and many of them are married. I am willing to sacrifice my time, my money and all my material profits for my country, but I cannot give my daughter in such a useless cause.

Well, I just thought you'd like to know what to expect when this melee is over.

—Pfc. James L. Scott
Camp Bowie, Texas

Dear *Yank:*

I have never wanted to be quoted publicly before, and this is the first time I have ever written to any publication, but this is also the first time I have ever been so burned up. As a native Texan, and mighty proud of it, I found the letter submitted by a Camp Bowie (Tex.) soldier, which had been written by a member of the Texas Christian Federation of Women's Clubs in Brownwood, Tex., the most disgusting piece of writing I have ever had the misfortune to read. It is certainly the least representative of any I have ever read about Texas women. . . . Brother, she is no real Texan.

—Lt. H. H. Montgomery
On Maneuvers

Dear *Yank:*

. . . And that remark about Deep in the Heart. We're proud of who wrote it, as we want our gals as we left them and we don't want them on the altar of sacrifice. We are glad the mothers of Texas are holding on to their daughters and that they hold their respect.

—Sgt. Delmos Daniels
Attu

Dear *Yank:*

. . . I have never known of a Christian person with such a nasty and inconsiderate attitude toward the men and boys that are serving their country in these trying times. Any girl that has to have a chaperon along on a date to remain pure and clean is not the type of girl that a soldier would like to be seen in public with. . . .

—Pvt. Dorsey Wiggins*
Hawaii

*Also signed by Sgt. Lester, T-5s Howell, Rouse, and Wilkinson and Pfc. Lemmens.

Dear *Yank:*

. . . The remark about selling daughters to American soldiers is one of the most stupid remarks any normal person has ever made. . . .

—S/Sgt. John Grider*
India

*Also signed by Pvt. Peter Manquacine.

Dear *Yank:*

Yank acted in good faith in publishing Pfc. James Scott's letter in regard to the feelings of the mothers of Brownwood—it was James Scott who acted in ill faith in submitting a letter without explaining the circumstances surrounding the letter. . . . [It] was written over three years ago by a woman who lived approximately 150 miles southwest of Brownwood and who, at that time, had probably not met a single one of our new brand of GIs. It was written to a woman who lived in Austin, Tex. A copy of that letter was sent to a Brownwood woman because it was outrageously dramatic enough to be funny. . . .

—Muzelle Stanley
City Recreation Supervisor
Brownwood, Texas

Mercy for Japs

Dear *Yank:*

As God is my witness I am sorry to read of the way two American soldiers treated the enemy on Makin Island; they shot some Japanese when they might have been able to take them alive. I don't believe in killing unless it has to be done. I am a servant of God, so when I get into battle I hope by His help to take as many Japs alive as I can.

If I am compelled to destroy lives in battle I shall do so, but when U.S. troops throw grenades into an enemy position and Japs run out unarmed we should make an effort to take them alive. I know that if I were in a dugout and forced to run out I would want mercy.

—Pvt. Ralph H. Luckey
Camp Davis, North Carolina

Dear *Yank:*

Brother, Pvt. Luckey better live up to his last name if he goes into combat with the idea of taking Jap prisoners alive!

—Sgt. Carl Bethea*
Port of Embarkation

*Also signed by 13 others.

Dear *Yank:*

We are all Navy men who are suffering from combat fatigue. Many of us have been strafed by Jap Zeros while floating helplessly in the sea and have seen what the soldiers and marines have gone through in this fight. If Pvt. Luckey heeds his own call for mercy for Japs, his soul will belong to God but his body will belong to the Japs. . . .

—Vets of World War II
Norfolk Naval Hospital
Portsmouth, Virginia

Dear *Yank:*

Has Pvt. Luckey ever seen his friends and buddies shot down by the Japs? Has he ever carried our dead out of the jungle for burial? I have—and more, during the eight months I spent on Guadalcanal. Pvt. Luckey will have no dead Japs on his conscience when they kill him.

—Pvt. C. E. Carter
Harmon General Hospital
Longview, Texas

Dear *Yank:*

Me and my buddies sure were mad as hell when we read Pvt. Ralph Luckey's letter. He sure shot off his mouth about our treatment of the Japs. The trouble is that he has had it nice and soft so far. . . .

—Pfc. Edward Staffin
Trinidad

Dear *Yank:*

. . . Wake up, Luckey. The Jap doesn't care if God is his witness or not.

—Pfc. Charles J. Nichols
Worthington General Hospital
Tuscaloosa, Alabama

Dear *Yank:*

It's evening. We're sitting about two feet from our foxhole thinking about a letter written by Pvt. Ralph H. Luckey from Camp Davis, N.C. in a recent issue of *Yank*. Do you mind if we ask him a question? Pvt. Luckey, you're now living in an Army camp, just as we did. Making friends, just as we did. Friends who, in time, will be much closer, dearer, to you than you would believe possible.

We bunked together, ate together, laughed and played together, worked and dated together. Recently we fought together. During the battle, Blackie was wounded and taken prisoner. When we advanced several hours later, we found Blackie. His cheeks were punctured by sharp sticks—pulled tight by a wire tourniquet, the sticks acting as a bit does for a horse's mouth. There were slits made by a knife along the center of his legs and on his side—just as if an artist had taken pride in an act of torture well done.

We continued to move on. Do you think that we also continued to remember the niceties of civilized warfare?

—S/Sgt. B. W. Milewski
Central Pacific

This is the last of a series of GI comments in reply to Pvt. Luckey's letter. Yank *has received a great number of letters on the subject, but only two readers supported the point of view advocated by Pvt. Luckey.*

"That's the new submarine crew."
—LEO SALKIN, PHO M 3C

NUDGE IN REAR CAME TOO SOON, SO HE BOMBED WRONG TARGET IN CHINA

—Sgt. MARION HARGROVE
September 17, 1943

SOMEWHERE IN China—This story has been held back for a while because the fellow was mighty sensitive about it, and he happens to be a tech sergeant, 6 feet 2 and weighing 200 pounds. He's cooled off a little, so now it can be told.

The tech sergeant is Karl May of Yakima, Washington, an aerial engineer and gunner in one of the local Mitchell B-25 bombers. The tale goes back to the time when he was still a buck private, working as an armorer in his squadron and bucking like hell for a job on a combat crew.

They finally let him go on a few missions to try him out. He got along fine until his third trip. That was the raid on the big Jap base at Hankow, former Chinese capital, on the Yangtze.

There were two minor defects that day in the bomber to which May was assigned: there were no racks in the ship for fragmentation bombs and the interphones were temporarily out of commission.

Well, they were working the thing out all right without frag racks or interphones. They had Pvt. May squatting by the photo hole with a stack of frag bombs and the understanding that when the turret gunner nudged him in the behind, he was to cut loose with all he had.

It happened that the bomber had a passenger that day—maybe an observer from Washington, maybe a newspaperman, maybe just a sightseer. This worthy person grew unaccustomedly chilly, saw that the draft came from the open photo hole, and decided to ask the private beside it to close it. The private—yep, it was May—had his back turned, so the passenger sought to attract his attention with a gentle nudge in the rear.

Pvt. May reacted like the eager beaver he was. He held one frag bomb over the hole and let it drop. Then he turned another loose into thin air. He was preparing to drop every bomb in the ship—until he was rudely and violently stopped. To May's dismay, he learned (1) that the ship was nowhere near Hankow, (2) that he had been given no signal, and (3) that he had just wasted a couple of hundred dollars' worth of U.S. high explosives.

The mission proceeded to Hankow, where May dropped the rest of his bombs through the photo hole, an armful at a time. But his heart was heavy at the thought of having goofed.

When the plane returned to its base, there was an intelligence report from the Chinese Army waiting for it. According to this report, two bombs dropped on a Japanese barge on the Yangtze had scored direct hits, sinking the barge and drowning 160 Japanese soldiers.

T/Sgt. May never tells the story himself, and he gets mad when he hears anyone else tell it. Only those who've seen the records will believe it.

1944

ELMER'S TUNE

MARLENE DIETRICH SANG for them beneath exploding shell fire, Al Jolson performed "Mammy" only two miles from the front, and Bob Hope did everything but put on goggles and bomb the Führer's bunker himself. Back home it was the same—New York had the Stage Door Canteen, Los Angeles had the Hollywood version. If you were a GI (even a private) you could dance with Lana Turner or Lucille Ball, order coffee from Ray Bolger or Alfred Lunt, and kiss Joan Leslie good night.

All of this was indicative of a new mood that had overtaken the American people by D-Day—if the first year of the war had been marked by bewilderment and the second by a grudging participation, 1944 was the year that an entire country finally succeeded in forgetting about itself and putting everything it had behind the kids who were laughing at Bob Hope in Italy. Taxi drivers, housewives, and bankers— it was all the same thing: women left their children with communal baby-sitters and assembled B-29 Superfortresses, guys in ties during the day put on overalls at night and riveted gun turrets to tanks, and little kids collected scrap metal. This is exactly what the Axis had feared. At the close of World War I, Paul von Hindenburg had warned his successors against American military production. "They understand war," he had said. We understood a lot more than that. By 1944, we were turning out one Consolidated bomber every hour (they were tested immediately, then flown off directly to combat), and a Liberty ship every 3½ weeks (normal construction time was 200 days). Overseas, the hands-across-the-water effect was unmistakable. Anzio was smashed in spite of a four-month siege; Rome became an Allied possession almost immediately; Kwajalein, Eniwetok, Guam, and Saipan fell, one after the other; and Normandy, in the most electrifying invasion of the Second World War, was taken by machinery and equipment not even envisioned two years earlier. Rosie the Riveter had performed well. So, by the way, had her boys.

In Los Alamos, New Mexico, Gen. Leslie Groves and physicists J. Robert Oppenheimer and Klaus Fuchs had long since determined that a workable uranium bomb was entirely within the realm of possibility. The American people didn't know about that, but if they had, they would not have cared. The war effort at home was what really counted —most people did not even take the *movies* seriously anymore. In fact, Hollywood had sensed that its audiences were growing up to the realities of combat and were no longer susceptible to such precooked pabulum as *The Purple Heart*, or to lines of dialogue like "Have you seen the look on a man's face when you tell him he can't fly anymore?" The changing winds were evidenced by the most popular film of the year—one that had no tail gunners, no U-boats, no saboteurs, and no plot. Instead it had something to do with growing up in a place called St. Louis at the turn of the century, and Judy Garland sang pretty songs about clanging trolleys. Except in real life, the boy next door was still on Bougainville, and the only thing that mattered at all now was bringing him back. Upright. Even Tin Pan Alley had caught the mood—"Oh, What a Beautiful Mornin'" was sung everywhere, as though repeating the lyric often enough would force it to come true. The one remaining constant in an otherwise unpredictable world was Madison Avenue, whose executives were now placing radio plugs for mortuaries immediately following the combat casualties and drafting advertising copy that featured the newest German war machine accompanied by the legend: "Who's Afraid of the Big Focke-Wulf?" One squadron of aviators wrote back, "*We* are," and included the name of every man in the outfit.

Roosevelt was returned to the White House for an unprecedented fourth term, defeating the ever-unfortunate Thomas Dewey by an electoral margin of 432 to 99. Yet it was the absentee vote that he cherished the most—two out of every three servicemen in the trenches had chosen to reelect the man who had put them there in the first place. It wasn't just that they worshiped him—though many of them did —but that they closeted an unshakable belief in everything he told them, even though they knew it was destined to be a long and ugly war. When he said they'd be coming home, they bought it. They even made up jingles to pinpoint the date: "Back in the Sticks in '46," "Back to Heaven in '47," "Golden Gate in '48," and "Back from the Line in '49" were among the favorites.

They didn't even consider "Home Alive in '45."

MAJOR BATTLES:
Kwajalein, Anzio, Eniwetok, Biak, Monte Cassino, Normandy, St. Lo, Arnhem, Philippine Sea, Guam, Leyte Gulf, The Great Marianas Turkey Shoot

HOLLYWOOD'S BEST:
Passage to Marseilles (Bogey, directed by Michael Curtiz)

HOLLYWOOD'S WORST:
The Master Race (George Coulouris, directed by Herbert Biberman)

MOST QUESTIONABLE CASTING:
Katharine Hepburn as Chinese, in *Dragon Seed*

MOST POPULAR WAR SONG (Nonracist):
"I've Got Sixpence"

MOST POPULAR WAR SONG (Racist):
"I'm a Cranky Old Yank in a Clanky Old Tank in the Streets of Yokohama with a Honolulu Mama, Singin' Those Beat-o, Flat on His Seat-o, Hirohito Blues"

MOST POPULAR SONG—GENERAL:
"Don't Fence Me In"

MOST READ BOOK:
Brave Men, by Ernie Pyle

LEAST READ BOOK:
Forever Amber, by Kathleen Winsor ("Her characters talk about as interestingly as brokers on the 8:19 from White Plains."—*Time* magazine)

THE ONLY THING THE OPA COULDN'T RATION:
V-mail

THE ONLY THING YOU WISHED THEY *COULD* RATION:
Telegrams

THE KIND OF PIE MOST SOLDIERS DREAMED ABOUT:
Blueberry, mince, and cinnamon with raisins, in that order

WHAT MADISON AVENUE CLAIMED HITLER WAS AFRAID OF:
Dictaphone recording equipment

WHAT MADISON AVENUE CLAIMED WAS HELL FOR HIROHITO:
Hoover ball bearings

WHAT MADISON AVENUE CLAIMED WAS BLASTING THE AXIS:
Colgate toothpaste in a throwaway tube

MOST MEMORABLE LINE FROM THE ETO:
"I feel like a fugitive from the law of averages."

MOST MEMORABLE LINE FROM THE PACIFIC:
"I got my ass out of there, swabbie. *There*'s my souvenir."

THE PLACE THAT MOST GUYS (EXCEPT TEXANS) CLAIMED TO BE FROM:
Brooklyn

THE PLACE WHERE EVERYBODY HAD A NICKEL FOR A HOT DOG AND A BEST FRIEND NAMED DOMINICK:
Brooklyn

THE PLACE WHERE THEY KEPT THE GREATEST GODDAMN BASEBALL TEAM IN THE WHOLE WORLD:
Anywhere but Brooklyn

MOST POPULAR LETTER (CIVILIAN):
V, for Victory

MOST POPULAR LETTER (MILITARY):
F, for just about anything

WHAT YOU SAID TO AN AMERICAN OF JAPANESE DESCENT:
(a) "You're drafted" (if he had just turned eighteen); or (b) "Shut up and get back in line" (if he hadn't)

WHAT YOU CALLED A BLACK CORPORAL WITH THREE PURPLE HEARTS:
"Edwards"

BEST VALUE FOR YOUR DOLLAR:
GI life insurance

BEST ANNIVERSARY PRESENT FOR MOM AND POP:
Breakfast in bed with real eggs

WHAT YOU GOT WHEN YOU TRADED TWO STEELIES AND AN AGGIE:
One glassie—and with a chip in it, so it didn't hardly roll

COMBAT DIALOGUE—HOLLYWOOD STYLE:
"Say your prayers, you Nazi bastard."

COMBAT DIALOGUE—THE REAL THING:
"Jesus, Willie—I think I just pissed my pants. Willie?"

MOST ADMIRED AMERICAN FEMALE (Limbs Only):
Rita Hayworth
MOST ADMIRED AMERICAN FEMALE (the Whole Package):
The gals who'd dance with you at the USO and make you believe they meant it

MOST CREATIVE SUBTITLE TO DER FÜHRER'S WORDS:
"Have war bonds in your pockets instead of Axis bonds on your wrists."
MOST SUCCESSFUL ACRONYM:
Woman Ordnance Worker—WOW!
MOST ADMIRED AMERICAN MALE:
The GI

Oh, how they hated him. And not just because he made their girls back home swoon, although that certainly had something to do with it. He was rich, he was famous, and he was 4-F. Oh, how they hated him.

WHAT AND WHY IS SINATRA?

When Frankie sings . . .

—*Yank* Staff Writer
January 12, 1945

IF YOU have been overseas long enough to have forgotten thoroughly the taste of fresh milk and the look of civilian clothes, you are probably baffled by the U.S. song-and-sex phenomenon known as Frank Sinatra.

All I knew about Sinatra was that he had been a better-than-average vocalist with Tommy Dorsey's band when I last heard him and that he had climbed, by the time I got back to the States, into a position as "King of the Baritones" and "Idol of the Bobby Soxers." Lord help me, I didn't even know what bobby soxers were! I learned by going to a theater where Sinatra headed the stage show. It was a school holiday, and the shrill little girls, packed into the theater and overflowing into a major traffic problem on the streets outside, were the bobby soxers.

When Sinatra—whom they call "The Voice" when they aren't calling him "Oh, Frankie"—came on the stage, they whistled and stamped and uttered odd cooing sounds and jumped up and down in their seats. Whenever he moved, the sounds got louder and the jumping more unrestrained. You couldn't hear his voice for the bleating of the soxers, so I can't judge whether he's better or worse than he used to be. I did get to meet him between shows and found, to my surprise, because I was braced to dislike him, that he was just a guy, nicer than not nice.

For your information, here are a few facts on "The Voice." He is draft age but is not draft material because of a punctured eardrum. He was born in Hoboken, New Jersey, and went to high school there, swimming on the school team and playing a little tennis. He kidded around some with boxing, but his old man, who had done some pro boxing himself, talked him out of going into the racket seriously. Instead he had a fling at sports reporting on the *Jersey Observer*. Then he started singing, and from there on in his voice was his meal ticket.

The bobby sox business—possibly begun as a press-agent stunt but now out of anyone's control, including Frankie's—got him his first big-time publicity. Today he has two radio programs, draws top money for personal appearances, and can write his own ticket in Hollywood. He has kept up his interest in boxing to a certain extent, the extent depending on what you think of Tami Mauriello, a boxer whom he is rumored to own. He married a hometown girl, and they have two kids—a girl going on five and a baby boy.

Sinatra makes violent love to the mike when he sings. His fans love it and the anti-Sinatra crowd hates it. A teenage boy threw an egg smack in his face during his last New York stage engagement, and Sinatra took it with as good grace as anyone can take an egg in the face. He and the egg thrower made up after the show. On his stage dates, Sinatra has to come into the theater early and hide there all day. If he goes out, he is mobbed by the bobby soxers. Between shows, he usually eats backstage and listens to a Victrola, frequently playing Sinatra records.

Nobody has been able to figure out to anyone's satisfaction why Sinatra has the effect he has on his bobby sox fans. One of his secretaries, a cute dish whose husband is serving overseas, said: "The doctors say it's just because he's got a very sexy voice, but I've been with him a year now, and his voice doesn't do a thing to me."

Maybe it's the war.

A million-dollar wound was one serious enough to send you home, but on your feet. Assuming, of course, that you still had feet. Many did not.

HOSPITAL SHIP

— Sgt. MACK MORRISS
February 4, 1944

AN EAST Coast Port—The USHS *Acadia*, her hull a startling white with huge red crosses blazing amidships, tied up at the pier, where a band and a fleet of ambulances awaited her.

The band played a march, and aboard ship the wounded said yeah, they knew there'd be a goddam band, but why didn't they swing it. The band played maybe a couple of more military pieces and then jived into something that was stronger on the reeds than on the brass.

And the wounded from Italy hobbled to portholes or swung up stairways to the open decks, leaned on the rail, and beat time to the music with whatever limbs they had left. From all over the port side of the ship, the battle casualties made like hep cats and watched as the *Acadia* discharged the first of her cargo, the commissioned cases who were able to walk.

They moved across the gangplank and stepped into waiting GI buses. Trained Negro litter bearers handled their luggage. Then came the psych cases, each one escorted by two men. Then the walking enlisted men, most of them with only a few personal belongings in little Red Cross ditty bags but some with barracks bags which they surrendered to the handlers. At the end of the gangplank, two Negro soldiers grabbed each man under the arms and helped him negotiate the low step down to solid ground, that last step he took to get back to the States. One of the casualties bent over and put both palms flat on the concrete pier, yelped in mock amazement, and danced rather uncertainly into his bus. He was the only one. The rest of the boys from Salerno and the Volturno and beyond hardly changed expression. Some of them seemed to relax tensed lips to let out the breath they'd been holding. But that was all. No dramatics.

The litter patients came last. The Negro handlers, who deserve the reputation they have as experts in the work, moved them into the ambulances in a smooth, effortless stream. In five hours the *Acadia* was emptied.

The whole business of getting back home was just about as simple as that. The swing music was as inappropriate, perhaps, as the marches for the men who couldn't walk—and none could walk very far—and there was a profound incongruity about it: but war is full of incongruities, and the wounded wanted the jive even if they did come ashore with dead pans. They were pretty solemn about it, those with an arm or a leg gone or the few who were blind, but there were no tears. Nobody bawled, no matter how much he felt like it, if he felt like it at all.

Earlier, several hours before the 800-patient hospital ship had docked, there wasn't a dead pan aboard. On B deck, Ward 31 was getting ready to disembark. Since every ward in every hospital has

No matter what his name is they always call him "Doc." Frontline portrait of a rifle company medic.

its comic, 31 had its paratrooper from the West Virginia hills. He and the Chief, an Oklahoma Indian, kept the bulkheads ringing with their patter.

There was an excess energy, pent up after days at sea, and the wounded sought safety valves for its release. The Chief calmly put his GI cane across his knee, threatened profanely to break it, thought better of the idea, and instead banged it merrily on the deck. The paratrooper, his face and arm scarred and an eye missing because of a hand grenade some now-deceased German used in a hand-to-hand fight at Salerno, looked out the porthole to see a launch chugging alongside. He erupted.

"The U.S. Navy—in dangerous waters. Look at 'em! Goddam! Let me off this boat. I wanna get at them USO soldiers," he howled, switching services. "Oh, let me at 'em!"

He registered a burlesque ferocity and, crouching into a fighter's posture, strode up and down the narrow passage between the tiers of bunks. It will take a while for him and the others to get over that feeling which he expressed as comedy but which he actually felt as a kind of tragedy. It is an emotion most returning soldiers have, for a while, regarding servicemen who of necessity are still on duty in the States.

A grave guy from Iowa stood on his one good foot and grinned at the paratrooper.

"Lookit him," spouted the 'trooper, still going strong. "Goddam infantry soldier. Went out, him and his outfit did, to fight the whole Jerry army. We had to come floatin' down to get him out of it. Goddam infantry."

The sober infantryman defended himself briefly: "We was trapped."

A Japanese-American captain limped through the ward. The paratrooper followed him with his one eye. "Goddam good fighters, them fellers. We used to send out patrols and the Jap boys would bring 'em back in. Our jumpsuits were too much like the Jerries'. Them Jap boys was takin' no chances. It was sort of rough on us. Rugged, but right, though."

"Rugged, but right," echoed the happy Chief. Then he started needling some kid about having been overseas 19 months and coming home now to a wife with a 2-month-old baby. The heckled soldier swore comically, boasted that for a guy like him it was easy, and invited the Chief to go to hell; it was his kid all right.

Meanwhile, the paratrooper threw his arms around a middle-aged nurse and asked for a date to get blind drunk ashore. The nurse tactfully refused and the 'trooper said well, he still loved her anyway. Among other nice things about the *Acadia* were 43 nurses who had a high average of good looks.

Two men, each with a foot encased in plaster casts that left only their toes uncovered, suddenly tumbled off a bunk and started whirling between the tiers. One was a Seabee, the other a soldier. They were trying to pull the hairs off each other's toes imprisoned in the casts. The ward looked on, half interested. The Seabee won.

A blind sergeant, his hands on the shoulders of another soldier, walked majestically toward his bunk. The ward fought its tendency to hush. Somebody reached out and tickled the blind guy under the arm. He grinned and felt for his bed. The two playful foot casualties came at him from either side and started tickling. The sergeant roared and lashed out in an arc around him, laughing. He had lost his eyes when a clip of cartridges exploded in his face, detonated by a hit on the chamber of his M1.

It was an hour before docking time. From the opposite ward came the smell of coffee and luncheon meat.

"When do we eat, goddam it?" yelled the wounded in 31.

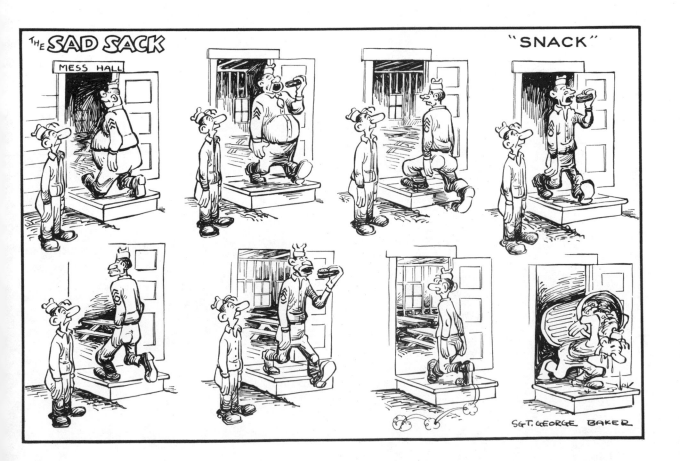

You never know what's coming over the next hill.

By all rights, the American invasion at Anzio and Nettuno on January 22, 1944, should have come as enough of a surprise to guarantee an unopposed Allied push on Rome. Instead it was a series of unexpected miscalculations—the beachhead took 10 days to secure, while roads and bridges previously thought to have been knocked out of commission by the U.S. Air Corps were in fact operational, as evidenced by the thousands of German troops pouring across them. Trapped by the coastline, the GIs were pinned to the beaches for nearly four months with virtually no cover, a condition made all the worse by the inclement weather—some of them actually drowned in their foxholes. The breakout finally came on May 11, but the number of casualties was appalling.

NIGHTMARE JOB AT ANZIO

—Sgt. Burtt Evans
Sgt. Burgess W. Scott
March 3, 1944

IT WAS now 0720. Just five hours ago I was sweating out this invasion in the first landing boat of the first wave with the Rangers, the tough, commando-trained, and experienced outfit that spearheaded the attack on Anzio.

We disembarked before midnight from a proud British ship, a former English Channel ferry that has seen them all—Lofoten, Dunkirk, Dieppe, Africa, Sicily, Salerno. As planned, we lay off shore in invasion barges awaiting H-Hour.

We had been briefed on the town until, as Pfc. Henry J. Corven of Ridgewood, New Jersey, put it, "I could pick out the town bootlegger's home."

It was perfect invasion weather, neither too bright nor too dark, with a calm sea glistening in the silver moonlight. Cramped in the only available space in the rear of the barge, I listened to the Rangers.

"Did you ever hear of Zip Koons?" asked Lt. Tom Magee of Springfield, Illinois. "He was the Ranger who got credit for killing 66 Germans at Dieppe. He went wrong—he's a lieutenant now, you know. We had a lot of fun with him in Sicily when he was my first sergeant. *Superman* magazine made him the Superman of the Month, so the fellows went around shouting: 'Let me be Koons today. You were Koons yesterday. After all, it's my gun!' "

"I wish to hell we would get going," came a voice from the darkness, expressing the awful nervous impatience all of us felt.

"Koons told me to watch out on my 3rd, 7th, and 13th invasions," said Sgt. Samuel Cooperstein of Malden, Massachusetts, who got the Silver Star for gallantry in action in Sicily and was twice awarded the Purple Heart for wounds suffered elsewhere. "This is my third."

"What worries me is those 300 yards of shallow water we have to wade through," said another voice through the darkness. "Funny thing about beaches. The boat pulls in until it can't move any more, and then you step out and it is only one foot deep. Then you move farther in and—*plop*—you're over your head. I hit that kind of a beach in Sicily. Damn near drowned and took my radio equipment with me."

"My feet are cold," complained Pfc. Edward Daley of New York City. "I'm going to take my time when I hit the beach—sit down and change into dry socks. May even shave."

It was now 0150; H-Hour was 0200. All was quiet except for the lapping of water against the barge. With no air interception or sign of the enemy, it seemed too good to be true.

Then at 0151 came the ear-splitting wave of sounds we were waiting for. The briefing officers had told us that a British ship would fire its guns at the coast at exactly 0151, and we were glad now to have that promise confirmed.

It was suddenly silent and black again as the guns halted and the steel barges crept in at three miles an hour toward the beachhead. I disobeyed SOP and peered over the side to see the beachfront. Typical white marble and stucco Italian buildings loomed up on the terraced hillside behind the beach.

We knew roughly what we were getting into. The beach, we had been told, was probably mined. Behind it was a barrier of "three to seven feet," a sea wall with barbed wire on top. There were also several gun positions, but these were believed to be unoccupied. Another version had it that

seven batteries of artillery had recently been moved into the vicinity.

We were all thinking of Salerno, and we thanked God for the relatively flat land, which didn't make the beach easy to defend.

The barge pulled up by the sand at the proper place and the proper minute. Almost the last man out of the boat because of my position in the rear, I followed gingerly while a score of others in squad columns sloshed through several hundred yards of knee-deep water toward shore. I had one hand on my helmet, ready to dig for quick cover if machine guns or artillery opened up. The others ran up that beach so fast I was almost alone. But, even though sidestepping driftwood that might be mines, I soon caught up.

Fortunately, the sea wall was only three feet, and the barbed wire was easily cut. I crossed the main highway, nicknamed "Hitler Road" in the briefing, and joined a squad searching one of the large resort-type homes.

Except for less than a score of German soldiers who were quickly taken care of, our immediate front had been hastily deserted.

Writing this story, I have dived dozens of times for shelter from Jerry bombers hitting the beaches, but our air force is also much in evidence. Outside is a sign pointing to Rome.

—B. E.

This little Allied colony on the shinbone of the Italian boot is only a few weeks old, but it is rapidly becoming one of the hottest corners of this struggling earth.

It measures only about 12 miles in length along the shore and averages about seven miles penetration inland, or about 84 square miles in area—every foot of it vulnerable to bombs, shells, and machine-gun and small-arms fire.

There is no relatively safe rear area as in most operations. One place is about as bad as another, inside or out. Men working on the ships and on the beaches are targets for artillery and bombs; men working in the front lines are exposed to shells and small arms; those in the middle frequently get a mixture of all of these.

The invasion area is humming with activity day and night. Kraut dive-bombers filter through the air cover and ack-ack regularly and lay their eggs along the beach. They do damage, but the work of landing supplies goes on. In fact, Pvt. Maxwell Remmick of Cincinnati, Ohio, member of an Army beach party, wasn't even interrupted; he stayed by his telephone even though his shoulder was dislocated by the concussion of a nearby bomb blast.

Men on the long pontons, who direct vehicles and men coming ashore, have to stick by their posts when the bombers come over because there's no place to go. At night, the men who guide the traffic over the pontons use blackout flashlights and keep hoping they won't see the terrible sight of flares in the sky. On shore the MPs take over, directing the vehicles to assembly areas. From there they are routed to their designated locations.

It is almost unbelievable that the great amount of men and materiel now beyond the beaches could have been unloaded in the few days since D-Day.

The quartermaster and signal corps, engineers, and medics are set up and operating as if they had been here for months.

The hospitals were set up the day after D-Day. One hospital is doing business—a lot of it—in spite of Jerry shells flying regularly overhead. One afternoon the doctors and medics performed an appendectomy with 88s swishing just above the ridgepole of the operating tent.

From the debris littering the beach, it's quite evident that Anzio and Nettuno were, in days past, the resort towns the guidebooks make them out to be. The Tyrrhenian Sea's mild surf tosses up strips of faded canvas and broken sticks that once were bright beach chairs; on the sand are battered hulls of runabouts and sailboats; the bathing beaches are littered with Italian suntan lotion bottles.

But more and more the sea washes up equipment that wasn't made for peacetime pleasure but for war. And sometimes what looked like a piece of driftwood turns out to be a corpse.

—B. H. S.

MAIL CALL

Dear *Yank*:
I have just received a new GI sleeping bag and thought that I would pass on a few simple instructions on the assembly and use of same. First of all, a few simple tools are necessary. These include pliers, wire cutters, hammer, screw driver, hack saw, monkey wrench and a bottle of Lydia E. Pinkham's Vegetable Compound. (The latter item is for the nerves.)

The first step is to put the outer covering over the inner covering, or, if you prefer, the inner covering over the outer covering. A blanket or two is then neatly folded and carefully tucked in the inside of the bag, or, if you like, you can pin the blankets neatly on the outside, using only the Little Giant No. 14176324 Nonskid Safety Pin.

Now you are ready to enter into your battle-front boudoir for an exhilarating night's repose. This is accomplished by entering feet first with a series of eel-like wriggling motions until your feet have hit bottom. The next step is to case your head into the snuggle-bunny hood which is attached and then reach forward and downward and firmly grasp the convenient loop which is attached to the zipper. If the zipper doesn't close with a smooth, gliding motion, the hell with it!

The next morning the bag should be neatly rolled and tied with your tent rope and then taken to that genial gent of service, your supply sergeant. Grasping the roll firmly in both hands, you bop him on the noggin with it and scream at least one of the following expressions at him: "You can take this and you know what you can do with it!" or "Gimme my goddam blankets back!"
—Pvt. John C. Davies
Germany

Dear *Yank*:
We, the mess hall personnel of this outfit, wish to know why the mess halls in the United States have all the can openers and no cans, and we over here have the cans and no openers. We would greatly appreciate your help in this matter.
—T/Sgt. Gido De Marco
and Mess Personnel
India

Dear *Yank*:
Our latest order is something I don't understand. Maybe you can help me.

We have been given an order to lace our shoes differently. I mean each pair. A cross lace and a block lace. We must wear the block lace pair of shoes on even-numbered days only. And the cross-lace shoes on the odd days only. The order says we must change shoes every day. But what do we do when the month has 31 days in it?

I've been in the Army over three years. And it's the first time I've ever been ordered how to lace my shoes. And I'm over 21 years of age. So do they actually pay people to waste time when there's a war on to tell someone how to lace their shoes and make it as uncomfortable for the poor EM as possible?

If you wish to check my statement you could ask any member of the 803d FA Battalion or look at the lace on the shoes on two different days, odd and even.

—(Name Withheld)
Camp Bowie, Texas

Dear *Yank*:
We can understand the reason for changing shoes every other day—so they may dry out; but what we want to know is just who in hell's idea is it that the shoes be laced differently and is there a regulation regarding same?

The insteps of one pair of our shoes are painted yellow, so as to know which pair of shoes to wear on what day, but now there is a notice on our bulletin board with a cartoon from *Yank* attached, stating that the shoes be laced accordingly. As long as one pair was painted yellow in the instep so as to distinguish one from the other, just why the idea of different lacing? . . .

Perhaps they would soon tell us which hand to place the toilet paper in. Kindly give us the low-down on this deal.

—(Name Withheld)
Camp Livingstone, Louisiana

Dear *Yank*:
It takes courage to buck against so many people, but we would like to know who the person was that started referring to a soldier as a "GI." Discussing it with all the fellows over here, I find that most of them hate to be called GI. Anybody can be a GI, but it takes a man to be a soldier, sailor or marine.

What would Washington have said if you asked him to send up a GI? Nathan Hale said: "As a soldier I'll gladly die." Abraham Lincoln said: "A soldier is more than just a man. He's a bearer of truth and faith in the things that go to make up everlasting decency of mankind." Gen. Pershing said: "Only as soldiers who know what they are fighting for, do my men push on." Francis Scott Key didn't know any GIs; he wrote only of the guys who kept the flag "still there."

When we walk over our dead buddies we wouldn't refer to them as dead GIs. And when we get home again, and see our buddies' loved ones, we just couldn't say: "Your son died a GI's death." When we think of GI we think of items of issue, but we are not issued; we are here for a cause.

When I got in the Army they told me I was a soldier, and that's what I have been. GI might be a term for some people in this Army, but not for us. I may not be all the way right, but lots of fellows are with me on it.

—Sgt. Frank K. Turman
Netherlands East Indies

Dear *Yank*:
In answer to T/Sgt. Gido De Marco's problem about not having can openers, we have found here in India that the best thing to use is the cook's fighting weapon, a meat cleaver. If T/Sgt. De Marco and his mess personnel would of been properly trained before they left the States for overseas, they would of never asked such a question.
—S/Sgt. Harvey E. Boyd
India

Dear *Yank*:
The War Department should award the designer of the troop sleeper some kind of medal—say for instance the Distinguished Service Cross with at least four Oak Leaf Clusters.

After spending four days and three nights, we still have a day and night to go, and we are all on the verge of physical collapse due to being tossed from one end of the car to another. Our hearing has long since been destroyed by the thunderous noise as we are dragged along (all wheels are flat) at speeds up to 75 mph.

The first night out, the rain came in the doors so freely that several of us awakened completely soaked. Fortunately no one contracted anything worse than a head cold.

Old-time railroaders claim a flat-wheeled boxcar rides much easier than one of these troop sleepers. Having made a couple of trips via the "rods," I'm inclined to agree.

We do appreciate the WD's generosity in paying our expenses to and from POE, but we feel that Uncle Sam has been swindled again when some "expert" designed this monstrosity. . . .
—First Sgt. H. W. Evans*
Hawaii

Also signed by four others.

Dear *Yank*:
My bitch is about that outrageous beribboned, be-collared, bebuttoned insult to a full-grown man, the Navy uniform.

The pockets aren't big enough, the collar gets in the way, the pants buttons are funny for just so long, the white stripes won't stay clean, the blue dress is too heavy for summer and the whites are a mess after 20 minutes. The neckerchief is as useless as the laces in the back of the pants, and that silly, stupid cry of "tradition, tradition" is ridiculous; not even authorities agree on the origin of the alleged customs. We're like Chinese women who bind their feet because their mothers and grandmothers bound *their* feet. . . .

I've been in the Navy for three years and I'm now on shore duty survey, so I'm not a new guy shooting off my mouth. I'm mildly proud of my branch of the service, but I'm intensely angered by the pajamas I have to wear to work.

—William C. Rand SK1c
FPO, New York

Dear *Yank*:
We have been reading *Yank* for many months, in North Africa, Iran and now here in India. We think it is the best damn weekly publication ever to receive ink from a printing press. However, we think a certain section is being highly abused and slightly degraded. This section is Mail Call. There are some darn good questions submitted from time to time and very good answers given in return. But we think that some of our fellow soldiers are just bitching in this column to see their names in print. . . .

—Pfc. H. Chamberlain*
India

Also signed by 56 others.

Dear *Yank*:
Just before I came into the Army my papa took me aside and told me where babies come from. I was quite surprised and shocked but really, in a way, quite thrilled. Now what I would like to know is where the hell officers and sergeants come from. . . .

—Pfc. C. R. McManus
Hawaii

They may not have seen eye-to-eye on the Cleveland Indians or Lana Turner's legs or whether Lucille Ball should have married a Cuban, but they all agreed on one thing: the best part about H-Hour was when it was over. At least for now.

AFTER THE BATTLE AT KWAJALEIN

—Sgt. MERLE MILLER
March 10, 1944

KWAJALEIN ISLAND in the Marshalls —Although there is still some occasional rifle fire and the smoke still curls from the ruined concrete pillboxes, the veterans of the Army's Seventh Division are now sitting under the trees or lying on the ground with V-mail blanks, writing their first letters home.

Most of the letters are short and simple. The men cannot say that they are on Kwajalein, cannot give details of the action they fought here, cannot name friends who were injured, cannot give the date, and cannot say where they came from and where they are going. They can't say much of anything except "I'm still alive and well." But that is enough.

The officers are wearing their insignia again. There are heated arguments about whether the First Platoon of Company A killed more Japs than the Third Platoon of Company L. Hardly anyone knows for sure just how many Japs he did kill.

"When it gets past ten, you lose count and lose interest," says Pfc. James Carrigan of San Saba, Texas, a BAR man who accounted for 12.

Down on the beach, about one man in 15 has succeeded in finding his own barracks bag in the disorganized piles there. Those who have located their own toilet articles are sharing their razors and soap with a dozen other GIs. Some of the soldiers are bathing in the surf, wearing shoes to protect their feet from the sharp, jagged coral.

Everywhere burial details are removing the remains of the last dead Japs. A few minutes ago, an unarmed private in a graves registration unit adjusted his gas mask and went into a small pillbox near the center of the island, an area that was supposed to have been completely cleared of Japs during the morning of the second day of the battle.

A split second later, the private ran yelling from the pillbox. He thought he had seen ghosts. Following him were two emaciated but very much

165

Another H-Hour, another beachhead . . .

alive Japs in shorts, their hands in the air. They are now changing into fatigues with PW painted on the back.

This morning hundreds of tropical white birds, driven away by the battle, have returned to the island and are resting again on the tops of what they still recognize as trees. A special service officer is looking for the best place to hang the screen for the outdoor movies that will begin in a few days. A site for a post exchange will be selected tomorrow.

Already a half dozen bulldozers are rolling the runways of the half-completed airstrip so hurriedly abandoned by the Japs. The engineers are surveying the site, discussing the best places to build hangars. The remaining skeletons of the Jap revetments are sadly out of line, they say.

A Negro port battalion is unloading food, ammunition, and supplies from newly arrived cargo ships. The men are putting up their shelter halves in the few cleared spaces, and AA crews are finding permanent positions for their guns.

Jeeps, half-tracks, and tractors are moving along the battle-torn main highway, passing medium and light tanks that are returning from the front area.

The few enemy bicycles here are too small and too mangled to ride. But T-5 Robert Fuller, a coast artilleryman from Kansas City, Kansas, started tinkering with the engine of a shrapnel-scarred truck with a left-hand drive. A few minutes later he was taking passengers all over the island.

Everywhere the foundations of blockhouses and the charred remains of barracks and storehouses are being searched for souvenirs. There are enough Jap rifles for everybody and once in a while a rare hara-kiri knife with a silver blade and a handle that some say might be gold.

No one who has acquired a complete Imperial Marine or Jap Navy uniform would consider selling it, but a pistol, carried only by the enemy officers, can be had for a month's overseas pay of a private.

Anybody can pick up right now the Jap postcards that make those of the French variety seem mild by comparison. There are also a few sets of travel prints of Australia, New Zealand, Pearl Harbor, and San Francisco, with Japanese captions under the photographs. The experts, of course, point out that these are the high points of a planned Nipponese tour of the Pacific, which somehow never came off.

Near what used to be a Jap food dump, there are piles of boxes of small, soggy crackers and a pasty stuff in cans that nobody will sample. Also there are 150 cases of beer, guarded by four MPs with guns.

No one cares about the beer, anyway. It isn't very good, much weaker than the PX stuff, and warm. There is no ice on this island. Besides, there are plenty of bottles of *sake* around here.

Hot coffee and hot chow are available for the first time in the company's CPs. Vienna sausages, beans, meat, and vegetable hash are being cooked over dozens of fires in shell craters.

There is a rumor that bacon and eggs will be served tomorrow. No one puts much stock in it.

Tonight it will be possible to sleep, but not many of us will. The sickening odor of the dead Japs still fills the air, and there may still be a live one around who is unwilling to surrender.

No one can do much sleeping 24 hours after a battle, anyway.

Every time they went up, the first thing they would think was "This is the one where I don't come back," and the second thing they would think was "Tough."

ROSIE'S RIVETERS

—Sgt. Saul Levitt
Sketches by Sgt. Howard J. Brodie
April 28, 1944

ENGLAND—For newspapers, bigger victories in this war are a simple problem—you just use bigger type on page one. Like the American daylight raids on Berlin. In somebody's 20-volume history of the Second World War, to be written in 1955, an aging crew chief like J. E. Woodard and a tailgunner like Bill DeBlasio will find the Berlin raids rating a paragraph or two on page 963. For the men concerned with them only yesterday, they meant another evening return of tired, living men—or another ship sloping down to the limbo of "missing in action."

Sometimes even a working airfield gets a sense of something special and enormous. On one field the crews had this feeling about the Berlin raids, when a certain plane came swinging low over the tower, home from Berlin, one late afternoon.

The plane was Capt. Robert Rosenthal's—*Rosie's Riveters*. Her crew came home to a sudden, unrestrained, crazy holiday greeting. It was a private party; nobody else was invited. It was their own hunk of bitter victory—for many were lost over Berlin, taking part of the *Luftwaffe* with them.

But Rosie, the pilot, had completed his tour of duty. The sky was filled with flares—the armament men had given them two extra boxes before takeoff that morning. They threw the Fourth of July up at the cold, gray sky; and the control tower, which is a grave and dignified institution at an airfield—something like the Supreme Court—came back with more flares.

The crew's request to the pilot that morning, when they learned it was to be Berlin, had been for a "beautiful buzz job" coming in. The pilot gave it to them with his low swoop over the tower. It is said—though J. E. Woodard, the husky crew chief, denies it—that big tears rolled down his face when *Rosie's Riveters* showed at last over the tower.

Then the crew rode off in great style to the interrogation, each man on a jeep. All except T/Sgt. Michael V. Bocuzzi, the radio operator; he rode on the rear of a proud MP's motorcycle.

Capt. (then Lt.) Rosenthal and his crew came

Rosie poses for a picture at his home base in England with some of the men who have sweated out many missions over Europe in his veteran Fortress.

Front row: Lt. R. C. Bailey, Capt. R. Rosenthal, Lt. C. J. Milburn, and Lt. W. T. Lewis.
Back row: S/Sgt. L. F. Darling, T/Sgt. M. V. Bocuzzi, S/Sgt. J. F. Mack, T/Sgt. C. C. Hall, S/Sgt. W. J. DeBlasio, and S/Sgt. R. H. Robinson.

overseas quietly enough last September. They brought with them their own crew name, to be duly inscribed on the nose of a Fort by some weary Joe who has seen all kinds of names tagged onto B-17s that can't answer back.

The pilot was a quiet, inconspicuous young man of 26 who wore his visor cap clamped down on his head and walked with the shambling gait of a countryman, although he hailed from the Flatbush farmlands of Brooklyn, New York. With him was one of those typical American "mongrel" crews that the Army arranges so well—as if in conscious answer to the "racial unity" armies of Nazi Germany. Their backgrounds were German, Irish, Scotch, Italian, and others, and their home places were scattered from the eastern seaboard to the far west.

In Dyersburg, Tennessee, Rosie had quietly canvassed his crew to find out how they felt about

combat. No one backed out. Yet no one could possibly have wanted the combat they got in their first three days of flying in this theater. As S/Sgt. Ray H. Robinson, the ball-turret gunner from Arkansas City, Kansas, put it, "The first night after Bremen we were too scared to sleep, the second night after Marienburg we were too tired. The third night after Munster we were bushed—finished."

Bremen was bad. On that one, the squadron lead crew, piloted by Capt. (now Maj.) Everett E. Blakely, had the hell smashed out of it. On the operations blackboard, Sgt. Jennings wrote after all the plane numbers "severe battle damage." Marienburg, with only a few hours' sleep intervening, was one of the longest flights ever undertaken in this theater. And then came Munster, the very next morning.

The haggard, griping crew of *Rosie's Riveters*

went down to the Munster briefing that morning in the company of experienced crews—men who had been on the first Regensburg shuttle raid to Africa and on the "longest flight in the ETO," to Trondheim.

Late that afternoon, as fog settled over East Anglia, *Rosie's Riveters* came back alone—the drone of its two engines a mournful elegy for those men who had been to Regensburg and Trondheim. Careful landing procedure for formation was unnecessary. There was only the one plane coming in—actually, half a plane—with two of its engines out. Thirteen planes had failed to return. The interrogation was very exclusive, like a consultation with a private physician. There was only the evidence of the dazed, battered men of *Rosie's Riveters*.

It had been a ferocious and concentrated attack. One by one the planes of the group had gone down. Left alone, Lt. Rosenthal had decided to go on with the bombing run.

"Shall I drop them now, Rosie?" the bombardier kept asking.

"Not yet."

"Now?"

"No."

"We're over Munster," Lt. C. J. Milburn, the bombardier, finally said.

"Now," said Lt. Rosenthal.

Then they fought their way back from Munster to the French coast, enemy fighters queueing up on them. S/Sgt. L. F. Darling of Sioux City, Iowa, crept up to the nose to help Lt. Ronald C. Bailey, the navigator, spot the landing field. At last came the landing.

Rosie came down through the bomb bay to look over his crew. Darling was wounded and so was the other waist gunner, S/Sgt. J. H. Shaffer. As Rosie stepped out and went along in the ambulance with his wounded, he got a glimpse of something new—the torn-down skin of the right wing where a rocket shell looping from above had plowed between empty gas tanks, cutting a hole a foot across.

Mike Bocuzzi, tumbling out white-faced, yelled: "I'm through flying these things. That's enough."

"C. J.," the bombardier, round-faced and amiable, a little quieter than Mike, didn't say anything, but he thought: "Well, if this is the way it is, they must get you sooner or later, but I'll go along until it catches up with me."

Young Bill DeBlasio, the tailgunner, wrote in his battle diary: "By the grace of God we were the only ship to come back. Our pilot brought us home safely."

That was Munster, and it was five months more until Berlin.

Mike Bocuzzi, who had yelled that he was going to quit, griped that way many more times—and never quit. T/Sgt. C. C. Hall of Perry, Florida, a pleasant guy with a sour puss, went on shooting down fighters that he was reluctant to claim. And Rosie, the pilot, went on making his laconic reports to interrogation officers when they tried to pump him.

"The flak was meager," he would say. "We landed with our flaps out."

"Flaps out? Were you hit?"

"A little bit. But if you get back, it's a milk run."

They flew to Bremen, Rostock, Brunswick. On the second Regensburg, the target area was snow-covered. Lt. Bailey, the navigator, gave the crew a little running lecture on European history and geography. Here were the Alps. Over that way was Switzerland. Those long, wide lanes below were the "six-laned highways built by the Germans for this war." And here was where the Germans had broken through in an earlier war with France, in 1870.

Before Rostock, Bocuzzi was tired and jumpy. Rosie came down to the line, put his arms around Mike's shoulders and said: "What's the matter, Mike? We're all nervous. I'm always scared myself. What's the matter?"

"Nothing," said Mike.

In his battle diary, DeBlasio wrote darkly: "They better give us a rest and a few short raids. I am very tired now."

The pep talks had mounted. "By this time we'd had 102 since Dyersburg," says Ray Robinson. "I counted them. Rosie always gave us a pep talk before a mission. After that he never spoke on a raid, except when he had to."

For Berlin, the briefing was like all the others. But it was for Berlin, the "Big B," to be hit in daylight. Last August, as a gag, someone had put up the red ribbon across to Berlin, and no return route was indicated. Now it was no gag, and there was a return route. Through the briefing room came the shuffle of heavy boots. Cigarettes were lighted. As the pointer touched Berlin, Bocuzzi said to somebody: "Who got drunk last night and dreamed this one up?"

They went down to the line. Behind them were more than 20 raids. They dove into the ground crew's kitty of cigarettes in the tent. Bocuzzi borrowed a pencil from the ground crew. "Number 12, this is. I owe you 12 pencils," Mike said.

It was a cloudy day. Berlin could always be postponed, couldn't it? Couldn't it wait for tomorrow? They looked toward the tower where the flare might go up announcing "mission scrubbed." There was no flare, only the dull gray sky.

A new navigator was along. Instead of Lt. Bailey, riding the bike and looking like a professor with his navigator's briefcase under his arm, there was a new man who had to be put at ease by Rosie.

The copilot, Lt. Winfrey (Pappy) Lewis of Houston, Texas, came down and did his premission job of checking equipment. Then he dived for the cot in the tent—a regular thing with him, this sack time before a mission. S/Sgt. Marion J. (Junior) Sheldon of Arkansas, who had replaced Darling, carefully hung his two rag dolls, "Blood" and "Guts," to the receiver of his gun. All the little things had been done, and pep talk number 103 took place—with Rosie's usual delivery: "You worry about your guns and let me worry about the plane."

The only changes this time were that they got into the plane a little earlier than usual and the silence over the interphone after the takeoff was greater than usual. Interphone discipline had always been strict, but this was quieter than it had ever been. "We were a shipload of nerves," says Ray Robinson.

As they came over the German coast, the clouds began to lighten. Moving into Germany, things were getting clearer. Pappy Lewis, the "bald eagle," looked over toward Rosie, beginning to sweat.

"It was only 30 below," says Mike. "Not too cold."

They got over the "Big B." It was clear below them, although smoke was already billowing high in the air. Flak was thick about them—"but not worse than Bremen," says DeBlasio. Nervousness disappeared with the first fighters.

"On this one," says Mike, "we didn't want them to get in close."

The bombardier got one and so did the top turret. *Rosie's Riveters* made its turn past the target.

Now the enemy coast was behind them. Over the interphone Rosie said: "Interphone discipline is now a sack of something." Voices broke in a frenzy of babbling, laughing noises. There was a hell of a squabble in the waist, and DeBlasio was refereeing between S/Sgt. Jimmy Mack and Junior Sheldon.

England again, after Munster, Bremen, Brunswick, Rostock, Stettin—and Berlin. After unloading bombs on the map of Germany. After 103 pep talks by Capt. Robert Rosenthal of Brooklyn and Brooklyn College.

They buzzed the field. Down below were friends. Maj. Blakely, the CO, was waving. The flares went up. It was a private victory, but in this roaring excitement, there was the knowledge of men who had not come back. In four raids on the "Big B," American bombers had dished it out, but they had taken it, too.

At the interrogation Capt. F. E. Callahan asked his questions, and the answers were, as usual, laconic. "We never get anything out of you," said Capt. Callahan gloomily. The new navigator told most of the story. Somebody was always pushing over to shake Rosie's hand, and the navigator said complainingly: "I wish this guy weren't so popular, so we could get through."

Lt. Col. Kidd and Col. Harding pulled Rosie aside to find out things. They found out little, and after he had downed a Scotch, Rosie asked po-

The bombardier got one and so did the top turret. Rosie's Riveters made its turn past the target.

litely: "Would it be all right if we had a couple of bottles of Scotch tonight at the barracks?"

It seemed very much okay.

One evening a week later, they went to get decorations at the Officers' Club. There were Capt. Rosenthal, Bill DeBlasio, Ray Robinson, and Mike Bocuzzi. They sat quietly, shoulder to shoulder, dressed in Class As. Lt. Gen. Spaatz and Maj. Gen. Doolittle spoke. It was brief and to the point about the war. Jimmy Doolittle, answering a question, said in his resonant voice: "After all, it's not a matter of you and me going out, it's a question of winning the war."

Rosie went out and walked down toward his hut in the dark. Capt. Putnam, a close and good friend, had gone down a few weeks before. This Berlin raid was a thing of the past; let its history be written elsewhere. And tomorrow was another day, another raid.

At the Aero Club some mechanic got to the piano and played boogie-woogie, and boys with

"Berlin" inscribed on their jackets tapped their feet to the music, standing around the piano.

Over in the BOQ Ray Robinson found Rosie in the midst of a lot of clothes, with his B-4 bag open. Robinson shook his head and said pityingly: "Someone always has to pack your stuff. How on earth do you ever expect to get off on that leave tomorrow?"

He packed Rosie's stuff carefully into the bag.

"You won't need that," he said, throwing an extra suit of underwear to one side, after counting out the number he thought Rosie would need for the leave. And then he zipped the bag shut.

"Thanks, Ray," said Rosie.

"What train are you taking?"

"Early one, I guess."

"It's at eight o'clock, so you better get out of the sack early—or do I have to come over and get you up? Good night, Rosie."

"Good night, Ray," said Capt. Rosenthal, settling into his sack.

Thought for Tomorrow

Now, here's a post-war problem
That's really apt to hurt;
How many GIs with civilian ties
Will stuff them in the shirt?
—Cpl. Marvin Lore
Sheppard Field, Texas

Nocturne

The world is filled with dying light,
The streets are shadow-filled,
The busy town is hushed at night,
The working hands are stilled.

The stars slink out of their gloomy dens,
A silent watch to keep;
From somewhere comes the sound of guns.
My mother will not sleep.
—Cpl. Jerome Hoffman
Camp Wheeler, Georgia

Pleasant Dreams

Breathes there a GI with soul so dead
Who never once to himself has said,
"Reveille, hell! I'll stay in bed,"
And then got up?
—Anonymous

Soap and Water

You might think this nonsense and so much pa-
laver
Till you've gone for a month and not even seen
lather.
I think someone said that a bath is a bath
When a man's in a tub and can both sing and laugh,
With no one to watch him and tell him to hurry
And soapsuds are flitting about in a flurry.
I've bathed in canteen cups and helmets and cans,
I've gone for three weeks without washing my
hands,
But I think if I ever get out of this war
I'll live in a bathtub for time evermore.

Just give me a tub that is porcelain-lined,
With nice tiled floors, and I'll soon be reclined
The full length of that lovely container of water
And neither my wife nor my son nor my daughter,
Through threat or enticement shall lure from his
lair
The father they love. They can pull out their hair,
They can rave, they can rant, they can scream,
they can roar;
But I'll smile and remember this bathtubless war,
And I'll lie midst the wonderful soapsuds, I think,
Till my skin and my soul are a rose-petal pink.
—Cpl. John E. Abel, Jr.
France

The Optimist

If the devil takes the hindmost,
No doubt I'll be behind;
The gold beyond the rainbow
Is the gold I'll never find;
I'm always on the other side
Of the cloud that's silver lined.

My life is rugged, really,
And yet I'm seldom vexed,
Because I'm stickin' round to see
Just what the hell can happen next!
—Pfc. John C. Mlocek
Station Hospital, Chico AAF, California

Quatrains on Brass

Rank Among Lieutenants
Proclaim the truth with flying pennants
    And nail them to your mental storehouse,
The thing of rank among lieutenants
    Is rare as virtue in a whorehouse.

Puzzler
Of all Army enigmas, one of the worst
    Is how ratings and ranks will be reckoned;
For instance, the second lieutenants come first,
    And the first lieutenants come second.
                        —S/Sgt. A. L. Crouch
                        Camp Selby, Mississippi

My Pre—Pearl Harbor Ribbon

I trim my chest with yellow, lest
    My friends should not remember
I got my gun in Forty-One
    Some time before December.

Through awful peace, through Lend and Lease
    I stood up like a man
And won the war a year before
    The goddam thing began.
                        —O/C Charles P. Graves
                        TCOCS, New Orleans, Louisiana

Army Chapel

The doors stand open for the files of men
Whose step is lighter at the Sunday dawn.
These are the ones who yesterday had been
All fierce and heavy with their weapons on.
They are the grimmest worshippers of all
Who come to sing the quiet songs today,
Who have the strident marches to recall
And who have knelt to fire, but not to pray.
Just what the troubled heart will call its own
And will remember from this steepled place,
If fully felt, but not precisely known,
And written only on the soldier's face.
It is a search for rightness, little more—
The strangest, strongest weapons of the war.
                        —Pvt. Darrell Bartee
                        Camp Crowder, Missouri

Jacket, Field

The jacket, field jacket,
When issued you rack it
Or carefully pack it
And stack it away.

Though Springtime is chilly,
An AR that's silly
Says nilly to "Willie"
The jacket's passé.

Can't wear it or share it
Or even fair-tear it
An MP will snare it
And bear it away.

Ransack it and sack it,
Evac to Iraq it
Donate to some yak it,
The jacket's passé.
                        —Sgt. Lee Allman
                        Wright Field, Ohio

Passing Comment

Advice to the Folks Back Home
Give thanks to the valiant Soviet,
But remember the war's not oviet.

On the Futility of Passes
If it catches my whim, it's
A cinch it's off limits.

Day Dreams
One guy I'd love to drop kick
Is the top kick.

Line-Outfit Blues
I've lugged a 60-mm
For many a damn-km.

GI Emily Post
To eat from a mess kit
You don't need a waistcoat.
                        —Cpl. Seymour D. Schneider
                        Italy

Beer Ration in New Guinea

Dig your ice box,
    Make your plans,
Drink your beer,
    Smash your cans.
    Go to bed
    In a mellow haze,
Wait another
Thirty days.

—Pvt. Jack H. Steinmann
New Guinea

Letter to Joe

It was a year of days, like any other,
A year of nights when the hunted heart
Panted out its fears in the baying dark
And the face that recurred in dreams
Most often was a face with numerals
And somewhere secret moving hands:

Was a year of midnight snow and lights burning;
Girls, petals of them brushing our lips
Filing our hands; jukebox music
Stained with a sailor's blood;
The river white with ice, hands frozen
To riflebutts, striding voices,
The squadroom lit with snow,
And the phone in the hallway ringing ringing
Like the insistent tender bells
In a girl's crying;
Was a year like this, like any other

The hut's lights glow like a jack-o-lantern
In the swamp. Carnivals of fireflies
Swarm the palms. And this
Is the dog-howl of loneliness, I know.
But—kiss Detroit for me, Joe.

—S/Sgt. Troy Garrison
Philippines

GOING

SOMEWHERE?

Then you'll need a set of our handsomely designed GI LUGGAGE, styled in the essence of simplicity. No buckles, straps or handles to become lost or broken..

It's roomy enough to hold more than you can carry, but you'll carry it anyhow, bub.

Illustrated here is the new BAK-BREAKER set, which comes beautifully embossed with your complete nomenclature at no additional cost.

It's Fun to Rummage

In GI LUGGAGE!

TOO GOOD FOR THE GUARDHOUSE

—Sgt. ANDREW A. ROONEY
Britain
June 16, 1944

Paratroopers are tough guys who tell tough stories about themselves. This is one they tell in Britain. And who are we to doubt it?

YEAH, THEM six holes up there is what the paratroopers left. Tough? They was plenty tough. Here six weeks before they pulled out.

One of 'em's name was Marcetti. Toughest guy I ever see. Damn, he was tough! Marcetti used to be a rigger in a steel mill at Pittsburgh, and when he come into the Army they made an engineer out of him. Sent him to Belvoir and taught him how to make bridges out of them little boats and how to dig. If there was anything Marcetti didn't want to know how to do, it was dig.

176

They kept him at Belvoir till they found out they'd got the wrong guy to teach digging to. He used to give half his month's pay to a guy named O'Hara to pull his KP for him, and the other half he'd spend on Scotch up to Washington. Hell of a guy he was; sergeants couldn't do nothing but put him in the guardhouse when he popped off. Too good a man for the guardhouse, Marcetti was, and them officers of his knew it.

After they had him about six months they decided they better get someone else to do their engineering, so they sent him to Paratroop School where he'd been trying to get since they got him. It wasn't so much they let him go where he wanted but they sure'n hell didn't want him, and the Army just don't send nobody back to a Pittsburgh steel company.

Marcetti got hooked up with this rugged paratroop outfit—one of the first. Hand-picked, them boys was, back in the days when you hadda be able to lick hell out of three Marines before they'd let you in.

They wasn't having no more trouble with him like they was having at Belvoir. He didn't get drunk much, and he began listening because he figured them babies in the paratroops knew more about stuff than he did. At Belvoir he'd always guessed he could dig as good a hole as the next man without a sergeant telling him how.

Well, hell, first thing you know this Marcetti gets to be the demolition expert of the outfit. Goes to demolition school and learns everything there is to know about blowing things up. Before long the outfit moves over here, and they're the babies that's going to drop right out of the ETO onto Jerry some day when he's still tryin' to figure out what day he's going to get dropped on.

Them six holes is a story. At night Marcetti, Hannock, Taragan, and the rest would be sitting around here playing poker for what they had. Marcetti would get restless, and without saying much he'd get up and wander into that little room at the end he had to himself. He'd start taking down all them bottles of stuff he had on the wall.

Damn, he had a pile of the stuff. TNT, nitro,

dynamite, everything. Had enough to blow this whole ETO to hell and gone. Under his sack Marcetti kept a hack saw, a bunch of them heavy English beer bottles, and three pieces of pipe that run the length of his bed. He'd saw himself off a foot or so of pipe, then he'd come back out here and, talkin' natural all the time, he'd smash himself up about six or eight of them beer bottles in a bucket. He'd go back to his room with the bucket of glass, and pretty soon you'd hear that sound like coal running down a chute when he poured the glass into a hunk of pipe.

Marcetti'd come out of his room with his pipe in one hand and a fuse in the other. He'd sit down with the boys again for a while, talking just like he was knitting a sock as he put the fuse into the moxie he'd packed into that length of pipe.

When he was satisfied with the job he'd lean back in his chair, finish what he was talking about, and then wander out. In five minutes he'd be back in his chair again, sitting there talking and smiling.

All of a sudden all hell would break loose. The whole damn hut would shake, and the rivets holding them corrugated-roof pieces together would snap off, a few of 'em. For 30 seconds you couldn't think what was happening for the noise of stones and dirt rattling down on the roof.

You shoulda seen the trees out here at the side. You can still see the scars on 'em. Big hunks of broken bottle stuck into them trees from all angles, and out in the field here they was a hole blown deep enough to bury a horse.

After looking around to see how Marcetti's concoction worked that time, the boys would go back to the hut and start playing cards again. In a few minutes this here meek little shavetail from the provost marshal's office would pull up in a jeep outside. He'd come every time, and I knew he hated to come in that but worse'n anything in the world. It didn't bother Marcetti and this paratroop outfit none. Nobody who wasn't a paratrooper bothered them guys none.

This second louey would knock on the door real light and then come into the hut. He'd stand there looking pretty helpless with a .45 on his hip and try to make the boys look up from the game by slamming the door. Hell, everybody that come in there slammed the door.

"Look, you fellows," he'd always say. "I asked you not to pull that stunt anymore," he'd say. "Cut it out, will you?" he'd say, pleading. Hell, it was funny. There wasn't anything he could do because no one give a damn. They knew where they were headed for, and what anyone but their CO told them didn't carry no weight.

One day they brought some new boys in. Fellows up from an infantry outfit. They'd been through a pretty rugged course, but they wasn't paratroopers. They'd got most of their training back in the States, and they was pretty cocky. Always showing these paratroopers how they learned it.

Things didn't go too well between 'em, and the CO decided something hadda be done. He gets Marcetti to fix up a bunch of tear-gas bombs under the sacks of a couple of these new Joes. They was in here then, and Marcetti and his bunch was over in the bigger hut next door.

That night the infantry boys come in after a speed march, pretty rugged they was, and a couple of 'em flops down on these sacks with the tear gas underneath. Boy, you shoulda been around. The bombs go off, and the hut starts filling with gas. The boys think they've been hit direct with HE.

They come hollering and screaming out of this hut like wild Indians. Marcetti is over there in the next hut, not even watching—just laying on his bunk, looking up at the ceiling and smiling.

This new crowd finally catches on. They get pretty mad but take it good. Can't get back into their hut, though. All their stuff is in there, and a man can't go near the place for the gas.

This shavetail from the provost marshal's office comes along to find out what all the excitement's about. It's getting dark, and he begins to worry about the lights in the hut. Doors and windows are wide open, and there'd been plenty of damn Germans around them nights.

Marcetti hears what's up and comes out of his hut. The louey looks at him pained and helpless like. He knows damn well who set them tear-gas bombs off.

"Can I do anything for ya, lootenant?" Marcetti asks, real casual.

"Well," says the lootenant, "I gotta get them lights out some way. If you'd put your gas mask on and put them lights out I'd be much obliged to ya, sergeant."

Marcetti disappears into his hut just like he's going in to get his mask like the lootenant said.

Well, the funny thing is that Marcetti does come out with his mask—last thing anyone expects to see him do. But on his hip he's strapped his .45.

He flips his hat between his legs like they taught him at Belvoir and starts fixing the straps on his gas mask. He gets his mask on, puts his hat on his head, waves at the louey, and starts towards the hut. Marcetti is smiling sure as hell behind that mask, but you can't see it.

About 20 feet from the door of the hut he stops, pulls out his .45, and starts aiming. Everyone's expecting something from Marcetti but not this. He just plugs away six times at them lights hangin' there from the ceiling of the hut, knocks 'em clear out, and then calmly walks back towards the louey.

Marcetti pulls off his gas mask. "There you are, sir," he says to the louey and walks back into his hut and lays down.

That's how them six holes got up there. Marcetti. Sorta sorry to see them paratroopers go, but damn! they was tough.

⭐

Anne Frank heard about it in a Dutch attic, Joe DiMaggio heard about it in center field, and James Dean heard about it in an Indiana classroom. Excepting only the Titanic and Lucky Lindy's solo landing at Le Bourget Field, the Normandy invasion set more headlines than any other news event of the twentieth century—yet no one was particularly surprised. Even an abortive failure like the 1942 raid on Dieppe had proven that a cross-channel leap into France was not only necessary, it was inevitable.

THIS WAS D-DAY

—Sgt. RALPH G. MARTIN
June 30, 1944

WHEN PVT. Charles Schmelze of Pittsburgh, Pennsylvania, stationed in England, had finished servicing a big troop-carrying glider of the Ninth Air Force, he was pretty well pooped. So he climbed aboard a glider, picked himself a comfortable corner, and went to sleep.

The glider, towed by a plane piloted by F/O E. G. Borgmeyer of St. Louis, Missouri, was next seen landing in France in a zone of heavy fighting. Pvt. Schmelze had slept his way into the greatest military operation in history.

Most of the plans were neatly filed in a fatfolder labeled "Operation Neptune." Everything had been figured out, on paper. There would be so many personnel and vehicles on so many boats, so much ammo, so many rations, so many stretchers. Each truck would have its gas tank full, carry enough extra for a 150-mile trip, and each soldier would carry a K and a D ration. All officers would send their trunk-lockers to storage.

There had been dry run after dry run, with soldiers seldom sure whether or not it was the real

thing. There had been a final date set, and changed, postponed a day because of bad weather. It all depended on weather, tide, and what the moon looked like.

This was the plan:

Simultaneous landing on two main beaches. V Corps would hit near St. Laurent-sur-Mer, on the northern coast of Calvados, with a regimental combat team of the 29th Division on the right and an RCT of the First Division on the left. Meanwhile, at the southern part of the east coast of the Cotentin Peninsula, the VII Corps would land near Varreville, with the Fourth Division making the assault by sea and two airborne divisions, the 82d and 101st, dropping inland the night before in the area around Ste. Mere-Eglise. The British and the Canadians would come in north of Caen near Le Havre.

There also would be a one-hour air bombardment and continuous naval bombardment of the 16 German coastal guns and the myriad of six-foot-thick concrete pillboxes, things the Nazis called *Widerstandsnets*. And there would be three companies of Rangers going in to destroy a battery of

155mm guns at Pointe du Hoc, which commanded both beaches. Engineer special brigades would have the big job of blowing gaps in the thick concrete wall lining the beach, cutting through the rows of barbed wire, bulldozing roads out of nothing, and sweeping the mines.

According to COSSAC (Chiefs of Staff, Supreme Allied Command), there would be a maximum of five German infantry divisions and one panzer division along our whole front on D-Day.

It was there in the folder, everything you could think of. Somebody had even sat down with a pencil and paper and figured out that by D-plus-10 we would have 43,586 casualties.

An invasion ship is a lonely ship. Downstairs in an LST you sit and sweat and nobody says anything because there is nothing to say. You look around and you wonder who will be dead soon. Will it be that tall, tough-looking sergeant who is busy double-checking his M1; or the guy stretched out in his upper bunk who keeps praying aloud all the time; or the kid sitting next to you who wet his pants? Who will be dead soon?

Then the thought comes, swelling inside of you, a huge fist of fear socking at your gut, hammering and hammering . . . "Maybe it's me. Maybe I'll be dead soon . . ."

Communiqué number one, Tuesday, June 6, 1944: "Under the command of General Eisenhower, Allied naval forces, supported by strong air forces, began landing Allied armies this morning on the northern coast of France."

The sea was choppy and Omaha Beach was a long seven miles away when the first wave of the First and 29th Division soldiers lowered into their assault boats. Coming in, there was naval gunfire bursting all along the beaches; large, medium, and fighter bombers swooping down by the dozens, dropping their loads on gun positions, troop concentrations, coastal batteries, bridges, highways, railroads.

With so much air-Navy pounding, everything looked easier. Somebody even thought that it might be a walk-in.

But nobody walked. They came in running fast, falling flat, getting up again, crouching, running fast, falling flat, hunting for a big rock, a shellhole, anything. Then digging in, because the Germans still had plenty of guns and ammo and defense positions behind the bluffs.

From these 100-foot-high bluffs, their guns not only commanded the beach strip of 7,900 yards but also the five small valleys reaching out into the beach. These five valleys were the keys to the tactical situation, because they were the only exits through which all of our troops and supplies would have to pass. If the Germans could keep these exits closed and pin down our troops and shoot up our ships and vehicles, the show would soon be over. But if we could force the exits, then our troops could fan out behind the hill defenses, neutralizing them and consolidating the beachhead.

We would be able to do that because the German defense was not in depth. They were concentrating their strength along the beaches.

It looked bad at first. When the Second Battalion of the 16th RCT landed on the billiard-table beach, near the mouth of the Ruquet River, they were supposed to get off the beaches in a hurry, but they couldn't go anywhere. The Germans were pouring in enfilading fire from 57mm and 75mm in concrete pillboxes in addition to mortars and 88s. They had been practicing anti-invasion maneuvers just two days before.

After a half hour, elements of the 16th and 116th Regiments, supported by 16 Army-Navy assault teams, had succeeded in establishing a ragged line on some sectors of the beach.

Everything was confusion. Units were mixed up, many of them leaderless, most of them not being where they were supposed to be. Shells were coming in all the time; boats burning; vehicles with nowhere to go bogging down, getting hit; supplies getting wet; boats trying to come in all the same time, some hitting mines and exploding; more than 30 tanks never reaching shore because of the high seas or because the German guns

June 6: "If you want to live, keep moving."

picked them off on their way in; only six out of 16 tankdozers reaching the beach; everything jammed together like a junkyard.

Soon, though, scattered units got assembled; one of the valley exits was forced open and trucks started moving off the beach. Some gaps were blown through the wire and concrete, and troops began pushing southward across the high ground, into a position near Colleville-sur-Mer. Landing farther to the left, the 164th RCT's Third Battalion fought inland, up a deep draw, moving eastward on the Anglo-American boundary.

"If you want to live, keep moving," everybody said.

When the British ship pulled slowly into port, all of the newspapermen crowded inside because it was the first boat back from the beach. The boat was loaded with dead and wounded. One of the wounded talked quickly, excitedly.

He told how he got soaking wet wading ashore with a load of explosives on his back. He was part of a demolition team of 28 that was supposed to blow gaps in the concrete wall.

"I was just coming out of the water when this guy exploded right in front of me. There just wasn't anything left of him except some of his skin, which splattered all over my arm. I remember dipping my arm in the water to wash it off. I guess I was too excited to be scared."

Farther up, on the same Omaha Beach, at the same time, the 116th RCT swept in north of Vierville-sur-Mer with two battalions in the assault wave. They had Rangers with them to help clear the beach through one of the planned exits. The First Battalion swung west along the enemy defenses occupying the western edge of Vierville, while the Second Battalion pushed into the western outskirts of St. Laurent-sur-Mer just before darkness. The Third Battalion had to fight through snipers and strong points that had been bypassed by the other two battalions.

It was expensive for them, too. Dead were scattered liberally—on the sand exposed by the low tide, in the fields below the bluff, on the bluff itself, and in the sea.

Still, an exit had been cut into the valley.

The infantry kept coming. At 0850, right on schedule, the 18th RCT was working its way across the beach, up the bluff to the edge of Colleville, cutting the Vierville-Colleville road, finally digging in on the high ground. Right after the 18th came the 26th RCT, getting into position to the right of the 18th and commanding the road between St. Laurent and Formigny. The major part of St. Laurent was soon occupied by the 115th RCT, which landed at 1045, battling its way to the south.

Twelve hours after H-Hour, only one of the planned exits was in operation. Most of our artillery was under water, but by 1600 the Seventh Field Artillery had five howitzers just off the beach, supporting the 16th RCT. Two hours later, there were 10 more howitzers of the 33d FA, backing up the 18th RCT.

During all this, the naval shore fire-control parties, which had come in with the doughboys, were talking to their big gray ships telling them what to bomb with how much.

By midnight, the tired, dirty assault forces of V Corps were spread out on a strip of free France about 10,000 yards wide, straddling the coastal road, with their deepest inland penetration estimated at 3,000 yards and their forward positions sitting on the high ground that divided the sea from the Aure River.

The two DUKWs floundered around in the rough waves, and shells kept plopping close. The big ships seemed far away, and the 15 guys in the two DUKWs kept working on their SCR-300 radio sets. At H-plus-15, they finally got through. "Testing . . . one, two, three, four, can you hear me . . . over. . . ."

There were four SCR-300s going into Utah. Two had been put in waterproofed jeeps which were knocked out long before they got onto the beach. The other two were in the DUKWs. If they got knocked out too, then the distance from shore to ships would be a million miles and a million years apart.

At H-plus-three, the two DUKWs wobbled for shore, tried to race up the beach behind cover. One was smacked square; one guy was killed, several others were wounded, the radio was smashed. For 15 hours, the single SCR-300 did the job of four, filling one hot-priority order after another: change of fire direction, more boats for the wounded, more this, more that, more everything.

For 15 hours, "Can you hear me . . . can you hear me . . . over. . . ."

They started dropping by the light of the full moon at 0130, five hours before the first waves of infantry hit Utah Beach. They started dropping from 800 invasion-decorated planes (black and white stripes) on six predetermined zones. Twenty planes never got back.

Of the two airborne divisions, the 101st was widely dispersed because of thick flak and fog. Even as late as June 8, the 101st still had only 2,100 combat effectives under unified control. But that didn't stop them from storming Pouppeville, a tiny town that was important because it blocked the causeway entrance from Utah Beach. Before glider reinforcements arrived the next night, they also had taken stubbornly defended Varreville, pushing down Purple Heart Lane toward Carentan, to link up Omaha and Utah. Purple Heart Lane went through canals and swamplands and across the Douve River. To get out of the swamps, they used bayonets for the first time in France.

Meanwhile, paratroopers of the 82d Division landed mostly west of the main Carentan-Cherbourg road, west of Ste. Mere-Eglise, which the troopers promptly walked into, cleaned out, and took over. That was the first town taken in France, and the Germans shoved in several tank attacks trying to get it back. There were two bazooka teams that took care of five tanks all by themselves. Finally the Germans pulled out. But they still tried to retake or knock out the paratroop-held bridge over the Merderet River, which the 82d was holding for the Fourth Division. They

called it Kellams Bridge, after a major who had been killed there, and they held it intact. Before the day was over, 500 planes and 500 gliders were on their way with more troopers.

They had done their job—elbowing enemy reinforcements away from the beaches.

Now they were waiting for the infantry.

"Just before we pulled out, the CO read us this message from Eisenhower about how we were all crusaders and all that, and it made us feel pretty good," said Sgt. Robert Miller of the 502d Regiment, who was in the 16th plane over France.

"It seemed like a long trip, but it was only two hours. It was a long two hours, though, because it was so hot in the plane, and with all that 120 pounds of stuff on us, most of the guys got a little sick.

"You don't talk much. I didn't say a damn word. And don't ask me what I was thinking, because I don't remember. I guess I was thinking a little about everything.

"And don't ask me what I saw when the chute opened, because I don't remember that, either. But I remember everything after I hit the ground. Seeing a guy burning in the air. Things like that.

"The most terrible thing is when you hit the ground and you don't see anybody and you don't hear anything and you're all alone. Being lonely like that is the worst feeling in the world."

The landing at Utah was smooth and quick compared with Omaha. That's because Utah was a mistake. With the Eighth RCT spearheading, the Fourth Division landed 1,500 yards southeast of the beaches at which they were supposed to land. They still got plenty of fire, almost continuous from some German battery in nearby Fontenay, but this was only a small sprinkling of the stuff they would have got if they had landed where they had intended to.

Here it was so smooth that 30 amphibious tanks of the 70th Tank Battalion, launched 5,000 yards ashore in two waves, came in with the loss of only

The waiting war . . .

Germany

one tank. Together with other regiments of the Fourth came a 90th Division RTC.

Soon after five forts were cleared around the beaches, the Fourth crossed some of the flooded area, the 12th RCT pushing through to Pouppeville to relieve the 101st Airborne, and the Eighth RCT heading for Ste. Mere-Eglise to do the same for the 82d. By midnight, they had cleared an arc-shaped area four to seven miles inland.

The expected Luftwaffe show of strength never materialized. Instead of an estimated 1,800 Nazi sorties over the beaches on D-Day, the ack-ack crews spotted several single planes that didn't stay around long enough to be shot at. The first ack-ack crew moved in at H-plus-17; the first barrage balloon was floating in the breeze at H-plus-225 minutes.

Even our artillery came in early, delivering supporting fire as quickly as H-plus-90.

But despite the smoothness and quickness of everything, there were still plenty of red crosses scattered along the beach (832 wounded were evacuated from France that first day, the others were stretched out behind cover somewhere). As for the dead, they lay where they fell. There was no time to bury the dead that first day.

This was his fourth D-Day, he said—Arzew in Africa, Gela in Sicily, Salerno in Italy, and now this one. He was a medic with the 3052d Combat Engineers, Pfc. Stanley Borok of Center Moriches, Long Island.

"If you're shooting dice," he said, "how many lucky sevens can you roll before you crap out? I figured that this time maybe I was gonna crap out, and I didn't want to crap out. But it was rough; it was sure rough."

The waves slapping and banging and the LCVP floating around in circles for two hours before H-Hour and everybody sits with a helmet between his knees, puking his guts out, so sick that he doesn't care what happens to him. But suddenly the boat starts moving in and somehow you stand up and swallow what you've got in your mouth and forget you're sick.

"I took five steps and this 88 lands about 30 feet to my left. Then I run to the right and bang! another 88, and this time my buddy is staring at his hand because his thumb is shot off. Then two more, just like that, and I found some backbone and ribs and the back of a skull with the whole face cleaned out, all of it right near the pack next to me."

His first patient was a guy who had his front tooth knocked out by a piece of shrapnel. His second was in a foxhole, buried up to his thighs.

"I didn't even notice it at first, but the blood was spurting from his chest. Two big holes. You can't plug up a guy's lungs, brother. We did all we could, though. I spotted this bottle of blood plasma we were giving some other guys and then I noticed this other one was dead, so I just took out the needle and put it in this guy's arm. But it didn't do much good. He died in my arms."

The British were having it tough those first few days. They had landed near Bayeux, two British divisions and one Canadian. Their foothold near Caen was the hinge of the whole beachhead. Three German armored divisions were hammering away at them, throwing in attack after attack. The Germans rightly figured that if they could crack through the British-Canadian position with tanks, they could race down the beaches, cut off our supplies, surround us, separate us, and chop us up.

The Germans were also particularly sensitive about our threat to Carentan and the possible linkup of the two beaches into a firm front. To keep the two beachheads separated, they threw in a single extra paratroop division, which was like adding meat to a grinder, because our buildup was steady, with more and more troops pouring over the beaches (the Second Division on D-plus-one).

But as late as June 9, the beaches still weren't completely secure. There were still plenty of sniper nests fringed all along the full length of the beach. A whole battalion got the job of housecleaning the area.

That same day, advance units of the 747th Tank Battalion rumbled into Isigny, following a terrific bombardment by artillery, tanks, and naval guns.

Rest came in increments of seconds.

Behind the tanks came the doughfeet of the 29th Division, with the dirty job of erasing the several hundred stubborn snipers who were scattered among the rubbled buildings.

At Isigny, divers of the 1055th Engineer Port Construction and Repair Group were the first to go below the surface of France, opening the canal locks to relieve the flooded countryside where our troops were fighting.

It was the continued pressure west of the Merderet River that temporarily cracked the Nazi line of resistance, and V Corps started fanning out, with the First and Second Divisions securing the high ground between the Aure and Tortonne rivers, putting the beaches almost beyond artillery range. It was near Agy that the First Division contacted the British on June 10.

Meanwhile, part of the 29th Division was securing the right bank of the Vire River, and troops of the 115th RCT began the slow crossing of the Aure. For almost two miles they waded through water three feet deep before they finally got onto the high ground on the southern side of the marshland.

"I'll never forget that swamp," said Pfc. Vito Dziengielewski of Company G, Second Battalion of the 115th Regiment of the 29th. "It was stinking, scummy, gray-looking water and it came up to our knees. I'll never forget that stink. It just made you kinda sick. As if a lot of things had died there. Then there were millions of bugs buzzing around, biting the hell out of you, and you were too tired to even shoo them away. You were so tired that you just wanted to fall down in the swamp and stretch out for a while. Some of the guys did slip and fall. If you didn't see a guy fall, it was hard to spot him because the weeds were so high and thick, just like Sea Breeze Bay in Rochester."

But even when you crossed the swamp, there was no time to sit down and take off your shoes and wipe your feet and wiggle your toes in the sun and change your socks. You could feel the wet socks sucking down in your shoes with each step, wet socks heavy with mud and scum. Some of the Joes threw their leggings away and rolled up their pants so that their legs would dry a little quicker. But nobody had a chance to change his socks for three days. Some of them didn't have to.

Back on the VII Corps front, our troops were sitting on the high ground looking down into the German flats, at the same time holding a line along the Merderet and Douve rivers. Somewhere between Carentan and Isigny, at the Auville Bridge,

a paratrooper from the 101st shook hands with a dough of the 29th, and newspapers back home headlined the fact that Utah and Omaha were now one solid front.

But they weren't. Temporarily, the junction was thin because troops on both beaches were heading away from each other, trying to swell out and make some elbow room for maneuvers. Besides, the Germans still held the high ground, which meant that they could throw artillery fire any time they wanted to on both the Isigny-Carentan highway and the vital Carentan bridge. It was the bridge we were particularly worried about, because if the Germans got the bright idea of breaking through in strength to retake it, it would have sliced an unhappy wedge into our supply line. For insurance the engineers built another bridge 2,000 yards downstream.

Troops and supplies were still flowing over the beaches in a steady stream (the Ninth and 90th Divisions), and one of the forgotten units with a private headache was the Traffic Headquarters Subsection of G-4.

"There was one vehicle for every six men in the invasion force, so you figure it out," said Sgt. Francis Scanlon, who used to be an accountant in West Medford, Massachusetts.

"Our phone used to ring all day and all night long, and people wanted to know where their unit was and which was the best way to get there and which roads were open."

He remembered something and smiled.

"The last question was the easiest to answer, because there were so few roads open to anywhere."

They had to make records of every vehicle hitting the beach, which unit, and where it was going. They did this 24 hours a day.

At certain critical sections of the road, there was an hourly flow of more than 1,700 vehicles.

"And there were only 17 men in our section," said the sergeant. Then he remembered something else.

"I'm the only one who's alive now," he said.

LEYTE, THE PHILIPPINES—Part of war has always been the exchange of conversation and dirty cracks between soldiers on opposite sides of the line, and that goes out here, too.

Usually, the American GIs come off first in the snappy dialogue department, possibly because they're dealing with their native tongue. But there is one Yank here who was bested in a brief verbal exchange, although the Jap died very soon afterward.

The Yank had the Jap cornered in a hole and courteously advanced the suggestion that he come the hell out and surrender.

The Jap had apparently met Americans before, because just before he died he shouted these imperishable words: "Come and get me, you souvenir-hunting son-of-a-bitch!"

FORT MONMOUTH, N.J.—A little GI wasn't satisfied with the size of his trousers. He kept pestering the supply sergeant to change them for him but failed to get any action. One afternoon he walked into the supply room and pleaded timidly: "Sarge, can I get a better-fitting pair of trousers?"

Without looking up the sergeant growled: "I don't see anything wrong with those pants."

Desperate, the GI replied: "Maybe you can't see it, but they're chafing me under the arms."

CAMP EDISON, N.J.—A grateful GI here wrote a letter to his election board: "Thank you for the ballot application. It came as a welcome and flattering surprise. This is the first time I have been invited to express an opinion on anything in 18 months."

FLORA ASFTC ORDNANCE PLANT, MISS.—When the librarian here sent out a card for an overdue book, it came back marked "Soldier AWOL." Title of the book: *A Farewell to Arms.*

CAMP ATTERBURY, IND.—Two days before payday, Pvt. Theodore L. Rich borrowed some money from Pvt. John H. Knodt. "That's funny," Rich said. "I'm Rich and he's Knodt, yet I'm borrowing from him."

MANILA—When a man hasn't had fresh eggs in a long time, he'll go through anything to get them. This was the case with the Eighth Regiment of the First Cavalry Division, while they were cleaning the Japs out of this area.

After long months of jungle fighting, the regiment finally got an issue of fresh eggs, and the chow line began forming several hours before breakfast. Then, just as the serving started, a Jap machine gun started peppering the area. Everyone ducked—but kept his place in line. The precious eggs were left sputtering on the stove. The only sounds heard above the Jap woodpecker and our own M1 fire were cries of "Don't let the eggs burn!"

One at a time, as their numbers came up, the cavalrymen left their cover, dashed up to the stove, hastily fried from two to four eggs and dashed off to safety to eat them.

Eventually somebody got around to knocking off the Jap.

A SOUTHWEST PACIFIC BASE—He had red hair and a likable grin that came with his face. We beat our gums casually, as two GIs from different outfits will.

He said he was 19. Temporarily he was working on the ground, but he was next in line for the tail gunner in his crew.

"Sweet planes, those B-24s," he said.

"You're right," I said. "We watch them all go

out in the morning. One of the prettiest sights I know around here."

He still had the smile.

"It's a lot prettier," he said, "when they all come back."

CAMP REYNOLDS, PA.—For seven years, Pvt. Bill Purdy of Ithaca, New York, had gone steady with a girl from Buffalo. While Bill was taking his basic at Camp Croft, South Carolina, the girl wrote him often and almost as often sent him packages of cookies.

Then another Bill Purdy came into the outfit. This one began to receive the other's letters and cookies. Finally he wrote to the girl to explain the error. Their correspondence blossomed into friendship.

Recently Pvt. Purdy visited his hometown and learned that his girl had married the other Bill Purdy. "I don't mind so much that he stole my girl," he commented, "but what about the cookies?"

NAVY NOTES—A Seabee in the Aleutians who lost a 100-pound bomb from the back of his truck found it later at another camp. It had been painted with red-and-white stripes and was being used as a barber pole.

"So that's France, huh? Well, I don't like it."
—PVT. THOMAS FLANNERY

Bougainville represented the last major link in the Solomon Islands chain not yet secured by Adm. Nimitz's forces. Operation Cherryblossom, intended to remedy that, was implemented on November 1, 1943; and though, by the end of the year, the Allies had established a workable defensive perimeter that included a naval base at Empress Augusta Bay, much of the island remained in the hands of the Japanese throughout 1944. So when you heard one of the guys say "It ain't over till it's over," you could be pretty sure he wasn't talking about baseball.

THE SECOND BATTLE OF BOUGAINVILLE

—Sgt. BARRETT McGURN
Sketches by Sgt. Robert Greenhalgh, South Pacific
April 19, 1944

EMPRESS AUGUSTA Bay, Bougainville, the Solomons—Battles are not like the ones they show in the movies; at any rate, the Second Battle of Bougainville was not. Most American soldiers, after all, are just civilians in uniform, who carry over to the battlefield many of their peacetime habits and points of view. The result is a strange melee of the grim and the unconsciously comic.

Like thousands of other Jap soldiers on the bypassed Shortlands, Choiseul, Buka, New Britain, and New Ireland, the Japs on Bougainville were faced with the choice of starving because their supply lines had been cut or of making suicidal attacks against the American military machine. Four months after our seizure of the Empress Augusta Bay beachhead, the Japs on Bougainville chose to fight. They were composed of handpicked Jap Imperial Marines and one of Japan's most celebrated army outfits, the Sixth Division, veterans of six years' fighting in China and of the rape of Nanking. The U.S. forces on the beachhead were the Americal Division, veterans of Guadalcanal, and the 37th Division, veterans of New Georgia and Vella Lavella. Both outfits have spent more than two years in the Pacific.

In the Second Battle of Bougainville, there were great numbers of maimed and dead on both sides. Some 7,000 Japs were believed killed in their assault on the prepared U.S. positions, and our forces counted 20 Jap dead to one American.

As I rode up to the battlefront, just past Coffin Corners on Major Fissell Highway, I was confronted by a bold sign: ALL SIGHTSEERS FORWARD OF THIS AREA WILL BE ARRESTED. Up at the front somebody explained that kibitzers from corps headquarters, service-command, and combat outfits not currently in the line had been scooping up all the best souvenirs and even getting in the way of the shooting. The fighting infantrymen were pretty bitter about it.

The matter came to head during the battle when a Marine darted forward under fire to relieve a fresh-killed Jap officer of his saber and pistol. A rifle poked out of a foxhole at the officer's feet and covered the Marine. "I killed that Jap to get those souvenirs," said the soldier in the hole, "and I'll kill you, if I have to, to keep them." The Marine retreated.

While the infantrymen were still too busy to hunt souvenirs, one fearless GI businessman trotted back and forth, bringing out fallen Jap rifles and selling them at $30 apiece. Another souvenir hunter refused $150 for a Jap light machine gun with bayonet attachment.

Eventually, order was established. Someone called in the MPs. Since then the fighters have been left more to themselves.

This bizarre souvenir-hunting during battle had a variety of explanations. For one thing, the Japs' tactics were to concentrate all their force at one point, throwing as much as a regiment against a 100-yard-wide stretch of wire. Consequently, battlefields were often only the size of a football field or even of a couple of tennis courts. This meant that sightseers could walk up almost to the scene of the fighting itself in comparative safety.

For another thing, the Bougainville beachhead in four months of occupation had become so American that it was sometimes easy to think of it as a secure corner of the States. A couple of hundred yards from the Americal Division front, for instance, ambulances and trucks rolling forward came upon a warning in red: DANGER. STEEP HILL. LOW GEAR.

But the principal explanation lay in the character of the enemy himself. In front-line pillboxes a popular subject for debate was whether the Japs were (a) crazy, (b) dumb or (c) literally dopey. Many thought c was the correct answer; a lot of Japs carried a soft brown pill believed to be a narcotic.

One Jap, not yet classified, walked down a trail outside our lines carrying an American helmet and (upon the word of the GI who shot him) whistling "Yankee Doodle." Another Jap, in a foxhole a few yards from American positions, raised his head to yell: "What's the score, Joe?" Before any unsuspecting Yank could put up his own head to reply, a GI off on a flank answered the Jap with an accurate shot.

During the fighting, I visited Bloody Hill (Hill 260) outside the Americal front. An acting MP came up, and I thought for a minute that I was back in basic training. A group of us had gathered around to hear about a Jap trick that cost us four dead and 22 wounded the day before, a couple of hundred yards down the east slope.

"Spread out, fellows," the MP interrupted us. "The colonel will get sore if he sees a lot of guys together. Too many get killed at one time."

We spread. We didn't want the colonel sore.

Then, at longer range, we heard the rest of the story: A patrol had succeeded in pinning down the Japs occupying several pillboxes. When five Japs raised their hands and stood up in full view, the Americans ceased firing and came out in the open, too. An interpreter told the Japs to throw down their weapons and promised them that they would not be harmed. Suddenly a wounded Jap in shorts, apparently an officer, screamed something, and the Japs dived back into their holes. Instantly, mortar fire lobbed out at the exposed Americans, hitting 26. The patrol had to withdraw.

The hilltop where we were chatting was jointly occupied by Americans and Japs at that very moment. The Japs were dug in 75 yards from us, beneath the roots of a banyan tree.

Down the hill below us resounded the "dat-da dat-da dat-da dat-da" of a machine gun, the "pow-pow" of M1s, the "pha-lot" of 4.2-inch mortars and the hammering "baa-da-da-banh" of 90mm guns. The Japs on the hill with us were quiet for a change, although two-inch slugs of shrapnel occasionally struck in our area.

A group of Americans off to one side had a burner going under coffee, and medics in an aid station in a log-covered pillbox were busy sprinkling sulfanilamide into the fresh wounds of soldiers who drifted in periodically. Getting hit was regarded as an occupational hazard, and nobody seemed to worry about it.

The colonel was not sore about anything when we met him. He volunteered to put a barrage of 4.2-inch mortar shells on the Jap positions just to show that the U.S. marksmen on Bougainville, shooting 1,400 yards from far below us on the flat beachhead, could lay shells 25 yards from our own men.

But before the colonel could put on his mortar show, the telephones from the beachhead reported that our 155mm guns were going to maul the Japs a little. Everyone on the hilltop got into holes to escape the 155 shrapnel. "On the way," shouted a fellow at the phones, and then the shells came over, crackling like ripped newspaper. The ground shivered as they hit.

Then the colonel called for his mortars. The shell bursts walked across the Jap holes, planting bushes of black smoke with brilliant blossoms of red-orange flame.

Another colonel, inventor of a Rube Goldberg flame thrower, agreed to demonstrate it. We scooted through shallow trenches to a spot 25 yards from the Japs. The colonel's invention consisted of cans of gasoline fastened to rods that fit into the mouth of a mortar. In quick succession he lobbed six cans into the Jap holes, but the mortar got so hot that the next can burst into flames and spilled only a few feet in front of the barrel. The colonel apologized; the device was not perfected yet, he said.

All of this finally succeeded in waking up the Japs or getting them sore. A Jap knee-mortar shell suddenly exploded 15 feet from us and sent me to the hospital along with two other GIs. The shell blast felt like a board slamming flat against my chest, but I didn't notice the small wounds from the fragments until moments later.

The shell served at least two purposes. It demonstrated to my satisfaction that you never know about the one that gets you until most of the damage has been done. And it labored the point that, for all the sporting flavor, this pocket-sized war was the real game and for keeps.

Among the GIs who thought the Japs were dopey was Pfc. John W. Colvard of Tallahassee, Florida, assistant BAR gunner in an Americal unit. He and Pfc. John C. Buntain of Paris, Illinois, were credited with killing 20 or 30 Japs with BARs, while mortars directed from the same pillbox took care of 50 more.

"You'd shoot one," Colvard said, "and he'd never look at you—he'd just keep on walking. Some were armed; some weren't. Most of them were just carrying sacks. We shot the Japs till they lay still. Then we shot them some more sometimes. I figured they were just doped up or dazed or something from so much shelling."

The two men did their firing from a pillbox alongside a Jap supply trail. Jap mortar shells finally drove them out after three days.

T/Sgt. Denis J. Fullerton of Lexington, Massachusetts, an Americal platoon sergeant who was converted into a stretcher case by the mortar shell that broke up the demonstration of the homemade flame thrower, leaned toward the theory that the Japs were bomb-happy. "We were picking them off all morning," Fullerton said. "The Japs would stand up there on the hilltop, shell-shocked, I suppose. My men got seven who did that today."

According to Pfc. Sebastian B. Porretto of New York City, the Japs acted "sort of happy-go-lucky, as if they didn't give a damn." Porretto set an ambush for the Japs 3,500 yards beyond our lines. With 12 bullets he killed nine and got one possible, although in training back in the States he had failed to win an expert rifleman's medal. "I didn't

Eyewitness drawing showing action against the Japanese by the 37th (Ohio) Division on Bougainville.

give a damn in the camp," Porretto explained. "But here I just shot when it counted. Just took my time, kept cool, and damn, I got them."

"I'd say they're a poor class of fighter the way they go at it," commented Pfc. Harold R. Mueller of Jamestown, North Dakota, who refused corporal's stripes to keep his BAR. "In a setup like this, they could never whip us. That's for sure." Mueller was credited with 35 Japs but insisted he and the two others in his hole got at least half the 158 Japs whose bodies littered their positions after an attack on that part of the line.

"It seems to me they don't give a damn whether they live or die, so long as they get in," said Mueller. He spotted one Jap officer trying to get into a pillbox, and he shot him. Instantly there was a terrible bawling, and Japs spilled wildly out of a banyan tree near the fallen officer. "It seemed they all wanted to get out at the same time," Mueller said. "I just mowed them down. I figured I got 25 or 30."

Some Japs came down a gully below Mueller's pillbox one night. "They were all columned up," said Sgt. Dominic Verde, a BAR man from Brooklyn. "They seemed to come in close-order drill." Maybe the Japs liked one another's company. Anyway, their close formation also pleased Mueller, Verde, and the third man in the box with them— Pvt. Jim Holtz. Mueller and Verde opened fire with BARs, and Holtz rolled grenades down the slope. Hearing the grenades, the Japs prodded for mines. Next morning, 54 Jap corpses lay there.

"The Japs are dumber'n hell," insisted S/Sgt. Delfred G. Sadler of Neponset, Illinois. "Either they've got lots of guts or they're dopey. I think they're dopey." One Jap officer tossed his pack over a fence and then climbed over the top after it. Sadler got him against the skyline.

Throughout the battle, the Japs seesawed between shrewd know-how and striking ignorance.

When the Jap artillery opened up, it directed some embarrassingly accurate fire on a number of key objectives. Several times each of the three airfields had to shut down for a few hours, and when 50 shells landed on it, an American regiment's rest area suddenly became an unhealthy place to rest.

The Japs also displayed an amazing ability to infiltrate. At one point they tunneled under the barbed wire and kept on crawling deeper into our area all night long, creeping from bush to tree, through our communication trenches and even from one heap of dead to the next. One group of Japs opened a grave we had dug for others killed two days earlier and huddled among the corpses. Still another Jap used a latrine hole as a pillbox; Sgt. Charles F. Kandl of Easton, Pennsylvania, got him with a rifle grenade.

Sadler told how the Japs sneaked through our wire with incredible stealth and silence. "But once they're inside," he said, "they stand up and give orders. One Jap shouted: 'All carbines, cease firing.' Unfortunately for him and his men, we didn't. Another Jap called out: 'Where are you, F Company?' They knew who we were, all right."

In contrast to this cunning, there were instances of stupidity. After penetrating 300 yards behind our lines and reaching a battalion CP, 50 Japs were dumb enough to sit down placidly for breakfast at dawn, the very moment our tanks rolled in for the counterattack. A point-blank hit with a 75 HE shell made one Jap vanish like a stooge in a magic show, and soon all the rest were dead. One of our major casualties was the battalion victory garden where the encounter took place.

The Japs broke most of the rules in the book. On Hill 600, they attacked frontally in waves, just what our machine gunners would have ordered. The overwhelming automatic firepower facing the Japs proved too much for them, and 700 were slaughtered in one day. Every time they pierced our lines they seemed to march into one of our 37mm antitank guns, mounted for antipersonnel use. They could hardly be blamed for that, however, because those guns were everywhere.

Pfc. Larry Haselhuhn of Rogers City, Michigan, said the Japs were afraid only of flame throwers. "They're not scared of our bullets," he said.

"Throw thermite bombs, and they'll throw them right back at you." All in all, he thought the Japs were "pretty slick" fighters, but that didn't keep him from getting seven verified plus "a lot banged up" with his light machine gun at the foot of Hill 260. Haselhuhn had plenty of respect for the Jap knee mortars. "They can lay them in on you," he said; "don't let anyone kid you about that. They can drop a shell in your hip pocket." I had good reason to agree with him.

Our tanks brought a varied reaction from the Japs. In the Americal sector, the big Jap Imperial Marines, ranging from five feet six to more than six feet, "laughed at the tanks, ran up to them, and threw grenades and Molotov cocktails on the backs to set them afire," according to Cpl. Fred Angelo of Schenectady, New York, commander of a light tank. "They couldn't harm the tanks, not with the bean shooters they had," he said. "We mowed them down with the bow gun."

In another sector, the 37th Division was facing Jap soldiers of the Sixth Division, some of them so small they looked like dolls. When the tanks struck, a few of the Japs jumped from their foxholes and ran, a maneuver that proved as fatal as the marines' daring.

What caused the most comment among the Americans was the Jap knack of digging in anywhere, anytime. "They dig in while you're shooting at them," said Haselhuhn. "I was firing with a machine gun at one fellow, and dirt was coming out all the time."

Sgt. Sadler agreed. "If they get three shovelfuls out," he said, "you can't hit them."

A few Japs tried to tunnel into tenanted American foxholes, but without success. The foxholes the Japs dug inside our lines after breakthroughs were not much wider at ground level than a man's torso, but at the bottom they were burrowed forward. Practically the only way for a GI to kill the Jap occupant with a rifle was to get behind the hole and shoot in at an angle.

Advance American patrols often heard the pounding of axes as Japs chopped logs for their dugouts. Second Lt. Carl D. Johnson of San Francisco, an American platoon leader, was 4,500 yards outside our lines when he heard a wood chopper, and presently he found himself in one of the battle's most remarkable hand-to-hand duels—a slugfest with rifle butts.

The lieutenant's carbine misfired as he leveled it at a little moon-faced Jap only an arm's length away. In too-cramped a position to return fire, the Jap swung his long Arisaka rifle as a club, slamming the flat side of the stock across the lieutenant's head. The last thing the lieutenant remembered doing before he passed out was pulling the butt of his own rifle out of the Jap's forehead. Mechanically he had dashed it in up to the oiler. He was out for 20 minutes but got back to the lines all right.

"The Jap officers may be brilliant," said Lt. Raymond H. Ross of Medford, Oregon, "but the men are sure dodos." Lt. Ross is head of the Dime-a-Dozen Club, a 10-man group of volunteer Americal snipers. The lieutenant has agreed to pay 10 cents out of his own pocket to each member of the club who kills 12 Japs, each kill to be witnessed by at least one other club member. So far the club has 21 victims, but no member has an individual total of 12. Two of the club members have been killed, and two are MIA.

"The Japs have always been so damned ignorant," Lt. Ross said. "We'll go behind their lines and kill three or four, and next day we'll go back and do it all over again. Out in the rear of Hill 260 on the fork of the Torokina River, four Japs came down the trail in their pajamas. It looked as if they had just had breakfast. They evidently didn't expect us until 0800 or 0900. We blew them all to hell with M1s. Not that they're not brave fighters. They fight like wildcats. But they're so easy to catch."

Some of the Jap officers also are far from model warriors, Lt. Ross said. On one patrol the Dime-a-Dozen Club, plus a large party that had gone out with them on the job, spotted a Jap officer and managed to surround him with 69 men before he suspected anything. Lt. Ross whistled because he felt guilty about shooting him in the back. Then, as the officer turned, the lieutenant shot him through the buttocks. He wanted to take him prisoner. The Jap officer played dead until Lt. Ross

From a jeep, an American watches curiously as a big MP takes a little Jap prisoner to the rear.

approached, and then leaped at him bare-handed. A BAR man sliced the Jap officer in two, from the belly through the head.

S/Sgt. Ralph E. Brodin of Spooner, Minnesota, who said he joined the Dime-a-Dozen Club to earn the down payment on a ring for his girl, a WAC corporal, was the leading enlisted man in the group, with three Japs to his credit. Lt. Ross was showing the way with eight, plus another five for which he couldn't get club credit because there were no club witnesses.

One Dime-a-Dozener, S/Sgt. Harry E. Schulte of Gary, South Dakota, was not a rifleman but a mortarman. "I joined the club," he said, "with the idea of getting a few Japs with the old rifle, I guess, instead of indirectly." He had two so far. Schulte was also doing okay at his platoon job. On top of Hill 608, he had a home of canvas, bamboo, and sandbags, labeled "Sky Room."

Across a 700-foot-deep ravine from Schulte was Hill 11-11, from which the Japs were firing 77s and 47s for a while, taking advantage of the jungle cover that prevented the Americans from locating them. But Schulte figured out a system. For hours he stared at the green slope, waiting for a gun flash. When it came, he fired instantly with his 50-caliber machine gun and kept up tracer bursts until

When Sgt. Greenhalgh sketched the stockade, one Jap inspected his drawing and chuckled, "Very good."

our heavy artillery could come in on the target pointed by Schulte's fingers of flame. A Jap 47 objected one day and threw several rounds at Schulte, but the gangling farmer boy said: "I got in the last shot. I don't know whether he ran out of ammunition or got tired or what."

Like everybody else on the beachhead who didn't want to go nuts, the Dime-a-Dozen Club looked for laughs even on patrol. Once they heard a noise in the jungle darkness and stealthily surrounded the spot from which the noise had come. As guns pointed, they flashed on a jungle light. A slimy-tailed, terrier-sized ball of fur blinked in the glare. It was a "banana bear."

Another time, Pfc. Richard Kowitz of St. Paul, Minnesota, had to lie still while a big green jungle spider with inch-long legs built its web under the peak of his helmet. A Jap was combing the area, and the slightest move would have spoiled Kowitz's camouflage. So he had to lie there and watch the spider spin. The club members thought the whole episode very funny.

The Dime-a-Dozeners worked out several new wrinkles in jungle fighting. In addition to blacking their faces and pulling their hats low over their eyes, the members painted their weapons OD. On large patrols, the men slept in groups, with a sturdy vine reaching under their arms so that a single jerk would awaken the whole party. That way, only three men needed to stay awake in a patrol of 40 or more.

Not the least odd feature of the battle scene was the behavior of Jap prisoners in the stockade. Our men preferred killing Japs to capturing them, until a case of beer was offered for each captive. Most of the Jap prisoners were deep brown and quite pleased with life as they washed their laundry or did other personal chores inside the wire. One Jap with a splitting grin offered sunglasses to a group of GIs who were squinting into the sun to stare at him. Another prisoner cut out the characters in an American comic strip and decorated his tent with them. When Sgt. Robert Greenhalgh, *Yank* staff artist, sketched the stockade, one Jap asked to see the drawing. "Very good," he chuckled.

Two other Japs threw the Bougainville panorama into what was probably the correct focus. The first Jap clutched his army's favorite weapon, the bayonet, and charged a tank with it. The tank ran over him. The second Jap, a prisoner, asked permission to broadcast a message to his comrades over a front-line PA system. "With our ancient ideas," he said to the other Japs, "how can we expect to win over the arms possessed by the civilized and world-prominent country of America?"

That seems to be just about the score. The Samurai swords, cruel weapons used for generations to lop off the heads of the Emperor's powerless enemies, are now mostly souvenirs for American curio collectors. Our automatic and heavy weapons are seeing to that.

Ironically, considering FDR's earlier concerns, it was the Japanese who wondered whether the Allies weren't utilizing Alaska as an eventual springboard to Tokyo. With that in mind, and with the Aleutians firmly in American hands, the Nipponese task force turned a substantial share of its ack-ack guns northward, in a perpetual search for any signs of air activity. To the bored GIs on Attu and Kiska, it was a periodic reminder that complacency can kill.

MESS HALL IN ALASKA

—Sgt. A. N. Maloff
August 4, 1944

ALASKA—He stood out by the side of the runway and waited, as he always did. When the weather permitted, the planes would take off in the morning and come back in the afternoon. Or they would take off in the afternoon and come back in the evening. He would always stand by the side of the runway and wait for them to return. Sometimes he would stand a long time, and they would never come back.

He was the only one who came out to watch anymore, and the others never understood it. "Joe Buza," they said, "he's nutty. He's plane-nutty." He used to tell them he had to know how many tables to set up in his mess hall, but they laughed at him. He himself didn't know exactly why he wanted to watch, but he was always there. Every day there was a flight, he would walk over to Operations and ask when the men were coming back. If it was Kiska, it meant he had to prepare an early lunch; if it was Attu, he would have the KPs set up a few tables in the middle of the afternoon. Then he would walk out to the runway and watch.

He dug his face deeper into his mackinaw, trying to shield the tip of his nose with his collar. He moved around a little to keep from standing still and shoved his back into the wind. The sound of footsteps behind him made him turn around. It was one of the cameramen from the photographic unit at the hangar line.

"You sweating it out, too?"

"Yeah," Joe said. "Will they be coming in soon?"

The man nodded. "In a minute, I guess. There's just one. A fighter. We took a gun out of the nose and put a camera in. Something about one of the boys spotting some Jap ships."

They heard the engine before they saw the plane. It must have been hidden in the fog. Then it circled slowly, dropped its wheels, gently lowered itself onto the ground and taxied down the runway. It pulled up at the end of the field, turned around, and moved back to the center again, where the mechanics were waiting for it.

The pilot lifted himself out of the cockpit and jumped down. He turned to the cameraman and grinned in satisfaction. "This is it, boy. Just what the doctor ordered. Develop them right away and bring them over. The colonel will want them right away." The pilot started unstrapping his parachute. "Right away," he said again.

Joe walked back to the mess hall. He never used to worry about feeding the men, but it was different now. He didn't like to set up the tables with all the food and watch some of them stay that way—clean and untouched. Some days some of the planes didn't come back, which meant some of the men would never eat again. Those were the days he hated, and he always made the KPs elbow the floor and told the cooks to make hamburgers or a stew so the unused meat wouldn't go to waste.

He kicked open the door to the kitchen and entered. The cooks had already started to prepare supper and the KPs were standing around, smoking and waiting to see whether they could get a couple of hours off. He sat down on a box and picked up the menu for tomorrow. One of the men came over to him. "Sarge," he said, "we set up the mess hall for supper already. Is it okay for us to take off for a couple of hours?" Joe bent his head toward the dining room and looked it over. "Okay, Sherwood. Be back by four. Don't make me send for you."

He half expected the telephone call that came in the evening. Lt. Johnson of the Operations Room. There was a big flight the next day, starting early. Could he have an early breakfast ready for about 30 or 35 men, early, say about 0430? "Sure, lieutenant, anything. Anything at all. Hot cakes and cereal and—Yeah, okay, lieutenant. Anything I can do—"

Something was up, something pretty big. He could see that by the way the men ate their chow the next morning, concentrating on every bite they put in their mouths. Maybe it was what that fighter brought in yesterday; he didn't know. There was too much quiet in his mess hall, and the

men passed the coffee too promptly. It bothered him. Then they got up and left. Joe liked it that the tables were dirty and the food bowls were mostly empty. That was the way it should be. No waste, and everyone in his place.

At Operations, after the rest of the squadron had eaten breakfast, they told him he could expect the planes back in time for dinner if everything went all right. You couldn't be sure, because you never knew how much flak and fighter opposition the men would meet. But dinner looked like a safe bet, maybe even a little earlier.

The clerk at the desk smiled. "Buza, I can't figure you out," he said. "You're like an old maid half the time. Always afraid you'll be missing something. Why don't you relax?"

"It's not that," Joe answered. "It's the tables. I got to get them ready, don't I?"

By the time he reached the mess hall again, the men were just finishing the cleaning. There wasn't so much to do after breakfast—clean off the tables and sweep the floor. Someone would bring out the silverware and the cups, enough for each man; then they would wait until just before the men came to put out the food and coffee. Joe walked over to the pantry and pulled out a pack of paper napkins. He saved them for special occasions, like Christmas dinner or maybe a squadron party sometime, but today was special—more special than other days, because 14 of the big boys took off today, and that was more than usual. He put the napkins under the silverware and made sure the forks were at the left. He lit a cigarette and took a long pull. In another hour or so he would walk out to the field to watch them come in. Another hour at least.

The wail of a siren jerked him to his feet. It took a second before he recognized it; then he ran to the window. A field ambulance tore down the company street, skirted the corner on two wheels, and raced for the runway. Everyone seemed to be running. Men streamed out of the hangars and pulled up sharply at the edge of the flying field. A jeep shot out of the headquarters enclosure and dashed toward the firehouse. The red light at the head of the control tower started blinking furiously, then remained on. A plane sitting at the end of the field spun around and pulled itself out of the way.

Joe shoved through the crowd. Then he saw it, limping in out of the fog. He saw it circle slowly and lose altitude. The wings leaned over to one side. The wheels edged into position and the plane started to level off. The engine whined in an unsteady cry, and the body quivered with the effort. Painfully the nose tilted downward, and as painfully the plane slipped onto the runway, bounced nervously into the air for a few feet, dropped onto the ground and rolled to a stop. It just lay there.

Joe pushed forward with the others. They watched the crew come out of the plane, bunched together as if for protection. The captain punched a finger through the black hole where a .50 caliber had struck. His face was blank and half-believing, tired beyond weariness. The crew stood around him, waiting for him to do something. Then the words poured out as if he couldn't stop them, as if he could tell his story only once and then forget it.

"They caught us. They were waiting for us and they caught us. We were like rats, caught, and we didn't know what hit us. In the fog and in the clouds, that's where they were. Forty, 50, something like that, and they hit us with everything. We didn't have a chance. They bombed us from above and then they passed over us with their machine guns. It happened quick, like I'm telling it. You could see how our men exploded with the ships. Only some exploded. Some burned. We got away. I don't know how. They hit us with everything they had."

He stopped and pulled his lips tight over his teeth. The crowd made room for him, and he passed through it. His crew followed after him, still not talking.

Joe Buza stayed there after everyone had gone. One out of 14! No one was coming back now, but he stayed there and waited. He pecked at the ground with the toe of his shoe. He didn't want to go back just yet, because the others would be eat-

ing and he didn't want to see them. Maybe another would return. He propped a cigarette between his lips before he remembered he couldn't smoke there. Overhead the sky was empty and the fog was thick.

But for the KPs clearing away the plates, the dining room was empty. Everyone had eaten. Tables were covered with patches of bread and half-used platters of butter. On the floor was a little pool of water where someone had spilled a cup. He pushed the water with his foot so it would dry quickly.

In the back were the unused tables where the combat crews were supposed to eat. They would have to be cleaned off now, just like the others. Just as if the men had eaten there, even though they hadn't. The floor was clean of crumbs and all the bread was still neatly piled. Joe toppled a pile so it wouldn't look so neat. Tomorrow the men would have hamburgers for dinner because he couldn't waste the meat. He picked up the meat dish.

A KP had been standing behind him. "Sarge," he said, "I think this butter ought to be put away. It's been standing pretty long." Joe looked at him for a minute before he understood. There was a lost mission in his voice. "Soldier, it's not your job to think here," he said. "It's your job to scrub this floor till it's clean enough to kiss." He moved into the kitchen and stopped suddenly. Muttering to himself, he turned, walked to the garbage can, and dumped the meat.

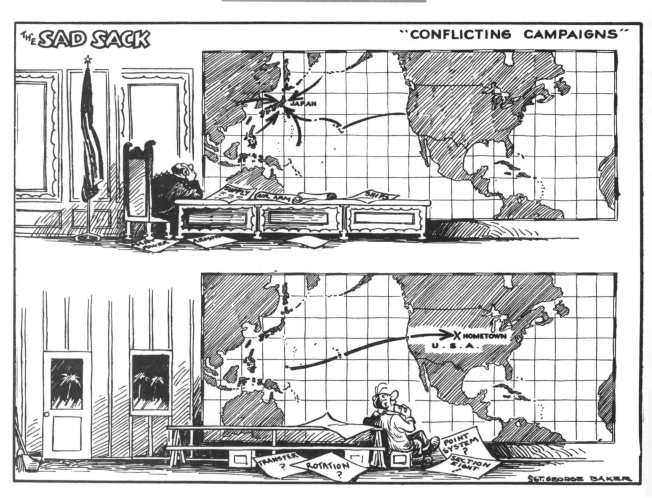

Despite the way their families had been treated back home—and perhaps because if it—their loyalty was, at the very least, remarkable. Proportionately, they were decorated more than any other American squad in the ETO, a distinction they earned the hard way.

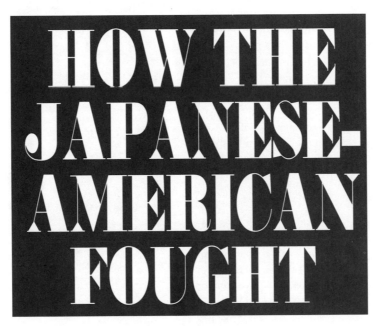

HOW THE JAPANESE-AMERICAN FOUGHT

—Sgt. JAMES P. O'NEILL
August 25, 1944

THERE ARE three outfits that will remember the little Tuscany town of Belvedere for a long while to come. One of them is a German *SS* battalion, the remnants of which continued on from Belvedere, spearheading a drive toward Naples and the nearest PW camp. The other two are the American 100th Infantry Battalion and the 442d Combat Team, both of them composed of Americans of Japanese ancestry.

The 442d was a recent arrival, but the 100th had been in Italy a long, long time. The men of the 100th went in at Salerno and had since fought through almost every major action from the Volturno to Rome. In a battalion of 1,300 men, they had more than 1,000 Purple Hearts.

The story of Belvedere really began after Rome fell, when the 100th was pulled out of the line and sent to bivouac in the pleasant countryside just north of the city. There it joined the 442d. It was a happy day for both outfits; most of the 100th's younger brothers, cousins, and friends were in the 442d, and they hadn't seen each other since shortly after Pearl Harbor, when the 100th left Hawaii, the home of many of its members, for training in the United States.

For three days, the brass hats left the two outfits alone. The kids of the 442d plied their older brothers with questions of war. The older brothers, like all combat men, dodged these questions and asked questions of their own about Hawaii and their families and girls. Together the outfits visited Rome, buying souvenirs and baffling the Romans, who decided they must be Japanese prisoners.

After the three days, the two outfits went to work. For 14 days, the men of the 100th drilled the 442d, sweating with the kids from morning to night, cursing and pushing and ridiculing and encouraging them, giving the final polish that makes a man as much of a combat soldier as he can be before combat. And in the evenings, they would sit around together and drink *vino* and sing their soft Hawaiian songs.

Then, on the 17th day after the fall of Rome, the 100th Infantry Battalion and the 442d Combat Team were pulled into the line, and two days later they headed for the beautiful little hilltop of Belvedere.

The 100th was the first to go into the line. Its objective was a small town about seven miles below Belvedere. The German strategy since Rome had been to fight in pockets on each sector of the front, and the mission of the 100th was to clean up one of these rear-guard pockets. The men of the 100th did it in two days, chasing the Germans up the inland road toward Florence and meeting little resistance until they neared the valley directly before Belvedere. There they were stopped by four 155mm cannons and by several self-propelled guns. The German artillery also was holding up a battalion to the right of the 100th. This battalion was trying to use a crossroad, but the Germans had it zeroed in. Division sent orders for the 100th to stop while division artillery tried to clear out the Germans. When the barrage was over, the 100th was pulled out and the 442d was sent in to assault the German positions.

It didn't work. The 442d made an initial breakthrough, but that was all. The Germans counterattacked against the 442d's left flank, throwing in a mess of mortars. They pushed the 442d out of the valley and pinned the outfit down in an exposed and highly uncomfortable position in a wheat field. Meanwhile, the German artillery had moved back and was still stopping the battle on the right of the 442d.

American soldier: Pvt. Henry (Slim) Nakamora.

Back in their bivouac areas, the men of the 100th heard what was happening to the 442d and began to get itchy. The enlisted men began to clean and oil their guns; the officers brought out their maps and began to think. And then, finally, the 100th had orders and a mission.

The mission was simple. All the battalion had to do was to infiltrate the German positions in the valley, the hill that Belvedere was on, and the town itself; to encircle and capture the town and cut off the main road out of Belvedere that runs north to Sasseta and Florence. That was all. Division intelligence said the position was being held by an SS battalion that had an OP in the town directing artillery and mortar fire on the 442d and the battalion on its right.

A and B Companies of the 100th were assigned to assault positions, with the rest of the battalion in reserve. The jump-off was at 1200 hours. By 1300, both companies had infiltrated completely around Belvedere and were behind the town at a farm called Po Pino. The rest of the battalion dug in among the olive groves at the edge of the valley. B Company was to initiate the attack, while A Company was to rendezvous at Po Pino.

Commanding B Company was Capt. Sakae Takahashi. He planned the attack this way: The First Platoon under S/Sgt. Yeki Kobashagawa was to take the town; the Second Platoon under Lt. James Boodry, a former Regular Army dogface from Boston, was to move on the main road leading out of town and cut it off; the Third Platoon under Lt. Walter Johnston of New York was to cover the northern position of the company. The heavy-weapons platoon was to move with the Second Platoon and cover the road north to Sasseta.

Sgt. Kobashagawa broke his First Platoon into three squads, two of which encircled Belvedere on each side while the sergeant led his squad into town. On the outskirts, Kobashagawa's squad located the Jerry OP wires, which were cut by one of the point men, Pfc. Seikichi Nakayama. Then the squad moved cautiously into town. It was quiet, and the men were almost up to the modern, three-story Fascist headquarters when two German machine pistols opened up on them. They

ducked behind some houses and settled down to work.

Kobashagawa and two men, loaded with grenades, moved toward the big building under cover of the others. The machine pistols were located in a doctor's office on the first floor. One of the men was hit, but the sergeant and the other man got to the house next door. They tossed four grenades in the window, and the machine pistols were through. Four Germans came out of the building, and the covering fire killed three and wounded one.

That left about 20 Germans in the building. They started to retreat the back way and out of town toward the valley. They fought from house to house and then ducked over a ravine and down into the valley. The two squads encircling the town caught some of these Germans coming out of the ravine.

When Kobashagawa's platoon assembled again at the edge of town, it ran into machine-gun fire from a German half-track located in front of one of the valley farmhouses. The platoon also could hear the noise of a battle opening up to the right. Kobashagawa decided to dig in and call for mortar support before jumping the farmhouse.

The mortar support didn't come. The heavy-weapons platoon had discovered a nice reverse slope and set up there to cover the road to Sasseta. The platoon was about to open up on some Germans trying to make a getaway when the point squad of the Second Platoon, preceding the weapons platoon, arrived at the edge of the hill and practically ran into the four German 155s that had been firing on the 442d and its flank battalion. The Germans had just moved into this position and were preparing to fire.

They never did. Lt. Boodry, commanding the platoon, had Cpl. Hidenobu Hiyane, communications man, get the weapons platoon on the radio. Cpl. Hiyane contacted T/Sgt. M. Nakahara and gave him the essential data. Their conversation must have sounded terrifying if any Germans were listening—it was conducted in a personal code, combining Hawaiian dialect with Japanese and American slang.

The plan worked, all right. While Lt. Boodry and his platoon moved in on the German battery with carbines and M1s, the weapons platoon cut loose with its mortars. In five minutes, 18 Germans had been killed and all four of the 155s were out of action.

The Germans knew they were encircled now and tried to make a break up the main road toward Sasseta. Capt. Takahashi ordered the Third Platoon to move up and cover the flank of the Second Platoon. He told both rifle platoons and the weapons platoon to hold their fire until the Germans made a break, which sooner or later they had to do. And they did.

Seventeen of their amphibious jeeps loaded with Jerries swung out of an olive grove and headed hell-bent for Sasseta. The three platoons let them get onto the road and then let them have it. All 17 jeeps were knocked out. Two light machine guns manned by Sgt. K. Yoshimoto and Sgt. Nakahara accounted for most of the damage, and the riflemen picked off the Germans as they ran from the jeeps.

Right after that, four German trucks filled with men broke from the olive grove and tried to swing around the knocked-out jeeps. The first two made it, but the other two were stopped. Lt. Boodry picked out one driver with his carbine and one of his riflemen got the other. The trucks piled up in the middle of the road, blocking it effectively and preventing any further German escape. "The next half hour," said Pvt. Henry (Slim) Nakamora, a bazookaman of the Second Platoon, "that valley was like a big box of chocolates and us not knowing which piece to take first."

The rest of the Germans retreated to the grove and dug in. Sgt. Kobashagawa's platoon on top of the hill picked off a few of them. The sergeant was good and sore about not getting his mortar support and kept calling for it, but the mortars were needed somewhere else. Capt. Takahashi had decided to make a frontal attack on the farmhouse with the Third Platoon. The First Platoon was assigned to keep the Germans busy in the grove, while the Second Platoon was to knock off any snipers on the platoon's flank.

When the Germans in the farmhouse saw the Third Platoon moving toward them, they opened fire. The Third returned the fire, aided by elements of the First and Second Platoons, and moved in and around the farmhouse. There was a German half-track there, with two Germans working its machine gun. Cpl. Toshio Mizuzawa, who had plopped a rifle grenade into the backseat of a jeep earlier in the day, scored another basket when he dropped one into the half-track and rendered it highly ineffective.

This was enough for the occupants of the farmhouse. They came out with their hands up.

Sgt. Kobashagawa had seen the Germans reforming in the olive grove and had spotted a PzKW IV tank there. He relayed this information to Capt. Takahashi, who didn't exactly relish the idea of running into a tank with so little ammo. The captain sent an urgent call for A Company and ordered the Third Platoon back to the reverse slope to join the weapons platoon, leaving a patrol to scout the area. The patrol consisted of Sgt. A. Governagaji and Pfc. Teneyshi Nakana, working as a BAR team, and Pvt. Nakamora with his bazooka. Snipers tried to get them but were silenced by Lt. Boodry and a squad from his platoon.

Then the German counterattack started. The tank rolled out of the olive grove and started up the slope. It was followed by a half-track, and behind that were some soldiers with two light machine guns and what was left of a rifle company. Sgt. Governagaji of the patrol crawled over to Pvt. Nakamora and asked him if he wanted to take a crack at the tank with his bazooka.

"Yeah," said Pvt. Nakamora, who is a man of few words.

Sgt. Governagaji nodded and started to crawl back to his position. On the way he was hit by a slug from the tank. Then the tank bounced into view about 15 yards from Nakamora. He aimed, fired, and hit the tank right in the belly. He reloaded and hit it in the same place. The tank moved about 10 yards and blew up. The concussion knocked out Nakamora and killed Sgt. Governagaji, who was lying about 10 feet away. Two Germans started out of the tank, but Pfc. Nakana, working the BAR alone, got both before they were halfway out of the turret.

The weapons platoon on the slope took care of the half-track, knocking off its tread. The Second Platoon had run out of ammunition and withdrawn; the weapons platoon had one box of machine gun ammo left. Now the German rifle company with the two machine guns started up the hill. The dogfaces didn't know what they were going to do, but they hadn't counted on Nakana with his BAR. Nakana waited until the Germans were within 50 yards, then knocked out the four Jerries carrying the two machine guns. The rest of the rifle company hightailed it back to the olive grove. The counterattack was over.

After that, the 100th mopped up. B Company called it a day; A Company moved through and chased the retreating Germans among the olive groves and up and down the ravines. When B Company took stock, they found they had one box of ammo left. It was now 1660 hours.

In the valley of Belvedere lay 84 dead Germans; headed for the rear were 32 prisoners and 29 wounded Jerries. By 1900 hours, A Company had accounted for 26 more German dead, 18 prisoners, and 9 wounded. The box score of Jerry equipment was: 13 motorcycles, 19 jeeps, 7 trucks, 2 half-tracks, 1 PzKW IV tank, 1 SP gun, 2 antitank guns, 4 155mms, 1 radio CP, and 1 battalion CP with 20 telephones.

The 100th lost one man and had eight wounded. The next morning the outfit was relieved. It bivouacked that day with the 442d.

After a couple of days both of them went back into the line.

"I don't beef about a heavy message, Captain, but let's not get too flowery."—Sgt. Edward Urban

—Sgt. Len Zinberg
October 5, 1945

THE TWO soldiers sat deep in the soft luxury of their Pullman seat, staring at the American countryside racing by the train window. They had been looking out that window for nearly four days. The pfc. said, "Joe, I'm getting a funny feeling in my guts, like before we go in the line. Think of it, in less than an hour I'll be home!"

The corporal smiled and said quietly, "It will be good to be home."

"Good?" The pfc. laughed. "Brother, it will be sensational! You got to be overseas for a couple of years to learn what home really means. One more hour . . . think of me walking down the old street, the kids looking at my Combat Infantryman's Badge, my battle stars, my girl and my folks asking all sorts of silly questions. Of course, it won't be nothing to the welcome you'll get, Joe. They'll have the band out for you. Silver Star, Bronze Star, Purple Heart with cluster . . . you're a damn hero!"

"Yeah, some hero," Joe said, looking out the window again.

For a while they were both quiet, then the pfc. yelled, "Did you see that little white house we just passed, the one with the funny green shutters and fancy garden? That's like my house, only mine's bigger. I got my own room."

"I shared a room with my kid brother," Joe said. "Our house is a small brown bungalow. Got avo-cado and orange trees growing in the back, and a big garden. Some garden, my father sure liked to fuss in it. Funny the way a guy keeps thinking of things. At Anzio, in France, in the mountains before the Po Valley . . . I spent a bunch of time dreaming about that house."

"Your folks don't live there," the pfc. said, hesitating. "I mean you told me . . ."

The corporal said, "My folks are in Arizona. I want to see the house first, then I'll hitch a ride down to see my folks. Country sure is green around here."

"You bet, that's my country," the pfc. said proudly.

As the train pulled into the neat little town, the pfc. got his bags and shook hands with Joe and said nervously, "Well, after all the times it was supposed to be 'it,' this is really it. So long, pal. Glad I met you on the train. Take care of yourself, and don't forget and pull any of that '*Dove casa?*' stuff over here!"

Joe laughed politely at the corny wisecrack, and they shook hands. When the train stopped, Joe watched the pfc. jump off into the arms of a kindly, stout woman who hugged him and cried. A gray-haired man kissed him and tried not to cry. A pretty young blonde girl shook his hand awkwardly, then suddenly hugged and kissed him. All the time, a big clumsy dog tried to jump on the soldier, kept running around and around, his tail going like a propeller. Other people stepped forward, anxious to slap the pfc. on the back, shake his hand.

As the train pulled out, Joe caught a quick glimpse of the soldier's face—he was laughing and crying, trying to hug them all at once.

It took another 12 hours before the train crossed the California line. Joe sat in his seat nervously, leaving it only to go to the dining car or the men's room. People stared at him politely, coldly, noticing his blue Combat Infantryman's Badge, his two rows of brag ribbons.

The town was full of the afternoon heat when Joe got off. It was the kind of heat he liked, and he was glad to be walking once more instead of sitting. There was no one to meet him; the few men at the station merely stared at him and whispered to one another as he passed.

Every detail of the town was exactly as he had so often pictured it: the big high school where he had played basketball, Shaw's Bakery with its wonderful, friendly odor of baking bread and cakes, the modernistic movie house, the firehouse with the bright red engines and the men lounging by the door—even the spotted fire dog looked the same.

He passed the drugstore and saw Pop Anders still behind the soda fountain. Joe grinned as he thought of the great sundaes Pop could whip up. The old man looked at him and didn't smile. Joe walked faster. Down the main street and its stores, turn right, past the crowded fruit market where he had once worked—all new faces staring at him, nobody there he remembered. Another right turn, and down a street lined with trees and orderly white bungalows, service flags hanging in the windows, women busy in the kitchens. A tiny redheaded girl was playing house on one of the lawns. She looked up at him, then said shyly, "Hello, soldier."

Joe smiled. "Hello, kid." Must be a new family living there, he thought. Pretty kid. Sure, they're new, that used to be Eddie's house. Eddie and his cute sister . . . wonder where she is now?

Joe turned another corner, his heart beating wildly. He stopped in front of *his* house. The small front lawn was full of weeds; somebody had chopped down the orange trees. The boarded-up windows had been smashed, the porch and steps were broken and burned, junk and ancient garbage had been hurled at the house, leaving stains on the brown walls. In crude letters someone had painted, KEEP OUT! NO DAMN JAP RATS WANTED HERE!

The corporal didn't even drop his barracks bag. He just stood there, staring at the house, sweat rolling down his yellow face. This wasn't the house he had dreamed of at Anzio. This house didn't have the warm, happy air of the others, it looked haunted and desolate. This was the worst house he had ever seen; it looked even more miserable than the shelled stone houses of Italy.

Joe stared at the house for a long time, then he turned and went away, walking with slow, weary steps.

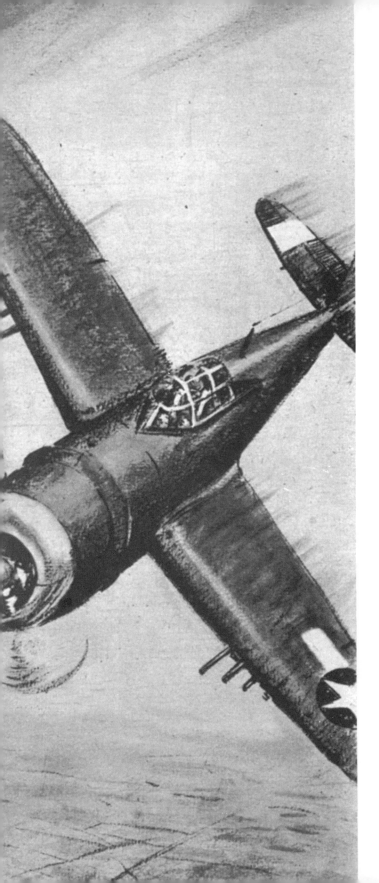

"BIG FRIEND"

—By Sgt. SAUL LEVITT
Yank Staff Correspondent
July 9, 1944

There was nothing remarkable in the relationship of the chubby bumblebee fighter and the crippled Fort, and it happened many times before in this theater—but some day the crew of a certain B-17 would like to meet the P-47 pilot who helped them home, and maybe stand treat at the local pub. It would be a nice way to cement a beautiful friendship, they think.

ENGLAND—For a certain long moment, seeing the speck in the sky, nobody could be sure. They were 350 miles from home, and this air they so sluggishly moved through was German air, those clouds spread underneath no real protection against the big flak guns below.

The bomber was in trouble. Minutes before, its formation had vanished over the horizon, going homeward. The bomber was 90 miles off course. It almost rolled in the air like a rudderless boat in a heavy sea. Its tail section was a sight—the upper part of the rudder and vertical stabilizer were sheared off. Head on, the view was even more interesting. Number-one engine had no prop, and number-two was feathered, with about a foot sheared off each of its three blades, as if steel scissors had been at work.

Both pilots were cagey on encountering each other in this enemy sky. The bomber pilot, a big young man, a veteran of combat, could only wait. But the fighter stood far off and above, made a couple of slow passes in the sky, inviting the guns of the Fort, just in case it was the enemy.

The navigator of the Fort thought, with a certain amount of embarrassment, I bet the guy is wondering how we stay up. Then the fighter swept closer, and identification on both sides was almost simultaneous. That big round nose, the chubby bumblebee shape of the fighter was unmistakable, and over the interplane frequency the bomber pilot heard that first calm call-up which was to be repeated all the way home:

"Big Friend, from P-47, what can I do for you?"

"P-47, from B-17 in distress, stay with us, stay with us."

The calm voice came back, "Big Friend, we will stay with you."

This was at X miles from the Ruhr. At 13,000 feet, just above the overcast, the B-17 labored on—its speed of slightly more than 100 m.p.h just around stalling point.

The fighter pilot glanced at his gas. The Fort was slow; it would take time to get him in. The fighter pilot would be close on gas; but he thought he would hang on.

Just to make sure it was real, the bomber pilot called again and the voice came back, "Big Friend, we will stay with you all the way to the English coast. Can you stay above overcast?"

"P-47, from B-17 in distress, we will maintain airspeed and altitude as long as possible."

In the enemy sky, nothing showed but the friendly fighter. Yet down below, the bomber pilot knew that the invisible but ever-alert radio knew him, knew where he was. However, he had his fighter now, and the fighter in command of a flight had brought his three other planes into a protective screen, which the B-17 pilot did *not* know, then.

The men of the bomber could afford to relax a

little now. Because the fighter was acting as their guns, they could get rid of the heavy weight of their own armament and ammunition, lighten their plane, pick up the plane's speed above that dangerous 105-m.p.h. crawl through space. The pilot called back, "Jettison all equipment you can, including guns."

The men were now just minutes past a bad dream, a bad dream of a terrific battle with a wind-milling prop that had threatened to tear a wing off. Twice, fire had leaped out of the engine cowling. A single piece of flak over Berlin, lodging in the oil sump of the number-one engine, had started this.

The copilot had called back, "All right, men, stand by for bailing out, this looks like it."

One of the gunners, thinking he was supposed to get out of the ship, was at the escape door before a crewmate pulled him back. The pilot had dived, then nosed his plane up, with the left wing vibrating like a seesaw until the prop of the damaged engine was torn off. But the free, rotating prop, still full of venom, had sheared off the tips of the number-two prop and then, still whirling, had cut off the upper half of the tail rudder and fin.

The pilot liked the sound of the fighter's voice. It was very calm, and it was always there. The B-17 went through clouds, and in the silence and darkness of the clouds the bomber pilot called again, "P-47, stay with us."

"Big Friend, we are still with you," said the fighter's voice.

And when the bomber came out on the other side of the cloud layer, there was the ferocious little bumblebee of the P-47 with its eight guns—and around the bomber but not so the crew could always see them—three more fighters with guns. That made thirty-two guns.

He was in the clear, thought the bomber pilot. Soon they'd "cross out" into the North Sea. The worst that could happen now would be a wetting if he had to ditch. He tried to transfer gas from his dead-engines to his working engines, but the fuel-transfer motor was burning, the fuel line leaking. There were 50 gallons in number four, 70 in number three—and they were still inside Germany.

The pilot called back to his radio operator, "radio, from pilot, can you contact Air Sea Rescue?"

"Pilot from radio, that damn vibration knocked out the liaison, it won't work."

The pilot called the fighter again.

"P-47, from B-17 in distress, we are low on gas, low on gas, may have to ditch. Can you contact Air Sea Rescue for us?"

"Big Friend, from P-47," said the calm voice, "I have already contacted Air Sea Rescue."

"Roger, thank you," said the pilot.

They were over the North Sea now—a dangerous little sea, this one. Without Air Sea Rescue you could come down and land in dinghies and float for a long time—so long, sometimes, that none of your friends would ever see you again.

"P-47, are you still with us?"

"Big Friend, we are still with you," said the fighter.

The B-17 crawled through the air over the North Sea.

"Rescue launch below you now," said the fighter, lightly.

"Roger, I'll keep going until I have to come down."

"Okay, I'll give you the launch's position."

And as the launch fell astern, the fighter called out its position.

"Launch off to the left . . . launch behind you now."

High above, the bomber pilot could see the fighter sporting, then coming by his window, but too fast for him to see the pilot.

"Big Friend, I can see the English coast, about thirty to thirty-five miles ahead of you."

"P-47, from B-17, many thanks."

"Roger."

The bomber pilot looked at his gas gauges. It seemed impossible that they could still be up there. Whether they would make the coast or land in the sea was a matter of drops of gas—

"Keep going, Big Friend," said the quiet voice, "you're doing fine."

"P-47, from B-17, do you think you can get us QDM to the nearest airfield?"

"Stand by."

The crewmen were clustered in the radio room, staring through the two small windows. The pilot, poking his way underneath the cloud layer at 3,000 feet, could see the shape of England's coast beneath him. Mudflats showed. This bomber pilot, a stubborn, skilful veteran who had brought battered planes home before and who was, moreover, a thrifty guy with Army equipment like a Fort worth a quarter of a million bucks, thought: son-of-a-bitch, they didn't get us, no ditching either, and at the worst now, we might have to land on these flats—

"Big Friend, from P-47, your bearing on nearest field to you is Y degrees. Will you make it now?"

"P-47, many thanks, I will try to bring her in."

The bomber pilot brought his ship in, almost dived his sick ship toward the runway. His number-four engine cut out as his wheels came down, and the ship rolled on the landing strip on one engine—home.

And he sat there for a single moment. He saw his fighters swooping low over him, climb again and off, a flight of four fast planes going home. He watched them for a long time, not exactly sure of what to think or what to say.

"Listen," said the fighter pilot, with just the slightest touch of irritation, "I didn't turn in any report on this thing because everything was all right. He set down okay. I covered him coming in and he was all right. That's why I didn't turn any report in."

"The bomber pilot said you got hold of Air Sea Rescue for him before he even asked for it."

"Hell, it was obvious enough," argued the fighter pilot. "I could see those port engines were out. I told my wing man, Lt. Leroy H. Sypher, to fly on one side of him, and I flew on the other. I sent my second element up above. They were Lt. Thomas F. Brubaker and Lt. Murray C. Bell. . . . It was clear enough the big guy was in trouble. I called my element leader and said, 'Brubaker, go up and get a fix.' Then I relayed it to the B-17. It was all pretty obvious."

He put his hands in his pockets and jiggled back and forth on his feet.

"You see them up there, like over Berlin, under fire from the FWs queuing up on one of the big guys slow as an ice wagon. I've seen the chutes come down like autumn leaves, and it gets you a little sick—so you go after the FWs. That's the job."

He shifted uneasily on his feet. He was a slim, small young man with very bright eyes and reddish-blond hair. He looked as if he had been, at one time or another, the kind of kid whom you call "urchin," and who, all his life, would never quite succeed in outgrowing it. Over his not unattractive, snub-nosed pan, written almost as clearly as over the hood of those sturdy one-man trucking enterprises you find over the United States you could read, "We give prompt, reliable, courteous service."

Though the fighter pilot had found nothing remarkable in the convoy job and though it had happened before in this theater, the names of the men who do them rarely break loose. And the name of this particular fighter pilot is Charles N. Keppler, and his rank is captain. He has been flying combat in this theater for about a year, having completed his tour of duty and then applying for "extensions."

He holds the Air Medal with three Oak Leaf clusters and the DFC with two clusters. Before the war, he went to the University of Wisconsin and studied engineering, but dropped out and tried to get into the Air Corps.

He was a GI in an infantry outfit for a year before getting his chance to fly.

He has knocked down three enemy fighters and has two damaged to his credit.

"That bomber pilot would like to meet you."

"I'd like to meet him myself," said Cpt. Keppler. "He sure did a nice job nursing that ship of his home."

"If you put down my hometown," said Cpt. Keppler, spelling it out, "it's Wauwatosa, but maybe you ought to put down Milwaukee because Wauwatosa is kind of a small town. . . . Is that all?"

That was all.

THE END OF THE LINE

—Pvt. JUSTIN GRAY
Yank Staff Writer
January 24, 1944

Telephone wires are more than mere lines of communication to the men of a Ranger battalion moving forward into action.

THE BATTALION was bivouacked about six miles behind the lines. We were divisional reserve. It looked as if we wouldn't get back into action right away, because the division was moving forward smoothly. They wouldn't call us unless the Jerries stopped them. It felt good to be resting. We hadn't had much rest in the past month. It was close to midnight and most of the boys were already sleeping, but I was still awake. I had just come off guard and was rolled up in my half-blanket under an olive tree, feeling good and wondering if I'd get some mail the next day. I hadn't heard from home in a long time. I thought about my girl. Funny how I wanted to see that scrawl of hers.

Hodal started to snore. That was a good sign. Hodal never snored when things were going bad for us. I was thirsty, but while I was making up my mind to go down to the water trailer, I fell asleep.

It must have been a couple of hours, but it seemed like a couple of minutes, when I heard Scotty, our first sergeant, bellowing at us to get ready to move. It took me a long time to react. I couldn't wake up. Miller was shaking me. "Get up, Gray, we're moving out."

The whole battalion was stirring. In the dark some of the men were filling their canteens, others were working on their packs or getting extra ammo. Everyone was awake. I must have been the last one to start getting ready.

"Hey, Cy," I called over, "where in the hell are we going? Back to a rest camp?" Miller groaned and looked at me with disgust. "Do you think they'd wake you up at midnight to get you back to a rest camp? You're going to do some mountain climbing."

I cursed myself for not washing my socks that afternoon. We'd had so much time. It had been a quiet, lazy afternoon. And how I hated those mountains. I'd never walk a step when I got home.

Miller was almost ready with his blanket roll and I hurried to finish mine. He went off into the darkness to fill our canteens. He always helped others—a rough fighter and a real friend. I wandered around in the dark and found the CP, then grabbed some rations and hurried back.

All the boys were ready when I returned to where I had been sleeping. They were smoking and kidding. Miller had lost all his ammo in a poker game that afternoon, and they were debating whether or not to give it back to him.

The captain would be calling us together any minute now to tell us about our job. I still had my pack to fix. The straps were all sweated up hard, and I couldn't fix them the way I wanted at first. I'd just finished when Scotty yelled: "Over here, guys."

We walked down the hillside to where the captain was bending over a map with a dim flashlight. Cy was right; we were not going back to any rest area. It didn't take long for the captain to tell us what we had to do. The division had met some unexpected resistance. A group of Germans was holding out in a small town way up in the mountains, a tough position to reach. We were to move forward, infiltrate behind the Jerry lines, and attack from the rear. It was a two-day job. We had done it before, many times, but I didn't relish this deal. It would be rough.

The other companies had finished their briefing and were forming. The captain dismissed us, and we hurried back to get our equipment. Someone was yelling: "Where's C Company?" We fell in. "First platoon, Second platoon, mortars in the rear." The battalion moved out. The colonel led off at a fast clip.

We moved down the mountain to the road below us and turned north. It sure wasn't the direction I'd have picked to go. We'd bypassed a clean little town, untouched by artillery, a couple of days before, and I was ready to go back and see what the girls were like there.

It was pitch black. We moved in two columns, one on each side of the road, the men about 20 yards apart. You couldn't really see the man in front of you. But you could feel him out. You knew that there were units bivouacked on either side of the road, but there was no sign of life—just a dark, desolate stretch of road ending in darkness. Everyone else was sleeping. Damn, didn't they know there was a war on? Well, I suppose their job would come up tomorrow. We'd rested the day before. I'd almost forgotten that.

Our artillery was unusually quiet, almost as if it were telling the Jerry to go to sleep so we could slip through. Every once in a while, Jerry lobbed a shell over us and we had to flatten down on the

Our artillery was quiet, but every so often Jerry lobbed a shell over us and we flattened down on the road.

dirt road. We were moving pretty slowly, even though still far behind the lines. What seemed to be hundreds of telephone wires stretched on the gravel past my feet toward the front. There was nothing to worry about yet.

A convoy of ammo trucks came by, and we had to pull off the road until they passed. I disliked this waiting. I started to count the strands of telephone wire, just to keep busy. The wire was a symbol of security and strength. The telephone is a wonderful invention, but the Rangers seldom take it with them. That's what bothered me most. It didn't seem so bad that we might be wiped out, but the thought that we couldn't let anybody know what was happening to us—that's what was bad. Then I laughed to myself, remembering how relaxed I had once felt on a night assault in Sicily. We had followed a thin strand of wire all night long, certain that infantry was in front of us. In the morning we attacked and only then realized no one was in front of us—we had been following a German wire.

The trucks had gone. We were moving again. It took all my energy to keep the guy in front of me in sight. I lost track of the wires. It must have been a half hour before the column halted again as some more Jerry shells landed, a bit closer this time. I hit the ground. Where had the telephone wires gone? I could count only about 10. It gave

me a bit of a turn. We must have really moved forward in that half hour.

The colonel started off again. I forgot about Gerhart in front of me. My eyes followed only the wires at my feet. One branched off into a field. Another suddenly stopped. It must have been hit by shrapnel earlier in the day. I tried to forget the wires by thinking of my girl. But it was no use; my eyes kept coming back to the diminishing number of wires. There was still no sign of our troops or fighting, and that convoy of trucks was completely swallowed up in darkness.

The telephone wires were my only contact with time or space. I couldn't tell how far we had gone or what time it was. But the telephone wires told the story. Only a few were left. There were no troops bivouacked by the road here.

We passed a lone weapons carrier, a divisional signal-company truck unable to go any farther because a bridge was cut. We had to go down into the riverbed and pick our way through a German mine field. There was only one strand of wire left now. I wondered where the infantry was—probably up on the mountain to our right. I strained my eyes to follow the last strand. And then that, too, ended. It led to a telephone in the ditch below us. A sleepy GI was telling headquarters we were passing his post. This was our good-bye. I wondered when headquarters would hear from us again. Our mission had begun.

★

"Dear Ike: Today I spat in the Seine. Patton." To the GIs who were there, the war in Europe ended on August 25, 1944. All that remained was to convince Hitler. On German soil.

THE FALL OF PARIS

—Sgt. RALPH G. MARTIN
September 22, 1944

WE WEREN'T supposed to go into Paris. We were supposed to outflank it.

But we hadn't counted on the FFI. Highly organized, spread out all over the city, the FFI started their own sniping and street fighting on a big scale on Aug. 19. For the Germans in Paris, the situation got so serious that Gen. von Choltitz arranged a verbal agreement. If the sniping would stop, he would permit food convoys to come into Paris. The FFI agreed not only because their food situation was critical but because they had an acute shortage of ammo and couldn't fire for much longer.

As soon as they learned all this, 12th Army Group Headquarters, under Gen. Omar Bradley, decided to enter Paris as soon as the armistice ended at noon, Aug. 23.

Selected for the entry was the Fourth Division of the First Army's VII Corps and the Second French Armored Division, detached from the Third Army. Both entered Paris at 0700, Aug. 25.

With the Fourth occupying the part of Paris north of the Seine and the Second French Armored in the southern sections and the FFI everywhere else, Gen. von Choltitz formally surrendered shortly after noon.

The Germans resisted only in a group of buildings east of Vincennes, shooting down both the German and American officers who walked toward

them with a white flag. It wasn't until the next morning that the Fourth reduced this strong point, and it wasn't until the day after that that all street fighting and sniping completely stopped and Paris was formally returned to the French.

When the rest of the V Corps started moving northeast, the 28th Division was paraded through Paris enroute to the front.

"We didn't have a damn thing to do with the taking of Paris," said Pfc. Verner Odegard of Gonvick, Minnesota, a rifleman with Baker Company of the First Battalion of the 19th Regiment of the 82nd Division. "We just came in a couple of days later, when somebody got the bright idea of having the parade, and we just happened to be there and that's all there was to it. What can you do, though—that's just the way it goes. And after all, we did a helluva lot of things that we didn't get credit for.

"As long as I live I don't guess I'll ever see a parade like that. Most of us slept in pup tents in the Bois de Boulogne the night before, and it rained like hell and we were pretty dirty, so they picked out the cleanest guys to stand up in front and on the outside. I had a bright, new shiny patch, so they put me on the outside. It was a good place to be, too, because every guy marching on the outside had at least one girl on his arm kissing him and hugging him.

215

Paris or not—it isn't over yet.

"We were marching 24 abreast right down the Champs Elysées and we had a helluva time trying to march, because the whole street was jammed with people laughing and yelling and crying and singing. They were throwing flowers at us and bringing us big bottles of wine.

"The first regiment never did get through. The crowd just gobbled them up. They just broke in and grabbed the guys and lifted some of them on their shoulders and carried them into cafes and bars and their homes and wouldn't let them go. I hear it was a helluva job trying to round them all up later."

GUAM—U.S. Marines have been distributing mimeographed copies of the following handbill among the troops on this island:

TONIGHT

BANZAI CHARGE

Thrills   Chills   Suspense

See Sake-Crazed Japs Charge at High Port
See Everbody Shoot Everybody
See the Cream of the Marine Corps Play
with Live Ammo

Sponsored by the Athletic and Morale
Office

Come Along and Bring a Friend

*Don't Miss the Thrilling Spectacle of the
Banzai Charge, Starting at 10 p.m. and
Lasting All Night*

ADMISSION FREE

Why work at your wash? Simply drop a cake of GI SOAP into a bucket of clothes and water, pull up a ringside seat and watch the battle.

GI's aggressive suds remove all dirt, grease, grime, color, buttons, fingernails, epidermis and hands.

For clothes without hope, use

GI SOAP

It's Pugnacious!

MAIL CALL

Dear *Yank*:

As a former Greek student at the citadel of classicism, Brooklyn Boys' High School, I really must set you straight on Pallas Athena, whose symbol is worn by the WAC. You stated, quite correctly, that she was the goddess of (a) War and (b) Wisdom. However, you failed to mention that she was even more famous as the goddess of (c) Virginity. (Perhaps virginity, in wartime at least, should be given a higher rating than "c.") Don't forget that when the Athenians built a temple for her, it was called the Parthenon—from the Greek word *parthenos* meaning "virgin."

I leave to you, or to some other modern Aristotle, the philosophical task of showing the relationship of (a) War and (b) Wisdom; (a) War and (c) Virginity; and (b) Wisdom and (c) Virginity.

—Maj. Franklin F. Russell
Arlington, Virginia

Dear *Yank*:

Recently you published a letter from Sgt. Al Forristol in your Mail Call column. It seems the writer was complaining of not having received mail for almost six months. He properly termed it a "crank letter," and little more need be said on the subject. However, since he is hitting the Army Postal Service decidedly below the belt line, I take it as a personal insult. The cases of people who do not receive mail for long periods are few and far between. In the majority, or about 99 percent of such cases the man concerned is at fault, as he has failed to cooperate with the Army Postal Service. . . .

The Army Postal Service has a lot of work, and that volume is rapidly increasing. We don't claim to be supermen, and have no time to give personal service to screwballs. If the personnel we serve will just use a little bit of common sense and cooperate with the various bulletins that are issued,

I am sure that there would be fewer complaints. . . .

—Sgt. R. C. Buckrucker
Egypt

Dear *Yank*:

We can assure Sgt. Forristol that there is no conspiracy to rob him of his precious mail. If his letters to the folks back home were written in the same vitriolic, bad-tempered and insulting tone, then what happened to his mail is no mystery. Who the hell would write to him?

—Sgt. Therman A. Tucker*
Trinidad

*Also signed by Sgt. Irving Caress, T-4s T. R. Kleinsasser and F. J. Eggen, Cpls. Clinton L. Clenny, Mead R. Johnson, C. M. Shorr and Nathan Finn and Pfc. K. V. Almirall.

Dear *Yank*:

After reading Sgt. Al Forristol's letter regarding the Army Postal Service we are inclined to believe that he was thinking only of himself when he mentioned fatheads and things that stink. If you can supply us with his complete address, we will see that he gets at least one letter, and we guarantee it won't have any lip prints on it, either. . . .

—Army Postal Personnel
India

Dear *Yank*:

Might I make a suggestion? The little pill they call atabrine—why couldn't the Medical Department, or whoever is making this stuff, color the pill red instead of yellow? Being as it's an added coloring they put in, why not red? It would help out on the appearance of us lads that are taking atabrine.

I don't mind looking yellow, but when the guys start ribbing you that you look like a Jap, I resent that. Besides how in hell would it look when I get home; the folks might think I'm on my last hitch of this dear old world. Especially the way my folks are, they'd call a doctor on the minute upon seeing me. Thanks pal.

P.S. Even purple, any damn color as long as it's not yellow. Red I still prefer, it would give you that added complexion that Mom would always like to see on her boy.

—Pfc. John De Fronzo
Burma

Dear *Yank*:
I have been eating 10-in-1 rations for quite some time and I haven't been able to find such rations in it as canned peaches, pears, fruit cocktail, vienna sausage, sardines and salmon. I have been trying to figure out for a long time just why they don't put that type of canned food in the 10-in-1 rations, but I haven't been able to do so. If they can put such canned food in them as chopped ham and eggs, corn beef, etc., why can't they put in the type of food I mentioned above?

Before I came overseas there was a lot of talk about food shortages, because they had to ship it to the soldiers overseas on the battle front. I don't think they really meant that, because unless we are stationed at a staging area or some place like Rome, we as front line soldiers do not get such food. Can you tell me why?

—S/Sgt. Lonzic Thomas
Italy

Dear *Yank*:
Read your article entitled "The Jap Soldier," and one particular paragraph caught my eye. It stated that the Jap cannot pronounce the letter *L* and gave an illustrative example "lollapalooza." Well, after an exhaustive test, I've found that they have no more difficulty with their letter *L* than with any other letter in the alphabet and can say "lollapalooza" just a shade better than a GI from Brooklyn. Who am I to argue with the OWI, but I only know what I hear and "lollapalooza" and "lullabye" are good enough for me.

—S. H. Blickman PhM3c*
Marianas

*Also signed by H. Isenberg PhM2c.

Dear *Yank*:
We saw in a John Wayne movie where we're supposed to be careful about capturing Japanese food and potables. Is that like in potable radios?

—Pfc. Clayton Landey*
Guadalcanal

*Also signed by Pvt. Mark Travis and Cpl. Eddie Frierson.

Shouldn't you guys be cleaning your rifles? Ed.

Dear *Yank*:
My buddy and I had an argument about the century we are living in. I claim that we are living in the 20th century and my buddy claims that we are living in the 19th century. Now, tell me who collects the ten bucks we bet.

—Pvt. Edward W. Schultz
Italy

You do, but you ought to be ashamed to take the money. Ed.

Dear *Yank*:
We here in France would like to see something done about the infamous malted milk and dextrose tablets found in our K rations. We can give the French almost anything and they will accept it but those tablets; they won't eat them. From hedgerow to hedgerow, from foxhole to foxhole, discarded dextrose tablets fairly litter the earth. They are just a waste of time and money since only about 2 percent of our boys eat them. We've been hungry enough at times to munch on the box, but never, never the tablets.

—Pfc. Harry Moore
France

STUDY IN SOUND

—Pvt. Justin Gray
October 6, 1944

Relentless barrages of artillery are hard to take, but long hours of silence in a forward position are even tougher on the nerves.

ITALY—It was a hot day in mid-September. We had expected that Italy would be cooler at that time of year. We had been fighting for 15 days—defensively, merely holding on to a thin peninsula of land that jutted into German territory, holding until the Army to the south could reach us. We held the high ground, a mountain ridge. Behind us we could see the invasion armada supplying the main Army at Salerno. There were thousands of ships, thousands of men. Ahead of us, great naval guns shelled Naples and airplanes bombed the valley below us. But we were isolated: two Ranger battalions facing what seemed to be the entire German Army.

At first the Jerries had attempted to beat us back. Failing this, they subjected us to an almost continuous mortar and artillery barrage. We were vulnerable. They knew exactly where we were. We had to dig in and take it, and we couldn't fight back. Directly below us, we could see a constant stream of German trucks on the way to Salerno to meet the main invasion thrust. At first we tried to harass these convoys, but now we no longer dared to go down into the valley. We didn't have the strength. All we could do was cling to the ridge. Our light mortars couldn't reach the German positions.

A few of us had dug a cave. We tried to play cards, but after days of sitting under artillery we were all too tense. When would they send us help? It was long overdue. They had told us we'd be in Naples in three days. It didn't look as though we'd ever get there. We were all nervous. Someone remarked: "Gee, I wouldn't mind getting a little wound. Get the hell out of this blasted artillery. If it keeps up much longer I'll be a Section 8 for sure."

We all remembered that young kid Cato a few days before. He burst out crying when he saw an infiltrating German come at him. He yelled: "What'll I do? What'll I do?" Then he was dead. That artillery did things to you. We weren't scared so much, just tired—tired of hugging the ground, of not being able to fight back. We'd been told not to duck when we heard the screaming of the shells; it would be too late. But we ducked anyway. Even the almost silent pop of the mortars was frightening. The sharper sounds of the artillery were always bad. We got to know exactly where a shell would land, and we played games, calling the shots.

It all seemed so futile. I'd have given anything to get out of it, to do something different, get another job, get moving. A combat patrol, maybe. Anything. Anything at all. Lucky the Germans didn't know how close to cracking we were. I wondered if I could stand another sleepless night. It would be the 14th. I knew I couldn't last much longer.

That evening, four of us got a break. We were called down to the CP and told we were to guard a mine field that night, about a mile and a half in front of the lines. We were anxious to go. Lt. Davey briefed us. At dusk we were to lay a series of mines completely covering the road leading to the pass. The position had already been picked. We were to cover the mine field with a light machine gun. Our mission was to fire as long as possible at any units that might attempt to infiltrate through the mines. Our firing would alert the Rangers.

The situation was not too clear. To cover the field effectively we had to set up the machine gun in an exposed position. To our left was a steep cliff some 80 feet high. Directly to our right the terrain broke sharply into a 50-foot drop. If we were attacked, we would have no place to go for cover. Even so, it seemed better than sitting on the mountain under artillery.

We collected the necessary equipment, and just before dusk we started out warily. We were burdened with a machine gun, ammunition, rifles, mines, grenades, and a few blankets we were able to scrounge. That was another break: we'd have blankets on this job. The nights were cold even if the days were hot. We carried no food. Ammunition was of greater importance. Along the way we laid the wire for our field telephone.

In an hour we had arrived, and everything was set up. The mines were laid and the machine gun was in position. The four of us decided to team up in pairs. There were still 12 hours before dawn. That meant six hours a team.

Rona and I took the first six hours. It would be a long vigil, but at least the artillery was going over our heads. We could see the shells landing in the positions we had just left. Rona swore softly: "Those poor bastards up there." He and I sat down back to back, next to the machine gun. The other two rolled up in blankets and went to sleep immediately. I had to smile. They had complete confidence in us.

I had done this many times before. It didn't seem like a very difficult job. It demanded a lot of self-control. Sitting back to back for six hours. Not saying a word. Not smoking. Not even chewing gum. Just searching with your eyes and ears for any movement that might give away the enemy.

Back to back for six hours. Not talking. Not even chewing gum.

It was dark now. And way off in the valley I could hear the almost constant hum of German motor transports rushing supplies under cover of night. The sound was irritating.

Then the moon came out suddenly, breaking over the mountain. It made us feel so exposed. I began to worry just a little bit. A child could have dropped a hand grenade on top of us from the cliff to our left. We certainly had chosen a stupid position. Jerry couldn't help but see us.

We were supposed to report back to the colonel's CP every hour. We couldn't talk on the phone. We just tapped on the mouthpiece, and they knew we were all right. That bastard on the phone back in the CP thought we needed a little morale and insisted on spitting out an endless stream of dirty stories. It was disconcerting. We couldn't listen to dirty stories and to the rustle of leaves at the same time. At last we shut him up.

My imagination started to work. Trees began to take human shapes. Scraping leaves on the ground sounded like footsteps. Two birds making love in a tree below us sounded just like an army. I wanted to throw a grenade, but that was out of the question. We had to be silent at all costs. I began thinking of the time I was out West on a ranch, when I used to guard the camp against bears. I began wondering if the Germans had gotten in behind our position, between us and the main lines. If they had, they'd surely find our telephone wire and trace it down to us. What if the Germans counterattacked and pushed the Rangers back to the sea? We would be trapped. We could never get out. I thought of a million things that could happen to us.

My rear end started to go to sleep. I just had to move. But Rona was as silent as ever, so I didn't dare. I could tell whenever he got tense. His back would stiffen up against mine, and I'd hold my breath so as not to interfere with his hearing. I didn't even dare swallow my spit; the sound would have seemed deafening. "Jesus," I said to myself, "I thought it was tense under the artillery fire. At least there we were all sharing it together." I

didn't like the isolation. What I'd have given to get back to my company. This was much harder on your nerves than the solid hammering of the artillery. I wondered if I'd have to do this again tomorrow night.

We could hear spasmodic firing back at the lines. I wished I could fire a couple of rounds with the machine gun. The noise would have been satisfying. It was too quiet. I'd be glad when dawn got here.

Our six hours were over. We woke up Stancil and Nichols. They took our place, and I tried to go to sleep. But it was no go. I was too tense. No sounds. No artillery. I couldn't sleep. I just had to sweat out the dawn.

By 0700 we were back at our lines. I began to feel nauseated and seemed to have a temperature. Suddenly I felt very weak and began to vomit, sweating. I could hardly move my legs and arms. I reported to the doc. He gave me a dose of medicine. Then they packed me into a jeep and drove me down to Maori on the waterfront.

The Rangers had taken over the largest Catholic church in town as their aid station. It was hot. The ward was stuffy. But sick as I was, it looked like something out of a Hollywood movie about the First World War. They carried me to a cot in front of the altar. The altar itself was covered with bandages and medicine. There was one American nurse, a beautiful girl. She was being helped by a number of Italian nuns. I looked around. One soldier was crying in the corner. A nun tried to comfort him. Another was getting blood plasma. The nurse washed my face with alcohol. It cooled me off a bit.

I suddenly realized that it wasn't as quiet as I had thought. The naval guns had opened up. The shells sounded like freight trains right overhead. The whole building shook. But I felt safe. Up on the mountain we had been so far from everything. This clearing station seemed to be a link with home, with the rest of the world. The noise was deafening but comforting. They were our guns, our shells. I fell asleep.

In order for the Allies to gain complete control of the South Pacific, the Philippines had to be retaken from the 350,000 Japanese who held it; on October 23, 1944, that beachhead was established at Leyte Gulf. Two years earlier, on fleeing Corregidor, MacArthur had said "I shall return." That promise was fulfilled in late December, after eight weeks of heavy combat had erased all Nipponese resistance in that area. The rest of the Philippine chain would follow suit, but not quickly and not without serious loss of American life.

WE LAND ON LEYTE

—Sgt. OZZIE ST. GEORGE
Art by Sgt. JOE STEFANELLI
November 17, 1944

FOR TWO and a half years, the men of Gen. Douglas MacArthur's command had said of our promised return to the Philippines, "That'll be the day!"

Now the day had come. The low, murky blue islands rising out of the sea to the northwest and southwest of our convoy were the Philippines, the promised land.

At midnight, when our APA (attack transport) entered possible Jap mine fields, troops had been moved out of the forward compartments to sleep the rest of the night on deck until reveille at 0230 hours. Chow was at 0400 hours. General quarters was piped at 0430. About an hour later, shortly before our own naval air cover arrived, a single Jap Betty appeared and circled lazily over the task force. From our APA in the middle of the force, we traced its course by the dirty black splotches of flak that peppered the sky behind and around it. And we cheered wildly for a few moments when the Betty went into a long, slanting dive, but it pulled out and disappeared unscratched. A Negro mess boy stretched flat on his back under an LCVP slept peacefully through the entire raid.

In our huge convoy were the First Cavalry Division (dismounted), veterans of the Admiralties; the 24th Infantry Division, which fought at Tanahmerah Bay, New Guinea; the Seventh Infantry Division, victors at Attu and Kwajalein; and the untested 96th Infantry Division.

Until 0700, when we were ordered below to our compartments, we watched the naval bombardment that the battlewagons, light and heavy cruisers, and cans were dishing out. It was a memorable show.

The fun, however, had worn off by the time we went below to our compartments, and H-Hour approached. We went down the cargo nets to our LCMs at about 0800 and circled with other landing craft until about 0900. Then we started slowly toward the beach. Six hundred yards offshore we passed two LCVPs that had been hit by mortars. One was nearly awash, the other down by the stern. A third LCVP was picking up the survivors.

MacArthur returns to the Philippines.

The Japs dropped half a dozen mortar shells in the vicinity of our APA, but none came close. About 100 yards offshore, we heard the crack of sniper fire and the "pop-pop" of Japanese machine guns.

As we splashed and floundered ashore in waist-deep water, the sniper and machine-gun fire grew louder. Between the edge of the coconut grove and the surf line, there was a two-foot drop. Most of us in the fifth wave joined those of the fourth and third waves huddled close against this bank. To our left, the Navy beach party had commandeered a crater and was crouched there trying, it seemed, to hide its brilliantly colored beach markers.

The number of bursts whining seaward presently grew less, and some of us slithered forward a few yards to the lee side of a tank. A lieutenant lying flat in one of the tank tracks asked where D Company was. "They got the captain's boat," he said. "It looks like I'm a company commander, and I can't find our mortars, so I guess we're infantry. We can be infantry if we have to."

He crawled forward and yelled at his platoon to follow. It did, crouching a hundred yards inland just seaward of a tank ditch.

Infantrymen were slowly getting up, fingers on triggers. As the firing gradually died down, the troops moved off the beach, working inland.

LSTs were coming into the beach when a Jap artillery piece opened up. Most of us dropped flat again as the shell whirred over our heads and struck the deck of the leading LST. In turn, three more Ts were hit repeatedly. Fires broke out in two of them but were quickly brought under control. Once a man's body was flung into the air. On another T, fire reached the ammunition, and smoking shells arched into the air.

Lying on the beach, we felt helpless and wondered where our naval gunfire was. The LSTs grounded and began to unload, and presently naval gunfire materialized. The Japs' artillery piece shut up, but they continued dropping mortars into the bay. A man crouched with us said, "I'm glad I came in on an early wave this time."

About 1300 we found the command post of the battalion assigned to take Hill 522, a steep, knobby eminence overlooking and commanding the beachhead area and the town of Palo. The battalion CO was trying to locate his companies. "We've wasted all that beautiful preparation on the hill," he said. "Everybody bogged down on the beach.

"Have you got C Company commander?" he asked the radioman at the CP. Somebody said, "The CO is missing, but there's a lieutenant right here." The colonel grabbed the lieutenant.

"Dick," he said, "you're commanding now. Move out and don't hold up for a machine gun or a couple of snipers. We want to sit on that hill tonight."

A runner came in and reported that A and B Companies were 300 yards ahead of us and moving slowly. The colonel went up to see for himself and speed things along.

When the colonel came back, he told the CP to start packing and sent an advance party out behind the companies to pick a new CP site. We followed them all afternoon without establishing another CP. A, B, and C Companies, with D in support, moved steadily through the coconut grove, meeting only light and scattered sniper fire. Eventually they broke into open country, mostly rice paddies knee-deep in water.

About 1600 it started raining. The battalion CP by this time consisted simply of those of the battalion staff who weren't running errands for the colonel, two or three enlisted men from each section, and the air-ground liaison party.

The attack companies reached the highway that connects Palo with Tacloban, crossed it, called for mortar fire on the hill, got it, and, seeing no sign of Japs, continued the advance.

The CP pulled up under a row of trees at the edge of a rice paddy, and the colonel surveyed the hill. "Hell," he said, "there's nobody up there."

D Company was moving up now and the colonel stood in the rain slapping the mortar men on the back as they passed and urging them on.

One soldier stopped. "Sir," he said, pointing to a native house half hidden by palms on the far side of the paddy, "something moved over there."

The colonel said, "Take a squad and investigate. But they may be Filipinos. Don't fire unless fired on. But be careful."

The squad leader called his scouts out, and they moved off and cautiously circled the house. They returned in about 10 minutes herding a family of Filipinos. Already a girl of five or so had her hands full of C ration candy, lump sugar, and a part of a D bar. Two or three Filipinos were smoking American cigarettes. One, a boy of about 15, had been accidentally wounded in the thigh by fragments during the day's fighting.

The colonel called for the battalion medics. With

smiles to reassure him, two medics dressed the boy's wound. Then grandma and grandpa and another lad stepped forward with cut feet. The medics fixed them up, too, and explained to a girl of 12, who spoke English as if long out of practice, that she should take them to the beach the next day to have the wounds dressed. Smiling, the Filipinos retired after telling us, "No Japs."

Battalion headquarters splashed on across three or four more rice paddies, past a deserted native dwelling whose owner had left a message —"Do not burn my house"—chalked on the door, until they came to the highway.

The highway was the first any of us had seen in two years of grabbing beachheads. It had a 10- or 12-foot hard-surfaced, blacktop center, somewhat in need of repair, six-foot shoulders, deep ditches, and the kind of single-span cement bridges found on the average country road in the States.

Again knee-deep in water, we waded through a large abaca-hemp field and reached the foot of Hill 522. A few men were already creeping up its nose toward the summit. More infantrymen were slowly spreading across the lower slopes. The Japs had evacuated all but the extreme southern shoulder, and the few still there held their peace for the moment.

Weary GIs dragged themselves and their equipment up the last steep slopes. A four-man litter squad carrying a man with a shoulder wound began a slow, painful descent to the battalion aid station. Mortars were mounted in gulleys on the reverse slope and MGs on the crest. The morning's bombardment and bombing had left the hill well pitted with holes. Some of the men improved these craters before tumbling into them. Others simply fell in.

The rain had stopped and the rocky earth was damp. It had been like other landings, but tiny, flickering lights in Palo at the foot of the hill were something new and different. The men, however, were too tired to make comparisons.

Sgt. Stefanelli's sketch of landing operations got wet as he waded in to shore.

THANKSGIVING 1944

—Sgt. AL HINE
November 24, 1944

IN 1941, if you happened to be in the Army in that good civilian year, you were probably on maneuvers for Thanksgiving.

The war play stopped for the holiday and you bivouacked in North or South Carolina. It was nippy the night before, but the day was bright and the mess sergeants cooked palatable turkey. In the rear echelon, you borrowed a couple of field desks from the company clerks and then took off to Camden, maybe, to buy a bottle of wine. You had your Thanksgiving in style and sprawled stuffed and happy on a still-warm patch of Carolina earth and shot bull till your dinner settled.

The maneuver problem didn't resume till the next day, so you could hitch into Cheraw or Springs Mills or Kershaw or wherever you were near and drink beer and bitch like hell because the local citizenry had hiked the price to 15 cents a bottle on account of maneuvers. If you wrote home you were very sad. . . . "It's no good to spend Thanksgiving away from home. I'll be glad when my year is up and I'm out of all this snafu. Remind me to tell you what snafu means when I get home. . . ."

Snafu was a new word then, in the 1941 maneuvers. As new as your uniform. As new as the Army that was just beginning to stretch and grow and get wise to itself.

Before the next Thanksgiving, you had heard Pearl Harbor boil out of the day-room radio. You had seen your Christmas furlough cut and had kissed good-bye to Wednesday afternoons off and shipped your civilian clothes home. By Thanksgiving 1942, you might have been in any one of a number of places very far from the Carolina maneuver area—waiting and training and training and waiting in Great Britain or Australia or Hawaii, holding a little piece of strange ground against the Japs on Guadalcanal, inching forward in North Africa.

Mostly you went without turkey. Your uniform was dirty, but nobody chewed you out for it. The Army wasn't so new, and snafu was a word that had been with you time out of mind.

You could be thankful, if you had time, that something had been started. You were past the war of posters and county-fair kisses bought with

defense stamps and into dirt and the slow, dirty business of winning.

You stayed in that business.

Thanksgiving 1943 saw you edging into the Jap domination of the Pacific the hard way on Makin and Tarawa. Rommel was out of all North Africa now. We were pushing up into Italy. Ragged newsboys in Persia, watching us truck supplies to the advancing Red Army, hollered *"Mussolini Fini!"*

Some places you even had turkey instead of the K rations, which had lost their novelty as quickly as the C rations you first bellyached about. Snafu was a word you could smile at again. It was a word the enemy was learning faster than you ever thought anyone could learn back in 1941.

There still isn't a hell of a lot of turkey going around this year, but you don't have to look in your mess kit to see who's winning. Any map will tell you. The increasing shrillness of the Axis radio will tell you.

It's a good feeling for Thanksgiving. It beats anything in a mess kit. It doesn't mean that everything is finished, but it does mean you can see the end, the end you sometimes wondered if you ever would see.

Maybe there will be another Thanksgiving of K rations, mess kits, and dirt. Maybe there won't. Even if there is, it should be a good one. Surer and surer we're building to the Thanksgiving we griped at missing in 1941.

If the hedgerows were bad, the Huertgen Forest was worse—only here they had land mines, too. But at least it was Germany, and Aachen already had been captured. Suddenly, Berlin was no longer something you joked about at bull sessions; proximity made it real—and put you that much closer to home.

WAR IN THE HUERTGEN FOREST

—Sgt. MACK MORRISS
January 5, 1945

THE FIRS are thick, and there are 50 square miles of them standing dismal and dripping at the approaches to the Cologne plain. The bodies of the firs begin close to the ground, so that each fir interlocks its body with another. At the height of a man standing, there is a solid mass of dark, impenetrable green. But at the height of a man crawling, there is room, and it is like a green cave, low-roofed and forbidding. And through this cave moved the infantry, to emerge cold and exhausted when the forest of Huertgen came to a sudden end before Grosshau.

The infantry, free from the claustrophobia of the forest, went on, but behind them they left their dead, and the forest will stink with deadness long after the last body is removed. The forest will bear the scars of our advance long after our scars have healed, and the infantry has scars that will never heal.

For Huertgen was agony, and there was no glory in it except the glory of courageous men— the MP whose testicles were hit by shrapnel and who said, "Okay, doc, I can take it"; the man who walked forward, firing tommy guns with both hands until an arm was blown off and then kept on firing the other tommy gun until he disappeared in a mortar burst.

Men of the 25th, 43d, and 37th Divisions would know Huertgen—it was like New Georgia. The mud was as deep, but it was yellow instead of black. Trees were as thick, but the branches were stemmed by brittle needles instead of broad jungle leaves. Hills were as steep and numerous, but there were mines—S mines, wooden-shoe mines, teller mines, box mines.

Foxholes were as miserable, but they were covered, because tree bursts are deadly, and every barrage was a deluge of fragmentation from the tops of the neat little firs. Carrying parties were burdened with supplies on the narrow trails. Rain was as constant, but in Huertgen it was cold, and on the line there was constant attack and a stubborn enemy.

For 21 days, the division beat its slow way forward, and there were two mornings out of those 21 when the order was to reform and consolidate. Every other morning saw a jump-off advance, and the moment it stopped, the infantry dug in and buttoned up, because the artillery and mortars searched for men without cover and maimed them.

There was no sign of glory in the green

There was counterattack, too, but in time the infantry welcomed it, because then and only then the German came out of his hole and was a visible target, and the maddened infantry killed with grim satisfaction. But the infantry advanced with its battle packs, and it dug in and buttoned up, and then the artillery raked the line so that there were many times when the infantry's rolls could not be brought up to them.

Rolls were brought to a certain point, but the infantry could not go back for them because to leave the shelter was insane. So the infantry slept as it fought—if it slept at all—without blankets, and the nights were long and wet and cold.

But the artillery was going two ways. The division support fire thundered into the forest, and it was greater than the enemy fire coming in. A tired battalion commander spoke of our artillery. "It's the biggest consolation we have," he said. "No matter how much we're getting, we know the kraut is getting more." So the infantry was not alone.

monument of Huertgen; it was a bitter thing.

Tanks did the best they could, when they could. In the beginning, they shot up defended bunkers and dueled with machine guns in the narrow fire-breaks, and they waddled down into the open spaces so that the infantry could walk in their tracks and feel the comfort of safety from mines. At the clearing before Grosshau, they lunged forward, and some of them still dragged the foliage of the forest on their hulls when they were knocked out.

One crew abandoned its tank, leaving behind all their equipment in the urgency of the escape. But they took with them the mascot rooster they had picked up at St. Lo.

The advance through Huertgen was "like wading through the ocean," said S-3 at the regiment. "You walk in it all right, but water is all around you."

There were thickets in the forest where two battalion CPs had been in operation for three days, and physical contact between them had been routine. Thirteen Germans and two antitank guns were discovered between them. The CPs were 800 yards apart. "Four thousand yards from the German lines," said S-3, who had been one of the battalion commanders, "and we had to shoot krauts in our own front yard. Our prisoner-of-war interrogation team got its own captives to question. The engineers bridged the creek, and before they could finish their work they had 12 Germans sitting on a hill 200 yards away, directing artillery fire on them by radio." These things were part of Huertgen, a green monument to the *Wehrmacht*'s defense and the First Army's power.

At that, the monument is a bitter thing, a shattered thing. The Germans had four lines of defense in the forest, and one by one those lines were beaten down and the advance continued. This was for the Fourth Division alone. There were other divisions and other lines. And these MLRs were prepared magnificently.

Huertgen had its roads and firebreaks. The firebreaks were only wide enough to allow two jeeps to pass, and they were mined and interdicted by machine-gun fire. In one break there was a teller mine every eight paces for three miles. In another there were more than 500 mines in the narrow break. One stretch of road held 300 teller mines, each one with a pull device in addition to the regular detonator. There were 400 antitank mines in a three-mile area.

Huertgen had its roads, and they were blocked. The German did well by his abatis, his roadblocks made from trees. Sometimes he felled 200 trees across the road, cutting them down so they interlocked as they fell. Then he mined and booby-trapped them. Finally he registered his artillery on them, and his mortars, and at the sound of men clearing them, he opened fire.

The first two German MLRs were screened by barbed wire in concertina strands. The MLRs themselves were log-and-earth bunkers six feet underground, and they were constructed carefully, and inside them were neat bunks built of forest wood, and the walls of the bunkers were paneled with wood. These sheltered the defenders. Outside the bunkers were the fighting positions.

The infantry went through Huertgen's mud and its splintered forest growth and its mines and its high explosives, mile after mile, slowly and at great cost. But it went through, with an average of perhaps 600 yards gained each day.

The men threw ropes around the logs of the roadblocks and yanked the ropes to explode the mines and booby traps in the roadblock, and then they shoved the trees aside to clear the way. The engineers on their hands and knees probed the earth with number-eight wire to find and uncover nonmetallic shoe mines and box mines that the Germans had planted by the thousands. A wire or bayonet was shoved into the ground at an angle in the hope that it would touch the mines on their sides rather than on the tops, for they detonated at two or three pounds' pressure. Scattered on that ground there were little round mines no larger than an ointment box, but still large enough to blow off a man's foot.

At times, when there was a clearing, the engineers used another method to open a path. They looped primacord onto a rifle grenade and then fired the grenade. As it lobbed forward, it carried with it a length of primacord, which was then touched off and exploded along the ground with enough force to set off or uncover any shoe mines or S mines hidden underground along its path. In other cases, when the area was known to be mined, it was subjected to an artillery concentration that blew up the mines by the force of the concussion. There could be no certainty that every mine was blown. The advance was costly; but the enemy suffered.

One regiment of the Fourth Division claimed the destruction of five German regiments in meeting 19 days of constant attack. The German had been told the value of Huertgen and had been ordered to fight to the last as perhaps never before. He did, and it was hell on him. How the German met our assault was recorded in the brief diary of a medic who later was taken prisoner, and because it is always good for the infantry to know what its enemy is thinking, the diary was published by the Fourth Division. The medic refers to the infantry as "Ami," colloquial for American. These are some excerpts:

It's Sunday. My God, today is Sunday. With dawn the edge of our forest received a barrage. The earth trembles. The concussion takes our breath. Two hundred are brought to my hole, one with both hands shot off. I am considering whether to cut off the rest of the arm. I'll leave it on. How brave these two are. I hope to God that all this is not in vain. To our left, machine guns begin to clatter—and there comes Ami.

In broad waves you can see him across the field. Tanks all around him are firing wildly. Now the American artillery ceases and the tank guns are firing like mad. I can't stick my head out of the hole—finally here are three German assault guns. With a few shots we can see several tanks burning once again. Long smoke columns are rising toward heaven. The infantry takes cover, and the attack slows down—it's stopped. It's unbelievable that with this handful of men we hold out against such attacks.

And now we go forward to counterattack. The captain is leading it himself. We can't go far, though. Our people are dropping like tired flies. We have got to go back and leave the whole number of our dead and wounded. Slowly the artillery begins its monotonous song again—drumming, drumming, drumming without letup. If we only had the munitions and heavy weapons that the American has, he would have gone to the devil a long time ago, but, as it is, there is only a silent holding out to the last man.

Our people are overtired. When Ami really attacks again, he has got to break through. I can't believe this land can be held any longer. Many of our boys just run away and we can't find them and we have to hold out with a small group, but we are going to fight.

Then, two days later, came the final entry:

Last night was pretty bad. We hardly got any sleep, and in the morning the artillery is worse than ever. I can hardly stand it, and the planes are here again. Once more the quiet before the storm. Then, suddenly, tanks and then hordes of Amis are breaking out of the forest. Murderous fire meets him, but he doesn't even take cover anymore. We shoot until the barrels sizzle, and finally he is stopped again.

We are glad to think that the worst is past, when suddenly he breaks through on our left. Hand grenades are bursting, but he cannot hold them any longer. There are only five of us. We have got to go back. Already we can see brown figures through the trees. As they get to within 70 paces, I turn around and walk away very calmly with my hands in my pockets. They are not even shooting at me, perhaps on account of the red cross on my back.

On the road to Grosshau, we take up a new position. We can hear tanks come closer, but Ami won't follow through his gains anyway. He's too cowardly for that.

Perhaps this German who called the infantry cowardly and then surrendered to it will never hear the story of one Fourth Division soldier in Huertgen. He stepped on a mine and it blew off his foot. It was one of those wounds in which the arteries and veins are forced upward so they are in a manner sealed, and bleeding is not so profuse as it otherwise would be.

The man lay there, but he wasn't able to bandage his own wounds. The medics tried to reach him but were fired upon. One was hit, and the trees around the man were white with scars of the machine-gun bullets that kept the medics away. Finally—after 70 hours—they managed to reach him.

He was still conscious, and for the medics it was a blessing that he was conscious; and for the man himself it was a blessing. For during the darkness the Germans had moved up to the wounded man. They took his field jacket from him, and his cigarettes. They booby-trapped him by setting a charge under his back, so that whoever lifted him would die. So the wounded man, knowing this, lay quietly on the charge and told the men who came to help him what the Germans had done. They cut the wires of the booby trap and carried him away.

The green monument of Huertgen is a bitter thing.

NOBODY KNOWS THE TROUBLE THEY'VE SEEN

Various Editions, 1944–45

IT HAD been such a long day. All day and all night riding in trucks with the same old K rations to eat, sleeping in your clothes, as usual, a single blanket maybe to cut off the night wind. Just some sniper fire and a few isolated machine guns to wipe out. Nothing much.

Two buddies stretched out together off the road.

"You know, Willie, I'm scared. I'm so goddam scared. . . ."

"Are you nuts? The way we're going now, the whole thing will blow over in a couple of weeks. Then you can go back to your wife and make babies and tell all your kids about what a wonderful hero you were."

"That's what I'm scared about, Willie. It's almost over and I'm almost home and I'm scared that maybe just a lucky shot will get me. And I don't want to die now, Willie, not when it's almost over. I don't want to die now. Do you know what I mean?"

"I know what you mean. . . ."

—Sgt. Ralph G. Martin

It is strange the way some people still think of war as all shooting and commando raids, when as a matter of fact it is nine-tenths grind with no excitement and a great deal of unpleasantness. Sometimes there is excitement, but mostly it is the loose-bowled kind that you would just as soon be without. Sometimes, of course, there is more than excitement; there is the good feeling that comes from being with men you trust and doing a job you believe in.

But most of the time, for the men who are really up there, the war in Italy is a tough and dirty life, without immediate compensation. It is cold nights and no sleep, the beard matted on your face and the sores coming out on your feet, the clothes stiffening and the dirt caking on your body.

It is digging and crawling and sweating out the 88s, inching forward over rocks and through rivers to mountains that no one in his right mind would ever want. It is doing the same filthy job day after day with a kind of purposeless insanity; and dreaming all the time of warm beds with clean sheets and a steak the size of your arm; and pushing, always pushing.

—Sgt. Walter Bernstein

Actor Brian Aherne had been touring Italy, France, and Holland portraying Robert Browning in *The Barretts of Wimpole Street*. He was standing backstage in Florence when a little dough came up and asked Aherne for his autograph. The dough mentioned he had met Aherne once before at Camp Wheeler in Georgia.

"Ah, yes, I remember that day at Camp Wheeler," said Aherne. "I went out on the range with you fellows there. And I remember one of your colonels telling me, 'We are making it very hard for these men, but when they get overseas they'll look back and thank us for it.' And you are thanking him for it now, aren't you?"

The little dough, who had come out of a rough sector of the 85th Division's line that morning and was going back into it that night, just glanced up at Aherne, lit a cigarette, and walked away.

—Sgt. Joe McCarthy

●

When the Bushmasters—the 158th Regimental Combat Team—landed at Sarmi, they encountered more Japs than anyone had figured. A big hump covered with a thick strand of trees and undergrowth rose along the shore. A good part of the time, the Japs and the Bushmasters were on top of each other without knowing it.

When the word came for the Bushmasters to pull back, Pfc. Dan French, an Indian BAR man in Company F, didn't hear the order. He stayed there and killed Japs until he lost count of how many he had killed. Maybe it was 30, or maybe it was 40.

The Bushmasters later retook the hill. The brass and everybody else pounded French on the back until it hurt.

But later on, whenever French got drunk, he'd wail and moan and beat his chest and feel bad because no one had had the common courtesy to tell him to get the hell off that hill.

—Sgt. Dale Kramer

At night before a big airborne operation you crawl deeper in your sack, but you can't get away from the noise. Over the roar of engines, somebody is shouting a bunch of names: Andrews . . . Burger . . . Edwards . . . Fairbanks . . . Jones, Jack Jones . . . and on down the roster. C Company is falling out to fit their chutes.

Tomorrow there will be an early breakfast—0400, the order said. Then we will climb into our parachutes as dawn breaks. We will trudge out to the planes and climb in, not saying much of anything about anything. The men will know where they are going and what they are going to do. Some have done it before; for others this is the first time. But they all know that this jump across the Rhine will be the end of the krauts.

They'll sweat a bit, as any paratrooper sweats before making a parachute jump. They will get the same old butterflies. But they'll jump.

—Cpl. Bob Krell

(Cpl. Krell was killed in action 12 hours after he wrote this.)

●

That night in New Georgia, the Jap worked by familiar formula, throwing in his little grenades which exploded with much noise and little effect, tossing in his knee-mortar shells, pouring in his fast-firing, brittle-sounding automatic fire.

Three times during the night, the Jap attacked in what would amount to platoon strength, and each time the attack was cut to pieces. In the morning, the air-cooled light machine guns looked as if they'd been in a fire, with their barrels burnt orange and flaking. But they kept on firing.

In the jungle, the first light of dawn always brings heavy fire, and this time it was heavy.

Once a man was gut-shot, and two medics picked him up and walked him, one on either side, through the fire to safety. Another man was shot, and as he raised up he said, "I'm hit." As he fell forward he said, "I'm dead." He was.

—Sgt. Mack Morriss

Rest periods in the ETO may have been short, but on occasion they gave a soldier a chance to get completely away from traditional Army life. No matter how wretched and dirty an Italian town happened to be, at least it was a change. In the Pacific, there are no civilian cities to visit or hot spots to gather in.

And these Pacific battlefields are of little interest to the average American. There seems to be a greater incentive to fight for Paris than to slug one's way toward Garapan, the capital of Saipan. Even fighting for the dirty North Africa towns had more personal meaning to the GI.

There is yet to be a case in the Pacific equal to the first hours at Salerno, where in the midst of flying shells, a man ran up to the beachmaster and cried, "Where's the pro station?"

—Cpl. Justin Gray

Sgt. Rafferty of the 101st Airborne sat at the Eagle's Nest overlooking Berchtesgaden and said that he wanted, more than anything else, to be home by Christmas. He said he had spent last Christmas at a place in Belgium called Bastogne.

"We were cut off there," the sergeant said, "and it was cold and there was snow on the ground. I was lying in the snow in a gully when I saw a German officer and six other krauts start running from one side of a field to the other side about two hundred yards in front of me. I had the officer in the sights of my M1 just as he started climbing over a fence.

"I squeezed the trigger, and this kraut officer just kind of folded across the fence, pressing his hands against his belly and screaming, real high pitched, like a hurt rabbit. I stood that for about five minutes, then I shot him again. He quit yelling. I got to thinking about it later.

"You know, that was the first time I ever had killed a man on Christmas Day."

—Sgt. Debs Myers

●

There was so much violation of the nonfraternization ruling that the GIs in Germany compared it with prohibition. A staff sergeant in the 30th Infantry Division said there was one big difference between nonfraternization and prohibition—in the old days, a guy could hide a bottle inside his coat for days at a time, but it was hard to keep a German girl quiet there for more than a couple of hours.

A tanker said: "Fraternization? Yeh, I suppose it's all right. Anyway, I've been doing it right along. But every now and then I wake up in a cold sweat.

"What do I dream about? I dream that we are at war again, and the German bastards I'm fighting this time are my own."

—Sgt. Allan B. Ecker

Italy

Manila was burning. The whole downtown section was smothered in roaring black billows of smoke. The Jap shells were coming in. A sprawling wooden structure across the street got a direct hit. A Filipino girl stood beside us shaking her head. She said her father and baby brother were inside the burning house.

A pretty, light-skinned woman dressed in a kimono was standing across the street. She scolded a little boy, who was pulling at her kimono. She pushed the child and yelled: "Get away from me, you little Jap bastard!"

The Japs threw in more shells. An MP said: "That goddam piece ain't a quarter mile from here! Why don't them spotters get on the ball?"

A middle-aged Filipino wearing a straw hat came up to a GI whose hands were trembling violently and said: "Have you heard any news about the war in Europe?" The GI dropped the cigarette he was trying to get into his mouth. "What the hell about that?" the GI asked, talking to himself. "The man asks me if I've heard any news about the war in Europe, and for three days and nights I haven't been able to find any news about fighting four blocks in front of me."

—Sgt. H. N. Oliphant

"Sure, there were lots of bodies we never identified," said T/Sgt. Donald Haguall of the 48th Quartermaster Graves Registration. "You know what a direct hit by a shell does to a guy. Or a mine, or a solid hit with a grenade, even. Sometimes all we have is a leg or a hunk of arm.

"The ones that stink the worst are the guys who got internal wounds and are dead about three weeks with the blood staying inside and rotting, and when you move the body, the blood comes out of the nose and mouth. Then some of them bloat up in the sun, they bloat up so big that they bust the buttons and then they get blue and the skin peels. They don't all get blue, some of them get black.

"But they all stink. There's only one stink, and that's it. You never get used to it, either. As long as you live, you never get used to it. And after a while, the stink gets in your clothes and you can taste it in your mouth.

"You know what I think? I think maybe if every civilian in the world could smell that stink, then maybe we wouldn't have any more wars."

—Sgt. Ralph G. Martin

1945

JUKEBOX SATURDAY NIGHT

RICHARD RODGERS AND OSCAR HAMMERSTEIN clearly had their fingers on the pulse of global history. Two of their biggest 1945 hits, "It's a Grand Night for Singing" and "It Might As Well Be Spring," were prophetically accurate indicators that closure was indeed drawing in upon a war-weary world.

At home, families watched with only muted interest as John Wayne went *Back to Bataan*, they pretended that food shortages and ration coupons were still funny, they mourned a president who had died of a cerebral hemorrhage brought about by a heart condition he'd never told them he had, and they pinned up photographs of six brave men raising a flag on some remote Pacific island that nobody had ever heard of. But mostly, they prayed.

The GI did his share of praying too. He knew that the longer the war, the greater the odds against him. Still, he was a hero who had a job to complete, and the idea of giving in now was unthinkable. He would have been hard-pressed to suspect that a year down the road, national apathy and a desire to forget would render him jobless, homeless, and one of millions who found themselves putting dimes in jukeboxes and commiserating with selections such as "Gee, I Wish I Was Back in the Army" and "Thanks for the Memory." That, however, was another story.

The Axis powers had all but disintegrated. In Europe, a last desperate burst of Nazi strength had held off the Allied advance in the Belgian Ardennes—a stretch of terrain also known as the Bulge—but the German respite was only temporary. Ever since the needlessly brutal firebombings of Dresden by the Army Air Corps, the Nazi High Command had begged the führer to capitulate. But Hitler would have none of it.

Likewise in the Pacific, the Japanese had withdrawn to Iwo Jima and Okinawa—the only two unconquered islands remaining between the Allied Fleet and the Japanese mainland. MacArthur was genuinely terrified—the Nipponese people, he knew, had been brought up under the code of the Bushido warrior: Surrender was disgrace. Even the incendiary raids over Tokyo, which had killed 125,000 (more than the combined casualties of Hiroshima and Nagasaki), had only served to stiffen the Japanese resolve. It indeed Operation Olympic—the planned invasion of Japan—were to proceed as scheduled, the war in the Pacific might easily drag on until 1950, or until every last Japanese had died. Whichever came first.

1945

MAJOR BATTLES (Fair Fight):
   The Bulge, Manila, Remagen, Iwo Jima, Berlin, Okinawa
MAJOR BATTLES (Below the Belt):
   Dresden, Tokyo, Hiroshima, Nagasaki
HOLLYWOOD'S BEST:
   G.I. Joe (Ernie Pyle)
HOLLYWOOD'S WORST:
   God Is My Co-Pilot ("Okay, you Yankee Doodle Dandy. Come and get us!")
MOST POPULAR WAR SONG (Nonracist):
   "Comin' in on a Wing and a Prayer"
MOST POPULAR WAR SONG (Racist):
   "When Those Little Yellow Bellies Meet the Cohens and the Kellys"
MOST POPULAR SONG—GENERAL:
   "June is Bustin' Out All Over"
MOST READ BOOK:
   Forever Amber, by Kathleen Winsor

LEAST READ PORTENT:
   A cloud in the shape of a mushroom hanging over Alamogordo, New Mexico, around 5:30 in the morning of July 16
WHAT SOLDIERS WERE WHEN THEY GOT MAD:
   "Browned off"
WHAT OTHER PEOPLE WERE WHEN THEY GOT MAD:
   "Sorer'n hell"
BEST WAY TO SPEND A SATURDAY NIGHT:
   Going to the show with the other girls, especially if Greer Garson was in it
WORST WAY TO SPEND A SATURDAY NIGHT:
   Trying not to remember that it had been two weeks and three days since his last letter, and what if something happened
HOW YOU KNEW WHEN SOMEBODY'S BOY HAD DIED "OVER THERE":
   Everybody whispered

WHAT MADISON AVENUE CLAIMED WAS BOMBING TOKYO:

Fresh eggs—on toast

WHAT MADISON AVENUE CLAIMED WAS KEEPING UP WAR PRODUCTION:

ScotTissue

WHAT MADISON AVENUE CLAIMED OLDSMOBILES GREW UP TO BE:

M-24 tanks

WHAT YOU SAID TO AN AMERICAN OF JAPANESE DESCENT:

"You can go home now, Jap."

HOW MANY OF THOSE HOMES WERE STILL THERE:

About ten

WHAT YOU CALLED A BLACK CORPORAL WITH THREE PURPLE HEARTS:

"Buddy"

THE TIME YOU MOST FELT LIKE A BABY:

When your big brother came back in one piece and you cried for three weeks, even though you weren't sad or anything

THE TIME YOU MOST FELT LIKE A BIG GUY:

When he showed you the hole in his foot, and you looked

BEST VALUE FOR YOUR DOLLAR:

Two on the aisle to *Oklahoma*—but in the balcony

BEST ANNIVERSARY PRESENT FOR MOM AND POP:

A new Victrola

WHAT YOU GOT WHEN YOU TRADED TWO STEELIES AND AN AGGIE:

Two glassies, a Carl Hubbell, and a Di Maggio (from his rookie year!)

MOST OVERSTATED COMBAT STEREOTYPE:

Douglas MacArthur trying to walk on water and getting his cuffs wet instead

MOST UNDERSTATED COMBAT STEREOTYPE:

Guys under shelter halves in the pouring rain who'd fall asleep holding on to each other just so they could feel somebody else's heart beating

WHAT YOU SAID TO YOUR TOPKICK WHEN HE TOLD YOU TO SHUT UP BECAUSE YOU FOUND A HOME IN THE ARMY:

"Yes, sir."

WHAT YOU SAID WHEN HIS BACK WAS TURNED:

"Shove it, you fart-headed sack of shit."

WHAT YOU SAID WHEN HE WAS DYING IN YOUR ARMS:

"jesusgodpleasenojesusgodpleasenojesusgodpleaseno"

MOST ADMIRED AMERICAN FEMALE (Limbs only):

Rita Hayworth, for Christ's Sake!

MOST ADMIRED AMERICAN FEMALE (the Whole Package):

The one you were married to—or would be as soon as this damned thing was over

MOST ADMIRED AMERICAN MALE:

The GI

The hell with Yalta and Potsdam—this story aroused more furor among the GIs than any statement that ever came out of the White House, the Kremlin, or Number 10 Downing Street.

HOMETOWNS IN WARTIME:
BROOKLYN, N.Y.

—Cpl. HYMAN GOLDBERG
Yank Staff Writer
January 26, 1945

BROOKLYN, N.Y.—Not long ago, a large number of bitter complaints poured into the New York City Health Department, the Department of Parks, the Department of Sanitation, and several other city bureaus about a terrible plague that was being visited upon the citizenry. It seems that some kind of vicious beast was attacking people by leaping on them from trees and biting them and goring them with two sets of horns. Strangely, all the complaints came from Brooklyn, and a very small part of Brooklyn at that. What investigators found was that some trees in the Bensonhurst section were infested with a spiny caterpillar that is apt to cause a rash when it comes into contact with human flesh.

A short time later, a subway train prosaically started out from Brooklyn, bound for the West Side of Manhattan, but to the amazement of the motorman and several hundred bewildered passengers, wound up way over on Manhattan's East Side after following a route that still has to be charted or satisfactorily explained.

Brooklynites recently were enraged almost to speechlessness—but not quite—when Noel Coward, a sort of British playwright, unfavorably compared the fortitude of soldiers from Brooklyn with that of soldiers from Texas and Arizona. At Salerno, Mr. Coward said, he had seen Brooklyn soldiers weeping because they had been hospitalized with such trifling disabilities as bullet wounds and broken legs. For once, to the acute embarrassment of Mr. Coward, Brooklyn's indignation was shared not only by the continental United States, but even by Manhattan.

And, at the close of the baseball season, the Brooklyn Dodgers were 42 games behind.

From the foregoing, Brooklynites who have been away from home for a long time can see that the spirit of Brooklyn hasn't changed. Not in any of the essentials. The Brooklyn mood, say students of the subject, would go on despite fire, flood, famine, and pestilence. A little global war hasn't even made a dent in it.

The Brooklyn *Eagle* and other newspapers in the borough over the river from Manhattan are still getting letters from indignant Brooklynites who say it was a great mistake for Brooklyn to have become part of New York City in 1898. Some of them say that Brooklyn will never receive its just recognition until it secedes from New York City or changes its name.

Not long ago, Park Commissioner Robert Moses did a restoration job on Grant's Tomb on Riverside Drive in Manhattan and decided that a statue of the Civil War general on a horse was needed to make the memorial complete. He looked around and found just what he had in mind in Grant Circle, Brooklyn, near the Public Library. He duly asked permission to move the statue to Manhattan. There were screams of rage in the Borough of Homes and Churches, where the forsythia, for some reason or other, is the official flower. "Why the hell," said Brooklyn with one raucous voice, "should we give Manhattan anything? Let them move Grant's Tomb over here." The park commissioner, usually a dauntless man, retired in confusion.

Although the spiritual quality of Brooklyn remains the same, physical changes have nevertheless been made. The city fathers of the borough and its business leaders have great things in store for *après la guerre*. The entire downtown shopping center is to be reconstructed and made into a flossy civic center, with grassy parkways and beautiful public buildings done in the classic Brooklyn style. A start toward this dream has already been made. The Myrtle Avenue El doesn't go over the Brooklyn Bridge to Park Row in Manhattan anymore. The entire section of the El leading from the bridge to Myrtle and Jay Street has been torn down. All the steel and iron in the structure went into war production, and Brooklyn is justly proud of this fact. "The Els that were torn down in Manhattan all went to the Japs," says Brooklyn, "but the only El that was torn down in Brooklyn is being turned

Despite the fire, Luna Park in Coney Island will be opened next year—bigger and better than you ever saw it before.

On Thanksgiving Day the kids still dress up in grown-ups' clothes and beg: "Mister, anything for Thanksgiving, Mister?"

Yes, sir! In Brooklyn a man can get the news without it costing him a penny.

into bullets for our boys to shoot at them."

The good citizens of Brooklyn, who have long been enraged because the world thinks that the only industry they have is the Brooklyn Dodgers, are more intense than ever, now that the borough has been making war on the Axis for more than three years. Brooklynites who are making such varied materials for war as surgical sutures and battleships number more than the entire populations of such cities as Topeka, Kansas, and New Haven, Connecticut. In the Navy yard alone some 68,000 persons were employed at last report.

Here are some other war statistics that the aggressive citizens of Brooklyn throw at you if you give them less than half a chance:

Forty-five percent of the war plants in the borough have been awarded the Army and Navy "E" or the Maritime Service "M."

About half the penicillin produced in the country is made at the Chas. Pfizer & Company plant on Bartlett Street, Brooklyn.

And Borough President John Cashmore, with a chest as proudly inflated as any sweater girl's, points out that more than 280,000 Brooklyn men and women are in the armed forces, and says without any apparent fear of successful contradiction that that's more soldiers and sailors and Marines than any of 39 entire states have given to the war.

Most any hour of the day or night there are a lot of uniforms in view, not only on native Brooklynites home on leave but also on a lot of service people passing through on their way to do a job on the Germans. Of course, most of the strangers in service head first for Times Square, but the next thing most Americans want to see when they hit New York for the first time—at least in summer —is Coney Island. And guess where that is.

"The Yiland" in 1944 had the busiest season in its history, and the way to the ocean from the beach was just as hard to find as ever. There was a big fire at Luna Park, and about one-third of the amusement center was burned out. That didn't close the place down, though. The burned area

became one of the big attractions of the place, and the owners announced plans for its reconstruction as a bigger and better Luna Park.

It was never very hard for enterprising young fellows to make new friends at Coney Island, and since Brooklyn decided long ago that nothing is too good for a serviceman, only a dope need be without the companionship of the other sex. The dim-out didn't hurt business at Coney Island. It was really dark there, and what with the benches all along the boardwalk, a fellow and his girl didn't have to get sand in their shoes.

In behalf of their Joes who have been called to a higher duty, many Brooklyn girls have gone into war work and some have become junior hostesses at the numerous canteens in the borough—or else, like a group of Flatbush girls who call themselves the GAMS, organized their own canteen. GAMS, these girls earnestly explain, stands for Girls' American Morale Service. Incidentally, it also means girls' legs. And what, they ask with modest pride, are a bigger morale builder?

But if you left a girl behind you when you marched off to Camp Upton and subsequent points east, west, north, or south, you can be pretty sure that she's still there waiting for you, because there's hardly a marriageable native male left in Brooklyn, and you know what chance a guy from the Bronx has of grabbing her off, because you know what a Brooklyn girl thinks of a guy from the Bronx. She thinks he stinks.

For some time now, the strange little men who had answers to all the problems of the world and who came every noon to spout their ideas from the steps of Borough Hall have disappeared. The only meetings held on the steps nowadays have something to do with the war, like war bond drive meetings and blood donor meetings. (In a stretch of 14 months, Brooklynites bought more than a billion dollars' worth of bonds and gave more than a quarter of a million pints of blood.)

The old men still come around to Borough Hall to play checkers on the steps and sit in the sun, and the kibitzers still crowd around them. And Old Bill Pierce still rings the Borough Hall bell every noon, and the "Angelus Club," whose members are the politicians and businessmen in the neighborhood, still rise and stretch during the 40 seconds it takes him to ring the bell 12 times.

Bill Pierce says someone accused him of ringing the bell 16 times one day last March, but he says it's a damn lie. He says he rang it 17 times, and it was on the 17th, for St. Pat, and if anybody didn't like it they could go take a flying leap for themselves. And he says that when the peace comes, he'll ring the old bell "till me arm falls off."

Brooklyn for the most part is still a nine-o'clock town, but there's plenty of gayety well after that hour in the downtown section and, of course, at Coney. They're still selling double shots of the few well-known brands of liquor left, and that's still a better buy than drinking them single.

The controversy that raged for a while about whether girls should be served at the bar has quieted down. Most places will serve the young dears at the bar if they're with a guy, but some of the neighborhood bars that stick to the old tradition, like Vogel's at Third Avenue and 68th Street in Bay Ridge, won't serve a woman a drink at the bar even if she has an escort when she comes in. If a dame wants a shot at Vogel's, she has to come in through the family entrance and sit down at a table like a lady, and she better not be loud about it, either, or she'll get run out on her, let us say, ear.

For a long time, the only burlesque houses open in New York were in Brooklyn, and all the art lovers in New York City used to make pilgrimages here. But some time ago, Mayor LaGuardia looked over and saw what was going on, and he shut the Brooklyn burlesque houses down, too. That added fuel to the argument about secession.

There's a shipyard once more at the foot of Calyer Street, where the *Monitor*, the first of the ironclad ships, was built during the Civil War. That's a change in the Brooklyn you left behind. But don't be too unhappy about how different Brooklyn is—the Gowanus Canal still stinks and so does Newtown Creek.

With the Siegfried Line breached and Aachen tucked away, the next objective was the Rhine itself. But on December 16, 1944, the American offensive was halted in the Belgian Ardennes when eight Panzer divisions unexpectedly attacked the weakest sector of the Allied line, breaking through to the key cities of Bastogne and St. Vith. The Allies were forced to withdraw to the outskirts, halting their own offensive in a desperate attempt to contain the Germans and to keep them from gaining any more ground. It was during the Siege of Bastogne that the Nazi High Command issued a surrender ultimatum to the Allies, which Brig. Gen. Anthony McAuliffe rebuffed with his now-legendary, "Nuts."

Through freezing temperatures and heavy snow, the Bulge was finally taken on January 4, 1945, due in no small part to the determination of the U.S. troops that held on by their teeth, stalling the German thrust until they were able to mount a counteroffensive of their own. Yet, victory had delayed Allied operations by six weeks and cut down 60,000 men.

BATTLE OF THE BULGE

—Sgt. ED CUNNINGHAM
March 2, 1945

IN THE first frantic days of mid-December, the newspapers called it Von Rundstedt's Breakthrough in the Ardennes. Then, as the American line stiffened and held from Elsenborn to Bastogne, it became known as the Battle of the Bulge. In between that time, it was probably the most frightening, unbelievable experience of the war.

At Corregidor and Bataan, it was a lack of men and equipment. At Kasserine Pass, it was inexperienced leadership. At Anzio and Omaha Beach, it was the natural advantage of the defense over the offense. But in the Ardennes, there was no alibi. The odds were all in our favor, yet we were being pushed back.

It was a nightmare of bewilderment for the first few days. Everybody knew we had superiority in men and equipment. There was no questioning the leadership on the grounds of experience. The Germans here were not exploiting fixed defenses.

What was it, then? Why were we falling back? Had the First Army leaders really been caught with their pants down? Were the Germans really turning the tide? Would they reach Liege, cutting off supply lines to the Ninth Army along the Roer?

Everybody asked himself those questions. And nobody knew the answers until the Second Division held at Bulligen, the 30th plugged the gap at Stavelot, and the 101st Airborne stayed put at Bastogne. The answers finally came from the people such answers always come from, the guys in the line.

In most cases, the fighting, the holding, and the winning were done by regular infantrymen and tankmen. But the Breakthrough also made infantrymen out of cooks and clerks and MPs. They gave a few answers to another question, the one about "rear-echelon commandos." More than one Belgian town in those days owed its continued freedom to Americans who never received a Combat Infantry Badge.

In the middle of December, the people of the town of Hotton, Belgium, heard frightening news. The Boche had driven the Americans from St. Vith and were rolling along relentlessly toward Hotton, just as they had done in the fearful days of 1940. Holiday spirits, bubbling over at the prospect of the first free Noel since 1939, quickly died down. The Boche was coming back for Christmas.

But new hope came to Hotton the week before Christmas, when American tanks and armored vehicles rumbled across the village bridge. Most of them continued north toward the approaching Germans, but some half-tracks and trucks and 100-odd U.S. soldiers stopped in the village. The burgomeister quickly gave permission for the Americans to occupy any buildings they might need.

The people of Hotton went to bed that night confident that the Americans had come back to protect their village from the Boche. They didn't know that the handful of U.S. troops were only rear-echelon men who were not rated as combat soldiers. They were Headquarters Company cooks and clerks, Signal Corps radio operators and linemen, Armored Engineer demolition men and mechanics, and half a dozen MPs from the division Provost Marshal's Office. They had been left behind in this safe spot when Maj. Gen. Maurice Rose took the rest of the Third Armored Division forward to meet the Germans.

Headquarters Company was eating chow in the schoolhouse at 0730 the next morning when eight rounds of mortar fire exploded 40 yards away in the schoolyard. That was Hotton's first warning

that elements of a Panzer grenadier division had rolled in from the east to take the main highway at Hotton running north to Liege.

Quick reconnaissance disclosed Jerry infantry and four Mark V tanks in the woods east of the village. Capt. William L. Rodman of Philadelphia, Pennsylvania, Headquarters Company CO, ordered a firing line built up along the hedgerows running from the school to the sawmill at the north end of the main street. Then he told T-4 Paul H. Copeland of Columbus, Ohio, Special Services noncom, to take three men and a half-track and set up an outpost at the north end of town to protect that flank. Copeland grabbed a .50-caliber and a .30-caliber machine gun and asked for three volunteers to help him man the buildings on the north edge of the village. The first volunteer was his buddy, Cpl. D. A. Henrich of Antigo, Wisconsin, followed by T-5 Peter Brokus of Shamokin, Pennsylvania, half-track driver, and Pvt. Carl Hinz of Chicago, Illinois. Meanwhile, the Armored Engineers under Maj. Jack Fickessen of Waco, Texas, had set up a defense of the southwest section of the village.

Following the heavy burst of mortar fire that ripped off part of the schoolhouse roof and wounded five Yank soldiers, two of the Mark Vs started moving on the village, supported by a small infantry force that stayed a safe distance behind the vehicles. One tank came down the ridge road on the east toward the engineers' CP; the other headed along the railroad tracks that bisected the village just north of the schoolhouse. A partly disabled American M4 tank, which had been left in Hotton for repairs, went out to meet the Jerry tank coming down the ridge road. They met directly in front of the engineers' CP. The U.S. tank threw the first punch and missed. It didn't get another. The heavier enemy tank knocked it out.

The other Mark V bulled through a stone wall and edged out onto the village main street. Waiting for it, game but overmatched, was a U.S. light tank that had stopped in the town the night before. The uneven battle was over in a matter of seconds.

Winter war: frostbitten feet and death by freezing.

Rumbling on, the Mark V stuck its nose up to the window of a house where two Yank bazookamen were firing at it. Firing point-blank, it wrecked the house, but the two bazookamen miraculously escaped injury. One of them, T-5 John Swancik of Melvin, Illinois, was scorched slightly by exploding powder that went off practically under his nose.

As the Mark V backed up, it was jumped from behind by two Headquarters Company bazooka-men, T-4 Philip Popp of Lincoln, Nebraska, and Pfc. Carl Nelson of Arcadia, Nebraska. They scored a hit on the turret, and the tank was abandoned by the Jerry crew.

While the tank battles were going on, Maj. Fickessen notified headquarters by radio that there were German forces trying to move into Hotton. He asked for instructions. He got them. They were: Hold the village at all costs until a relief force arrives.

Hotton, the sleepy little crossroads village, had become an important military objective. Control of it meant control of the road net running west to Belgium's important cities and vital U.S. supply installations. Until combat troops could reach the village, its defense depended on rear-echelon men who'd been left behind while their troops went off to fight.

Loss of the patrol tanks discouraged the Jerries. Instead of following through with an infantry assault, as the outnumbered Americans expected, the Germans started building their own firing line on a ridge that overlooked the village. That gave the Americans time to organize their forces. Maj. Fickessen, senior officer in the village, took over the defense setup and started posting his men—the cooks, clerks, mechanics, and radio operators—in strategic locations. He established strongholds in the schoolhouse, in the sawmill, in the Hotel de la Paix, and in the buildings that commanded the road branching off to the east, where enemy armored attacks might be expected.

Meanwhile, the people of Hotton readied themselves for a siege of their village. With the men unable to work in the sawmill and the children unable to go to school, whole families moved into cellars to sit out the war that had come back.

The Germans continued pouring massed mortars into the village during the afternoon, scoring hits on the theater, where the treatment station was located, and severely damaging several other buildings and homes. The Yanks defending the sawmill area had to take shelter behind piles of lumber to escape the intense mortar fire. The other defenders of the outposts around the village traded small-arms fire with the enemy. But the attack that the Americans expected momentarily failed to develop. It was learned later from PWs that the Germans had sent back a hurried call for reinforcements when their four tanks and company of infantry failed to overrun the 100-odd American rear-echelon men. When they finally made their big bid for Hotton the next night, they had a full battalion of infantry plus 14 tanks and supporting artillery.

Next morning, the village defenders were reinforced by a platoon of 81mm mortars and four medium tanks which came in from the division forward CP. The tanks set up roadblocks on a road east of the village, the most likely route for a German armored attack.

During the night, the Signal Corps had laid a wire net to all the strongholds for constant intra-defense communications. A mortar OP was set up in the schoolhouse under the direction of First Lt. Clarence M. McDonald of Long Beach, New York, who happened to be around only because he was in the treatment station suffering from a mild case of pneumonia when the Jerries first struck. He didn't stay in bed long.

The mortar platoon had only 150 rounds, and the men had to make every one count. The OP was located on the top floor of the schoolhouse, the roof of which had been ripped off by mortar fire. It was cold, but McDonald stayed there all day directing the use of the few precious shells.

All day long, Signal Corps maintenance men moved from one stronghold to the next to keep the phone net in operation. Despite mortar fire and MG fire that frequently pinned them to the ground, Pfc. Max D. Troha of Hamtramck, Michigan, and Pfc. Stanley R. Presgrave of Arlington, Virginia, kept the phones working. One mortar burst landed in the Ourthe River only 15 feet from where they were repairing a broken line. They were unhurt by the blast, but several ducks swimming nearby were killed.

Late that afternoon, a Jerry mortar sailed through an open window of the mortar OP in the schoolhouse. Lt. McDonald was knocked 15 feet across the room and suffered minor abrasions of the legs and arms. He was returned to the treatment station he had visited briefly a few hours before. Another officer took over the mortar platoon.

An hour later, the Germans launched a heavy attack—later identified as a full battalion in strength—against the Americans defending the sawmill and lumberyard. First Sgt. Denver Calhoun had 35 men armed with bazookas, a few machine guns, and small arms. The attackers overran part of the position and started infiltrating into the houses on the outskirts of the village. That split the defending force in two, leaving Copeland with 23 men cut off in the north outpost.

Then the Jerries on the ridge brought their newly arrived artillery into action for the first time. They scored three hits on Hotton's main industrial building, leveled the sawmill, and set fire to some of the lumber piles. Two of the Americans were killed and three others wounded in the blast.

Maj. Fickessen ordered Sgt. Calhoun to withdraw his forces to the railroad tracks and told T-4 Copeland to cut back to the west and try to get around the Jerry spearhead set up around the sawmill. An hour later, the special services noncom brought his men, who now numbered 23, including two wounded, and all equipment back to Maj. Fickessen's CP. He had swung 300 yards west, then infiltrated through gaps in the Jerry positions without the loss of a single man or weapon.

Setting up their line along the railroad track, the reconsolidated force of cooks, clerks, and mechanics awaited the next enemy attack. It came about 0200 next morning with an estimated force of two Jerry companies driving against the defenders' line. This time the cooks and clerks held fast.

After their second failure in trying to overrun the Hotton positions, the Germans withdrew to houses on the outskirts of the town. Just before dawn, five U.S. medium tanks with infantry support rolled into Hotton from division headquarters, and more came in later in the day. The cooks, clerks, and company barber had combat support at last. Although they remained at their positions for the next two days, Hotton's original defenders had finished their job. It included the destruction of four Mark IV tanks and five Mark Vs, plus more than 100 German casualties. They pulled out of Hotton on Christmas Day to rejoin the Third Armored Division Headquarters, which had left them behind in this safe place while it went forward to meet the Germans.

Early in the afternoon on the second day of the counteroffensive along the Western Front, a convoy of Battery B, 283d Field Artillery Observation Battalion, was moving along three miles south of Malmedy, Belgium, on a road leading to St. Vith. About 300 yards beyond the crossroad of the cutoff to St. Vith, the convoy was ambushed by riflemen, machine gunners, and mortarmen hidden in the surrounding woods. All the American vehicles halted immediately. The men jumped off and took cover in the ditches lining both sides of the road. Several minutes later, they were flushed out of their hiding place by Tiger tanks from an armored column that lumbered along the ditches spraying machine-gun fire. Other tanks quickly knocked out some 24 American trucks and other vehicles. Armed only with small-caliber weapons, the Americans had no alternative but to surrender. They were ordered by their captors to live up in a snow-covered field south of the crossroads.

While the Americans were lining up, an enemy half-track mounting an 88 gun made an effort to swing around and cover them but was unable to do so. In lieu of that, the Germans parked tanks

GIs infiltrate through the gap in Jerry lines.

at either end of the field, where their machine guns had a full sweep over the prisoners. Just then, a German command car drew up. The German officer in the car stood up, took deliberate aim at an American medical officer in the front rank of prisoners, and fired. As the medical officer fell, the German fired again and another front-rank American dropped to the ground. Immediately the two tanks at the end of the field opened up with their machine guns on the defenseless prisoners who were standing with their hands over their heads. No effort had been made to segregate the noncombatant medical corpsmen, all of whom were wearing medic brassards and had red crosses painted on their helmets.

When the massacre started, those who were not wounded dropped to the ground along with those who had been shot. Flat on their stomachs, with their faces pushed into the snow and mud, the Americans were raked by withering machine-gun and small-arms fire from the column of tanks that began to move along the road 25 yards away. Each of the estimated 25 to 50 Tiger tanks and half-tracks took its turn firing on the prostrate group.

Of the approximately 150 American prisoners who were herded up as human targets, only 43 were definitely established as having escaped the German slaughter. More than three-quarters of those who escaped had been wounded. Only 25 men of Battery B's 138 were reported safe.

Pvt. James J. Mattera was the first American to make a dash for freedom and one of the six members of the surviving field artillery men who escaped without injury. Here is his sworn account of what happened when his outfit was ambushed by the Germans:

About three miles outside of Malmedy on the road to St. Vith, our convoy was forced to stop because of machine guns shooting at us and also 88 shells hitting the trucks and blowing them off the road. Everybody dismounted and lay in the ditch along the road for protection. We were forced to surrender because we were not armed heavy enough to stop the tanks.

The outfit was put into one group and a German

officer searched us for wristwatches and took our gloves and cigarettes. After the officer was through, we were marched to an open field about 100 feet from the road where the German tanks were moving by. There were about 150 of us. counting officers and medics. We all stood there with our hands up, when a German officer in a command car shot a medical officer and one enlisted man. They fell to the ground. Then the machine guns on the tanks opened up on the group of men and were killing everyone. We all lay on our stomachs, and every tank that came by would open up with machine guns on the group of men lying on the ground. This carried on about 30 minutes and then it stopped all at once.

Then about three or four Germans came over to the group of men lying on the ground. Some officers and noncommissioned officers were shot in the head with pistols. After they left, the machine gunners opened up. I lay there about one hour sweating it out. My buddies around me were getting hit and crying for help. I figured my best bet would be to make a break and run for my life.

I was the first one to raise up and I yelled, "Let's make a break for it!" About 15 fellows raised up, and we were on our way. About 12 of the men ran into a house, and myself and two other soldiers took out over the open field. They fired at us with their machine guns, but by luck we made it into the woods, where we hid until dark. The house into which the 12 men ran was burned down by the Germans. Anyone who tried to escape from the fire was shot by machine guns. After it was dark, my buddy and I made our way back to our troops. We landed with an engineering battalion, told them our story and what had happened. They gave us chow and a safe place to sleep.

Pfc. Homer D. Ford, an American MP of the 518th Military Police Battalion, was directing traffic at the crossroads when the shelling started. Along with several American soldiers who had abandoned their trucks, he took shelter behind a nearby house. Then the Germans knocked an ambulance off the road, and on hearing the blast, Ford and his companions came back to the barn and tried to hide in the hay. They saw the Germans continue on toward the American armored men, who were marching with their hands up at the point of Nazi bayonets. After searching and disarming their prisoners, the Germans ordered them to line up in the field. Then they surrounded the barn where the MP and others were hiding. Realizing they had been spotted, the Americans came out and surrendered. They were herded into the fields with the others after having been disarmed and robbed of their valuables.

Here are excerpts from Ford's sworn testimony as to what happened after the firing started:

They started to spray us with machine-gun fire, pistols, and everything. Everybody hit the ground. Then, as the vehicles came along, they let loose with a burst of machine-gun fire at us. They said: 'You dirty bastards! You will go across the Siegfried Line!' Then they came along with pistols and rifles and shot some that were breathing and hit others in the head with rifle butts. I was hit in the arm, and of the four men who escaped with me, one had been shot in the cheek, one was hit in the stomach, and another in the legs.

The men were all laying around moaning and crying. When the Germans came over, they would say, 'Is he breathing?' And would either shoot or hit them with the butt of the gun. The closest they came to me was about ten feet. After they fired at us, I lay stretched out with my hands out and I could feel that blood was oozing out. I was laying in the snow, and I got wet and started to shiver, and I was afraid they would see me shivering, but they didn't. I had my head down and couldn't see, but they were walking around the whole bunch and then they went over toward the road junction. I heard them shoot their pistols while next to me; I could hear them pull the trigger back and then the click. Then men were moaning and taking on something terrible. I also heard the butt hit their heads and the squishing noise.

As I lay there, I saw about 25 big tanks, and I would hesitate to say how many half-tracks—they went by for two hours. When all the armor and stuff had cleared the road, we got up and ran, and two Germans sprayed us with tracer bullets, but we kept on running. We ran through the field toward Malmedy, and after running for approximately two and a half miles, a jeep picked us up and brought us in.

Testimony of German PWs captured since the massacre has substantiated the account of atrocities as related by the Americans who escaped. Here is an extract of testimony given by a German Prisoner, Pvt. Fritz Steinert, a member of the First *SS* Panzer Division:

On Dec. 17, 1944, at about 3:30 p.m., I saw approximately 50 dead American soldiers lying in a field near an intersection where paved roads radiated in three directions. This point was near Malmedy and between two and three kilometers from Stavelot. The bodies were between 30 and 40 meters from the road and were lying indiscriminately on the ground, and in some instances bodies were lying across each other. There were a burning house at the intersection and a barn and shed.

Questioning the German PWs, together with evidence of *SS* uniforms and insignia supplied by the Americans, convinced First Army officials that members of an *SS* Panzer division were responsible for the atrocity at Malmedy.

During the interrogation of two of the prisoners, both members of the First *SS* Panzer division but not of the outfit near the burning house, one of them—Pvt. George Conrath—was asked about the appearance of the bodies that had caused him to think something improper had happened. "It was such an unusual sight, I thought it was murder," he said.

Asked if anyone told him how these American soldiers met their death, Conrath replied, "No, no one told us. We were all *SS* men on the tanks, and it was strictly forgotten."

The second prisoner, Cpl. Hans Strasdin, who had not personally seen the bodies but who had been told the story by German comrades, was asked if he knew why the German soldiers had killed their American prisoners.

"I have no idea," he replied. "Of course, there are people among us who find great joy in committing such atrocities."

The evacuation of a city is an awesome thing. It gives you the same feeling you get at a wake; you go in, mumble some incoherency to bereaved relatives because you can't think of anything really satisfactory to say, take a brief, self-conscious look at the corpse, and then tiptoe into another room, where you converse with fellow mourners in whispers, even though you know you couldn't possibly be disturbing the person you came to see for the last time.

That's how it is when you are present at what appears to be the last hours of a city before it falls to the enemy. There's no really satisfactory answer when a frightened Belgian woman tearfully asks you if the Americans are going to leave her town to its fate before the advancing vengeful Boche. She doesn't understand when you try to explain in mixed English and French that it is only the rear-echelon troops who are being evacuated, and that the combat men are staying behind to fight, and that this whole thing is really just a consolidation of American lines to stop the German advance before it gains too much momentum. Rear echelons and consolidated lines and the military wisdom of moving back to take advantage of natural defense terrain mean nothing to her. She only remembers the four years the Nazis spent in her town and what their return will mean to her and her people.

It is hard to look at the clusters of old men and women and children standing silently on every street corner, watching the U.S. Army six-by-sixes, command cars, and jeeps assembling in convoy for evacuation. They remind you of a bereaved family at its father's bier.

Then suddenly there is the sound of planes overhead and bombs being dropped on the convoy road that runs west of the town. On a street corner nearby, a little girl with blonde curls buries her head in her mother's coat and cries. The mother pats the blonde curls tenderly and keeps repeat-ing: "*C'est fini. C'est fini.*" But there is no belief in her voice.

A little farther down the street is a U.S. Army hospital, formerly a Belgian schoolhouse, which was evacuated this morning. The wounded and sick who slept there last night are now in ambulances and trucks, bouncing over that road which has just been bombed.

The whole population of the town seems to be lining the cobbled streets to watch the Americans leave. The men stand silently, but some of the women and young girls cry softly. Only very small children still smile and wave as their elders did a few short months ago when the Americans first came to town.

Out on the convoy road, the traffic going west is already jammed. Stretched for miles ahead are the six-by-sixes, half-ton trucks, command cars, ambulances, jeeps, weapons carriers, and heavy-ordnance vehicles linked in the moving chain of the bumper-to-bumper escape caravan.

Our jeep stalls beside a bomb crater on the right side of the road. Hanging on a fence post is a pair of torn and muddy OD pants. Half-buried in the mud below are the remains of a GI shirt, matted with blood and torn as if whoever took it off was in a great hurry. In the muddy crater are two American bodies and an abandoned stretcher. They had been pushed off the road so that the passing vehicles would not run them over. An Army blanket covers each corpse. Beside one body is a helmet with a medic's red cross painted on it. There is a hole drilled clean through it.

On the other side of the road, going east, is a long convoy of tanks, TDs, and half-tracks of an armored unit moving up to the front. Our jeep passes slowly through a village, wedged between a weapons carrier and an ordnance truck, and the people of the village line both sides of the street, watching the movement of war. The people on our side are silent and grave, and their eyes have a mixed expression of dread and reproach. They look at our column without warmth, because it is going west. But on the other side there are young girls waving and laughing at the Americans in the tanks

A visit from Ike.

and half-tracks who are going east to meet the Germans. Older men and women smile behind their fears and give the V-salute to the men in crash helmets. An old lady stands in the doorway of a house by the road, urging a little boy by her side to wave at the Yanks.

At the edge of the village, still going west, are long lines of refugees, carrying suitcases and blankets and tablecloth packs, plodding slowly and painfully along the shoulders of the road. Some of the more fortunate ride bicycles with their packs balanced on the handlebars. Others push carts loaded with lamps and favorite chairs and loaves of bread and sacks of potatoes. A baby too young to walk sits on a sack of potatoes and smiles at everything.

There is a feeling of security along the road when it gets dark, and there is no longer the fear of planes. The convoy travels blacked out, with only cat's eyes and taillights to mark its progress, and the drivers are very careful to avoid the tanks and half-tracks on the left and the long lines of

256

civilians on the right. Suddenly there is a murmuring from the human line on the right. Everyone turns to the east. There is a low humming sound that grows gradually more ominous, and a long fiery streak flashes through the black sky. It is a German buzz bomb headed toward the Belgian cities to the west. Everyone breathes in half-takes until the flaming arrow has passed over the slow-moving convoy.

Finally the rolling country gives way to scattered black buildings, which can be sensed rather than seen. A city is coming up, far enough away from the lines to be a city of refuge. But it's not that now. Enemy planes are overhead; sirens are moaning, and red and yellow and green anti-aircraft tracers are reaching up through the blackness. They make you think of a giant Christmas tree in an enormous room, blacked out except for the red and yellow and green lights on the tree. The lights suddenly shoot up, spend their brilliance, and then sink back into blackness.

Now you start to think about the people who said so confidently that the European war would be over by Christmas, and when you think about them you begin to laugh. You can laugh now—in spite of the ack-ack Christmas tree before you, the little blonde girl who cries at the sound of bombs, the old men pushing rickety carts on a convoy road running west, the Americans in crash helmets and combat overalls who ride east, and the people of the evacuated town that gives you the same feeling you get at a wake.

The battered Belgian village, with its narrow, rubble-heaped streets and worn, cold-looking houses and barns, was a far cry from the spaciousness of the Champs Elysées and the war-forgetting warmth of Paris' swank nightclubs and bars —too damned far for the men of the 82d Airborne Division regiment who had held off on their 48-hour passes so they could spend part of the Christmas holiday in Paris.

Marshal Karl von Rundstedt's counteroffensive screwed up that deal, leaving the paratroopers with nothing more than Paris rainchecks redeemable once the Jerry drive had been rolled back. But the guys in the regiment had one consolation. They, in turn, screwed up a few of Von Rundstedt's holiday plans—and they didn't issue him any rainchecks, either.

According to German prisoners taken since the counteroffensive started, Von Rundstedt had promised they would have Aachen and Antwerp for their Christmas stockings and would spend New Year's Eve in Paris. The Jerries were heading for New Year's Eve in Paris by way of Belgium. That's where they met up with the Yanks, who had similar plans for ushering in 1945.

The meeting took place on a hilly road that leads down into this Belgian village. B Company of the First Battalion started out at 1500 to look over the town, which was reported to be lightly held by the Germans. That was a slight understatement. When the Americans got within half a mile of town, they were promptly tied down by Jerry flakwagons that came out to greet them. Lacking artillery and tank-destroyer support and armed only with M1s, light machine guns, flak, grenades, and bazookas, B Company was in no spot to start trading punches. Regimental headquarters was notified of the situation and urgently requested to send something to get the German flakwagons off B Company's tail. Just about that time, somebody hit on the idea of sending in a previously captured Jerry half-track, mounting a 77, as a pinch-hitter till our own TDs and artillery arrived. A hurry call was sent out for five volunteers to man the German vehicle.

The first guy to stick his neck out was Pfc. Russel Snow of Burbank, California, a regimental code clerk. Snow, who was a clerk in the Los Angeles Board of Education office before the Army got him, volunteered to drive the half-track, although he had never handled one before. Two members of the regiment's 57mm antitank squad —Pfc. Harold Kelly of Chicago, Illinois, and Pfc. Harry Koprowski of Erie, Pennsylvania—offered to work the 77. Pvts. Thomas R. Holliday of Henderson, Kentucky, and Buland Hoover of Hobbs,

New Mexico, two BAR men, volunteered to cover the driver and the 77 gunners.

After Kelly and Koprowski had been given a brief orientation on how to operate the 77—they had never fired one before—Snow drove the half-track onto the frost-hardened rutted road and they went off to relieve the pressure on Company B. For three hours, the Yanks operated their one-vehicle armored patrol up and down the hilly road that led into the German-occupied village. Seven Jerry flakwagons, mounting 20mm guns, and several heavy machine guns were deployed around the edge of the village, well hidden by thick underbrush and heavy ground fog that reduced visibility to 100 or 200 feet. Most of the time, Kelly, who was at the sights of the 77, was firing practically blind, aiming in the direction the 20mm and machine-gun tracers were coming from. Once, however, the men on the half-track saw a column of German infantrymen coming down the road toward positions taken up by B Company. Moving in for the kill, Kelly raked their tanks with his 77, forcing them to abandon the attack. Another time, Hoover, the BAR man, spotted a Jerry machine-gun nest through the fog and silenced it permanently.

Just before dusk, a blast of a 20mm hit the brace of Kelly's gun. He got several pieces of flak in his lower lip and chin. At that point, Snow, the clerk, started doubling in brass. He maneuvered his vehicle into position against the tracers coming from the enemy 20mm or machine gun, then moved back to take Kelly's place on the 77. A moaning German half-track got into Snow's sights on the crossroads just outside of the village and went up in flames, and there were two probables on the machine-gun nests, but Snow couldn't be certain because of bad visibility. Finally, with his ammunition almost gone and Kelly in need of medical attention, Snow turned the captured Nazi vehicle around and headed back to the command post to resume his regular duties there as regimental code clerk.

After determining the real strategy of the German occupying force, Lt. Col. Willard E. Harrison of San Diego, California, battalion commander, ordered an attack on the town that night. The battalion kicked off at 2000 after a 10-minute artillery barrage, with two TDs for support.

It had started to snow, and a thick veil of white covered the huge fir trees that lined the hill road leading into town. B Company, advancing on the right side of the road, yelled over to C Company on its left: "The last ones in town are chicken. Get the lead outta your tails, you guys!"

C Company made contact first, taking on a column of 100 German infantrymen who were supported by 19 flakwagons, several tanks, and a big gun. The first wave was pinned down by murderous fire from Jerry advance machine-gun emplacements. But when the second wave came up, they overran the enemy position and wiped out both guns and crews. S/Sgt. Frank Dietrich of Detroit, Michigan, emptied his tommy gun on a machine-gun crew, and when the last Jerry started to break and run, Dietrich threw the tommy gun at him. The shock of being hit by the gun slowed up the fleeing German just enough for another C Company man to finish him off with a BAR.

Meanwhile, B Company had attacked the flakwagons with bazookas and hand grenades, mixed in with spine-freezing Texas cowboy yells and self-exhortations to "get those bastards!" It was not phony heroics, as one B Company man proved by the way he finished off a Jerry flakwagon gunner who wouldn't surrender. The kraut was injured, but he still leaned over his gun, firing at the advancing Americans. Suddenly, one tough, battle-maddened GI made a direct break for the flakwagon, yelling: "You German sonuvabitch!" He jumped up on the vehicle and stabbed the German with a knife until he fell over dead.

Another Company B man, S/Sgt. William Walsh of Winnetka, Wisconsin, had sneaked up on a flakwagon, ready to throw a grenade inside, when he was hit on the left arm and side by small-arms fire. Unable to pull the pin, Walsh had another GI pull it for him, then turned and hurled the grenade into the flakwagon.

The battalion got into the first building on the outskirts of the town that night, set up a CP there, and dug in. The Germans launched a five-hour counterattack supported by flakwagons and a tank. This failed, but only after the tank had hit the CP three times.

During daylight hours, the Yanks and Jerries fought it out at long range, with nothing particularly startling happening except for the experience of S/Sgt. Edgar Lauritsen, Headquarters Company operations sergeant from Limestone, Maine, and Pfc. Theodore Watson, a medic. While a German tank was shelling the CP, two jeeploads of soldiers in American uniforms—a captain and eight enlisted men—pulled up in front, got out, and started walking around the other side of the building toward the German lines. Watson hollered to them that they were going too far, but they ignored his warning. That aroused the medic's suspicion. He demanded to know what outfit they were from.

"The 99th," said the captain, and he continued on his way.

Sgt. Lauritsen, who had just come out of the CP, caught the tone of the conversation, got suspicious, and shouted: "What outfit in the 99th?"

"Headquarters," replied the captain in a slightly guttural voice as he kept on walking.

The accented answer convinced Lauritsen. He hollered, "Halt!" and when the eight American-uniformed strangers started running, Lauritsen opened up with his M1. The captain staggered, shot in the back, but his companions grabbed him and hurried him toward a steep embankment that led down into the woods.

The other Americans in the CP, attracted by the firing, thought Lauritsen had gone flak-happy and was shooting Yanks. They were all set to drill Lauritsen himself until they realized what had happened. By that time, the eight fugitives had escaped into the woods, presumably making their way back to German lines.

Regardless of any information the phony Americans may have carried back to the German lines, it didn't do the Nazis who were there much good. That night, the Third Battalion came up the valley and joined with elements of the First Battalion to clear the village, destroying one Mark IV tank and seven flakwagons in the process.

The Joes in the 82d figure that's some solace for the 48-hour passes they didn't get to Paris—but not enough. Mark IV tanks are poor substitutes for G-stringed blondes at the Folies Bergère, and flakwagons and dead Germans will never take the place of champagne and cognac.

The Ardennes campaign was more than a fight against the strongest German attack we had faced since the early days in Normandy. It was also a fight against almost daily snowstorms in near sub-zero temperatures and face-freezing winds which doubled the difficulty of rolling back the German advance.

We learned a lot about winter warfare in the Ardennes. Some of it was learned the hard way, by frostbitten hands and feet, pneumonia, and even death by freezing. Besides physical difficulties, there was the added trouble of frozen weapons, equipment, and even food. But out of it all came the GIs' usual improvising and homemade remedies.

Line-company men of the 83d Division, who cleared the Bois de Ronce of German opposition in a continuous eight-day push that enabled the armored spearheads to follow through to the vital St. Vith–Houffalize highway, learned a lot of ways to fight winter weather during that operation. Their methods were often makeshift and crude, because there was no time to waste on details. But the men of the 83d are sure those hastily improvised methods of keeping themselves moderately warm and dry and their weapons and equipment workable played an important part in the ultimate success of the operation.

T/Sgt. Wilbur McQuinn of Helechawa, Kentucky, a platoon sergeant in the 331st Regiment, used the usual method for frostbite prevention in his platoon by insisting on frequent toe and finger-clenching exercises to keep the blood circulating. But he and his men learned some other tricks, too.

"Some of the men took off their overshoes and warmed their feet by holding them near burning

GI heat rations [fuel tablets] in their foxholes," McQuinn said. "Others used waxed K ration boxes, which burn with very little smoke but a good flame. Both GI heat and K ration boxes are also fine for drying your socks or gloves. I also used straw inside my overshoes to keep my feet warm while we were marching. Some of our other men used newspapers or wrapped their feet with strips of blankets or old cloth."

McQuinn's company commander, Capt. Robert F. Windsor, had another angle on keeping feet warm. "We found our feet stayed warmer if we didn't wear leggings," Capt. Windsor explained. "When they get wet from snow and then freeze, leggings tighten up on your legs and stop the flow of blood to your feet. That's also true of cloth overshoes which are tight-fitting.

"Another must in this weather is to have the men remove their overshoes at night, when that's possible. Otherwise their cloth arctics sweat inside, and that makes the feet cold. Of course, the best deal is to have a drying tent set up so you can pull men out of the line occasionally and let them get thoroughly dried out and warm."

The drying tent to which Capt. Windsor referred is nothing more than a pyramidal tent set up in a covered location several hundred yards behind the front, with a GI stove inside to provide heat. There, an average of seven men at a time can dry their clothes and warm themselves before returning to their foxholes. This procedure takes from 45 minutes to two hours, depending on how wet the men's clothes are. All the front-line outfits in the 83d Division used this method.

Because of their almost continuous advance, it was all but impossible to get sleeping bags and straw up to the front-line troops. In place of straw, the men used branches of trees as matting for their foxholes. Logs and more branches were used as a roof to protect them from tree bursts. GI pioneer tools, which include axes and saws, were issued to each outfit for foxhole-construction work. Raincoats, overcoats, and the usual GI blankets were used for covers. Two or three men slept in each hole, close enough so that they could pool their blankets. Some slept with their helmets on, for an extra measure of warmth.

The chief difficulty men had in carrying their own blankets was that they got wet with snow and then froze, making them hard to roll and heavy to carry. The same was true of GI overcoats, which became water-logged after several days in the snow and slush.

On some of the more frigid nights, the men abandoned any hope of sleep and walked around and exercised all night to keep from freezing.

The front-line troops of the 83d were issued a pair of dry socks each day. However, wading through icy streams and plodding through knee-deep snowdrifts often resulted in men soaking two or three pairs of socks within a few hours. In such cases, the men wrung out their socks thoroughly and placed them inside their shirts or under their shirts or under their belts, where the heat generated by their bodies gradually dried them out. Another sock-drying method was to put them under the blankets and sleep on them at night.

Marshlands in some sections of the Bois de Ronce added to the infantrymen's troubles. When digging in for the night, they hit water two feet down. That meant two or three inches would accumulate in their foxholes before they were ready to go. This also forced them to move around gingerly on branches to avoid sinking into the water. One night, a platoon of the 83d had to dive into muddy foxholes without any preliminaries when a German tank came along a forest path spraying MG bullets. By the time the tank had retreated, every man in the platoon had had the front of his field jacket and pants, plus shoes and socks, thoroughly soaked. Enemy pressure that night was so strong that none of the dripping soldiers could be spared to go back to the drying tent. They spent the entire night in wet clothes with the temperature less than 10 above zero.

The standard GI gloves proved unsatisfactory for winter fighting, 83d men reported. When wet, they froze up and prevented the free movement of the fingers. Nor were they very durable, wearing out in a few days under the tough usage they

At last the reinforcements came.

got in the forest fighting. When their gloves wore out, many of the men used spare pairs of socks as substitutes.

Another improvisation was the use of sleeping bags for combat suits. To be sure of having their bags with them at all times, some of the men cut leg holes in them and drew them up tight, like a pair of combat jumpers. During the day they made a warm uniform; at night they served the original purpose as sleeping bags.

Web equipment was a problem. It froze solidly on cold nights and had to be beaten against a tree in the morning in order to make it pliable enough for use.

Frozen weapons were one of the most dangerous effects of the winter warfare in the Ardennes. Automatic weapons were the chief concern, although some trouble was experienced with M1 rifles and carbines. Small arms had to be cleaned twice daily because of the snow, and none of the larger guns could be left unused for any length of time without freezing up.

"The M1s were okay if we kept them clean and dry," said T/Sgt. Albert Runge, a platoon sergeant from Boston. "You had to be careful not to leave any oil on them, or they would freeze up and get pretty stiff. But you could usually work it out quick by pulling the bolt back and forth a few times. Sometimes the carbines got stiff and wouldn't feed right, but you could always work that out, too."

However, during the fighting at Petit Langlier, Pvt. Joseph Hampton found himself in a spot where he had no time to fool around with the above method. Just as his outfit started into action, Hampton found that ice had formed in the chamber of his M1. With no time to waste, Hampton thought and acted fast. He urinated into the chamber, providing sufficient heat to thaw it out. Not five minutes later, he killed a German with his now-well-functioning rifle. Hampton's company commander vouches for that story.

"The BARs gave us the most trouble," Runge said. "They froze up easily when not in use. Ice formed in the chamber and stopped the bullet from going all the way in, besides retarding the movement of the bolt. We thawed them out by cupping our hands over the chamber or holding a heat ration near it until it let loose."

Some other outfits reported that the lubricants in their light machine guns and antitank guns froze. Heat tablets were ignited to thaw out the machine guns that couldn't be cocked. But blow-torches were needed before the antitank guns were put back into firing condition.

Communications men of the 83d had headaches in the Ardennes fighting. Breath vapors wet the inside of their radio mouthpieces and then froze, cutting off transmission of their speech. Most of the time, the mikes were thawed out with cupped hands or by placing them inside sweaters.

Pfc. Frank Gaus of Pittsburgh, Pennsylvania, solved the problem by inserting a piece of cellophane inside the mouthpiece to prevent the moisture from accumulating there.

Other communications difficulties were experienced when radio batteries froze up and went dead. Signal Corps wire-maintenance crews were kept on 24-hour duty by numerous torn-out lines that resulted when tanks and other vehicles slid off the icy roads and ripped out wires.

The 83d medics also were hampered greatly by winter wartime conditions. Not only did snow-drifts make their litter-bearing jobs doubly difficult, but the severe cold caused their morphine syrettes and blood plasma to freeze. The medics remedied the morphine situation by keeping the syrettes under their armpits, thawing them out with body heat. When stoves were not available to melt the frozen plasma, they stuck it under the hood of a jeep whose motor was running. Slippery roads and snowdrifted fields often stymied jeeps, half-tracks, and tanks, which were pressed into service to haul supplies and evacuate the wounded. Some units improvised crude toboggans made of strips of tin taken from shell-shattered roofs with two-by-four planks as runners.

The 83d men found only one compensating factor amid all the misery of the Ardennes. That was when they occasionally plodded across snow-covered German mine fields without incident because the mines failed to explode. Melted snow seeped down around the firing pins of some of the mines and then froze them up when the temperature fell at night, thus preventing them from detonating. Chemicals in other mines turned to mush and failed to go off.

That was the only good thing the 83d men could find about winter war in the Ardennes.

★

MILK RUN

—Pfc. Mack Williams
June 8, 1945

ITALY—It was Christmas Eve when I found out that Jimmy was missing in action. I was hurrying back to headquarters through the icy rain, and right in the middle of the little Itie village, somebody yelled at me. I didn't know the guy's name, but I remembered he was from Jimmy's group. "Say," he said, "did you hear about Jim?"

I knew then. It couldn't be anything else when he said it that way. "What happened?" I asked.

"Nobody knows for sure. There's always different stories. Somebody said they ran into a mountain because of the fog, and somebody else said the plane was shot to hell and they had to bail out over enemy territory."

I wasn't really listening to him. I was thinking back to last night when Jimmy, Al, and I had been sitting in a little wine joint drinking *muscato* and singing with the lousy little three-piece orchestra. All of a sudden, Jimmy had asked me how the mission was for tomorrow. That had gotten to be a kind of joke between us. Because I was in headquarters, the guys from the groups always seemed to think I knew all about everything. Even when I did know what their target would be the next day, which wasn't often, I couldn't tell them, so I always gave the same answer, "It's a milk run, boy."

That's what I'd said to Jimmy, and he had laughed and said, "That's good, because I want to spend Christmas Eve with you and Al." Well, here it was Christmas Eve, and Al would be meeting me soon.

Al and Jimmy were from the same little town in the States and had known each other most of their lives. I'd only known them for a few months, but we seemed to hit it off right from the start. We spent all our free time together, even though we were in different outfits. Men get to know each other faster overseas; maybe because they're lonely as hell and need to feel close to someone.

263

Anyway, it wasn't long before the three of us felt like we'd been friends for years. We'd try to help each other, advise each other, and all that. There was the time Al got some bad news from home and went off the deep end. Jimmy and I followed him to every wine joint in town, telling him he was drinking too much, and he finally put us both to bed.

"Well, I've got to go," I said. "If you hear anything, let me know, will you?" I went back to the office and tried to do some work, but I couldn't concentrate on it. All I could think about was that Al would be waiting for me in a couple of hours, and I didn't know what to say to him.

A captain came in with a bottle of Scotch and offered me a drink. I had a couple of shots, but it didn't make me feel any better.

At five o'clock, I went over to the wine joint. Al was already there and had three drinks on the table. The first one there always ordered a round. I stood at the end of the crowded room for a few minutes, watching Al. He was talking to Mario, the waiter, and laughing. The orchestra was playing "I'll Be Seeing You." I went over and said, "Hi boy, *che si dice?*"

"*Niente,*" Al said. "What's new?"

I wondered if he was really looking at me kind of funny or if I just imagined it. I started to light a cigarette and dropped my lighter. "What's the matter?" Al asked. "Nervous in the service?"

"Must be, I'm sure not crackin' up from shackin' up." We'd used that routine a hundred times, but it was always good for a laugh.

"Well, here's a go," Al said. "Bottoms up."

I downed my drink and motioned to Mario to fill 'em up. A couple of headquarters men came by and said Merry Christmas. "Have a drink," I said. They pulled up chairs and one of them brought out a bottle of cognac. We drank from the bottle and used the wine for a chaser. Al asked, "What time is it?" Somebody told him 5:30, and he said, "Jimmy must have missed the 4:30 truck."

"Order another round," I said. "I'll be back in a minute." I went out in the rain and walked down the street a ways. I was sick as hell. I leaned against a tree and vomited.

"What's the matter?" Al said. I hadn't heard him come up behind me.

"I'm sick," I said. "I'll be okay in a minute."

"What the hell?" he said. "How much have you had to drink?"

"Not much. Guess I ate too much or something." I blew my nose and turned around to face him. He was looking at me now, all right. He was looking straight through me. "Al," I said. "Al—"

"Come on, let's go back," he said suddenly. I could see the hard line along his jaw he always got when he clenched his teeth.

When we got back, the other two guys were gone and there were three glasses of *muscato* on the table. "Well, here's a go," Al said. "Bottoms up." He drank and then he picked up the third glass, poured half the wine into my glass and half into his, and smashed the empty glass on the floor. Mario started toward us, saw Al's face, and stopped.

"Here's a go," Al whispered.

MAIL CALL

Dear *Yank*:

In two of your recent British editions you put the pinup girls on the back of the maps. How in hell can you look at the maps and pin up the girls, too?

—Pvt. Lawrence A. Peterson
Britain

We were beginning to think you didn't care. Ed.

Dear *Yank*:

In a recent issue, *Yank* featured lovely pinup Sheila Ryan perched atop the hood of an automobile, but being automotive men we were drawn to notice the exquisite lines of the partly hidden vehicle. Miss Ryan leaves no room for disagreement as to the type and model that she is, but we don't quite agree as to what make the automobile is. Enlighten us.

—Pvt. Philip E. Lass*
Alaska

*Also signed by S/Sgt. Warren, Sgt. Saul, T-4 Weckbucker, T-5s Pullman, Gavin, Martin and Fox and Pvt. Cravin.

It looks like a Lincoln Continental. Ed.

Democracy?

Dear *Yank*:

Here is a question that each Negro soldier is asking. What is the Negro soldier fighting for? On whose team are we playing? Myself and eight other soldiers were on our way from Camp Claiborne, La., to the hospital here at Fort Huachuca. We had to lay over until the next day for our train. On the next day we could not purchase a cup of coffee at any of the lunchrooms around there. As you know, Old Man Jim Crow rules. The only place where we could be served was at the lunchroom at the railroad station but, of course, we had to go into the kitchen. But that's not all; 11:30 a.m. about two dozen German prisoners of war, with two American guards, came to the station. They entered the lunchroom, sat at the tables, had their meals served, talked, smoked, in fact had quite a swell time. I stood on the outside looking on, and I could not help but ask myself these questions: Are these men sworn enemies of this country? Are they not taught to hate and destroy . . . all democratic governments? Are we not American soldiers, sworn to fight for and die if need be for this our country? Then why are they treated better than we are? Why are we pushed around like cattle? If we are fighting for the same thing, if we are to die for our country, then why does the Government allow such things to go on? Some of the boys are saying that you will not print this letter. I'm saying that you will. . . .

—Cpl. Rupert Trimmingham
Fort Huachuca, Arizona

Dear *Yank*:

. . . I'm not a Negro, but I've been around and know what the score is. I want to thank *Yank* . . . and congratulate Cpl. Rupert Trimmingham.

—Pvt. Gustave Santiago
Port of Embarkation

Dear *Yank*:

I am writing to you in regard to the incident told in a letter to you by Cpl. Trimmingham (Negro) describing the way he was forced to eat in the kitchen of a station restaurant while a group of German prisoners were fed with the rest of the white civilians in the restaurant. Gentlemen, I am a Southern rebel, but this incident makes me none the more proud of my Southern heritage! Frankly, I think that this incident is a disgrace to a democratic nation such as ours is supposed to be. Are we fighting for such a thing as this? Certainly not. If this incident is democracy, I don't want any part of it! . . . I wonder what the "Aryan supermen" think when they get a first-hand glimpse of our racial discrimination. Are we not waging a war, in part, for this fundamental of democracy? In closing, let me say that a lot of us, especially in the South, should cast the beam out of our own eyes before we try to do so in others, across the seas.

—Cpl. Henry S. Wootton, Jr.*
Fairfield-Suisun AAF, California

Also signed by S/Sgt. A. S. Tepper and Pfc. Jose Rosenzweig.

Dear *Yank*:
You are to be complimented on having the courage to print Cpl. Trimmingham's letter in an April issue of *Yank*. It simply proves that your policy is maturing editorially. He [Cpl. Trimmingham] probes an old wound when he exposes the problem of our colored soldiers throughout the South. It seems incredible that German prisoners of war should be afforded the amenities while our own men—in uniform and changing stations—are denied similar attention because of color and the vicious attitude of certain portions of our country. What sort of a deal is this? It is, I think, high time that this festering sore was cut out by intelligent social surgeons once and for all. I can well understand and sympathize with the corporal's implied but unwritten question: Why, then, are we in uniform? Has it occurred to anyone that those Boche prisoners of war must be still laughing at us?

—S/Sgt. Arthur J. Kaplan
Bermuda

Dear *Yank*:
Just read Cpl. Rupert Trimmingham's letter titled "Democracy?" in an April edition of *Yank*. We are white soldiers in the Burma jungles, and there are many Negro outfits working with us. They are doing more than their part to win this war. We are proud of the colored men here. When we are away from camp working in the jungles, we can go to any colored camp and be treated like one of their own. I think it is a disgrace that, while we are away from home doing our part to help win

the war, some people back home are knocking down everything that we are fighting for.

We are among many Allied Nations' soldiers that are fighting here, and they marvel at how the American Army, which is composed of so many nationalities and different races, gets along so well. We are ashamed to read that the German soldier, who is the sworn enemy of our country, is treated better than the soldier of our country, because of race.

Cpl. Trimmingham asked: What is a Negro fighting for? If this sort of thing continues, we the white soldiers will begin to wonder: What are *we* fighting for?

—Pvt. Joseph Poscucci (Italian)*
Burma

Also signed by Cpl. Edward A. Kreutler (French), Pfc. Maurice E. Wensen (Swedish) and Pvt. James F. Malloy (Irish).

Dear *Yank*:
Allow me to thank you for publishing my letter. Although there was some doubt about its being published, yet somehow I felt that *Yank* was too great a paper not to. . . . Each day brings three, four or five letters to me in answer to my letter. I just returned from my furlough and found 25 letters awaiting me. To date I've received 287 letters, and, strange as it may seem, 183 are from white men and women in the armed service. Another strange feature about these letters is that the most of these people are from the Deep South. They are all proud of the fact that they are of the South but ashamed to learn that there are so many of their own people who by their actions and manner toward the Negro are playing Hitler's game. Nevertheless, it gives me new hope to realize that there are doubtless thousands of whites who are willing to fight this Frankenstein that so many white people are keeping alive. All that the Negro is asking for is to be given half a chance and he will soon demonstrate his worth to his country. Should these white people who realize that the Negro is a man who is loyal—one who would gladly

give his life for this our wonderful country—stand up, join with us and help us to prove to their white friends that we are worthy, I'm sure that we would bury race hate and unfair treatment. Thanks again.

—Cpl. Rupert Trimmingham
Fort Huachuca, Arizona

Since Yank *printed Cpl. Trimmingham's letter we have received a great number of comments from GIs, almost all of whom were outraged by the treatment given the corporal. His letter has been taken from* Yank *and widely quoted. The incident has been dramatized on the air and was the basis for a moving short story published recently in the* New Yorker *magazine.*

Eight and a half square miles of volcanic ash, it represented the next-to-last steppingstone to the Japanese mainland. But the price was unusually steep, especially for heroes. On February 23, 1945, Michael Strank, Franklin Sousley, Harlon Block, Ira Hayes, Rene Gagnon, and John Bradley raised a now-legendary flag on Mt. Suribachi. Four weeks later, half of them were dead.

BATTLE FOR IWO

—Sgt. BILL REED
March 30, 1945

ANYONE WHO landed at Iwo Jima will tell you that naming the stretch of beach just north of Mount Suribachi "Green Beach" was inaccurate, to say the least.

The sand of Green Beach got into the eyes of members of the Fifth Marine Division who landed there and caked around their eyelashes. It became mixed in their hair like gritty dandruff. It invaded small cans of K ration ham and eggs as soon as they were opened. It crept over the tops of men's leggings and worked to the bottom of their shoes. The sand was both friend and enemy. It made foxhole-digging easy, but it made fast movement impossible for men and vehicles.

For two days, the men who landed on Green Beach were pinned to the ground. Murderous machine-gun, sniper, and mortar fire came from a line of pillboxes 300 yards away in the scrubby shrubbery at the foot of the volcano. No one on the beach, whether he was a CP phone operator or a front-line rifleman, was exempt. The sight of a head raised above a foxhole was the signal to dozens of Japs, safely hidden in concrete emplacements, to open up. Men lay on their sides to drink from canteens or to urinate. An errand between foxholes became a life-and-death mission for the man who attempted it.

For two days, the Marines stayed pinned to the beaches in what seemed to many of them a humiliating stalemate. Hundreds of green-clad bodies hugged the ground, spread out helplessly in a scattered pattern, furnishing marksmanship practice for the Japs on the mountain with their telescopic gunsights.

The Marines had been hopelessly cut up and disorganized when they hit the beach. Their vehicles bogged down in the sand when they were brought in. Their supplies were ruined. Many of their wounded still lay where they fell, in spite of the heroic efforts of the tireless medical corpsmen. Bad weather and a choppy ocean prevented the landing of many small boats on the second day and held up the supply of new ammunition and equipment and evacuation of the wounded. Though scores of dead Marines lay everywhere, few of our troops had seen a single Jap, dead or alive.

Towering over them was Mount Suribachi, a gray, unlovely hulk with enemy pillbox chancres in its sides. Marines on Green Beach grew to hate the mountain almost as much as they hated the Japs who were on it. Reaching the summit was almost as much of a challenge as destroying the men who defended it.

The supporting air and naval fire did much.

268

Their objective was a gray, unloving hulk.

The Japs were cleaned out with flame throwers.

Hour after hour of surface and air bombardment couldn't fail to wipe out many emplacements, imprison many Japs in their caves, and slowly eat away the mountain fortress itself. But when it came to the specific four-foot-square machine-gun emplacements and the still smaller snipers' pill-boxes, there was little the offshore and air bombardment could do except silence them for a few minutes. Everyone knew that in the end, the troops would have to dig them out.

The foot troops made their drive on the third day. They were aided by a naval and air bombardment so terrific that the Tokyo radio announced that the mountain itself was erupting. They also were aided by our own artillery and rocket guns, landed with superhuman effort the previous day in spite of a choppy ocean and the enemy's guns.

But the foot troops were aided most by the tanks that advanced with them and lobbed shells into the stone-and-concrete revetments that blocked the way of the foot troops. The Japs were afraid of our tanks—so afraid that they ducked low in their shelters and silenced their guns when they saw them. They dug dozens of tank traps, but that is all they did. They didn't dare challenge our tanks with their guns.

As soon as the tanks had passed on or had been blown up by mines, the Japs came out of their holes and attacked our men from behind with machine guns and mortars. Between the foot of the volcano and Green Beach, the enemy had hundreds of pillboxes and emplacements connected by a network of tunnels. When the Japs were driven from one pillbox, they would disappear until the Marines advanced to another, and a moment later they would appear at their old emplacement, lobbing grenades at our men who had just passed.

By early afternoon of D-plus-two, the Japs at the foot of Suribachi had been silenced. However, everyone knew there were still Japs around. There were Japs in the tunnels between the caves and there were Japs in the "spiderwebs"—the one-man sniper pillboxes—who would lift the camouflaged lids of their shelters and take pot shots at Marines trying to reorganize.

There were also many Japs who were dead. There were dead Japs in every conceivable contortion of men who meet death violently. Their arms and legs were wrenched about their bodies, and their fists were clenched and frozen. Those who had been killed by flamethrowers were burned to a black darker than the ashes of Suribachi or scorched to a brilliant yellow. Their clothes had been burned off, and the heat vulcanized their buttocks together with ugly black strips. It was good to see these sights after having been pinned down to Green Beach for two terrible days.

There were dead Marines, too. Some platoons had been entirely stripped of their officers and noncoms. Some had lost more than three-fourths of their men since morning.

But the worst of the battle for Suribachi was over. Our men had fought their way in under the guns higher up on the mountain. Many of these guns had been knocked out by our tanks and artillery and our naval and air bombardment. Many others couldn't be depressed far enough to menace our new positions.

There was still much to be done at the foot of the volcano. There were still many emplacements to be cleaned out with flamethrowers and tanks, and there were still snipers sneaking through the subterranean tunnels. The third afternoon, a detachment of Marines fought around one side of the mountain and another detachment fought around the other. Then they dug in for the night. At 0100 hours the Japs counterattacked. They kept coming until daybreak, but the Marines held them back. And all day, the Americans were busy cleaning out the tunnels, caves, and concrete emplacements at the mountain's base.

On the fourth night, S/Sgt. Ernest R. Thomas of Tallahassee, Florida, led a platoon whose officer had been killed; it was accompanied by the company's executive officer, First Lt. Harold G. Schrier of Richmond, Missouri. They dug in for the night at the base of a tortuous path leading to the top of the mountain. It was a bad night. Rain streamed down the mountain in small rivulets that trickled under their clothes and washed sand across their bodies. The cold wind made them shiver.

They huddled in foxholes, keeping their weapons dry with their ponchos.

At 0800 hours the following morning, they began the ascent. The volcanic sand on the steep path offered poor footing. Stubby plants broke off in the men's hands or pulled out by their roots. But the only resistance encounterd was the occasional *ping!* of a sniper's bullet. As the men reached the summit, they found a few more emplacements that were manned by live Japs. These were cleaned out with flamethrowers, BARs, and satchel charges.

At 1131 hours the Marines were in undisputed control of the top of the volcano. Sgt. Henry O. Hanson of Somerville, Massachusetts, looked around for a pole and found a lead pipe on the ground. At 1137 hours he, together with Lt. Schrier and other Fifth Division Marines, raised the American flag on Suribachi.

Far below, Green Beach was rapidly taking on the appearance of any other beachhead. The volcanic sand was littered with abandoned equip-

ment, and the shores were lined with boats delivering more supplies and evacuating the wounded.

Iwo Jima was far from being secured. But the Marines were on the summit of Mount Suribachi, the fortress that had made them wallow in sand for two days. Not far from where the flag flew, a communications man shouted. "This is easy!" into his field phone.

The Marines intended to stay. Green Beach had been avenged.

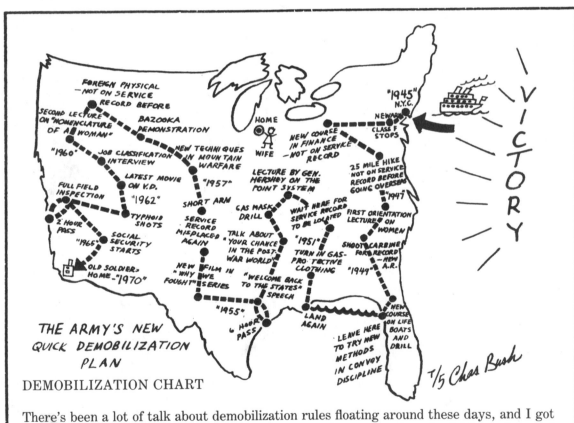

THE ARMY'S NEW QUICK DEMOBILIZATION PLAN

DEMOBILIZATION CHART

There's been a lot of talk about demobilization rules floating around these days, and I got to doing some thinking, too. So, with malice toward none, here's a chart I have dreamed up about those United States that we hope to be seeing again soon.
—T-5 CHARLES L. BUSH

The POETS CORNERED

Aleutian Lament

We've all got paper dollies;
    They're pinned on every wall,
From a pistol-packin' mama
    To luscious Lucille Ball.

We always find 'em waiting,
    True as any pearl,
But we'd trade our paper dollies
    For a fickle-minded girl.

They've got no animation
    Though posed to hypnotize,
Displaying dainty breastwork,
    Hips and knees and thighs.

We never have to worry
    About 'em doing wrong,
They're only paper dollies
    Like that one in the song.

We're getting out of practice
    At winking flirty eyes;
We need some real live dollies
    To make us flirty guys.

But we pin 'em up as often
    As we find a shapely lass,
And cuss the Frank Sinatras
    Enjoying all that class.

We'd take our chance on losing
    A dolly that was real;
A blonde, brunette, or redhead
    Would have the same appeal.

We are no longer choosy—
    For a short one, fat or long,
We'd trade our paper dollies
    To the guy who wrote the song.
                    —Cpl. James R. Gardner
                    The Aleutians

The Death of Private Jones

Let's say that Pvt. Jones died quietly.
Let's say that when the first wave stormed the
        shore
A single shot went through his heart, and he
Slipped lifeless to the sand. Not one man saw
Him die, so busy they with lying hid
And crawling on, yet all men felt the breath
Of leaden wings come close, and when they did,
It made his passing seem a public death.
So much for Jones. He died as one of scores,
And on a distant beach. But when they bring
The news to those who count the cost of wars,
A private's death becomes a private thing.
How strange that war's arithmetic discounts
The spread of sorrow as the sorrow mounts!
                    —Sgt. Harold Applebaum
                    Camp Butner, North Carolina

Time

Time on a tropical island
    Far from combat and strife,
Lush, equatorial stillness,
    Unstilled by Army life.

Simmering heat of the tropics
    Tempers, tests, and anoints.
Monotony measured by patience,
    Pays off in discharge points.
                    —S/Sgt. Irving Caress
                    Trinidad

The Radio

The radio, in days of yore,
    The days before the draft,
Caused family rows and quarreling
    Which almost drove me daft.

Soap op'ra swung dear Mama's vote
    And Papa wanted Bing;
My sister screamed for Frankie's voice
    And brother wanted swing.

But now, up in Alaskaland,
    As Uncle Sammy's guest,
I've never heard a single tiff
    On where the dial should rest.

Hell no! No fight, no dial to turn;
    But here's the situation;
There ain't no choice, no choice at all;
    We've only got one station.
                    —Sgt. William Armbruster
                                    Alaska

Supply

Back in Texas where I took my training,
I had no galoshes when it was raining.
Straight to supply and down on my knees.
"No soap," said the sergeant. "It's all overseas."

Then to England we finally sailed.
"No supply troubles now," I wailed.
Went to the sergeant with my song and dance.
"TS, my boy, it's all in France."

Someday soon I'll cross the Rhine,
Everything then should really be fine.
The supply angle will be terrific,
When I get there it's in the Pacific.
                    —Pfc. Bob Timrick
                                    France

Query

Breathes there a GI
    On the face of the earth
Who possesses the rating
    He thinks he's worth?

                    —Anonymous

Travel Note

From London to Tahiti,
From Attu to Port of Spain,
From Bougainville to Martinique,
You'll hear a new refrain;
From Frisco to Pearl Harbor
The legend will appear
That during World War No. 2
Mrs. Roosevelt slept here.
                    —Sgt. Jack N. Carl
                            Southwest Pacific

The Reconversion

When bugles sound their final notes
    And bombs explode no more.
And we return to what we did
    Before we went to war,
The sudden shift of status
    On the ladder of success
Will make some worthy gentlemen
    Feel like an awful mess.

Just think of some poor captain
    Minus all his silver bars
Standing up behind some counter
    Selling peanuts and cigars;
And think of all the majors
    When their oak leaf's far behind
And the uniform they're wearing
    Is the Western Union kind.

Shed a tear for some poor colonel
    If he doesn't feel himself;
Jerking sodas isn't easy
    When your eagle's on the shelf.
'Tis a bitter pill to swallow,
    'Tis a matter for despair;
Being messengers and clerks again's
    A mighty cross to bear.

So be kind to working people
    That you meet where'er you go,
For the guy who's washing dishes
    May have been your old CO.
                    —Pfc. Edward Blumenthal
                            Fort Knox, Kentucky

Re: Your Letter

V-mail is quicker,
Air mail is thicker.

—Pvt. Raymond Carlson
Southwest Pacific

Rank Reflection

I vow that I
   Would never gripe
Could I but wear
   Just one more stripe.

But then again
   It seems to me
I felt that way
   As pfc.

—Cpl. G. G. Dowling
Camp Atterbury, Indiana

In Memoriam
(Freeman Nimhauser, Killed in Action)

From pen to rifle
It was a long way,
From Greenwich Village to New Guinea
Yet it was the same.

Mourn for the dead who died in vain,
But not for him.

When the poems gave out,
When it wasn't enough
To sing of freedom,
He fought for what he wrote for,
He died for what he lived for.

Mourn for the dead who died in vain,
But fight for him.

—Pvt. John E. Brown
ASTP, Atlanta, Georgia

"You realize, Ludlow, this goes on your service record."
—SGT. AL JAFFEE

★

___

By now they were unstoppable, smashing down the Moselle and Roer rivers into the Rhone River Valley toward a rendezvous with the Russian troops pushing toward them from the north. Key bridges at Remagen and Nijmegen had been destroyed, Dresden had been incinerated, and the entire Nazi war machine teetered on the brink of collapse. Unbeknownst to the GIs, a German surrender was already under negotiation.
But first, the Roer.

ASSAULT ACROSS THE ROER

—Sgt. Howard Brodie
April 13, 1945

I JOINED K Company, 406th Regiment, 102d Division, the night before the shove-off, as an artist, not an infantryman.

We were part of a reserve regiment several miles behind the line and would not be committed until after the Roer had been crossed by forward elements.

I felt every one of us sweated it out as we went to sleep that night. At 0245, our barrage awoke us, but we stayed in our sacks until 0400. After hot chow, we saddled our packs and headed for an assembly area in a wrecked town about five miles away. It was a silent company of men spaced on either side of the road—the traditional soldier picture of silhouettes against the crimson flashes of shells bursting on the enemy lines in the distance.

In the assembly town, we waited in the shattered rooms of a crumbling building. It was not pleasant waiting, because a dead cow stank in an adjoining room. We shoved off at daylight and came to gutted Rurdorf. I remember passing crucifixes and a porcelain pee pot on the rubble-laden road and pussy willows as we came to the river. A pool of blood splotched the side of the road. We crossed the Roer on a pontoon bridge and moved on. The forward elements were still ahead of us a few miles.

We passed a still doughboy with no hands on the side of the road; his misshapen, ooze-filled mittens lay a few feet from him. Knots of prisoners walked by us with their hands behind their heads. One group contained medics. In their knee-length white sacks, emblazoned with red crosses, they resembled crusaders. In another group were a couple of German females, one of them in uniform. Mines like cabbages lay on either side of the road.

We entered the town of Tetz and set up the CP in a cellar. Two platoons went forward a few hundred yards to high ground overlooking the town and dug in. We were holding the right flank

**They passed a still doughboy with no hands
by the road; his misshapen mittens lay beside him.**

of the offensive finger. Several enemy shells burst in the town. Some tracers shot across the road between the CP and the dug-in platoons, seemingly below knee-level. Night fell.

The CP picked up reports like a magnet: "The Jerries are counterattacking up the road with 40 Tiger tanks. . . . The Jerries are attacking with four medium tanks." Stragglers reported in from forward companies. One stark-faced squad leader had lost most of his squad. The wounded were outside, the dead to the left of our platoon holes. It was raining. I went to sleep.

The next day, when I went to our forward platoons, I saw a dough bailing his hole out with his canteen cup . . . saw our planes dive-bomb Jerry in the distance . . . saw our time-fire burst on Jerry, and white phosphorus and magenta smoke

bombs. I saw platoon leader Lt. Joe Lane playing football with a cabbage. I saw a dead GI in his hole, slumped in his last living position—the hole was too deep and too narrow to allow his body to settle. A partially smoked cigarette lay inches from his mouth, and a dollar-sized circle of blood on the earth offered the only evidence of violent death.

Night fell, and I stayed in the platoon CP hole. We didn't stay long, because word came through that we would move up to the town of Hottdorf, the forward position of the offensive finger, preparatory to jumping off at 0910.

K Company lined up in the starlit night—the CO, the First Platoon, MGs, the Third Platoon, heavy weapons, headquarters, and the Second Platoon in the rear—about 10 paces between each

A partially smoked cigarette lay near his mouth.

man and 50 between the platoons. The sky overhead was pierced by thousands of tracers and AA bursts as Jerry planes flew over. Again it was a silent company.

At Hottdorf, we separated into various crumbling buildings to await H-Hour. We had five objectives, the farthest about two and a quarter miles away. All were single houses but two, which were towns of two or three houses. We were the assault company of the Third Battalion.

H-Hour was approaching. A shell burst outside the window, stinging a couple of men and ringing our ears. We huddled on the floor.

It was time to move now. The First Platoon went out on the street, followed by the MGs and the Third Platoon and the rest of us. We passed through doughs in houses on either side of the street. They wisecracked and cheered us on. We came to the edge of town and onto a broad, rolling field. The Third and First Platoons fanned out in front of us. Headquarters group stayed in the center.

I followed in the footsteps of Pfc. Joe Esz, the platoon runner. He had a light aluminum case upon which I could easily focus the corner of my eye to keep my position and still be free to observe. Also, I felt that if I followed in his footsteps, I would not have to look down at the ground for mines. He turned to me and commented on how beautifully the company was moving, properly fanned and well spaced.

Several hundred yards away, I noticed Jerries running out of a gun position waving a white flag. A black puff of smoke a few hundred yards to my right caught my attention, then another closer. I saw some men fall on the right flank. The black puffs crept in. There were whistles and cracks in the air, and a barrage of 88s burst around us. I heard the "zing" of shrapnel as I hugged the earth. We slithered into the enemy 88 position from which I had seen the prisoners run. Somebody threw a grenade into the dugout.

We moved on. Some prisoners and a couple of old women ran out onto the field from a house, objective one. There was the zoom and crack of 88s again. A rabbit raced wildly away to the left. We went down. I saw a burst land on the running Jerries. One old woman went down on her knees in death, as though she was picking flowers.

A dud landed three feet in front of T/Sgt. Jim McCauley, the platoon sergeant, spraying him with dirt. Another ricocheted over Pfc. Wes Maulden, the 300 radio operator. I looked to the right flank and saw a man floating in the air amidst the black smoke of an exploding mine. He disap-

On the right flank, men fell.

peared just in front of the squad leader, S/Sgt. Elwin Miller. A piece of flesh sloshed by Sgt. Fred Wilson's face. Some men didn't get up.

We went on. A couple of men vomited. A piece of shrapnel cut a dough's throat as neatly as Jack the Ripper might have done it.

The right flank was getting some small-arms fire. I was so tired from running and going down that it seemed as though my sartorius muscles would not function. The 300 radio wouldn't work, and we couldn't get fire on those 88s. Pfc. George Linton went back through that barrage to get another one from Hottdorf. Medic Oliver Poythress was working on wounded in that barrage.

Objective two loomed ahead—a large building enclosing a courtyard. A cow shed, stables, toolshed, hay loft, and living quarters opened onto the inner court. I saw an 88 explode over the arched entrance.

We filtered into the courtyard and into the sur-

rounding rooms. The executive officer started to reorganize the company. The platoons came in. First Sgt. Dick Wardlow tried to make a casualty list. A plan of defense was decided on for the building. A large workhorse broke out from his stable and lumbered lazily around the courtyard. T-4 Melvin Fredell, the FO radio operator, lay in the courtyard relaying artillery orders. An 88 crashed into the roof. The cows in their shed pulled on their ropes. One kicked a sheep walking around in a state of confusion.

A dying GI lay in the toolshed; his face was a leathery yellow. A wounded GI lay with him. Another wounded dough lay on his belly in the cow shed, in the stench of dung and decaying beets, and another GI quietly said he could take no more. A couple of doughs started frying eggs in the kitchen. I went into the toolshed to the dying dough.

"He's cold, he's dead," said Sgt. Charles Tur-

Dud shells landed close, spraying men with dirt.

pen, the MG squad leader. I took off my glove and felt his head, but my hand was so cold, he felt warm. A medic told me he was dead.

Lt. Bob Clark organized his company and set up defense. FO Philip Dick climbed the rafters of the hayloft to report our artillery bursts. The wounded dough in the cow shed sobbed for more morphine. Four of us helped to carry him to bed in another room. He was belly down and pleaded for someone to hold him by the groin as we carried him: "I can't stand it. Press them up, it'll give me support." A pool of blood lay under him.

I went to the cow shed to take a nervous leak. A shell hit, shaking the roof; I ducked down and found I was seeking shelter with two calves. I crossed the courtyard to the grain shed, where about 60 doughs were huddled.

Tank fire came in now. I looked up and saw MG tracers rip through the brick walls. A tank shell hit the wall and the roof. A brick landed on the head of the boy next to me. We couldn't see for the cloud of choking dust. Two doughs had their arms around each other; one was sobbing. More MG tracers ripped through the wall, and another shell. I squeezed between several bags of grain. Doughs completely disappeared in a hay pile.

We got out of there, and our tanks joined us. I followed a tank, stepping in its treads. The next two objectives were taken by platoons on my right, and I don't remember whether any 88s came in for this next quarter mile or not. One dough was too exhausted to make it.

We were moving up to our final objective now —a very large building, also enclosing a courtyard, in a small town. Jerry planes were overhead but for some reason did not strafe. Our tanks spewed the town with fire and led the way. Black bursts from Jerry time-fire exploded over our heads this time. We passed Jerry trenches and a barbed-wire barrier. Lt. Lane raced to a trench. A Jerry pulled a cord, setting off a circle of mines around him, but he was only sprayed with mud. S/Sgt. Eugene Flanagan shot at the Jerry, who jumped up and surrendered with two others.

Jerries streamed out of the large house. Women came out, too. An 88 and mortars came in. I watched Pfc. Bob de Valk and Pfc. Ted Sanchez bring out prisoners from the basement, with Pfc. Ernie Gonzalez helping.

We made a CP in the cellar. The wounded were brought down. Stray Jerries were rounded up and brought to the rear. Jittery doughs relaxed for a moment on the beds in the basement. Pfc. Frank Pasek forgot he had a round in his BAR and frayed our nerves by letting one go into the ceiling. A pretty Jerry girl with no shoes on came through the basement. Doughs were settling down now.

Two doughs had their arms around each other.

The CO started to prepare a defense for a counterattack. Platoons went out to dig in. L and M Companies came up to sustain part of our gains.

Most of us were too tired to do much. The battalion CO sent word that he was relieving us. All of us sweated out going back over the field, although this time we would go back a sheltered way. We were relieved and uneventfully returned to a small town. The doughs went out into the rain on the outskirts and dug in. A few 88s came into the town.

Early the next morning, K Company returned to its former position in the big house, with the courtyard as the final objective. Just when I left, Jerry started counterattacking with four tanks and a company of men.

⭐

1293D SCU, UNIVERSITY OF BUFFALO, N.Y.—When Pvt. Charles DelValle of Company B reported on morning sick call to complain of hemorrhoids, the doctor told him to report for an eye examination. He came back to company headquarters at 1100 with a dislocated knee and at 2100 he was operated on for acute appendicitis.

WITH THE FIRST CONVOY TO CHINA OVER THE LEDO-BURMA ROAD—At one of the many parties thrown for officers and men of the convoy on its way through China, a member of the Chinese Army was placed as host at each table of GIs.

At one table a GI driver began calling the Chinese Army man "Butch" and getting very chummy, although neither could speak more than a few words in the other's language. Finally the host asked the GI, "What is your commission in the Army, sir?"

The GI grinned and replied, "Corporal. What's yours, Butch?"

The Chinese Army man had to get an interpreter to find out what the GI said, then he answered, "Lieutenant general, sir."

"Geez," said the GI later. "It's a good thing he doesn't know what a corporal is."

FORT DIX N.J.—The lieutenant, calling the roll of the men getting their discharges at the Separation Center here, rattled off the names Lathrop, McKeon, etc., and the men concerned answered with their first names. Finally, he called "Justice."

There was a silence; then Pfc. Ullsberger, a member of the permanent party of the post, spoke up.

"There *is* no Justice," he said.

NORTHERN IRAN—MPs at a GI camp here have developed a secret weapon—a foolproof method for stopping Russians.

When Red Army truck drivers refused to slow down at the gate, the MPs—used to having eagles come to a dead stop and present dog tags—were vexed. As one MP said, "We were vexed."

They put their heads together, seeking some great common denominator to hurdle both the linguistic barrier and the natural impetuosity of a Russki in the driver's seat. Next morning Russian trucks skidded to a meek halt. Cheerfully Red Army soldiers showed their passes.

"We pinned up a pitcha of Ann Savage on the outside of the gatehouse," said the MP corporal. "Cut it outta *Yank*. Everybody stops—Russian drivers, doggie drivers, old guys on camels. Now we gotta figure some way to get them moving again."

CAMBRIDGE, MASS.—Acting 1st Sgt. George C. Vaughan, inspecting the quarters of the Harvard ASC Unit, came upon a neglected window sill and in the dust he printed the word "dirty." Returning next day to check the room, he found the "dirty" still undisturbed, but underneath it someone had written "where?"

ANGUAR, PALAU ISLANDS—When the 81st Division hit Saipan Town on Anguar, they noticed a shed piled high with bottles. "Sake," guessed the troops, and an MP was appointed to keep an eye on things. Near Suicide Hill more bottles were found lying outside Jap dugouts.

But instead of Japanese characters, the labels were lettered in English: TOMATO CATSUP. And inside the bottles, instead of sweet-tasting sake, was a thick something that looked and tasted just like the ketchup it was alleged to be. One GI guessed the Japs used it as a flavoring for the sacks and sacks of rice piled on the island. But another had a simpler solution to the mystery: "They just like ketchup, I guess."

New Caledonia—It's kind of lonesome these days at a certain Army dispensary here. Pfc. Stanley Pryzbyla has quit coming around.

This healthy-looking 190-pound typist in a Signal Corps photographic lab has been on sick call exactly 103 times in five months. He is proud of his record but resents being known as a goldbrick.

"It was always legitimate stuff," he says. First he got some sort of fungus in his armpits. That was cured in a few months. Then someone brought a cat into his tent, and Pryzbyla broke out in flea-bites. After the fleabites the fungus came back. All in all, it was just one damned thing after another.

None of this made life any easier for Pryzbyla. His lieutenant jumped on him for missing so much work. And his friends all called him a goldbrick.

"Things got so bad," Pryzbyla says, "that I asked the doctor to give me some salve to treat myself. In the meantime, the lieutenant went to the Old Man about me missing so much work. Well, you know the regulations—they can't keep a man off the sick book, but they can make it tough for him. So the Old Man put out an order that the sick truck was to quit stopping off at the service club. After that, things were pretty boring."

Pryzbyla is a well man now and hasn't seen the inside of the dispensary for several weeks. The company clerk is a little sorry. "I was just getting to the point where I could spell his name," he says.

Commander-in-Chief, 1933–1945.

To most of them, he was the only president they'd ever known. He'd bailed them out of the Depression, found work for their fathers, reopened their stores, and fed them again. Now, with the war all but won, the shattering news from Warm Springs, Georgia, was practically inconceivable.

"SO LONG, SIR"

May 11, 1945

MOST OF us in the Army have a hard time remembering any president other than Franklin D. Roosevelt. We never saw the inside of a speakeasy, because he had prohibition repealed before we were old enough to drink. When we were kids during the Depression, and the factories and stores were not taking anybody, plenty of us joined his CCCs, and the hard work in the woods felt good after those months of sleeping late and hanging around the house and the corner drugstore, too broke to go anywhere and do anything. Or we got our first jobs in his ERA or WPA projects. That seems like a long time ago.

And since then, under President Roosevelt's leadership, we have struggled through 12 years of troubled peace and war, 12 of the toughest and most important years in our country's history. It got so that all over the world, his name meant everything that America stood for. It meant hope in London and Moscow and in occupied Paris and Athens. It was sneered at in Berlin and Tokyo. To us, wherever we were, in the combat zones or in forgotten supply and guard posts, it meant the whole works—our kind of life and freedom and the necessity for protecting it. We made cracks about it and told Roosevelt jokes and sometimes we bitterly criticized his way of doing things. But he was still Roosevelt, the man we had grown up under and the man whom we had entrusted with the staggering responsibility of running our war. He was the commander in chief, not only of the armed forces but of our generation.

That is why it is hard to realize he is dead, even in these days, when death is a common and expected thing. We had grown accustomed to his leadership and we leaned on it heavily, as we would lean on the leadership of a good company commander who had taken us safely through several battles, getting us where we were supposed to go without doing anything foolish or cowardly. And the loss of Roosevelt hit us the same way as the loss of a good company commander. It left us a little panic-stricken, a little afraid of the future.

But the panic and fear didn't last long. We soon found out that the safety of our democracy, like the safety of a rifle company, doesn't depend on the life of any one man. A platoon leader with the same training and the same sense of timing and responsibility takes over, and the men find themselves and the company as a whole operating with the same confidence and efficiency. That's the way it will be with our government. The new president has pledged himself to carry out its plans for the successful ending of the war and the building of the peace. The program for security and peace will continue.

Franklin D. Roosevelt's death brings grief but should not bring despair. He leaves us great hope.

"This Is the First Uncensored Daily Express *in Six Years!"*—London headline.

THE FALL OF GERMANY

—Sgt. ALLAN ECKER
June 1, 1945

The two weeks that ended with the Germans' signing an official surrender at 2041 hours, U.S. Eastern War Time, Sunday, May 6, 1945, were crammed with more important happenings than any other equal period of the war. From the fall of Cologne and the massing of Russian assault forces on the east bank of the Oder, the fact of final German defeat had been obvious. The climax came in these last two big weeks, and when it came, news flash tumbled upon news flash, rumor upon rumor, surrender upon surrender, so quickly that the average GI or civilian could hardly grasp one Allied triumph before he was caught up by the impact of the next.

These two weeks began with the Russian battle for possession of Berlin in full swing. Below Berlin, near Torgau on the Elbe, tankmen of the U.S.

First Army were beginning to pick up snatches of Russian combat directions on their mobile radios. Marshal Ivan Konev's forces were moving to meet them. All along the Western Front, an Allied nutcracker was breaking up the vaunted "hard core" of German defense, U.S. Lt. Gen. William H. Simpson's Ninth Army was pushing east from Magdeburg, Gen. George S. Patton's tankmen were cowboying toward the Czech border, the First Canadian Army was at Emden, the First French Army was past Stuttgart, Lt. Gen. Alexander Patch's Seventh U.S. Army was south of the Danube near Lauringen, Gen. Jacob L. Devers' Sixth Army Group threatened Bavaria, British Field Marshal Sir Bernard L. Montgomery's

Twenty-first Army Group was bringing complete freedom to the Netherlands and Denmark. From their side, the Russians continued the same inexorable squeeze that had forced the Germans back from their high tide of Eastern aggression before Leningrad and Stalingrad. Marshal Gregory Zhukov's First White Russians were in Berlin. Konev was almost to the Elbe River. Gen. Fedeor Tolbukhin's Third Ukrainian Army cut into the Nazi redoubt. Gen. Rodion Malinovsky had pushed through Vienna and was following the Danube deeper into Austria. In Italy, the long, dull stalemate of Lt. Gen. Mark W. Clark's polyglot armies had been broken. The U.S. 10th Mountain Infantry Division had spearheaded a breakthrough, and the war in Italy had a moving front again—a moving front of Fifth Army veterans, including American Negro troops and Japanese-Americans and Brazilian Allies and free Italian troops, and British and Indian GIs of

the famous Eighth, which had swept across Africa in 1943—all of them aided by the sabotage and behind-the-lines action of Italian partisans in the north and by the sharp, constant pressure against the German eastern flank from Marshal Tito's Yugoslavs. Hitler's Germany was going down in flames.

Moving forward with the U.S. Ninth Army into the confusion of a dying Reich, *Yank* staff correspondent Sgt. Allan Ecker observed the symptoms of collapse:

A FERRYBOAT, a big barge propelled by the hand-over-hand cable system, was loaded to the gills with about 60 displaced persons, German nationals and American GIs crossing west over the Elbe from a strictly unofficial American 35th Division bridgehead on the other side of the river. A patrol of K Company of the 137th Infantry under Lt. Howard Pierson of

Huntington, Oregon, and S/Sgt. Denzil Lindbom of Peoria, Illinois, had made a crossing to the eastern bank for a brief reconnoitering, but they'd run into a peculiar situation.

Everybody and his uncle in the little town of Ferchland insisted on going back with them. So the boys set up a ferryboat. One of the passengers when we went back was a German woman with four kids, the youngest five months old, all of them waiting to beat the band. We asked where she was coming from and where she was heading, and her answer seemed to sum up the whole plight of the German nation crushed between two fronts: "We left Brandenburg two days ago," she said, "because the Russian bombs and shells leveled our home there. Where are we going? To a big city where we have relatives.

"Perhaps you've been there? It's called Aachen."

Among the prize catches of the 102d Division was an attractive and much-married female Gestapo agent whose current and fourth husband is an SS major general. Interrogated at her hideaway house in the woods by German-born Edward Hoffer of New York City, the *frau* was much embarrassed by one question. She couldn't remember the first name of her first husband with whom she had lived for seven years, until 1929.

As Russian and American forces converged on the Western Front, a rumor started back among the Eighth Armored Division men around Braunschweig that a junction had already been effected. "Just take a look at those two guys if you don't believe it," GIs advised cynics.

"Those two guys" were honest-to-God Red Army first lieutenants, one of them an ex-member of the Crimea General Staff. They were, to be sure, a trifle out of uniform: GI ODs and field jackets, German leather boots and Lugers, Russian shoulder insignia, and GI helmets with big red stars and the words "Soviet Union" painted on them.

Picked out of a horde of Russian slave laborers and war prisoners wandering along the highways and byways of Germany, the two officers had been given razors, baths, and equipment by the Eighth Armored's 88th Cavalry Recon Squadron. Thus transformed, they were ready—with the aid of Russian-speaking Pfc. Frank Ilchuk of New York City—to organize some of the thousands of their countrymen into orderly communities in each village. Many starving Russians, newly liberated, have taken to pillaging and cluttering up important roadways. The use of Red Army officers to control them and the requisitioning of rations from local German *burgomeisters* was put into effect to take the load off American combat units until military government authorities arrive in sufficient numbers to take over.

In the news, as the first of the two last weeks wore on, you heard less about Adolf Hitler and more about Heinrich Himmler, his Gestapo chief. There were increasing rumors of Hitler's disappearance or his death or his madness, and with them, increasing rumors of a Himmler bid for peace. The peace rumors reached a climax in a false armistice announcement in the United States on April 28. Newspaper headlines screamed "Germany Quits!" and premature celebrations were set off in some communities. They didn't last long in the face of a sharp denial from Supreme Allied Headquarters and the White House.

The facts behind the false armistice—Himmler's attempt to surrender to the United States and Great Britain and leave Russia holding the bag— were true. But the chief fact behind the Himmler trial balloon was fear, German fear before an assault the Germans now knew they could not withstand.

Lt. Gen. George S. Patton's Third Army was an arrow aimed at Hitler's Berchtesgaden mountain hideaway. U.S. troops took Italy's chief naval base at La Spezia. Genoa fell. Aged ex-Vichy chief, Marshal Petain, came through Switzerland to give himself up for trial in liberated France. The Germans in Italy were shoved back into the Alps and their lines of possible retreat were all but cut off. Great Britain and the United States refused to be parties to any peace overtures that did not include their Russian ally. At Torgau, advance groups of the First Army's 69th Division made contact with the 58th Guards Division of Konev's First Ukrainian Army.

Sgt. Ed Cunningham, Yank staff correspondent, was with the First Army to report the meeting:

A 28-man, 6-jeep patrol of 69th Division Yanks under the command of First Lt. Albert Kotzebue of Houston, Texas, and his platoon sergeant, T/Sgt. Frederick Johnston of Bradford, Pennsylvania, and a Russian cavalry patrol made the first linkup between the Eastern and Western Fronts. The meeting took place on a hill outside the village of Zauwitz just before 1330 hours on April 25.

The jeeps roared up the hill smack into the middle of a group of hard-riding Cossacks who were patrolling the area in search of stray pockets of German resistance. Both units recognized each other, so there was none of the confusion that attended some later Russki-Yank meetings.

The Cossacks detailed a Russian civilian to guide Lt. Kotzebue and his men to where the CG of the Russian division was waiting to greet them on the other side of the hill. Then they galloped off in search of more Germans.

The American patrol crossed the Elbe in jeeps ferried on a platform raft and fell headlong into a lively Russian celebration.

A Russian major who spoke a few words of English set the tone of the celebration with a toast. "Today," he said, "we have the most happy day of our lives. The years 1941 and 1942 were a most difficult time. Germany was at Stalingrad. It was the most difficult time of our lives. At that time we do not think of our lives, we think of our country.

"Just now, our great friends and we have met one another, and it is the end of our enemy. Long live your great leader. Long live our great leader. Long live our great countries."

Maj. Fred Craig of Friendship, Tennessee, and Second Lt. Thomas R. Howard of Mississippi were in command of the second patrol to meet the Russians. They made contact at 1545, April 25, at Clanzchwitz with a column of Russian cavalry.

The Russians galloped across an open field to meet them, throwing their helmets in the air. Maj. Craig was ferried across the river and taken back to the Russian corps headquarters to meet the lieutenant general commanding. The general asked him if he was the highest American officer available to greet him, and Maj. Craig explained that his was only a patrol, not the official greeting party.

The major and his men had two meals with the Russians, one at 1900 and one at 0930 the next morning. Once again, there were toasts and mutual greetings. The Russians had several cameramen and correspondents on hand to record the meeting and seemed sorry we didn't have any of our own. The general told the major he was sending a message direct to Stalin to inform him of the meeting. The Russians and Yanks fired each other's weapons and criticized them. Red Army men found our M1 too heavy for their taste but liked our carbine and .30-caliber machine guns.

During the night, the radio operators at the major's CP on the west bank of the Elbe relieved each other so they could cross and enjoy the Russian party. A Cossack column stopped by the CP and put on a two-hour serenade of Russian songs with harp, mouth organ, and accordion accompaniment.

In the morning, a Russian barber shaved the Yanks in bed. It was quite a meeting.

The third U.S. patrol to contact the Russians had a more confusing time of it. It was led by Second Lt. William D. Robertson, First Battalion, 273d Regiment, 69th Division, who had studied Japanese as an ASTP man, a factor that was as useful as an extra toenail in establishing friendly relations.

Robertson and his three-man patrol reached the town of Torgau on the banks of the Elbe after a 27-mile jeep ride through the no-man's-land then separating our forces. He spotted Red Army men on the opposite bank and shouted to them: "Amerikanski! Come over. Friends! Tovarisch." But the Russians weren't having any, since a German patrol had tried to get next to them by pretending to be Americans the day before.

Robertson and his three-man GI patrol weren't daunted and proceeded to manufacture an American flag from cloth and red, white, and blue paint procured at a Torgau store. They waved their flag at the Russians from the tower of a castle. The Russians fired two colored flares, the agreed linkup signal. But Robertson had no flares to fire back.

The Russians were now thoroughly convinced that something phoney was afoot. They opened up with an antitank gun and small-arms fire on the castle and scored two direct hits.

An American naval lieutenant, a newly-freed PW, came up about that time. He spoke Russian and so did a Russian liberated slave worker who was nearby. Between the two of them, they managed to shout the news across the Elbe that the patrol was really American and wanted to meet the Russians.

Then and then only did the Russians relent and allow Robertson and his men to cross to their bank.

Once across, the meeting followed the pattern already set. There was vodka and backslapping; there were toasts and mutual congratulations. This third meeting by Lt. Robertson's patrol was the one credited as the first contact in early news dispatches.

The climactic meeting, of course, was when Maj. Gen. Emil E. Reinhardt of Decatur, Georgia, CG of the 69th, made his official visit to Lt. Gen. Rosakov, CG of the 58th Guards Division. The major general and three staff officers crossed the Elbe and returned in a slim German racing boat, so delicately balanced that all the officers had to sit at attention in order not to tip themselves over into the drink. The shell had been designed for sport, not transportation, but it was the only craft available at the section of the Elbe where Gen. Reinhardt crossed and where the Germans had blown the only two bridges.

Sgt. Andrew Marriack of Hudson, New York, served as interpreter for a Russian captain who told some of the Americans gathered by the river how his men had taken Torgau. Marriack had learned his Russian as an ASTP student at City College in New York.

"They took this town two days ago," he trans-

Left: *Russian and American soldiers had a celebration after they met near the town of Torgau, Germany, April 25.*
Center: *The bodies of Benito Mussolini, the "sawdust Caesar," and his Clara Petacci lie in a square in Milan after their execution by partisans.*
Right: *German officers meet Montgomery on May 3, to surrender forces in Netherlands, northwest Germany, and Denmark.*

lated. "It wasn't much of a fight, but the captain got sore because the Germans ambushed one of his patrols. He says a gang of Krauts held up a white flag, and when his patrol came over to take them prisoner, they threw down the flag and opened fire, killing two of his men. He says the Germans don't fight like human beings; they're treacherous and they destroy towns and civilian populations without any cause. He says the Russians will stay in Germany until the Germans are capable of respecting the rights of other people. He doesn't—"

The roar of an exploding grenade, which landed in the river several yards away from the party, interrupted. Some of the Americans who had just arrived hit the ground. Marriack, who didn't seem disturbed, said, "That's nothing to worry about. Just one of the Russian soldiers showing one of our guys how their grenades work. They always fire their weapons when you ask about them; they figure a demonstration is the best answer they can give."

Outside of the actual meetings, the unoccupied area that separated the Russian forces on the Elbe from the American forces on the Mulde River was the most interesting and the screwiest part of the linkup picture. Hundreds of German soldiers streamed along the roads leading to the American lines, unguarded and all but forgotten in the excitement of the Russki-Yank junction. They had been disarmed by advance American patrols and ordered to make their own way to our PW cages because we didn't have enough GIs around at the time to escort them. Most of them seemed to be happy to be out of the fighting.

Unlike the reception we got in the dash from the Rhine to the Mulde, where the civilians accepted our entry in sullen silence, the people between the Mulde and the Elbe welcomed us like returning heroes. They stood on the curbs of no-man's-land towns, waving and laughing.

None of their waves and smiles were returned. The $65 question—the fraternization fine—had nothing to do with the Americans' passive reaction to the sudden German welcome. The Yanks could see through the waving and the smiles. It wasn't that the Germans hated us less; they just feared the Russians more.

Fear was becoming an all-pervading thing in Germany. No matter which way the Germans turned,

Left: *On May 7, Col. Gen. Gustav Jodl, German chief of staff, signs formal surrender terms at SHAEF Headquarters in Reims, France.*
Right: *After the surrender at Reims, Gen. Dwight Eisenhower holds up the pens with which the documents were signed.*

they found the Allies moving in on them. On April 29, the 12th Armored Division, the 20th Armored Division, and the 42d Infantry Division of Lt. Gen. Patch's Seventh Army took Munich, birthplace and shrine of the Nazi party. The Fifth Army took Milan and the British Eighth took Venice, and from the north of Italy, from the village of Dongo on Lake Como, came word of the death of Mussolini, tried and executed by Italian partisans. The ex-Duce's mistress, Clara Petacci, was executed with him, as were 16 other captured Fascists. The bodies of Mussolini and Clara Petacci were brought to Milan in a furniture mover's van and displayed to the people of the town.

Pierre Laval, the "honest trader" who had sold France out to Hitler, fled from Germany to Spain and was interned. The Seventh Army took Dachau, the most infamous of all Nazi concentration camps and one of the oldest. The Ninth Army made its contact with the Russians just north of the First near Wittenberg. Yank correspondent Sgt. Ecker was still with the Ninth and observed sidelights of this second junction of Allied armies:

It doesn't take a second look to know the Russians are planning to stick around for awhile in Germany. In our area, American flags are few and far between, mostly on military-government offices, but over on the Russian side, almost every window of the occupied town buildings flies a red flag instead of the white surrender flags we leave up. There's another more conclusive proof of permanence of Russian intentions: German signposts, left up in our area, have been torn down by Russians and new ones in their language substituted.

Among the many other things that the Russians can do better than the Germans is the fine art of sloganeering. The Germans in many cities have painted a vast number of inspiration mottoes on the walls of the houses and public buildings, but none can quite measure up in concise impact to this Soviet slogan lettered in white on red banners flying in the street here: DEATH TO THE FASCIST AGGRESSORS. For the benefit of the American allies, a special two-language flag was displayed in Wittenberg, scene of a meeting between the Russian and American corps generals. This is the way it read in English: LONG LIVE THE GREAT LEADERS, PRESIDENT TRUMEN, MARCHALL STALIN, AND PREMER CHURCHILL. Lots of wiseacres bet Stalin's name came first in the Russian version of the same slogan, but they were wrong.

The Allied flood rolled on. It was a great period for capturing Nazi field marshals like Wilhelm Ritter von Leeb and Wilhelm List, both of whom had been kingpins in the Nazi drives that overthrew Poland and France, and both of whom had had less luck in the invasion of Russia. Adm. Nicholas Horthy, Nazi-controlled dictator of Hungary, was captured. All three were picked up by the Seventh Army. Lt. Gen. Kurt Dittmar, leading German military commentator, surrendered to the Ninth. And then came the biggest story of all. The German radio announced that Hitler had died in action in Berlin. The Russians, who had by this time freed Berlin of all but street fighting, agreed that Hitler was dead, not as a fighting soldier but as a suicide. They said that Josef Paul Goebbels, his warped little propaganda minister, had also died by his own hand. Tired of too many German tricks, most Allied authorities reserved comment; they would believe Hitler dead when they saw his body. But a dead Hitler made for cheerful talk.

In Paris, Sgt. DeWitt Gilpin, Yank field correspondent, took a sample of public opinion on the subject of Hitler's death:

Lt. William J. Cullerton of Chicago, a fighter pilot who was left for dead a few weeks ago after a German SS man fired a .35-slug through his stomach, sat in a Paris hotel and talked about the late Adolf Hitler.

"I hope the sonuvabitch was as scared of dying as I was when that SS officer let me have it through the stomach," he said. "I thought I'd had it.

"Now they say Hitler is dead. Maybe he is. If he is, I don't believe he died heroically. Mussolini died at least something like a dictator, but somehow I can't figure Hitler dying in action. And I don't think Hitler's death changes anything about Germany. It just might be part of a deal to soften us up so they can stick another knife in the soft spot."

Two Eighth Air Force aerial gunners, who like Cullerton were sweating out a ride back to the States from the same hotel, said that they hadn't believed the news of Hitler's death when they first heard it shortly after the 104th Division liberated them from the Alten Grabow PW Camp.

S/Sgt. Henry J. Smith of Scranton, Pennsylvania, said: "I came down near Stutlitz about nine months ago, and I just had time to get out of my chute before German civilians started beating me up. One old man of about 60 broke a .22-rifle over me. But when we left Germany, all the people were forcing smiles for us. And that old guy would smile, too, now. Mussolini is dead, Hitler is dead —but what's the difference? There are lots more."

S/Sgt. William Cupp of Tipton, Iowa, who came down in Belgium and beat his way within 200 yards of the American lines—then near Paris—before the Germans got him, said: "They want to make Hitler a martyr for the German kids. Most of them are pretty much for him as it is."

At the 48th General Hospital, Sgt. Allan Pettit of Verndale, Minnesota, and the 78th Division, was well enough to be going out on pass. He had been hit twice before on the Roer River, but this time it was only concussion, and now he had a chance to see Paris.

"Why waste words on Hitler," he said. "And how do you know for sure? Anyway, he picked a damned good Nazi to take his place. That crazy Doenitz fought us in the last war."

Over in another ward filled with combat men just in from the front, it was the entertainment hour, and as a special favor to Cpl. Peter Stupihin—a Red Army man suffering from prison camp malnutrition—a singer rendered "Kalinka." The GIs thought that was fine, and those who felt strong enough called for tunes like "Stardust" and "I'll Be Seeing You."

A redheaded Southerner from the Fourth Division was feeling good because the doctor had finished dressing the shrapnel wound in his chest, and he had something to say about Hitler and his Germany between songs.

"I wish I was the guy who killed him," he said. "I'd have killed him a little slower. Awful slow."

In the Tout Paree Bar, some men from the 101st Airborne and the 29th Divisions worked at having a good time with pilots from the Troop Carrier Command. There were WACs in the party, too, but the attention they were getting came mostly from pilots. Some infantrymen were arguing about what their outfits did and where.

A pianist was pounding out what he considered American swing, and it wasn't the place for a name-and-address interview. An infantry captain who'd had a few drinks didn't waste much time on Hitler.

"Yeah, I guess he's dead," he said, "but so are a lot of *good* guys. And you just remember that."

Then the infantrymen went back to arguing about what had happened at Bastogne.

And in a very different setting, in the PW section of a Third Army post in Bavaria, Yank *correspondent Cpl. Howard Katzander got a very different slant on what might lie behind Hitler's death from a source a little closer to* Berchtesgaden:

The colonel was out of uniform—regrettably so for an officer of his rank in the Third Army area —but he carried it off well. He was average in height, slim, and blond-haired. He carried a crooked cane and was dressed in green cotton trousers and a pepper-and-salt sport jacket zippered up the front. He wore gray suede gloves, and as he talked, he sat cross-legged, occasionally slapping at one trim brown oxford, composed and nonchalant as if he were back on his father's East Prussia estates in the heart of Germany's Junkerland.

The story he was telling was the story of why the war did not end last July. It was the story of the attempt to assassinate Hitler, and he knew all about it. Because this was Lt. Col. Wilhelm Kuebart, a member of the *Wehrmacht* General Staff and one of the original plotters.

Kuebart was a *Junker* gentleman of the Prussian militarist class with a long military tradition behind him. His wife was the daughter of a *Junker* general. His uncles were *Reichswehr* officers and before them his grandfather and great-grandfathers as far back as his memory went. Only his father had departed from the tradition to embrace a profession as an architect.

In the fall of 1932, Wilhelm Kuebart entered the *Reichswehr* as an officer candidate. He was commissioned as a second lieutenant in the fall of 1934.

From then on, his rise was rapid and in the best *Junker* tradition. He participated in the Polish campaign in the late summer of 1939 as a first lieutenant, and in the summer of 1940, he became a captain and was transferred to the staff of the 18th Panzer Division. In the early spring of 1941, his talents and family background received due recognition and he was sent to the *Kriegsakademie*—the General Staff School—after which he joined Von Leeb's staff in the Central Army Group on the Russian front.

It was there that Kuebart was inoculated with the anti-Hitler virus in its most violent form. Almost the entire staff of this army group was anti-Hitler.

This was not unusual. The *Junker* officer class was probably the most exclusive club in the world. Its members regarded the military as the only career fit for a gentleman, and it regarded the *Wehrmacht* as its own private sphere.

Kuebart had taken a pretty dim view of the Nazi regime from the beginning, the way he tells it, and had never joined the National Socialist Democratic Workers party. Kuebart and his fellow officers felt that their ranks had degenerated under Hitler and they were particularly resentful of Himmler's attempt to spy on the officers and impose *SS* control over them. Hitler's spectacular failures as general and supreme commander of the armies led to open revolt. The disaster at Stalingrad was the last straw.

From that time on, the most popular subject of conversation among officers of the old school was the question of how to get rid of Hitler and Himmler. Kuebart had been sponsored for a place on the general staff by Col. Hansen, chief of the *Wehrmacht* Intelligence Service, and Hansen was the brains behind the plot against Hitler's life. The *Burgemeister* of Leipzig, Boerdler, was to take political control. Hansen went to Zeitzler, chief of the general staff, and persuaded him that immediate action was necessary.

The date for the assassination was set for July 13. The weekly conference between Hitler and his generals was to be held as usual on that day. But, at the last minute, there were two hitches. Himmler was not going to be present, and Hitler decided to hold the conference in a flimsy wooden barracks.

The bomb that had been prepared to wipe out Hitler and Himmler was designed for use in Hitler's underground headquarters, where heavy concrete walls and the earth itself would confine the force of the blast to the small room.

When the bomb was exploded in the frame building aboveground—it had been brought to the conference in a briefcase—its force was dissipated. Hitler was injured, but not seriously. The attempt had failed.

It could not be proven definitely that Kuebart had plotted against the supreme commander, but it was felt that he had betrayed his trust as an officer of the *Wehrmacht*. Accordingly, a crushing blow was dealt him. He was expelled from the *Wehrmacht* as "*unwürdigkeit*," unworthy of the honor of wearing the uniform. He was forbidden to reenter the army even as a buck private. He was kept under constant Gestapo surveillance, apparently in the hope that his movements would betray others who had taken part in the plot.

Kuebart says that 120 high German officers were hanged as a result of the plot, and 700 others are waiting execution.

When American troops overran the area where Kuebart had been living with his wife and two children since his expulsion from the Army, he calmly walked into the CP of B Battery, 551st Anti-aircraft Artillery Battalion, and told his story. He expected to speak his piece and go home to his wife and kiddies. He had papers to show that he had been expelled from the German Army. He assured his interrogators that his group had been prepared to sue for peace immediately if their plot had succeeded.

But he did not go home to the wife and kiddies. Somehow or other, the Third Army did not feel that his expulsion from the Army relieved him of responsibility for the part he had played up to that time. He is now in a PW cage and knows no more than anyone else of what actually happened to Hitler this time.

Adm. Karl Doenitz was named as Hitler's successor—the new Führer. It was asserted that Hitler himself had nominated the grand admiral of the German Fleet to carry on his job. It was possible, Doenitz was a devout Nazi; he was also the man who had helped perfect wolf-pack submarine warfare. Göring, once head of the Luftwaffe, was no longer a factor in anything except guessing games—he was crazy; he was a suicide; he had escaped abroad. Von Ribbentrop was out as German foreign minister and cagey Count Lutz Schwerin von Krosigk was in. Berlin fell on May 2. Field Marshal Arnim von Runstedt had already been added to the list of captured field marshals by the Seventh Army. Also on May 2, it was announced that German forces in Italy and southern Austria had surrendered at Caserta. Free Czechs started their own revolt and battled Germans in Prague. The Fifth and Seventh Armies met at Vipiteno, Italy. On May 4, all the German forces in Holland, Denmark, and northwestern Germany surrendered to Field Marshal Sir Bernard L. Montgomery.

By now, the allied advance had gathered unstoppable force. On May 5, the First and Nineteenth Armies, comprising German Army Group G, surrendered to Gen. Jacob L. Devers' U.S. Sixth Army Group in western Austria and Bavaria; the German First and 19th surrendered to the U.S. Seventh and French First; the German Twenty-fourth Army surrendered to the French First. The Germans were preparing to give up Norway.

On Sunday, May 6, at Reims, France, Col. Gen. Gustav Jodl signed a formal surrender for all German armed forces. Yank's Sgt. Gilpin was at Reims when GIs there got the news:

The 201st MP Company, whose members handled the guard details when the Germans came to Reims to surrender, is a celebrity-wise outfit. Gen. Eisenhower knows many of the men by their first names and some of them have dined at Churchill's home. They have been the gun-carrying soldiers on hand during a succession of visits to high headquarters by Nazi bigwigs like Franz von Papen, who was described by one of them as looking like "an old goat in golf knickers."

"And this is Col. Gen. von Kleeb, who is scheduled for execution in no less than 12 different countries after the war."

Left: *Crowds swarmed down Broadway in New York on VE-Night, and bright lights were turned on again.*
Center: *Hitler's henchman Marshal Göring, captured in Austria, posed in his favorite uniform.*
Right: *Marshal Keitel, German commander-in-chief, signs ratified surrender terms at Russian headquarters in Berlin.*

The MPs said Col. Gen. Jodl looked and acted more like the popular idea of a German militarist than any of the other German officers with him at the surrender meeting. He walked and talked with the arrogance that the *Junkers* have developed through a long series of wars. He didn't seem to drink as much as some of the others, and before and after each conference, the MP outside his bedroom window could see him examining his face in his mirror. After the last conference session, Jodl came back to his room, threw open the windows, and looked down at Pfc. Jack H. Arnold of Lancaster, Pennsylvania. After peering at Arnold, he inhaled deeply and then twisted and pulled at his face before the mirror.

Adm. Hans von Friedeburg, of all the Germans, seems to have impressed the MPs most as what they called a "character." In the words of Pfc. Joseph Fink, who used to build Burroughs adding machines in Detroit, "The admiral had enough medals hanging on his chest to decorate a Christmas tree."

Fink rode in the car that took the admiral to the German billets. During the ride, a British major riding with them brought Friedeburg up to date on current events. He told him the lights were on again in London and Friedeburg, remembering air raids in Germany, replied in English that he hadn't had a good night's sleep in a month. He went on to explain that he had been bombed out of his headquarters three times.

While he stayed in the billets, Friedeburg consumed great quantities of cigars and liquor, but none of this seemed to make any improvement in his testy disposition. When he saw photographs of German atrocities in a copy of the *Stars and Stripes* during a between-conferences discussion of U.S. Army publications, he banged his fist on the table in a temper.

The house in which the Germans stayed during the conference looked like a shack on the outside and a palace on the inside. There were paintings on the walls and a grandfather clock, inlaid tile in the bathrooms, and comfortable double beds in the bedrooms. There was a bit of a fuss over the first meal, because someone had forgotten to get the red wine. Pfc. Frederick A. Stones of Pittsburgh, Pennsylvania, commented privately, "If I was running this show, I'd throw them a can of C rations."

Stones says that his proposed diet had a practical as well as a vindictive side in that it might have helped shorten the negotiations.

Once Pfc. Joyce Bennet, WAC manageress of the German billets, asked two of the GI orderlies to straighten up the beds of the German officers. The GIs complied but bitched. "We're usually assigned to British Air Marshal Tedder," one of them said, "and he straightens up his own bed, and so could these guys."

Speaking of the Germans, a little black-haired WAC from Tarentum, Pennsylvania, said, "I felt terribly uneasy serving them coffee. Some officer made a crack about my waiting on Germans while my husband was still shooting them. He didn't stop to think that I'd have preferred to have been spilling the hot coffee down their necks."

On the last day before the Germans signed the piece of paper that officially ended what was to have been Adolf Hitler's New World Order, Col. Gen. Jodl and Adm. Friedeburg were watched by the MPs as they walked in the little garden beside their billet. Friedeburg had relaxed a little, but Jodl was just as stiff necked as ever.

Later, when it was all over except the publicity, the MPs went back to their barracks and had a bull session about the war, the Germans, and "Ike." They talked most about Ike.

Sgt. Henry Wheeler of Youngstown, New York, said, "The windup was pretty much what we expected. 'Ike' didn't have anything to do with those phonies until they were ready to quit. Then he went in and told them to sign up.

"And what does he do as he comes out of the meeting? He shakes hands with the first GI he comes to."

And that is the way the war in Europe ended for the 201st MPs.

The news of the surrender was to have been held up for a simultaneous announcement by President Truman, Premier Stalin, and Prime Minister Churchill, but, in spite of censorship precautions, it leaked out and set off celebrations in all Allied capitals. Yank reporters in overseas posts from Saipan to Cairo heard the good news as it spread from soldier to soldier, in combat, in camp, and on the streets of pass towns:

The announcement came as an anticlimax to men of the Ninth Army, just as it did to most of the rest of the world. They had been relieved for the last time on the Western Front some days before the signing at Reims, and their relief was to them the real end of the war in Europe. Pfc. S. L. Gates, who has a brother in the Marines in the Pacific, figured he'd be heading there soon. Most of the talk was like that—either of home or of possible Pacific duty.

In Paris, where the news had begun as a phoney rumor and then turned true, it was an anticlimax, too. A photographer staged a shot with some French babes kissing some over-happy doughs in front of the Rainbow Corner. "I keep telling everybody that it's over," said an MP at the door of the Red Cross Club who was no longer even checking passes, "but nobody believes me."

Finally, when Paris believed the news, it was just a big-city celebration—crowds and singing and cheers and lots of cognac and girls. People stopped work, and airplanes of all the Allied forces buzzed the *Champs Elysées*. Pvt. Ernest Kuhn of Chicago listened to the news come over the radio at the 108th General Hospital. He had just been liberated after five months in a Nazi PW camp, and he still had some shrapnel in his throat. "I listened to Churchill talk," he said, "and I kept saying to myself, 'I'm still alive. The war is over here and I'm still alive.' I thought of all the guys in the 28th Division Band with me who were dead now. We used to be a pretty good band."

In London, there were crowds, too, and singing and kissing and cheering. Everybody you spoke to said the news was swell, but they all added a postscript about the Japs. The end of the war in Europe seemed to bring the Pacific war closer than ever to GIs here. Cpl. Robert M. Rhodes of Kittanning, Pennsylvania, who works in a base ordnance depot in the United Kingdom, said, "I just can't believe it's over on this side. That is, I can't realize it yet. I figure this VE-Day is just one step nearer New York and the Statue of Liberty. I figure it'll take 10 to 12 more months to get rid of the Japs. I'm just going to write home to my wife, 'So far, so good. I'll be seeing you.' "

GI reaction to the surrender was calm in Cairo. There was no singing or dancing in the streets, no great spontaneous demonstration, no fights. T/Sgt. Holis B. Miller of Benedict, Nebraska, leaning against a staff car parked in front of a downtown hotel, watched the crowds stopping to read the announcement in the extra of the *Stars and Stripes* posted on the hotel wall. "Most of the GIs don't quite know what to make of it," he said. "It doesn't mean much of a change. We won't be getting out of the Army tomorrow or going home." In the Cairo bars, which didn't even enjoy a business boom, men thought mostly of what the celebration might be like in the United States. "I'll bet they're having a hot time at home tonight," said Cpl. Paul Furgatch of the Bronx, and he ordered another drink.

In the Aleutians, there wasn't much formal celebrating either. Mostly there were rumors on "How much better are my chances of getting off this island?" Unit commanders banned "boisterous or disorderly demonstrations" and forbade "discharge of small arms," but many outfits arranged the monthly beer ration to coincide with VE-Day. Back of all reaction to the news was the thought that the theater might be due to become important again, that it might live up actively to its slogan, "The Northern Highway to Victory."

In Hawaii, there was almost complete lack of interest. The men there were too close to the continuing Pacific war to be unduly jubilant. The ones who got the biggest kicks were those who had close friends or relatives in the European theater. There wasn't even much talk about VE-Day among the GIs. And when they did talk, they were usually saying, "Now maybe we can wind *this* war up sooner."

Nobody got very excited on Saipan when the news came over the B-29 squadrons' loudspeakers in the morning. It was like the Hawaiian reaction only stronger. M/Sgt. Wilbur M. Belshaw, a flight engineer from Vesta, Minnesota, said what was uppermost in GIs' minds: "The Japs thought they could lick the world. Well, now they've got their chance."

There wasn't much war left in Europe. Germans in Norway moved toward Sweden for internment. The German heavy cruisers Prinz Eugen *and* Seydlitz *were turned over to the British Navy at Copenhagen. A few die-hard groups like the German Seventh Army in Czechoslovakia made a last stab at organized resistance. The official time set for the laying down of all guns in Europe was 2001 hours Eastern War Time, Tuesday, May 8. After that, what fighting remained was unofficial and sporadic. The Russians, justifiably suspicious after earlier Nazi attempts to sign a separate peace with the two other allies, forced Field Marshal Albert von Kesselring to sign a special ratification of surrender in Berlin. Göring turned up, not crazy or dead, but as a prisoner of the celebrity-collecting Seventh Army. Lights went on again in London; the "brownout" was relaxed in New York.*

VE-Day had come. People in America had been waiting for it so long they didn't know whether to believe it, and when they did believe it, they didn't quite know what to make of it.

To get an overall view of VE-Day in America, *Yank* asked civilian newspapermen and staff writers in various parts of the country to send in eyewitness reports. From these OPs, the reports were much the same. Dallas was quiet, Des Moines was sober, Seattle was calm, Boston was staid.

In some towns, crowds gathered and tried to think of something to do to celebrate. Mostly they didn't seem able to focus their thoughts. Two weeks of spectacular rumors and even more spectacular events had taken the edge off the official victory over Germany. And the press and radio kept saying: "There's still one war to go."

From Portland, Oregon, came a report of a conversation between a Broadway streetcar conductor and a young woman passenger wearing a service star.

"So this is VE-Day," the motorman said. "But we'll have to lick the little yellow men before I go on a toot."

The young woman said: "And my husband will have to come home before I go on a toot."

In Cleveland, crowds stood on downtown corners and moved aimlessly along streets where hawkers were selling flags, pompoms, lapel buttons, and tin horns. The streets were littered with torn papers and long streamers dangled from office windows and hung from trolley wires—all this the evidence of a brief, wild hubbub following President Truman's 8 a.m. radio announcement on May 8 that victory in Europe really had come.

A man in the Cleveland suburb of Parma painted a fireplug red, white, and blue; girls in a candy store threw candy kisses to the crowd; Hitler was burned in effigy at Lakeside and East Ninth Street; girls danced on the sidewalk; church bells rang; factory whistles blew. But on the whole, it was a quiet day, ending with well-attended services in all churches.

Houston's reaction was summed up in one sentence: VE-Day came to Houston like Christmas morning to the kid who peeked in the closet the week before and saw his electric train.

New Yorkers milled around the Wall Street district and Times Square, and over a loudspeaker Mayor Fiorello H. LaGuardia told them to behave

THE ARMY WEEKLY

VE ISSUE
JUNE 1, 1945
VOL. 3, NO. 50 · 5 CENTS

FADE-OUT

themselves. In a bar, a man said: "I betcha they act like this only in New York and Chicago and San Francisco. Back in Vermont, where I come from, I betcha they're acting different. I betcha the people are behaving decent, and going to church and praying and not carrying on."

In Chicago, a gray-haired man weaved up to the woman behind the cigar counter in the Stevens Hotel lobby. "Aren't you going to celebrate?" the man asked. "Celebrate what?" the woman said. "My two boys are on Okinawa."

San Francisco took it easy. Schools closed an hour early, the Bartenders Union voluntarily shut the saloons. The Junior Chamber of Commerce sponsored an "On to Tokyo" rally in the Civic Auditorium. The United Nations Conference on International Organization went right ahead working in the Opera House and the Veterans' Memorial Building.

In Atlanta, the big Bell bomber plant that turns out B-29s operated full blast. Officials said there was no increase in absenteeism.

Des Moines old-timers noted that it was a lot different from the way it had been 27 years before. On Armistice Day, 1918, rioters had filled downtown streets and overturned automobiles, dancing and singing to celebrate the U.S. Army's first victory in Europe. This time, except for a truckload of boys with musical instruments touring the heart of town, there was no revelry.

St. Louis church leaders held services in Memorial Plaza. Emerson Electric Manufacturing, Scullin Steel, Monsanto Chemical, and other plants said full crews showed up. Retail stores closed and so did most bars and taverns.

Rain fell in Baltimore during President Truman's speech, and streets were as empty as they usually are when it rains at 9 a.m. In the harbor, there were impromptu celebrations aboard Norwegian and British vessels.

In Boston, office girls sang, "Hi, ho, the merry-o" in Liberty Square, and workmen tearing down the old New England Mutual Building in Post Office Square tolled the bell in the tower. It was the first time the bell had rung in two years.

Minneapolis sounded its central air-raid warning siren atop the Northwestern National Bank when President Truman officially proclaimed VE-Day. For 17 minutes, the pigeons in the Loop area wheeled in a capricious wind. Till midday, the police and fire department kept extra men on hand in case of celebration trouble, but when it was clear that there wasn't going to be any celebration, the extras were sent home. Schools and colleges continued classes, and appointments at the Red Cross blood-donor center were kept.

Los Angeles celebrated by launching a 445-foot Victory ship in the California Shipbuilding yards —the 438th ship the yards have turned out. Churches of all denominations held special services, and public offices, retail stores, and banks remained open as usual.

Springfield, Massachusetts, stores barricaded their show windows with American flags to protect

"What's so funny about this Sad Sack cartoon!"—
SGT. SYD LANDI

them from VE-Day crowds, but there weren't any crowds. The Springfield Armory took down the HELP WANTED sign which had become almost a landmark at State and Federal streets. Officials said demands for the Garand rifle had fallen and that layoffs were expected.

In Thomaston, Connecticut, an employee of the Seth Thomas clock factory, which has been converted to war production, said: "I don't like to be a fussbudget, but this doesn't mean much to me. When I stop making fuse parts for shells and start making clock parts again, that will be a wonderful day."

Some German prisoners interned at Fort Oglethorpe, Tennessee, near Chattanooga, broke down and cried when they heard it was all over. There was no other display of emotion and no disturbance inside the compound. The post commandant, Col. Howard Clark, made a brief talk at a special retreat ceremony. Thirty minutes later, he learned that his son, Lt. William A. Clark, had been killed in action on Luzon on April 18.

Flags were still at half-mast for FDR.

On Okinawa, GIs and Marines continued to kill Japs and to be killed by them. It was raining when the VE announcement was broadcast over loudspeakers, and the artillery and the noise of planes made it hard to understand. Besides, almost everybody was too busy to pay much attention to it.

"All right, men, you all have your instructions."
—CPL. WILLIAM TEASON

It was the ugliest of all of them; the one from whose nightmares its surviving Marines still awaken, trembling with sheer terror. Okinawa was the last island before Japan itself, the end of the ladder that had begun in the Solomons three years earlier. Sadly, however, its carnage was wholly needless; before the wreckage could be cleared or an operable base established, events of an atomic nature would render Okinawa entirely unnecessary.

A BAD NIGHT

—Pfc. JUSTIN GRAY
Yank Staff Correspondent
July 6, 1945

WITH THE 96th Division, Okinawa—The captain had just been killed. A Jap sniper's bullet caught him in the neck as he was giving us the final instructions for tomorrow's attack. He died instantly.

Many of the men cried. They didn't try to hide it. They had really loved their CO. "The company won't be worth a damn now," one said.

This happened in the late evening. The captain hadn't given all the dope before he was hit. The company would have to advance in the morning without the full plan.

All we knew when we went on outpost for the night was that the battalion was going to attack Kakazu Ridge at dawn and the company was to be in the center of the assault. Jap positions on Kakazu had held us up for over a week. The high command was determined that we would storm over the ridge the next day. There was to be no halting until the objective was ours. No company was to be pinned down. Casualties were expected —lots of them—but Kakazu had to be taken. If we had only had more information.

The company was understrength. I was sent to help fill one of the Third Platoon's holes. Wyatt and Geark were the only men available from the platoon's Third Squad. A "flying boxcar," one of the Japs' 320-mortar shells, had just landed about 50 yards to the rear of the company. Wyatt and Geark were lucky. The two other men who had held the hole with them were badly wounded by rocks and dirt. Those rocks were as bad as shrapnel.

The hole was on the extreme left flank of the company. It was literally perched on the rim of the ravine which the company held. Company headquarters was down at the foot of the ravine and the line platoons had dug in at the top. Four men were needed to hold our hole. There were two directions from which the Japs could move in on us, and two men had to be on the alert all the time. Mitchell was brought over from the First Squad to help us.

The hole wasn't really in such a good spot. The "skibbies" (Japs) on Kakazu were actually breathing down our necks. You didn't dare stick your

"I wish to hell I knew what we were supposed to do tomorrow," said Geark, as he sat down.

head up while there was still daylight. Snipers and machine guns were sighted in on our position.

This was my first time up there, and as soon as it was dark enough to be reasonably safe, I took a good look about me to get my bearings. The hole was right in the midst of a group of pine and palm trees. There were also some tree stumps about as high as a man. The Japs must have cut down some of these trees for use in their pillboxes. In the dark it would be hard to tell which was a Jap and which was a stump. I tried to get the location of the stumps in my mind so I could pick them out later.

The hole wasn't actually a hole. The ground was so rocky that you couldn't dig down any depth. What had been done instead was to build up a foxhole with rocks. Around the top were a number

of palm fronds which were an attempt at camouflage. That was a worthless bit of effort, for the skibbies knew exactly where we were.

The two of us who were on guard stood near the front of the hole. One watched to the left, parallel with the rim of the ravine, and the other covered the front. A path led up toward our position directly to the front, which passed between two of those huge stone Okinawan graves that cover the hillsides all over the island. Those graves are tremendous and will make wonderful amphitheaters for GI movies once the garrison forces take over. I kept my eyes on that path.

At first it wasn't so bad, even though I was a bit jumpy. I kept thinking of tomorrow's attack. It was bad enough just worrying about being on out-

post. But not to know what was expected of the company in the all-out assault that was to follow at dawn was almost too much of an unknown quantity. I tried to concentrate on the present job of guarding the outpost.

The moon was about a quarter full, and it lighted up the hillside pretty well. It didn't seem logical that the Japs would try to infiltrate or counterattack until after the moon went down. I leaned over to Wyatt and asked nervously, "When the hell does that moon leave us?"

He smiled back and answered: "Not for a couple of hours yet. We don't have to worry until about 2300. Have you got a watch?"

No one had a watch. It was decided that since Wyatt and Geark were the experienced ones, having spent a couple of nights in this hole already, they should be split up, enabling at least one of them to be on duty all the time. I teamed up with Wyatt, and Mitchell worked with Geark. Wyatt and I took the first shift. We were supposed to stay on for what we thought was an hour, then wake up the other two. I doubt if any of us knew just what an hour was without a watch, but that was the plan.

"Give me a kick if you see anything—just any-

thing," said Geark before he sat down in the back of the hole. "I don't think I'll be able to sleep much tonight, anyway. I wish to hell I knew what we were supposed to do tomorrow." He sat down and threw a poncho over his head to cover his lighting a cigarette. Wyatt and I were scared of what might happen now and wondering what was supposed to happen in the morning.

Even with the moon up, more or less protecting us, I felt very exposed. If the Japs shelled us, with all those trees around, there would be high bursts right over the hole. Shrapnel would rain down on us.

Wyatt was looking down off to the left. I put my hand on his shoulder to indicate I wanted to whisper something to him. I held my hand there until he turned to me. "What's the countersign, in case we have to get out of here?" I asked.

Wyatt shook his head. "I don't know. It doesn't make any difference, anyway. We can't leave here until dawn. If we tried to go back down into the ravine, they'd shoot us first and ask questions later. We'll have to stay here until the attack."

I just had time to digest that thought when he turned back again and added: "If we do have to get out of here for some reason, run back and yell as loud as you can, 'Rolph, I'm coming down.' Rolph's the squad sergeant down there. He'll let you through—maybe."

I went back to looking down my sector, wishing to God the lieutenant hadn't sent me up here. If morning would only come. I didn't like this lack of movement at night. We kept the initiative during the daytime but seldom moved at night. In Europe, we kept the Jerries guessing plenty by hitting them at night. It could be done out here too.

Another thing occurred to me, and I laid my hand on Wyatt's shoulder again. He must have been watching something, for he didn't look toward me for a full minute. I began to stare into his sector, but I couldn't see anything. It must have been the wind. I asked him: "Why didn't you people put out some concertinas and trip flares in front of this hole? We wouldn't have to worry so much then."

Wyatt whispered back: "We tried to get out there, but the Japs fired on us every time they heard someone move from here. It was just impossible to do it."

The wind began to blow up from the east. I thought of what the book on Okinawa had said about typhoons every month. It would be rough next month when the typhoons are supposed to come. It was hard enough to hear a Jap moving in on you now, when it was only a breeze. Once those storms hit, a man on outpost wouldn't be able to hear a thing. We'd better get this Okinawa campaign over quick, I thought.

Over the ridge to our left front, the Japs began to send a stream of mortar shells into what seemed

He died as he was giving final instructions.

to be their own lines. I knew none of our troops were there. The Japs were using a smart technique on Okinawa. Their troops were so well dug in that they were actually shelling advancing infantrymen even after we reached the Japanese positions. I wondered if we were supposed to overrun those mortar positions in tomorrow's attack. Somebody had better take care of them. If we only knew what the brass expected our company to accomplish. Knowing merely that we had to attack wasn't enough.

I didn't know if an hour had passed yet, but I could hardly see anymore. Geark and Mitchell took our places. Neither of them had slept a wink. I didn't expect to do any better. Wyatt, not daring to leave the hole, urinated into an empty tin that used to hold a bottle of blood plasma and threw the water over the wall.

It wasn't very cold yet, and the mosquitoes were out in force. I poured a bottle of Skat over myself, but it didn't seem to do much good. I didn't mind the bites so much, but the constant buzzing around my ears upset me. I began thinking again of what was in store for us in the morning. Wyatt wasn't sleeping, either. We were dreaming up schemes that would make whatever might happen in the morning turn out okay.

I didn't think I got any sleep at all, but I must have gotten a little, for the moon had gone when Mitchell shook me and said another hour had passed. I could hardly believe my eyes when I took my place at the edge of the hole again. It was pitch black. I couldn't hear anything above the wind. I couldn't see how we could defend ourselves if we couldn't see or hear. Wyatt took off his helmet so he could hear a little better. I followed suit.

I leaned over to Wyatt and told him: "Take a look over into my sector every once in a while. I'm not certain I can see at all."

Wyatt nodded a yes but didn't take his eyes off whatever he was watching. That Wyatt was a steady one. Between the two of us were two M1s with bayonets already in position. As I leaned up against the wall I could feel six good, solid fragmentation grenades under my arms. Just to the right were a couple of bandoliers of ammo for the rifles. We had enough stuff to stop the Japs if we could only see them or hear them.

Our own artillery began firing. The noise from our guns made it even more difficult to hear. I began wishing the guns would remain silent. With all the good they did, it was probable that any number of Japs could still hit at us.

The wind shifted and I began to smell an awful odor. Wyatt leaned over and pointed right in front of our hole. It was a dead Jap. He had been there all the time and I never saw him. He had been killed the night before. It was a sharp reminder of how close the Japs could get to us. I began to watch even more closely.

Wyatt watched me strain a bit more and then said reassuringly: "It's better with the wind this way, even with that smell. You can hear the Japs now before they hear us."

His logic might have been correct, but it didn't comfort me a bit. I was scared. I remember standing outpost in Sicily and Italy, but I don't think I was as scared then. Even though I knew the Germans were fanatical in their attempts to destroy us, I always felt confident they also had a strong desire to live. From everything I have heard and seen so far in the Pacific, the Jap doesn't place such a high value on his life. The Japs crawl into our lines even though they know they have no chance of getting out alive. One lone Jap with that attitude might not hurt the company as a whole, but he sure could wipe out our outpost.

Wyatt and I were relieved by the other two, and in turn we relieved them again. The shifts became shorter and shorter, for it was getting darker with each passing hour. It was almost impossible to keep your eyes focused on one spot for a full hour.

Soon it would be getting lighter. Just before dawn, our artillery would open up in earnest, and then we would jump off on an attack in which we

I must have dozed off then Mitchell shook me.

didn't even know what we were supposed to accomplish. I was worn out, first worrying about the present and then worrying about what might happen in the future.

I must have been asleep when Mitchell shook me. I jumped up with a start. Someone was calling softly from our rear. What could have happened? Had some Japs gotten in behind us? Then we relaxed. It was Rolph calling.

We were to leave our positions. Our artillery was about to send in its preparation for the attack. The shells would be landing too close to our hole for safety. And while they were shelling, the new CO would finish our instructions. Everything was turning out okay—without the confusion we had dreaded.

MAIL CALL

Dear *Yank*:
Through all of the months that I have been reading *Yank* and looking at that "Hometowns in Wartime" feature, I have awaited just one thing. Suddenly there it was, in all its glory—Brooklyn! And where in Brooklyn? My neighborhood! Borough Hall with its old tower and the noontime bell. The Tivoli, the first movie house I ever went to; the Star, my second home—where I cut classes and invested my carfare in a ticket for a front-row seat. Fulton Street, with the Milk Bar on the corner—strange without its El, but still Fulton!

The *Citizen* scoreboard, where I amazed and infuriated many a Dodger rooter by cheering for a Giant score. And that spot where the building comes up to a corner, where they'd hang up the diamond to re-enact the World Series and all-star ball games. Kennedy's Bar, and Gallagher's, where I took my first tottering steps down the road to alcoholism. The old fire house, with its long, odd shape and the big, grand G-E building which all Brooklynites point out with pride. Luna Park, grandpop of all amusement parks.

No kidding, though, it was really a thrill. Despite the kidding the old borough takes from radio comics—and despite the undeniable wackiness of daily routine there—you still get a certain attachment for the old place that you don't feel anywhere else in the world, and that two-page spread in *Yank* brought it all back to me.

Thanks a lot from a really grateful GI. We don't have pin-ups on our walls here, but Linda Darnell is coming off the inner top of my foot locker as of now and up goes Brooklyn!

—Pvt. Dick Cavalli
Camp Howze, Texas

Dear *Yank*:
Even though the Brooklyn Dodgers were 42 games behind, they were still the best team in both leagues. Also I would like to remind you that the Dodgers come from Flatbush, a section which you did not mention in your article.

We are not feuding with the borough of Manhattan; most of our trouble has come from the borough of the Bronx.

—Cpl. Donald Speisman
Lake Lure, North Carolina

Dear *Yank*:
In your article on Brooklyn, N.Y., you mentioned about what the Brooklyn girls think of us Bronx fellows. Well, I don't know if you are from Brooklyn or where, but as far as I'm concerned I wouldn't be seen with a girl from Brooklyn on any account. . . . From what I've seen of Brooklyn they can give it back to the Indians. And as for making Brooklyn a different state, I'm all for it. . . .

Why don't Brooklynites be quiet like the people from Staten Island?

—Pvt. I. H. Wolfson*
Kessler Field, Mississippi

Also signed by Pvt. A. Kaplan.

Dear *Yank*:
Not that it would interest anyone in particular, but I'd like very much to record the following events for posterity:

World Affairs	My Contribution
Attu invaded..........	On KP
Kiska occupied........	Latrine duty
Tarawa landing........	Barracks orderly
D-Day in France	Signed 104th for having sleeves up
Return to the Philippines............	Squadron meeting
Nazis murder 150 Yanks in cold blood..	CO spent 2 minutes on war news and 20 minutes

on keeping your shoes shined

Great Russian offensive .... Worked on B-24s (someone must have slipped up that day)

The topper? My wife, an Army nurse, is in France and I am in the States.

—Cpl. Albert Baron
Tonopah, Nevada

Dear *Yank*:

It is time that someone told our patriotic writers that some of us GIs don't like the Army. The radio serials, the movies and the newspaper and magazine stories would have the reading public believe that every young man is just crazy about Army life.

If the young man in the story hasn't already enlisted (usually he enlists Dec. 8, 1941), he's very bitter about not getting drafted. He hates to be a civilian making $150 a week and curses the medical

"It's the apartment below. They want to know is all this noise necessary?"—T. Sgt. Frank Barth

officers who rejected him. His ailment of course is indefinite and doesn't render him less attractive to the girl. Personally, I didn't see any such rejections at Grand Central Palace. Also, the rejectees I have seen haven't shed tears when turned down.

The writers work it differently if the hero is already in the Army. If he has been in combat, been wounded and in general gone through hell, he's dying to get back into that muddy foxhole, just can't wait until he leaves his cuddlesome wench and the other comforts of civilization. If he's up for a CDD (with at least three big-time jobs waiting for him), he's grief-stricken.

If the soldier in the story has a nice soft job in a service outfit in the States, he's busting a gut trying to transfer to the infantry. Never yet has the gent in the story decided that he has a pretty good proposition and will sit tight until ordered elsewhere.

Now, don't get me wrong. It is commendable to be anxious for the fight. I'm only saying that there aren't so doggoned many anxious guys as the writers would have us think. Otherwise why did they have to draft us? The stories could be a little more realistic. Just once in awhile let's have a veteran who is tickled pink when he gets an honorable discharge.

—Sgt. Kirk Faris
Letterman General Hospital, California

Dear *Yank*:
We have been receiving quite a few air raids and some of them had been carried out by the Japs in such a way that we didn't know they were here until shooting of our AA guns had begun, or after they dropped their eggs and started strafing.

Many of the men began to sleep fully dressed, minus shoes, to be somewhat prepared. One night, when the raid signal started, one man, who was sleeping with his clothes on, ran out of the tent and didn't realize his shirt tail was out. His only thought was to reach a shelter. The next day we found out that our commanding officer had caught him with his shirt tail out and busted him from corporal to private.

We would like to know if our CO has the authority to bust a man for being out of uniform at a time such as this? As far as we are concerned a man thinks more of his life than he does of his shirt tail.

—(Name Withheld)
Marianas Islands

Dear *Yank*:
I am enclosing one of your "super deluxe" rejection slips, which you can blow out of your right eye. If I've gotten one of these things, I've gotten 300. I've never tried so hard to get into a damned magazine before in all my life, and I'm entirely fed up with these idiotic certificates you insist upon sending me—"Marching and Spam Club." What a laugh! I see red. What a bunch of heads!

Maybe my stuff isn't good enough to be printed in *Yank* and I don't give a damn about that, but for God's sake quit sending me these latrine pin-ups. The editors of *Yank* may be wiser than a tree full of owls, and I don't know about that, but as far as I'm concerned you can count me out of your practical jokes. My nerves are on edge and not from pounding a typewriter!

—S/Sgt. N. A. Urda
Britain

The GIs didn't think of him as a reporter, but as a friend who knew exactly how they felt. And his death hit them as heavily as had Roosevelt's.

THE DEATH OF ERNIE PYLE

—EVAN WYLIE CSp (PR), USCGR
May 18, 1945

ERNIE PYLE covered Okinawa on D-Day with the Marines. Many of them did not recognize him at first and stared curiously at the small, oldish-looking man with the stubby white whiskers and frayed woolen cap. When they did recognize him they said, "Hi, Ernie. What do you think of the war here in the Pacific?" And Pyle smiled and said a little wearily, "Oh, its the same old stuff all over again. I am awful tired of it."

The men watched him climb from the boat, his thin body bent under the weight of his field pack and draped in fatigue clothes that seemed too big for him, and they said, "That guy is getting too old for this kind of stuff. He ought to go home."

Ie Shima, where Pyle died, is a small, obscure island off the western coast of Okinawa. The operation was on such a small scale that many correspondents didn't bother to go along. Pyle had been in the ship's bay, sick for a week with one of his famous colds. The weather was perfect, with balmy air and bright sunshine. Pyle was ashore on D-plus-one. He stretched out on the sunny slope with Milton Chase, WLW radio correspondent, soaking up the sun and gazing at the picturesque landscape and gently rolling fields dotted with sagebrushlike bushes and clumps of low pine trees.

The country, he said, was the way Italy must be in summertime. That was only a guess, he added, because he was in Italy in the middle of winter. Most of all, it reminded him of Albuquerque.

"Lots of people don't like the country around Albuquerque," he said, "but it suits me fine. As soon as I finish this damned assignment, I'm going back there and settle down for a long time."

A young officer came up to report that the Japs were blowing themselves up with grenades. "That's a sight worth seeing," he said.

Chase asked Pyle what his reaction to the Jap dead was. Pyle said dead men were all alike to him, and it made him feel sick to look at one.

A wounded soldier with a bloody bandage on his arm came up the slope and asked Pyle for his autograph. "Don't usually collect these things," he told Pyle sheepishly, "but I wanted yours. Thanks a lot."

The operation was going so well that most of the correspondents left that night. There had been hardly any casualties, and only a very few of these were killed. Pyle was in the midst of preparing a story on a tank-destroyer team, so he stayed on. He was wearing green fatigues and a cap with a Marine emblem. He was with a few troops when

He was a small, gray, weary little guy, and the men called him Ernie.

he died, standing near Lt. Col. Joseph B. Coolidge of Helena, Montana. The Jap machine gun that got him took the group by surprise.

Pyle had proceeded to the front in a jeep with Col. Coolidge. As they reached a crossroads, still some distance from the front lines, the Jap machine gun, hidden in a patch of woods, suddenly opened up on them. The gun was a sleeper. Our troops had been moving up and down the road all morning and most of the day before. This was the first time it had revealed itself.

Pyle and the others jumped from the jeep and took cover in a ditch beside the road. The machine gun fired another long burst, and Pyle was dead. The rest withdrew. Several groups attempted to recover his body, once with the support of tanks, but each time they were driven back.

At 1500, Chaplain N. B. Saucier of Coffeeville, Mississippi, received permission to attempt to recover the body with litterbearers. T-5 Paul Shapiro of Passaic, New Jersey, Sgt. Minter Moore of Elkins, West Virginia, Cpl. Robert Toaz of Huntington, New York, and Sgt. Arthur Austin of Tekaman, Nebraska, volunteered to go with him. The crossroads lay in open country that offered no cover. The men crawled up the ditch, dragging the litter behind them. Army Signal Corps photographer Cpl. Alexander Roberts of New York City preceded them and was the first man to reach the body.

Pyle lay on his back in a normal resting position. His unmarked face had the look of a man sleeping peacefully. He had died instantly from a bullet that penetrated the left side of his helmet and entered the left temple. His hands folded across his chest still clutched his battered cap, said to be the same one he carried through his previous campaigns. The litterbearers placed the body on the stretcher and worked their way slowly back along the ditch under sniper fire. The battle for Ie Shima still remained to be won.

The island probably will be remembered only as the place where America's most famous war correspondent met the death he had been expecting for so long.

THE LONELY ROOMS

—Cpl. Bill Feinberg
August 31, 1945

ITALY—you know what it's like overseas. Up at the front, you spend so much time being tired and cold and scared that you don't think too much about things. Oh, maybe you think about home and a woman or two a lot, but it seems like a waste of time to think about anything else. Anything serious, like what to do with Germany now, and how can we prevent another war, and stuff like that. The sort of stuff we get pamphlets about. They're pretty good toilet paper when they're not glossy.

And the same thing in the rear areas. You don't think much. It's not the cold or the fatigue that gets you, and you're not scared about anything. You may worry a little when the MPs approach in town and you've got no pass. But, brother, you're not scared. No one's scared till they feel like crying inside.

But just the same, you don't think much. Maybe it's because you've got too much time, 24 months of it for me so far. You're so tired of waiting and waiting and doing the same goddam thing day in and day out that you don't want to think any more. Because when you do think, you always get around to the same things.

So you go to town and get a drink, or spend a hot time in the Red Cross, eating buns and talking to a wholesome Red Cross girl. Exciting, isn't it?

Now don't get me wrong; I know you knew all this without being told. I'm really telling it to myself because I'm impressed about something and I wonder if I'm losing my perspective. Like the guy who told me he was going to shoot himself in the leg the next time he got on guard. He wasn't right; too many guys were fighting and dying who hated the Army, too. But like I say, perspective is sort of putting things in their proper places. So they look like they really are. I've been thinking a lot about something that seems bigger and bigger.

I've been seeing these atrocity pictures in all the newspapers and magazines and they made me pretty sick. They got me mad, probably did the same thing to you, but I didn't do any real thinking about it. Except to feel sorry for the poor devils who spent any time in those camps.

Then, the other day I bumped into Stone on the street. Stone's a pretty old guy, about 40. I guess he'll be getting out now. When I saw him, he was waiting in line for a Red Cross movie to start. He looked peculiarly right waiting in line. He has that beaten look.

"Hi, Stone," I said when I saw him.

"Hello, Steve," he said. "Where you going?"

"Over to the Palace movie. How ya doing?"

"So-so," he said. "We're all still together."

For a minute I didn't know what the devil he meant. "Well, I'm glad to hear that," I said, trying to be polite.

"Yeah," he said. "We're still together."

"Well—so long, Stone," I said.

"So long, Steve."

Not exactly an epic conversation, but while I was walking away, I realized what he was talking about, and 18 months faded back in a flash. It's amazing what memory can do sometimes. Like it was last week, I saw us getting off that boat, fresh from the Italian invasion, and being assigned to this signal outfit in the hills back of Algiers. No one knew why we were there or what the four of us were supposed to do, so the first sergeant stuck us in with this special detachment that was on DS to the company. They monitored telephone conversations or something like that. There were some other guys living with us, too. They all had some sort of job that took them out of the ordinary company routine, so they lumped us all together in one big room.

It was nice living there. I remember the first morning when I woke up. We had come in at night, and the first thing my eyes saw in daylight was a long line of little girls filing right past my bunk through the room. I did one of those double-takes you see in the movies and wondered if it was time to hit the wagon. It wasn't. The company was quartered in an old school, and the little girls were on their way to morning class. After a while, I got

"Shut up or I'll hit you," Lefty said real nasty.

used to seeing them pass through in the mornings. They were cute little kids.

There were 16 of us in that room. In no time at all we got to know one another pretty well. You know how it is in the Army. You've got to be friendly with the guys you live with. There's no one else to be friendly with.

Four of us had been together for a long time, and we were the newcomers. Then there was Briggs, a fuzzy-haired little kid who was drinking himself to death. I don't know why. Maybe it was just the Army, but the kid was losing his wavy blond hair already, and there was something about his eyes that didn't look right in a 23-year-old guy. They looked too old. I heard recently that they finally sent him to a repple depple.

There was Archer, a simple kid from the farm country. Easy to get along with and strong as a bull. And Blore, from somewhere in the Middle West, who used to complain all the time. He had a picture of his girl standing on a chair. I think they had been engaged for nine years.

Jack used to sleep right beneath me. A good kid, with fire in his face. He used to burn because the WACs thought he was a little child. Hell, he was only 19.

Right across from me, Lefty slept. Lefty was a peculiar guy. Hard to get along with. But inside he was basically all right, if you know what I mean.

Then, of course, there was Stone, the guy I met waiting for the movies, and five or six others.

The four of us only lived there two months, and then we moved on, but two months seemed like a long time. It was winter and cold and rainy outside, and we used to spend most of our spare hours in the room, shooting the bull, or reading in the sack, or sleeping. I wouldn't say that everything was always peaches and cream in there, but by and large the bunch of us got along fairly well.

We had some good times together. I remember one night when for some reason, six of us got rhythmical and started singing and beating out every number we could think of. Lefty made believe he was the drummer, banging on a foot locker, and I did like a bass fiddle. When I look back now, it seems sort of foolish saying "doomp, doomp, doomp" in time and going through the motions of hitting a bass fiddle, but when I was doing it, it seemed all right. Lefty was good as a drummer. Once that was what he wanted to be.

We used to talk quite a bit and kid, too. One of the guys was running around with some French girl he met in town, and between no sleep and plenty of loving he was gradually getting thoroughly pooped. We used to kid him and say that he was going to wake up some morning dead. And he would ask us if we could think of a better way to die. In the morning, when the rest of us would get up, it took about five minutes to wake him up. We'd push him and call his name and shake him, and then finally he would slowly come to. "Huh?" he'd say, looking at us all as though he were waking from the dead, which he practically was. Then comprehension would come, and he'd grin.

Naturally, living in close quarters the way we were, with not too much to do, and lonesome inside to begin with, we got on one another's nerves, too. Blore had a high-pitched querulous voice and used to argue with Stone a lot about nothing. Briggs used to come in late drunk about three or four times a week, and he and the guy who slept beneath him would carry on a conversation in whispers loud enough to wake us all up. Which it usually did.

"Hey."

"Yeah."

"You there?"

"Of course I'm here."

"What a time!"

"Yeah."

"You're drunk, you drunken bastard."

"The hell I am."

"Sure you are."

For hours, sometimes, this would go on. And other times they'd go to sleep right away.

No one used to shout much at Briggs, though. We liked him. I guess it's because everyone sensed that there wasn't an ounce in him that ever wanted to hurt anybody. I mean, we all sort of felt sorry. You know how first sergeants are, even the good ones. Well, once the MPs called up about midnight to say that they had some kid down at the Hotel St. George, drunk as a lord, and if someone didn't come down to get him, they'd have to pull him in. Even the MPs like him, I guess. Anyway, the first sergeant got dressed, took out his jeep, drove down to the St. George, put Briggs in, and took him back to the company.

We got close in that room, too, which isn't odd. When 16 guys live in a room, you can't help seeing when a guy is happy and when he's sad, and if there's any capacity inside of you for it all, you get so that you understand one another pretty well. For one thing, you learn to leave one another alone.

Lefty surprised me one day. We were in the back, taking in a little of the sun that somehow came out one of those January days. Everything was peaceful. I had the day off and was thinking of home. The kids were playing in the courtyard around the corner and the sun was warm. He came over.

"Mind if I sit down for a while?"

"Hell, no, Lefty. Take a load off your feet."

We sat for a few minutes without saying anything. The sun usually shuts me up. But then, for some stupid reason, I started to talk about home. I guess I should have known better. I went on for about five minutes telling him that this sort of day

reminded me of my backyard, where I used to climb trees when I was a kid.

After a while I shut up. Lefty didn't look very happy.

"I don't have so much to look back to," he finally said. I didn't say anything. I had said too much.

"When I was about 14, I was all alone. My old man died when I was a kid and my mother went when I was 14."

"What did you do, Lefty?"

"What did I do? I nearly went nuts. That's what I did. I lived in a room all by myself, and sometimes I used to come back from work to that room and look at the walls and want to scream." He was getting a little worked up when he said it.

"You know what it's like to be all alone?" he asked me fiercely.

"I didn't before I came into the Army," I had to admit.

"Well, it ain't good," he said, "not to have no one."

For a couple of seconds, neither of us talked. That sun was really warm. He started again, and this time he was really living in the past.

"I used to sit for hours in that goddam room all alone. No brother, no sister. Then, when I couldn't stand it anymore, I'd go out and look for the girls on the block that played around. Hell, I had to have someone."

All I could do was listen.

"I don't know," he said. "Maybe that's why sometimes I do funny things now. I get nervous inside. Some of the guys don't like me."

"Oh, hell, Lefty, don't imagine things."

"Take that kid Jack. He don't like me. I like him. I think he's a swell kid. But he don't like me."

"He likes you all right, Lefty." It was a lie, though, when I said it, and I knew it. Lefty always irritated the kid.

Lefty didn't say any more. I guess he knew I was lying, too. We talked for a few more minutes and then it was time for chow, and I never mentioned the conversation to him.

About a week later, though, something happened that made it stick in my mind. One morning, when we all woke up, Lefty didn't get out of bed. We all kidded him about being lazy, and then he said he couldn't move. At first I thought he was joking, but when I went over to speak to him, I saw the look in his eyes and I knew he was serious then. We called the dispensary and they sent down a captain. He made us all leave the room and talked to Lefty alone for a while. Then they took him away. A few days later, Lefty was back, moving all right. He didn't mind talking about it. He said that this wasn't the first time it had happened. He would just wake up and couldn't move at all. He didn't feel any pain at all, just couldn't move. He said that it happened the first time while he was still a civilian, and that when he went into the Army and came overseas, he had been terrified all the way across that it would happen to him in one of the holds when the ship was hit by a torpedo, and no one would know. That must have been a nice thought to have with you for 13 days.

From what he said, the doctors thought he was pulling a fast one, at first. But after a while, when he told them about the other times, they believed him. Apparently, their only treatment for him was to tell him that he was all right, and that he could move if he really wanted to.

It must have worked, because here he was back.

After a few more days, the excitement wore off, and things were back to normal again.

Then about a week later, it happened.

It was night and cold. There were about 10 of us in the room, most of us stretched out in the sack. I was reading some stupid story in *Cosmopolitan* about how a GI in Algiers met romance. I knew it was silly, but I was reading it, anyway. There wasn't much else to do.

Jack was playing casino with one of the guys, the way they did almost every night, for 10 francs a game.

Lefty was the only one out of bed. He was getting dressed up to go out. He didn't have any girl that we knew of, so I guess he was going into town to a movie, or for a couple of drinks, or just to walk the restlessness off. He was restless, all right, and looked more nervous than usual.

For some reason, Stone was kidding Lefty, and Lefty didn't seem to like it much, though Stone really wasn't saying anything.

"Where ya going?" Stone said. And Lefty didn't answer him.

"Got a French babe on the string?" Stone asked.

"What business is it of yours?" Lefty snapped.

I don't know why Stone didn't shut up. As a matter of fact, none of us were paying much attention to either of them. This sounded like routine kidding.

I guess Stone was jealous or something that night. Maybe he was getting sick of being beaten by life and wished he were going out like Lefty was. Lefty was only 24.

Stone got out of bed to get a cigarette. After he got it, he walked over to where Lefty was by the door, tying his tie in the mirror.

"Well, you're looking like a dude, all right," Stone said.

"Shut up or I'll hit you," Lefty said, real nasty.

That one cracked through the rest of the room. We all looked up, and I guess everyone wondered why Lefty was so sore.

"Whatsa matter? Can't you take a little kidding?" Stone said. He knew Lefty meant what he said, and he was scared. But he had a little pride, too, and hoped to be able to get away with it and still save his face. He didn't want to shut right up, but he would have in a couple of minutes if Lefty had let him.

"Listen," Lefty said. "I'm warning you. Shut up."

"Aw, forget it, Lefty," one of the guys called out. "He doesn't mean anything."

Lefty kept fixing his tie without saying a word. I could tell from the way his face looked that he was all worked up inside. All of a sudden I thought of what he said that day in the sun about when he was a 14-year-old—"Sometimes I used to come back from work to that room and look at the walls and want to scream."

Stone was standing near Lefty, not knowing what to do. He looked small next to him. Lefty was a big guy. I guess Stone thought that if he could get in one more jab and then shut up, that would show everybody he was no coward.

The rest of us sat by like fools. I knew what was going to happen but somehow couldn't believe it. Like when people talked about what the Nazis intended, and everyone would listen but it wouldn't sink in, not really.

Finally, Stone said something. For the life of me, I don't know what it was. All I know is that Lefty stopped tying his tie and socked him hard right in the mouth. Stone staggered back against the wall, holding his hand to his face. For a moment, no one moved. I was looking at Lefty, and he was almost out of his head.

"Well, any of you guys got anything to say?" he said, fists ready. His mouth was sort of crooked.

I made my brilliant remark then and said, "Jeesus, Lefty, you shouldn't have done that."

He looked at me and said, "You looking for a fight, too?"

This time I had sense enough to shut up.

Lefty looked at all of us for a minute, and I guess the accumulated shock we all felt soaked into him. His expression changed and he put down his hands. Then he walked out of the room.

Stone walked over to his bed, tears in his eyes, his face down. He had been stripped of all his pride in front of all of us. That hurt more than the blow. He got up on his bed and lay face down for about an hour. No one spoke to him.

Everyone else tried to go on as we were before, but we couldn't. Lefty's hitting Stone was ugly, and we knew it. But we all felt so goddam helpless. I guess we should have stopped it before it went

that far, but most of us, I imagine, didn't think it would. I didn't have that excuse. When I first looked up, I knew Lefty was going to do what he did, but I just felt helpless, like I would be trying to stop something that began 10 years ago when Lefty was sitting in his room all alone and Stone was just beginning to realize he was beaten.

Well, I guess you can say it passed over, but it never really did. Lefty was sorry afterward like I knew he would be. He even apologized to Stone, but for a long time Stone wouldn't speak to him. We left shortly thereafter, and I didn't think about it until I bumped into Stone the other day.

And that's when I got those crazy thoughts. That little room was like a world in a way, and we were getting along okay in it. Till suddenly, something happened, and you had to go way back to find the reasons why. I mean the years in his lonely room had fixed Lefty up for life so that he was always going to be poking somebody somewhere. He was no good now, though. But that isn't all. A funny kind of question kept popping into my mind.

Don't countries, I mean people, have lonely rooms, too? I guess that sounds funny. But are we ever going to stop killing one another until we do away with all the lonely rooms? No one hungry, no one frustrated.

No one all alone.

That's what I was trying to tell you before. That lonely room idea. It keeps running through my head. Maybe I'm losing my perspective. But whenever I read about German murder camps, I see Lefty.

★

★

_____

In early 1945, 75 crack airmen were handpicked to form the 509th Composite Group of the 313th Wing of the 21st Bomber Command, 20th Air Force. They trained in highest secrecy at Wendover Field in Utah and on the remote island of Tinian in the Marianas, now in Allied hands; yet, what should have proven an honor was anything but. For soldiers accustomed to combat, their daily routine was not only inexplicable, it was mortifying. Practice runs were conducted over clearly unoccupied terrain for the sole purpose of dropping a single dummy bomb. As though that were all it would take. Inevitably, of course, the 509th became something of a joke amongst other bomber squadrons presently engaged in real battle.

Up in the air, the secret rose,
Where they're going, nobody knows.
Tomorrow they'll return again,
But we'll never know where they've been.
Don't ask about results and such,
Unless you want to get in Dutch.
But take it from one who's sure of the score,
The 509th is winning the war.

The verse was intended as a taunt. But not for long.

ATOMIC BOMB AWAY

—ROBERT SCHWARTZ Y2c
September 7, 1945

IT WAS 0245 when the colonel eased forward on the throttle. The B-29 with *Enola Gay* printed in big block letters on her nose vibrated and began to roll forward. She reached 100 m.p.h. in a hurry, then picked up additional speed more slowly. She had used up half the runway, and she was still bearing down hard on her spinning tires.

The tail gunner, S/Sgt. George Caron, up near the waist for the takeoff, began to sweat it out. Cpt. Robert A. Lewis, who usually piloted the *Enola Gay*, would have had her off the ground by this time. But Cap Lewis was only copilot on this trip, and Caron didn't know the colonel, Col. Paul W. (Old Bull) Tibbets, Jr., who had the controls now.

The *Enola Gay* neared the end of the runway and was almost on the gravel when she lifted gently into the dark sky. Caron realized suddenly that the colonel had been fighting to hold the ship on the ground the whole length of the runway just to be absolutely safe. And Caron remembered the bomb.

The men of the crew knew about the bomb— that it was something special—but they didn't know exactly why it was so special. It must be important, they felt sure, for in addition to Col. Tibbets' taking over for the trip, there was a Capt. William S. Parsons of the Navy aboard. He was a bomb expert of some kind and had come along as an observer.

Sgt. Joe Steiborik, radar operator, a dark, husky Texan who was almost uncannily adept at operating his precision instruments, called the pilot on the intercom and told him he would find a large cloud north of the next island. "Better stay away from it, colonel," he said. "It's pretty turbulent."

Fifteen minutes later, the colonel came to the rear to use the tube. Before the trip was over, he was to make a dozen or more such trips. "Coffee," was all he would say. "Drink so damn much of it."

Pfc. Richard H. Nelson, a boyish redhead who looked like a kid in a breakfast cereal advertisement, settled down to read *Watch Out for Willie Carter*, a boxing story. Nelson was teased pretty constantly about his reading, just as he was teased about almost everything. The youngest man on the crew ("I've been 20 for over two months"), he had been nicknamed "Junior" by the four other men of the plane crew. Before the flight was over, Junior finished the Willie Carter novel.

The flight engineer, S/Sgt. Wyatt E. Duzenbury of Lansing, Michigan, a quiet, 32-year-old, thin-faced fellow with big ears, sat at his control panel reading innumerable gauges. A pure, undiluted flight engineer, Deuce's only concern during the flight was to wonder how the big explosion would affect his gauges. "He's dial happy," said the others.

Up front sat Col. Tibbets, a 33-year-old with an accumulation of war flying experience. He had been the pilot of the first B-17 to fly over the English Channel on a bombing mission; he flew Gen. Mark Clark and later Gen. Jimmy Doolittle to Gibraltar; he flew Gen. Clark and Canada's Gen. McNaughton to Algiers, landing on a field he knew would be bombed and was actually under attack before he stopped taxiing; he led the first mission to bomb North Africa; returning to the United States, he flew the first B-29 on test missions; he was made CO of the atomic-bomb outfit forming at Wendover, Utah; and now, sitting at the controls of the *Enola Gay*, he was on his way to drop the first atomic bomb in history.

The copilot was Cap Lewis, the plane's usual pilot. He had flown four missions against Japan in the *Enola Gay* with his crew. The crewmen all called him Cap, and he is an easy man to know and an easy one to like.

The navigator was Capt. Red (Dutch) Van Kirk, a young Pennsylvanian with a crew haircut that gave him a collegiate look. Van Kirk was a good friend of Maj. Tom W. Ferebee, the bombardier. They had flown together in North Africa and England, usually as navigator and bombardier for Col. Tibbets. They were in on most of the colonel's firsts, and he had brought them into his atomic unit as soon as he was put in command.

The flight was well along now, and Caron, the tail gunner, remembering Cap Lewis' prodigious appetite, crawled forward through the tunnel to get to the food before the copilot ate it all.

Caron found six apples among the food up forward and threw these back the length of the tunnel, hoping that they would roll out of the tunnel and fall on a sleeping lieutenant who was flying this mission as special observer. He was Lt. M. U. Jeppson, an electronics officer. Caron wanted

The B-29 Superfortress—already a military legend.

to wake him and get him to sit erect, thus taking up less space in the waist, but none of the apples went the length of the tunnel, and the lieutenant kept on sprawling.

The flight to the target was routine, and only the thought of what they were going to see kept the crewmen active. They read, ate, and talked a little, and said little more historic than "move over, you bastard, and give me some room."

Occasionally they consulted various charms and talismans, of which the *Enola Gay* had an inordinate number. These included the following items: Three pairs of silk panties from Omaha,

stowed in one corner with a booklet on VD. One picture of Wendover Mary, a group companion during training in Utah—Wendover Mary had on a pair of high-heeled shoes. One Good Conduct ribbon, fastened on the radio set and owned by Junior. Six prophylactic kits, presented by the ground crew in case of forced landing in territory "where the natives are friendly." One ski cap, purchased in Salt Lake City and worn by Steiborik. One picture of the lobby of the Hotel Utah at Salt Lake. One lipstick kiss print on the nose, signed "Dottie" and bearing a dateline, "Omaha, one time," placed there by a civilian girl who worked at an Omaha air base; it had been shellacked over promptly for permanence and was the source of the crew's common prayer, "Omaha, one more time."

These things were a binding force to the men of the *Enola Gay*. A series of good drunks together in the States had helped weld them into a unit, and they were all very close friends.

They were getting near the target now, and Caron went back to the tail, taking his K-20 along. The plane began to climb, and they pressurized the cabin. The bombardier and the navigator, veterans of 54 and 63 missions, weren't worried about their imminent work, though it dawned on the navigator, Van Kirk, that "I'd be the biggest ass in the Air Forces if I missed the target." They passed over several secondary targets and found them visible, then continued into Hiroshima. They saw it, lined it up, opened the bomb-bay doors, made the bomb run, and let the bomb fall. The plane banked sharply to the right, and everyone craned to look out.

Back at the right waist window, Sgt. Bob Shumard, the assistant flight engineer, turned his Polaroids to full intensity and prepared to take advantage of the fact that he had the best seat for the show. When the bomb went off, it looked blue through his Polaroids, but he noted that the interior of the plane lighted up as though flash bulbs had been set off inside the cabin. He adjusted his Polaroids to mild intensity and looked down at Hiroshima. A large white cloud was spreading rapidly over the whole area, obscuring everything and rising very rapidly. Shumard shouted into the intercom: "There it goes, and it's coming right back at us!"

Looking way down again, he noted that outside the smoke circle and racing ahead of it were three large concentric circles. These appeared to Shumard to be heat rings, since they looked like the transparent wavy vapor seen coming off hot objects. He craned to see what happened to them,

The smoke of Hiroshima holds hope of end of war.

but the lieutenant who had been asleep was now awake and was climbing all over Shumard's neck.

He lost the rings during this interval and could not find them again.

The engineer noted that his instruments were still functioning normally, and then he looked out his little hatch. He said nothing.

When Steiborik got no instrument reaction to the blast, he looked, too.

"Jesus Christ!" said Lt. Jeppson. "If people knew what we were doing, we could have sold tickets for $100,000."

Ferebee, the bombardier, felt only one reaction: He was damn glad to be rid of the bomb. Then he set to work filling out the strike-report form, which was to be radioed in.

Back in the tail, Caron noted the turbulence and called to the pilot: "Colonel, it's coming towards us fast." He got no reply, but the plane changed its course and outdistanced the cloud.

They looked after it as long as they could see it, a great ringed cumulus-type shaft rising higher and higher through the clouds. Then they flew on, and it was gone. The tail gunner called to the pilot: "Colonel, that was worth the 25-cent ride on the Cyclone at Coney Island."

The colonel called back, "I'll collect the two bits when we land."

"You'll have to wait till pay day," said the tail gunner.

Maj. Ferebee filled out the strike report and gave it to Capt. Parsons, who had been in charge of the bomb. Parsons took it to Junior.

"This report," said the captain, "is going directly to the president."

The Navy captain wondered aloud: "How can you destroy so much and sacrifice so little? We didn't even damage the plane."

They talked about the bomb. Some of the men wondered how many it would take to make the Japs surrender; everyone wondered if the one bomb would end the war. Finally they dozed off a little, talked a little, and ate a little and engaged in brief flurries of speculation. But the *Enola Gay*, the plane that had been named by the crew for the colonel's mother as a gesture for the flight, flew on and on. "She sang," they said later, with the deep pride that airmen feel for a ground crew that can make a plane sing.

Deuce worried about fuel, but Cap kidded him out of it. Time dragged. Everyone got hungry. But then they saw the field and were alert again.

"I looked at the Old Bull," said Cap Lewis, "and his eyes were bloodshot and he looked awful tired. He looked like the past 10 months, at Wendover and Washington and New Mexico and overseas, had come up and hit him all at once.

"I says to him, 'Bull, after such a beautiful job, you better make a beautiful landing.'

"And he did."

WHAT'S YOUR PROBLEM?

Return to Overseas

Dear *Yank*:

I am 38 years old. They told me, when I was over in North Africa last summer, that I could get out of the Army if I applied for discharge before Aug. 1. I fulfilled all the requirements and eventually found myself hanging on the rail of a transport sailing for home. Well, *Yank*, when I saw Liberty's statue in New York Harbor—and I know this sounds corny—I got to regretting I was gonna be a civilian. And that's what I told my new CO; I told him I wanted to withdraw my application for discharge. He blew up like an ammunition dump. When the smoke cleared, I found out that he had orders fixed up for me to be shipped right back to the North African theater—to my old command! At this very moment I'm looking at the transport that is probably going to take me back across the Atlantic. But what I'd like to know is, can this CO *legally* do this to me?

—S/Sgt. Joe Morton
Port of Embarkation

He sure can. Ours is the sad duty to refer you to Sec. IV, WD Cir. No. 10, 6 Jan. 1944. Subparagraph 2 says that any man 38 years old serving overseas who has asked for a withdrawal of his approved application for discharge after he has already been returned to the States will be packed off in the first shipment heading back to his old command. One of the reasons for this circular, the Army says, is that some GIs were using the over-38 discharge rule, not as a way to get out of the Army, but simply as a pretext to get back to the States.

Lost Teeth

Dear *Yank*:

Does a GI have to sign a statement of charges if he loses the set of false teeth issued to him by the Army? Some guys say you do, and I'm worried. While we were crossing on the ship I was put on a detail as a sort of "bucket brigade" member who passes cardboard cases down to the galley below. One wise guy threw a box at my chest and the jolt bounced my false teeth into the Pacific. It wasn't my fault, and I'll be one damned sore dogface if I am expected to pay for them.

—Pvt. Dominick Atrellia
Australia

False teeth are not considered "property" in the usual sense of the word, and the Judge Advocate General has ruled that a GI who accidentally loses his dentures does not have to pay for them on a statement of charges.

Allotment Muddle

Dear *Yank*:

I have been overseas since June 1942. My pay was stopped in October 1942 because my mother was supposed to have been overpaid by the Office of Dependency Benefits. Since then I have had a few partial payments amounting to about $200.

Now the ODB has cut off my mother's allotment entirely. They have also cut off my six-year-old son's allotment. My mother is 68 and in very poor health. I can't understand why I get no pay and why the allotments were cut off. I've tried writing to the ODB and seeing my first sergeant, but it doesn't do any good. What can I do to get some money?

—Name Withheld
Italy

You'd better get used to living on partial payments, brother; you owe the ODB a wad of dough. ODB's records show that your mother has been overpaid to the tune of $1,292. Here are the facts:

In May 1942 you made a Class E (voluntary) allotment of $25 a month to your mother. Later that month you discontinued that allotment and set up one for $45. Your orderly room failed to

notify ODB about your discontinuing the $25 allotment, so ODB paid both amounts through September 1943, at which time the $45 allotment was stopped. The $25 check kept on going to your mother until January 1944. A third Class E allotment, based on an incorrect serial number, was also paid to your mother from October 1942 to September 1943. Total overpayment: $1,760.

You made out still another Class E allotment in June 1942 for $18 a month. The ODB never paid this one, however, so in theory at least they owe you $468. After this is deducted from the overpayments, you still owe ODB $1,292.

In January 1943 you applied for a Class F (family) allotment for your mother and son, retroactive to June 1942. This allotment was granted, costing you $27 a month back to June 1942, so that for over a year your mother received almost $200 a month in allotments. The ODB says that your wife, who you say died in 1941, is very much alive and has applied for a family allowance, claiming that your son lives with her. Your mother contends that boy is with her. Both claims are being investigated now.

Don't worry, though. Money isn't everything.

Tire Retreaders

Dear *Yank*:

I am going nuts retreading tires. I am getting and despondent. Only *Yank* can help me. You I have always wanted to get into the Infantry when I heard about that new *WD Cir. 132* ma it practically mandatory for COs to approve GI's request for transfer into the Infantry, I r eted over to the Old Man here. Smiling blissf I told him to get me outa this unit pronto. Shoc I heard him say he wouldn't let me transfer, yet with my own eyes I had read in that circ where only the War Department could say " on such a deal. *Yank*, it's up to you now.

—Pvt. F. L.
Aberdeen Proving Grounds, Maryla

Sorry, but we have to fail you. WD Memo. W61 44 (29 May 1944) lists tire rebuilders among t specialists who "are and have been for an e tended period of time critically needed by t Army." The memorandum goes on to say th such critically needed specialists "may not vo unteer for assignment and duty in the Infantry under the provisions of Cir. 132.

HIROSHIMA: ATOMIZED

—Sgt. JOE McCARTHY
September 28, 1945

IN THE bombed-out cities of Europe there were always plenty of eyewitnesses who were only too eager to tell you exactly how it was the day their house fell in. It wasn't like that in Hiroshima when I came here with the first group of Americans to enter the city since it was almost completely destroyed by our atomic bomb on Aug. 6. For the first two hours, as we walked through the utterly demolished downtown section, we couldn't find a single Jap on the streets who had been here when the bomb landed. Practically all eyewitnesses seemed to be dead or in the hospital.

"I knew lots of Hiroshima people, but only one of my friends survived safely," said the Japanese naval officer who acted as our interpreter. "He was at work in the second floor of a building. He fell through to the basement. Everybody else in the building was killed or injured, but he wasn't hurt."

The scarcity of healthy survivors gives some idea what our first and most effective atomic bomb did when it struck Japan. There's no doubt when you look at it that Hiroshima is the greatest man-made disaster in the history of the world.

You can stand at its center and for four square miles around there is nothing left but total destruction. The only things left standing are a few concrete-reinforced buildings, with their insides charred and ruined, an occasional bare chimney, and trees with every limb and every leaf torn off.

The fire engines that the city needed so badly are still standing in the fire station, their radiators folded inward like accordions and their mechanisms scattered on the floor.

The hospital which people tried to reach is a hollow, blackened shell.

In parts of the outskirts the smell of the dead under the debris is unbearable. In the center of the town there are not enough ruins to hide a corpse. Everything is level ashes.

We found that the few surviving Japs who had been in Hiroshima the day the bomb fell became inarticulate when we asked them to describe what they had seen and done during the blast and during the few hours that followed the explosions. In reply to our questions, they would stare at the ceiling and stare at the floor. Then they would make a helpless gesture with their hands and say things like, "The town was in the worst condition you can consider," or, "It was terrible beyond imagination."

One of the Japs we talked to was a Government official named Hirokuni Dazai, a little fellow with a bandaged head who described his job as Com-

. . . there was nothing left but total destruction.

missioner of Public Thought Control in the Hiroshima district. Dazai returned to Hiroshima from a trip to Tokyo only 40 minutes before the bomb fell. There had been an air-raid alarm shortly before eight o'clock that morning, but Dazai doesn't remember seeing or hearing any planes overhead. The all-clear signal sounded about five minutes past eight, and the people came out of the shelters and started home to have their breakfast. Dazai was standing in front of his house between ten minutes and a quarter past eight when he saw a light moving across the sky.

"It looked like some sort of electric flash," he told us. "It was arc-shaped and bright orange." Then he was knocked to the ground by a wave of concussion. His house shook and fell apart, some of the rubble landing on top of him. That's how he got the bandage on his head. He picked himself off the ground and got his wife and two children out of the ruins.

Dazai took his wife and children to the home of a relative two kilometers away and tried to get downtown to his office, but the heat of the fire there was too overpowering.

The whole city burned steadily for the next two days. Dazai and other officials found relief work almost impossible, since the fire-fighting equipment and the hospitals were destroyed and almost every telegraph pole and wire was flat on the ground. Finally the Government managed to get some help and supplies up the river boat, but it wasn't enough.

Later the trains came into the town. We noticed that railroad tracks and bridges had been completely undamaged by the atomic blast. Evidently it doesn't affect things close to the ground."

We asked Dazai how many bombs he thought we'd dropped on Hiroshima. He said that at first he thought the city was hit by several hundred, but that shortly after the blast, when he saw the whole area in burning ruins, he thought it was some new variety of "aerial torpedo." One thing that baffled him and other Japs who had experienced the bombing was the complete absence of noise in Hiroshima before and after the bomb landed. One Jap said he was deaf for a week afterward from concussion but heard no explosion. The Japs at the naval base in Kuri, about 12 miles away, however, say they heard a terrific roar. Vice Adm. Massao Kanazawa said the effect in Kuri was like a tornado. There was a "great wind," he said, and trees around the naval base were bent to the ground by it.

The Japs who went to Manila to arrange the peace signing said their dead at Hiroshima numbered 11,000. That was a great understatement. Reading figures to us from his black notebook, Dazai estimated that the Hiroshima dead so far number around 80,000.

Hiroshima was made to order for effective atomic bombing. It is built on a river delta like New Orleans, and it is as flat as a billiard table. There are none of the hills that protected part of Nagasaki from the blast of our second atomic bomb. Hiroshima was a new and modern city, the home of many Japanese who had lived in the States and had brought back with them American ideas about houses and gardens. It had a population of 343,000 in the 1940 census. Now the population is about 120,000. Most of the residents who are injured or sick as a result of the bombing are living in battered and misshapen houses on the edges of the city.

Dazai said that when the Japs took the first count of the Hiroshima casualties on Aug. 20 there were 3,000 known dead and 30,000 missing persons who had been given up for dead. There were 13,960 "seriously wounded" and 43,500 injured. On Sept. 1 the toll of known dead was up to 53,000.

Japanese doctors who have been attending Hiroshima casualties say that a lot of the weird stories about the effects of the atomic bombings on the civilian population are apparently true. They say that people who were only slightly wounded when the bomb fell and some others who didn't enter Hiroshima until a few hours after the bombing have died from loss of white blood corpuscles. The effect of the atomic bomb as far as they have been able to determine is about the same as overexposure to the rays of a very powerful X-ray machine. Sufferers, say the Japanese doctors, develop a temperature of around 105°; their hair begins to fall out, and they feel ill and vomit blood.

The doctors also say that the severely blistering X-ray-like burns are generally found only on the side of the body which faced the atomic blast. They say two men were fencing in Hiroshima the morning of the bomb exploded. One of these was facing the direction of the blast and died almost instantly. The other, burned only on the back of the neck, lived for a week.

The native doctors also say that clothing serves as protection against atomic burns. People wearing thick undershirts didn't get it as badly as those who had on only a kimono or a shirt. There was a strong rumor, both among Jap civilians here and among GIs back in the Philippines, Okinawa, and the Marianas, that anybody walking into an atomic-bombed area even a week or more after would be sterilized by the radioactivity in the soil. Jap doctors haven't had time to check that one yet. They think the victims who were exposed to the bombing itself may not be able to reproduce again, but they don't know for sure. Nor do they know yet how long it will be before Hiroshima will be an absolutely healthful place to live in. Some scientific writer back in the States has declared that Hiroshima's soil would be barren and radioactive for the next 70 years. One Jap doctor says this is the malarkey. He made tests of soil in Hiroshima a few weeks ago and found no radioactivity in it.

Walking into Hiroshima in broad daylight, wearing an American uniform and knowing that you were one of the first Americans the people in the utterly ruined city have laid eyes on since the bombing, was not a comfortable feeling. I couldn't help wondering what would have happened to me if I'd been a Jap entering Brooklyn after Japan had dropped an atomic bomb, or, for that matter, any kind of bomb, on Flatbush. I was accompanied by the crew of a B-17 who were wearing Air Forces insignia all over themselves the way an Irishman wears green on St. Patrick's Day, and that didn't help matters. But the Hiroshima Japs—men, women, and children, gave us exactly the same treatment we got in Yokohama, Tokyo, Kuri, and all the other Jap towns we have visited—the same prolonged, unabashed, curious stares unmixed with any expression either of hatred or welcome.

All through Hiroshima we've passed close to men and women pointing at ashes that evidently used to be homes of relatives or friends. We've seen them at the wrecked police station trying to locate missing people and walking toward their shrines to pray. I noticed one woman leaning over a water faucet, the only thing left of her home, filling a pan to wash some clothes. There was no wreckage around her, no broken walls or glassless windows—just the water pipe, with the faucet on the end of it, sticking up out of the ashes. "It's tough on them, sure," said a GI with me, "but it saved a lot of guys' lives."

One of the Jap Navy officers acting as our interpreters was born in Sacramento, Calif. We asked him if the people in this part of Japan accepted the atomic bomb as one of the misfortunes of war and held no particular resentment against us for it. Or, we asked, do they hate us?

The officer studied his boots and then peered quizzically through his tortoise-rimmed glasses.

"They hate you," he said.

"Quick! A tourniquet!"—PVT. THOMAS FLANNERY

'Oh, some slip-up somewhere. I imagine we'll be back on our regular rations in a day or two."
— SGT. DOUGLAS BORGSTEDT

FALL OF JAPAN

September 28 and October 5, 1945

THREE YEARS, eight months, and seven days after Pearl Harbor, total victory came to the United States of America and all the Allies. On the 14th of August 1945 the last Axis enemy went down to that total defeat which the democracies, some of whom had faced up to Rome-Berlin-Tokyo aggression long before the 7th of December 1941, had solemnly pledged themselves to bring about.

In the United States and throughout the Allied world the contrast between those two days was the contrast between shock, dread, and near-defeat, and relief, thanksgiving, and unqualified triumph. There was another difference, too.

To the citizens of the United States—and indeed of all the countries that later became the United Nations—Pearl Harbor had been a blow-without-warning. In its unexpectedness it had brought a mental shock almost as severe as the physical shock of the bombs that fell on Hickam Field and on the ships in harbor. VJ-Day came to a nation waiting for and well-schooled in victory.

America's armed forces had had a major share in Allied triumphs all over the globe. The weapons forged in its factories and carried on its ships and planes to every part of the world had proved its industrial supremacy. VJ-Day had come sooner than most Americans had dared hope, but for months none had doubted that it would arrive.

When it did come, after a five-day wait while the *samurai* fumed and quibbled over the details of defeat, there was such an outpouring of emotion as Americans had never known. Wherever Americans were gathered together—whether in Louisville, Kentucky, Berlin, or Manila—the pattern of celebration was much the same. There were roars of rejoicing, high hopes for reunions, and prayers. The prayers were offered in gratitude and in remembrance of those who had died for a day they could not mark.

In America the celebration outdid anything within the memory of living men. It made VE-Day seem silent; it far overshadowed Armistice Day 1918. On the continent of Europe and on continents and islands where the end-of-war had never found U. S. troops before, it was a day without precedent. A chapter, perhaps a whole book, of history had ended, and a word that had figured much in American thoughts for three years, eight months, and seven days—a word often spoken, but always in terms of the past or of an unsure future—could be spoken now in terms of the living present. The word was peace.

—Sgt. Hilary H. Lyons

For a while it looked as though the proceedings would go off with almost unreasonable smoothness. Cameramen assigned to the formal surrender ceremonies aboard the battleship *Missouri* in Tokyo Bay arrived on time, and, although every inch of the turrets and housings and life rafts above the veranda deck where the signing was to take place was crowded, no one fell off and broke a collarbone.

The ceremonies themselves even started and were carried on according to schedule. It took a Canadian colonel to bring things back to normal by signing the surrender document on the wrong line.

No one had the heart to blame the colonel,

though. A mere colonel was bound to get nervous around so much higher brass.

The other minor flaw in the ceremonial circus was that it was something of an anticlimax. Great historic events probably are always somewhat that way, and this one, to those of us who had taken off three weeks before with the 11th Airborne Division from the Philippines, was even more so. We had started out thinking in terms of a sensational dash to the Emperor's palace in Tokyo, only to sweat it out on Okinawa and later off Yokohama.

When it did come, the signing aboard the *Missouri* was a show which lacked nothing in its staging. A cluster of microphones and a long table covered with a green cloth had been placed in the center of the deck. On the table lay the big, ledger-size white documents of surrender bound in brown folders.

The assembly of brass and braid was a thing to see—a lake of gold and silver sparkling with rainbows of decorations and ribbons. British and Australian Army officers had scarlet stripes on their garrison caps and on their collars. The French were more conservative, except for the acres of vivid decorations on their breasts. The stocky leader of the Russian delegation wore gold shoulder-boards and red-striped trousers. The Dutch had gold-looped shoulder emblems. The British admirals wore snow-white summer uniforms with shorts and knee-length white stockings. The olive-drab of the Chinese was plain except for ribbons. The least decked-out of all were the Americans. Their hats, except for Adm. Halsey's go-to-hell cap, were gold-braided, but their uniforms were plain sun-tan. Navy regulations do not permit wearing ribbons or decorations on a shirt.

Lack of time prevented piping anyone over the side, and when Gen. MacArthur, Supreme Commander for the Allied powers, came aboard he strode quickly across the veranda deck and disappeared inside the ship. Like the other American officers, he wore plain sun-tans. A few minutes later, a gig flying the American flag and operated by white-clad American sailors putted around the bow of the ship. In the gig, wearing formal diplomatic morning attire consisting of black cutaway coat, striped pants, and stovepipe hat, sat Foreign Minister Namoru Shigemitsu, leader of the Japanese delegation.

Coming up the gangway, Shigemitsu climbed very slowly because of a stiff left leg, and he limped onto the veranda deck with the aid of a heavy light-colored cane. Behind him came 10 other Japs. One wore a white suit; two more wore formal morning attire; the rest were dressed in the pieced-out uniforms of the Jap Army and Navy. They gathered into three rows on the forward side of the green-covered table. The representatives of the Allied powers formed on the other side.

When they were arranged, Gen. MacArthur entered, stepped to the microphone, and began to speak.

His words rolled sonorously: "We are gathered here, representatives of the major warring powers, to conclude a solemn agreement whereby peace may be restored." He emphasized the necessity that both victors and vanquished rise to a greater dignity in order that the world might emerge forever from blood and carnage. He declared that his firm intention as Supreme Commander was to "discharge my responsibility with justice and tolerance while taking all necessary dispositions to insure that the terms of surrender are fully, promptly, and faithfully complied with."

The Japanese stood at attention during the short address, their faces grave but otherwise showing little emotion. When the representatives of the Emperor were invited to sign, Foreign Minister Shigemitsu hobbled forward, laid aside his silk hat and cane, and lowered himself slowly into a chair. The wind whipped his thin, dark hair as he reached into his pocket for a pen, tested it, then affixed three large Japanese characters to the first of the documents. He had to rise and bend over the table for the others.

The audience was conscious of the historic importance of the pen strokes, but watched for something else, too. Gen. MacArthur had promised to present Gen. Wainwright, who had surrendered the American forces at Corregidor and until a few

Shigemitsu's Japanese brushwork makes it official.

days before had been a prisoner of war, with the first pen to sign the surrender. Shigemitsu finished and closed his pen and replaced it in his pocket. There could be no objection. He had needed a brush-pen for the Japanese letters.

When the big surrender folders were turned around the table, Gen. MacArthur came forward to affix his signature as Supreme Commander. He asked Gen. Wainwright and Gen. Percival, who had surrendered the British forces at Singapore, to accompany him. Gen. MacArthur signed the first document and handed the pen to Gen. Wainwright. He used five pens in all, ending up with the one from his own pocket.

Sailors have been as avid souvenir collectors in this war as anyone else, but when Adm. Nimitz sat down to sign for the U. S. he used only two pens. After that the representatives of China, the United Kingdom, Russia, Australia, Canada, France, the Netherlands, and New Zealand put down their signatures.

As the big leather document folders were gathered, a GI member of a sound unit recorded a few historic remarks of his own:

"Brother," he said, "I hope those are my discharge papers."

—Sgt. Dale Kramer

The reception was uneventful at Atsugi Airfield in Japan. C-54s carrying elements of the 11th Airborne Division were coming in low over the coast of Japan in history's gentlest invasion. The narrow beaches, probably the very stretches of sand we would have stormed, were gray and empty. Crowding the beaches were hills and fields, very green and rolling gracefully out from the base of a range of eroded carpets. Here and there were clumps of trees—willows, evergreens, maples, and cherries. Hedges laced the rice paddies. Houses with thatched roofs were built close to the dirt roads. Most of the people walking along the roads carried heavy bundles or pulled carts. They didn't bother to look at the planes.

Atsugi Airfield looked somewhat like the Indiana Country Fair. Two long dirt runways were in the center of some feebly camouflaged hangars and ramshackle barracks. Wrecked Jap planes, glinting silver where their green paint jobs had worn off, lay like broken toys at one end of the field, having careened over on their wingtips and noses.

Waiting to meet the ships were members of the 63d Airdrome Squad and the 31st Air Freight Transport, who had arrived on D-minus-Two to ready the field.

These advance elements had expected to be massacred. Instead, they had been greeted by docile Jap officials, plus a few enthusiastic Russians who had apparently stayed in nearby Tokyo after their government's entry into the war.

Hundreds of square old Jap trucks stood at one end of the runway, lined up at close intervals, and hundreds of cars were in a big open field at the other end. It looked like the parking lot outside a college football stadium around 1938.

The baggage was piling up in front of the hangars, and troops heavy with packs were climbing into trucks. Jap interpreters, dressed in uniforms or suits or parts of each, stood around in nervous little groups. They had on yellow armbands to denote their calling. Like the Jap truck drivers and work parties, they tried to be impassive. One skinny interpreter wore a faded uniform of black crepe from which dangled bits of dirty gold braid. He looked like a cross between a scarecrow and a kid at a costume party.

On the far side of the field, around the administration buildings, stood armed Jap soldiers. They saluted every American who happened to come within 100 yards of them. Black-uniformed cops, carrying small sabers in silver scabbards, guarded the roads, looking sinister and self-important. A squad of Jap soldiers lay on thin straw mats in a car barn off one corner of the field. Their shirts were off, but they wore leggings. The squad's lieutenant lay on his back, his feet up against his buttocks, making nervous, wavy movements with his knees.

The barracks and administration buildings were weatherbeaten and somber. They had a bleak look that indicated they had been left to sag in rain and sun. Here and there a hangar roof had been burned off—or maybe never had been put on.

The D-minus-Two men were housed in a big barracks. The Jap Government had supplied them with the services of some waiters from Tokyo's Imperial Hotel. The atmosphere was practically lousy with the quiet selflessness that characterizes the breed of good waiters all over the world. "Hail the conquering hero!" said one GI as he snapped his fingers for more ice water.

American soldiers stood around and cracked about the broken-down automobiles. "I understand Henry Ford is coming over to get the cars out of the ditches by Christmas," a corporal remarked dryly. The MPs didn't like to let the ancient vehicles cross the field because of their tendency to fall apart in the middle of the runways.

In a deserted "shadow factory" dug into the side of the hill next to the field someone found a tissue-paper blueprint; it was a design for a homemade air-raid shelter. Standing on the roads that criss-cross the barracks area beside the field, you could feel the ground tremble as trucks rumbled past. Underneath was a huge network of electric-lighted tunnels where the Japs had set up a complete machine shop.

As MacArthur's entourage pulled out from the field a car loaded with Jap officials broke down. An officer squatted on the fender and peered under the hood, his *samurai* sword dangling grotesquely between his knees. Other Japs stood by helplessly while a truckload of GIs wheeled past.

"Why don't you trade that sword in on a screwdriver?" called one GI.

—Sgt. Knox Burger

At 0800 on Aug. 15 it was announced over the radio that the Japanese surrender had been accepted in Washington. At 1000 a force of Japs made a banzai charge on the command post of Company A, 128th Infantry, on Luzon. Our casualties were one killed, one wounded.

Aug. 15 was the 654th day of combat for the 32d (Red Arrow) Division and wasn't much dif-

ferent from any other day. The 32d had been celebrating premature announcements of peace for four days, and when Aug. 15 came the only loud or emotional voices to be heard were the voices of the men of two platoons arguing over the ownership of a small pile of lumber.

As one rifleman of the division said, "Them Japs out in the hills don't know the war's over."

The Japanese whom the 32d was fighting were believed to be out of contact with their higher headquarters and with Domei, and the division dropped leaflets telling of the war's end, sending over Cub planes with amplifiers to broadcast the news, and sent Jap prisoners back into the hills to spread the word. One of the prisoners stayed in the hills.

"You know that Jap we turned loose a week ago and he said he'd bring back his captain?" the chief clerk asked the major. "Well, the sonuvabitch ain't come back yet."

"If he don't come back tomorrow," said the major, "you might as well mark him AWOL."

From all indications, the Japs were taking the leaflets, the loudspeakers, and the returned prisoners for so much propaganda, and it was pretty much taken for granted that the fighting might go on for weeks.

Such celebration as there had been in the 32d was over. It had come and gone the Friday night before, when the movie was cut off in the middle of a newsreel showing the fall of Baguio and a voice said over the loudspeaker, "We have just received word from Division G-2 that Japan is willing to accept the surrender terms . . ."

The announcer's voice was lost in a roar of whooping and hollering that lasted for a minute and a half, during which time one man fainted from emotion. The announcer broke in to finish his sentence: ". . . provided it can keep the Emperor." This had no effect on the general enthusiasm. Then another voice came in, this one tense and excited. "All guards for the beer dump will report to their posts immediately!" The projectionist's voice was next. "All right," it said, "all right. Do you want to see the movie—or what?" Most of the men wanted to see the movie, so the fall of Baguio continued. The main feature was a Fred Allen picture titled *In the Bag.*

After the show the men went back to their tents, talked late into the night, listened to the orderly-room radios, or dipped into the beer that had been issued that morning. One man had been hoarding his beer and had a reserve supply of four cases when the announcement came. He put on one hell of a toot.

The first sergeant of a rifle company looked off down the road. "August the fifteenth," he said, "nineteen hundred and forty-five." He spoke the date slowly and a little wonderingly. "It's mighty goddam quiet around here to be the day the war ended."

"The base sections are the place to see the excitement," said the T-5 inside the orderly tent. "I hear there were big doings down to Corps the other night. They were shooting holes through the roof—and it was raining to beat all hell."

The first sergeant gave a tolerant laugh. "It was probably the first time some of those boys ever got to shoot off a gun."

The afternoon sun was hot and the air was still and drowsy like an August afternoon in the Deep South. There was an occasional snatch of distant conversation from a bunch of GIs working on a road detail and now and then an excited shout from a nearby court where some junior officers were knocking themselves out in a game of handball. A small group of men leaned against the wall on the shady side of a battalion headquarters.

"Two weeks ago," said a man stretched out on the ground, "you could have got any kind of odds betting that the war would be over in August. Be damned if I thought it would be over any time this year. I thought we'd be digging Japs out of their houses six months after we invaded the homeland."

A scattered force of riflemen on the ridge moved back to let the artillery register on the Japs. The Japs did some quick shifting, and the riflemen were cut off on three sides and part of the fourth. Some supplies were moved up to the riflemen, but the men's position wasn't particularly enviable. When word was sent up that the war was all over the reply came back down: "Yeah, it's all over. It's all over this bloody hill."

On Balete Pass, the jeep hit a good-sized stone and bounced toward the embankment. "He's got a forty-foot road and one little eight-inch rock," said one of the corporals in the back seat. "That's what I call real shooting."

"It's the guys who get killed after the war's over," said the other corporal. "They're the real sad cases."

"Goddammit," said the pfc. at the wheel, "any time you want to do the driving yourself you can take over."

Two PRO men showed up at the antitank outfit to photograph eight veterans of the Buna campaign who were leaving that night for the States. The eight Buna men climbed into the back of a truck, and the photographer scratched his chin thoughtfully. "It'd make a better picture," he said to the first sergeant, "if we had a few men standing here saying good-bye to them." "Right here?" said the first sergeant. He went to the head of the company street and blew a terrific blast on his whistle. "All right!" he shouted down the line. "Everybody outside!"

At sundown a cold, penetrating rain came up, and a hard wind drove it in through the doors and under the sides of the tents. The order to cease firing still hadn't come down from Corps, and a battalion commander, presumed to be bucking for a silver leaf, sent two rifle companies out into the rain on a night problem. The two companies had been out on the road for possibly two hours when Division heard about it and sent down word that basic training could be dispensed with for the time being.

The crowd at the supper table was discussing the immediate postwar world. "The way I understand it," said the man at the near end of the table, "athletics and recreation are going to be the thing until they decide to send us home. And if you want to study French or learn how to build birdhouses for money, that'll get you out of calisthenics. Build the body and build the mind; that's the ticket. Let 'em go ahead and see what good it'll do. When I get home I'm cutting body and mind both adrift to go to hell."

The man at the far end of the table broke in. "The way they ort to do it," he said, "they ort to serve breakfast in bed every morning for all the troops. I ain't had breakfast in bed since we left Australia."

The man in the middle looked out the mess hall door at the relentless rain that separated the mess hall from the kitchen. "Let's odd-man," he said, "to see who goes for coffee."

An elderly private from division headquarters got in late from a 40-mile drive over the mountains in an open jeep. It had rained all the way, and he was soaked to the skin. The first man he met gave him the message that he was supposed to go on guard duty in 45 minutes.

At 0700 on Aug. 16, Company A of the 128th was attacked again by a force of 60 or 70 Japs. Our casualties were one killed, five wounded.

It was the 655th day of combat for the 32d Division.

—Sgt. Marion Hargrove

The headline, in type so big that the words ran together across the top of the page, said: "NIPS QUIT." The Japanese prisoners of war crowded around the Jap private who held the paper. They stood in the sun-baked courtyard of the new Bilibid Prison south of Manila, where some 8,000 former soldiers of the Emperor are confined.

An elderly Japanese civilian interpreter lifted his eyebrows, adjusted his spectacles, and translated.

"*Nippon*," he said. "*Nippon Kofuku.*"

The private glanced sidelong at the older man and laughed at him. The civilian thumbed the paper with his forefinger and repeated the translation.

The private frowned and stared at the page that said that the war was ending and that his country was offering to surrender. The Japs behind him chattered and stuck their heads over his shoulder to see for themselves. The private left the paper with them and walked into the long concrete building where he lived.

I followed with the interpreter.

The room, which was part of the processing center for incoming prisoners, was about the size of a Stateside army barracks. The windows were barred, but the door was unlocked and open. About 30 Japs, most of them newly arrived at the prison, lay or sat on blankets spread on the concrete floor. On one side of the room were the day's crop of newcomers. Most of them were just skin and bones, and the GI shorts they wore hung loosely on their flanks as they lay with their thin arms clasped behind their heads, their dead eyes staring at nothing.

On the other side of the room were healthier specimens waiting to be assigned to work companies. It was easy to tell how long they had been prisoners by the amount of meat on their bones.

When the visitors were seated around the private's cot (he had a cot because he was a trustee and in charge of this part of the processing center), the interpreter asked him how he felt about the news of Japan's capitulation.

The soldier rubbed his eyes with the palm of his hand and figured out just what he wanted to say.

"I'm not sorry," he told the interpreter. "I'm in a happy mood." He smiled cheerfully to show how happy the mood was. There was a murmur in the room as the word passed from pallet to pallet, and some of those who had been lying down sat up and watched.

He was asked if he wanted to go home now. This was a ticklish one. He wanted to go home, and he didn't want to go home. His relatives and his friends at the aluminum plant where he worked in Tokyo might point at him, he said, and he didn't want to be pointed at. The Japs who had edged into the group all looked at the floor. Nobody said anything for a moment. The private looked up and smiled again—his happy-mood smile. He was happy that the war had ended and that the world could know peace again, he said.

The others, watching him, all smiled too. They

put on their happy-mood smiles, and there was the sound of polite hissing.

A muscle-jawed Jap sergeant joined the group. He'd been a prisoner for about a month and was in pretty fair condition. He, too, had been aware of what was going on.

"I'm much relieved," he told the interpreter. "All my friends [he indicated the Japs along the wall], all my friends have such a mood of mind." The Japs along the wall stared impassively. The sergeant gave his name and said he had no objection to having it published in an American magazine. He was a medical sergeant about 40 years old, and he had an abscess on one leg. He had given up after four months of hiding in the hills.

After he told the interpreter about his surrender he spoke rapidly for a moment, and the interpreter laughed.

"He wants to go to America," the interpreter said.

"Houseboy!" yelled the sergeant in clear English, the first English that he had spoken.
                                        —Sgt. Robert MacMillan

The people of Rome—Italian civilians and U.S. GIs—took the news of the Japanese surrender in their stride. There weren't any parades, bells didn't ring, and there were few drunken soldiers. People went about their business as usual, including the girls on the Via del Tritone.

In front of the Ristorante San Carlo, a GI restaurant on the Corso Umberto, there was the usual line of hungry soldiers waiting to eat. Aside from the fact that most of them were grinning as if they'd just heard a joke, they showed little reaction to the news. A big, beefy corporal wearing a Bronze Star ribbon and a blue Combat Infantryman's Badge, with the Red Bull patch of the 34th Division on his shoulder, said, "I don't know. Can't believe it. Only two bombs, and they give up. Don't sound like all that stuff we heard about the Japs fighting to the end. Seems to me there's a catch somewhere. Hey, what the hell's holding up this line?"

Outside the PX Italian kids were begging for cigarettes with "Joe, war *finito*. You give me one cigarette?"

A Nisei staff sergeant from the 442d Regimental Combat Team came out, carrying a paper bag full of rations. He grinned and said, "Wonderful news. Almost too good to be true. I'm anxious to get home. I hope people there'll realize the war's over. But it's sure fine news—best ever."

In front of the Red Cross a gray-haired tech said, "The best news I've ever heard on the radio. It's a funny thing. I came out of an Engineer outfit that's headed for the Pacific. They pulled me out because I got 95 points. I wonder if the boys have left Italy yet. They'll sure have the laugh if they beat me home."

At a sidewalk cafe on the Via Nazionale stood a bald-headed GI who was getting a buzz on. Laughing and sweating, he showed two Italians the well wallet-worn pictures of his wife and kids.

". . . and this garage here, you can just see part of it sticking out from the side of the house. I got the sweetest little Buick, what a car! You *capito* Buick?"

Inside the Florida Club, a GI hot spot, things looked about the same—a band giving out with some strictly Roman-version hot jazz, about 30 couples dancing, and several soldiers singing at their tables. A private who said he was attached to the 34th Station Hospital was drinking with an over-bright thin blonde. The private said, "I don't know why, but the thing sort of sneaks up on you. I started out to raise hell tonight, but somehow I can't get started. It seems hard to believe. No more worrying about points, stripes, or anything. Bud, when I get home now, it's to stay. Maybe when I get home I'll celebrate, really pitch some hell."

"War *finito*," the blonde said. "*Buono*, Americans leave Rome, no?"

It was hard to tell from her voice whether she thought the GIs' leaving Italy would be a good or a bad deal.

The private put his arms around her and said, "Yessir, baby, from now on it's home, sweet home."

"Play 'Home, Sweet Home'," he shouted at the orchestra leader.

A GI at the next table said, "That ain't dancing music."

Near the Calleria Club a Negro sergeant from the 92d Division, wearing a Silver Star ribbon under his Combat Infantryman's Badge, said, "I'm glad we didn't have to invade Japan. That would've been a bitch. Got a brother in the Navy in the Pacific, and I bet he's shouting now."

Inside the club somebody yelled over the music: "When you guys get papers from home now you better start reading the want-ad columns!" The crack brought a wave of laughter.

The Negro GI smiled. "That's a fact. Start thinking about jobs, but after the Army it'll be a pleasure."

It was a little after midnight, and St. Peter's looked very solemn and impressive against the stars. The church was shut. GIs kept coming up and then standing and looking at the church as if they didn't know what to do. One soldier said, "I thought it would be open tonight."

An elderly Italian said that in Italy all churches close at dark.

"I know, but tonight . . ." the soldier said.

At the entrance to the Swiss Guard barracks a heavy-set guard in the ancient uniform of this small army was standing at the gate. His face was expressionless—his army life not dependent on the war's ending or beginning.

On the day when the greatest and most terrible war in world history came to an end, on the day when fascism was finally broken in the world, Rome—where fascism was born—was quiet and orderly. Rome has seen its share of this war. Maybe there should have been a lot of noise and great rejoicing. Here, where people know war, there wasn't shouting, ticker-tape showers, or hysterical parades, but the people were happy. In Rome most people were merely smiling quietly.

—Sgt. Len Zinberg

Berlin, the city that had seen its own brand of fascism and international banditry tumble only a few months before, had little energy left for reaction to the fall of Japan. The Armed Forces' network broadcast the first authentic VJ news at 0210, and most of Berlin's polyglot occupation population, as well as most native Berliners, were asleep.

The U.S. Army newspaper *Allgemeine Zeitung* was the only Berlin paper that carried the news the next day. But the four days of false alarms made even the real thing seem unexciting.

Russian GIs interviewed had the same responses as their American counterparts. Said one of them, typically: "Now maybe I can get home to see my wife and children."

—Sgt. Georg N. Meyers

MAIL CALL

Dear *Yank*:
This is not a gripe; we are only seeking information concerning our pet, a tree-climbing wallaby. We belong to a parachute unit and would like to know how to jump him. We have a chute for him, but we're afraid he'll climb the suspension lines and collapse his chute, killing himself. Now how do we jump him?

—Pfc. A. G. Lukcik
New Guinea

Have you considered a heart-to-heart talk with the wallaby? Ed.

Dear *Yank*:
In a friendly sort of way I would like to ask you why you insist on printing incorrectly such abbreviations as "m sgt, s sgt, Tec 3, Tec 4 and Tec 5" and why you insist on putting a period after each? For authority on the correct use of abbreviations as used in the Army I refer you to AR 850-150 and C1, C2 and C3. It is very difficult to get the officer candidates here to learn correct usage when they see abbreviations misused so often in *Yank*.

—Second Lt. Louie W. Walter
Fort Monmouth,
New Jersey

REULET and ops o/a adm sub Yank sd WP the ex disch of SOP long cont w/ no app by pers at orgn Hq. In other words, we like our own system better. Ed.

Dear *Yank*:
I am 6 feet 7 inches tall and I cannot seem to get placed in any branch or outfit where I fit. When I was drafted they put down my height as 6 feet 4 inches, and I have never been able to get it changed.

I have never been issued any clothing that comes within inches of fitting. I have bought all my class A clothes in order to get off the post on a pass. Since the OD season came on I've been confined to the post because I do not have a proper fitting uniform.

Is there any way I can be discharged on account of my height?

—(Name Withheld)
Fort Monmouth, New Jersey

Dear *Yank*:
I'm only 10 inches short of being six feet tall and have trouble getting clothes to fit. I condemn the practice of basing sizes on "average" measurements. Sizes should conform to actual personal requirements.

Too many people have a cock-eyed view of this problem. They say, "You are too short." I say, "Horsefeathers!" Human beings come in a whole range of sizes.

When asked what size mackinaw I wanted I wasn't sure so I ordered size 38 because I measure 38 inches across the chest. I received a 38, yes, but it fitted me like an Arab's blanket.

—Pfc. Andrew Vena
France

Dear *Yank*:
On the troop carrier I was on, the PX rationed chocolate. One day I purchased a Hershey bar with almonds, as did the soldier in front of me. It developed, upon eating our chocolate bars, that his Hershey contained nine almonds while mine only had seven.

Is this fair?

—T-5 F. O. Nebling
Hawaii

Dear *Yank*:
Several of the boys in Hut 169 at an ATC base in the ETO were distressed after reading an account of an egg-throwing exhibition in New York where Frankie "The Voice" Sinatra was the target.

After perusing said account we have reached

the opinion that the civilian population have damn little to do when they have to resort to eggs for a missile to throw at poor Frankie, especially after these boys have to sweat out a breakfast line seven days a week in order to be served "mechanical eggs."

If they persist in tossing things at poor Frankie why not toss rotten tomatoes or bricks?

Let us save the old-style eggs for the lads overseas.

—T/Sgt. James E. Fitzgibbon
Britain

Dear *Yank*:
I do not like your magazine! It is a "trade" paper for professional soldiers. I am not a professional soldier. There are comparatively few professional soldiers. I like civilian life. I like civilian life pictures. So I can see what I'm missing and fight a bit harder to get back to it. Sad-Sack is O.K. I am O.K. We're all O.K. But *Yank* isn't.

—Cpl. W. H. Dundas
Britain

Dear *Yank*:
I've often heard that three on a match is bad luck. If that is true, what happens to a guy who lights ten on a match? Will he have the same bad luck or more?

—Pvt. A. M. Shirm
Philippines

He would probably burn his fingers. Ed.

Dear *Yank*:
The other day I received this card from a postmaster. My wife sent me a card and the stamp fell off somehow. Now they say if I want this one-cent card I have to send them a one-cent stamp with the card in an envelope with a three-cent stamp on it. Now just to get this card I have to send them four cents. My wife has already put a one-cent stamp on it. This one-cent card will cost us five cents.

I have been overseas 13 months and in two operations and to think they have the nerve to stop a card or letter to a serviceman just for a one-cent stamp. That card would have made me feel very good.

A letter or card from someone we love means more than a good meal to us. Now if I don't send them the one-cent stamp right away they will dispose of it. Why can't they send the card when they know we need writing from home?

Where the hell do they think I can get a one-cent stamp out here?

—Cpl. Francis E. Scully
Ryukyus

Dear *Yank*:
In a recent issue of *Yank* T-5 Nebling stated that the man preceding him in the chocolate bar ration line received nine almonds in his Hershey bar whereas he himself only received seven. We feel that we can clearly clarify the situation by pointing out that through some gross and unpardonable error the other soldier undoubtedly received an officer's Hershey bar.

—Capt. Frank L. Kirby*
Baker General Hospital

Also signed by Lt. Andrew J. Lisman and Lt. Gerard M. Nordone.

Dear *Yank*:
I've been thinking about this demobilization plan. The best way it could be handled is to discharge the men alphabetically.

—Cpl. Robert L. Adams
Tennessee

Dear *Yank*:
Quite a few of us over here would like to say how very sorry we are to be saying good-bye to your boys.

We've had them in our homes ever since they first came over so we feel we're losing many good friends.

Their never-failing cheeriness helped us in our bad times; they were fairy godfathers to our children, and they gave the girl friends the time of their lives.

Their lack of convention was maybe startling at times but it did us good and melted some of our reserve!

We're all very grateful for all you've done for us—and to the memory of those brave boys who will never leave Europe.

Please write to us and in the meantime good luck and Godspeed to a happy journey's end. In your language, it's sure been swell meeting you guys.

—Mrs. E. Wilkinson
Norfolk, England

"Just carry the messages we give you. Never mind the peace propaganda."—CPL. LOUIS JAMME

"Now, before we go any further, is there anyone who doesn't understand what we're doing?"—PFC. JOSEPH KRAMER

When you're on that last lap of Army before getting out, the air is as tense as at induction.

SEPARATION

—Ex-Sgt. MERLE MILLER
Former *Yank* Staff Writer
December 28, 1945

EARLY IN 1942 when I reported to Ft. George G. Meade, Maryland, for induction, fell into my first awkward formation, stripped, was shouted at, jabbed and endlessly questioned, I rather forlornly hoped something would happen to keep me out of the Army of the U.S.

When, recently, I reported to Ft. Dix, New Jersey, for separation and went through what is essentially the same process, I was sure something would happen to keep me in. A friend had been unceremoniously yanked off to an Army hospital for a month when the doctors at Dix decided he had high blood pressure; another had had to stay an extra week to have several cavities filled; a third had been returned to his outfit because, it was discovered, five of the points his company commander had approved were illegal.

But nothing of the sort happened to the 14 men from my outfit who stopped at a bar in Grand Central Station for two quick drinks before buying tickets for Dix.

On our arrival at Dix, we were hurried into a cluttered barracks marked "Incoming Personnel" where a captain, apparently anxious to prove that we were still EM and not civilians, treated us with a studied rudeness, ordered a sergeant to take our records, pointed disdainfully at a bench on which we were to sit and, in a speech of welcome to ourselves and a hundred other prospective dischargees who soon gathered, several times screamed at us to "pipe down, dammit, or I'll keep you here all day."

Then a corporal who wore a Third Division patch handed each of us a white tag on which, he explained, we were to print our last names, initials and serial numbers before tying the tags to our left breast pockets.

After that, the corporal called out our last names; we shouted our first names and middle initials and stepped up to a counter, where we were given our clothing records and then shown down a long corridor, also lined with counters.

Since my clothing had already been turned in at my previous station, I simply showed a bored private the clean shirt, undershirt, shorts and two pairs of socks in my civilian overnight bag.

"Me," said the private, rather testily, "I'm a lucky bastard. I got 20 goddam points. Twenty." Then, as I turned to leave, he added, "Good luck, chum."

At the end of the corridor, we were met by a pfc. who gave us blue cards on which we again printed our names, ranks and serial numbers; then we were herded into a bus and driven to what looked like the company area of any Army post anywhere.

Here we were assigned to a barracks and, once inside, lined up for the usual sheets, pillow cases and GI blankets. As I was making my bunk, slow and easy and being careful to make hospital corners, a weary-looking Fifth Army sergeant said, somewhat sadly, "I'd almost forgotten how, you know, and pretty soon I won't even have to remember."

A sergeant and a corporal were pacing up and down the barracks nervously, chain-smoking but being careful to put each butt in the GI cans conveniently and familiarly placed in front of strategic bunks.

"Anything might happen," said the sergeant. "I had malaria once; they might keep me in for that. Anything might happen."

"A day or so won't matter," the corporal added. "Not after all this time. I mean, even a week or so isn't so much after four years."

They each lighted another cigarette and continued pacing. A few minutes later a permanent-party corporal, who wore a Combat Infantryman's Badge but was obviously on the defensive, came in to tell us there would be a formation at 1645.

"That's 4:45, civilian time," he said.

"How long's it take, corporal?" someone asked him.

"Forty-eight hours," he answered, "after you get on a roster. But it might be a week before you get on one. Might be longer." He said the last somewhat gleefully, as if he hoped it would take longer.

When the corporal left, I dropped off to sleep for what seemed a few minutes, but when I awakened, it was time for the formation. We lined up outside the barracks, almost a hundred of us, and listened to a brash young first lieutenant with a mustache, steel-rimmed glasses and almost no chin.

He talked in what he obviously hoped was GI jargon, repeating a number of stale jokes and advising us as if we were rather backward children that "pitching woo" (as he called it) in the nearby guest house was frowned on. Then, rather quickly, he told us that the Army was as anxious to get rid of us as we were to get out and that we should be on a roster in the morning.

When he dismissed us, an elderly technical sergeant wearing a patch of the Ninth Division gave him a mock salute and muttered, "Thanks a lot, sonny boy."

By then, it was time for chow, and we fell into a fast-moving line in front of the mess hall.

"I hear the KPs are krauts," said the Ninth Division sergeant. "Dirty krauts." They were krauts, looking surprisingly healthy and well-fed.

"Dirty bastards," the sergeant said, but that was all.

The food was good enough, substantial and unimaginative but plentiful, and after chow we looked at the bulletin boards outside our barracks on which the rosters were posted. We knew our names could not possibly be there until morning, but we looked anyway. It made us feel better.

Then we walked to the PX, bought our cigarette ration and waited at a table in the beer garden until it opened. The beer was warm and not very good, but we drank a lot of it.

"Relaxes you," someone said. "That's the only thing about beer. It relaxes you."

We all agreed that it did, and we spent the evening talking about what we planned to do when we got out, and about officers we'd like to meet again, a few because we suspected that they would really be good guys when they weren't officers any more and a good many more with whom we wanted to settle a score.

When the beer garden closed, we were all a little high, but relaxed, really relaxed. I went to sleep as soon as I hit the sack.

After chow the next morning, we hurried to the bulletin boards, and, sure enough, there were most of our names. Those whose names were missing walked slowly back to the barracks.

"I can't prove I'm not still in Casablanca," said one of them. "I'll probably still be here for the next goddam war."

At 10:15 we lined up outside the barracks, and in a careless, desultory formation walked to a Post Theater. It was the old routine again, like basic training.

Everyone filed into the theater quietly and sat down, nobody talking much.

First, there was the chaplain, a huge, hearty man who boomed at us that we were about to be discharged from the Army, and he supposed we were all pretty unhappy about that. It was a bum gag, but everyone laughed appreciatively. Then he explained about our discharge pay, pointing out that it would be paid in monthly installments, one when we got out, another a month later and, for the great majority of us (those who had been overseas), a third payment a month after that.

He bellowed that we probably wouldn't have too much trouble getting adjusted to civilian life —but that we must be patient with other, more settled civilians. Also that dischargees had a lot of trouble with what he called "pitfalls" in and around Trenton, New Jersey. He warned us to hang on to our money.

"I hung on to a hell of a lot more money than he's ever seen long before I got in the Army," said a somewhat dispirited man in the row ahead of me.

When the chaplain had finished, a young lieutenant rather diffidently explained that in the afternoon we would meet our counselor, who would tell us about our insurance and the GI Bill of Rights and answer any questions. Then we were handed a card on which to check the questions we wished to ask our counselors.

A few men made checks on theirs, but many of us didn't.

"If they don't know the answer, they may keep you here until they find out," said a corporal. The majority seemed to agree with him.

My own counselor was a large, red-faced Irish private who obviously enjoyed beer and drank a good deal of it and explained to me that he had been a newspaper man once himself—and, when he got out of the Army, hoped to be again.

"I guess it's kind of a crowded field, though," he said, rather hopelessly. I agreed that it was.

"You want to know anything?" he asked. I said I didn't.

"Hardly anybody does any more," said the Irishman.

Then he carefully filled out my Form 100, listing my jobs in the Army and my civilian experience.

"It might come in handy sometime," he said. "I doubt it, but it might."

Then, quite brusquely, he asked: "You don't want to join the Enlisted Reserve, do you?"

"No," I replied.

"You know," said the private, "I once had a man who did. He was a pretty smart fellow, too. He thought there was going to be one hell of a depression in this country, and he wanted to keep on eating."

The private paused, then added, "But he was the only one, and I've talked to a lot of guys."

After the counseling, we were through for the day and returned to our barracks. On the way, we passed a formation of men carrying their baggage and with the bright golden discharge emblem on their shirts. They grinned at us.

"Hiya, soldiers," one of them said, then repeated, "soldiers," making it sound like a dirty word.

"A lot of things could still happen," said the sergeant with whom I was walking. "The medics hold up a lot of guys."

"I've got varicose veins," said someone else. "I wonder if that'll make any difference." No one answered. We were thinking of our own minor ailments, wondering if they would matter.

We all drank more beer that evening, but it wasn't as much fun as the night before. Civilian life was too close, and there was still the chance that maybe, somehow, for some obscure Army reason, we wouldn't get out at all.

"We might be civilians tomorrow night at this time," said the technical sergeant from the Ninth Division. "Let's drink to it." We did, but it wasn't much of a toast.

When we marched to the dispensary next morning nobody talked much, and once inside we took off our clothes and waited. The examination was much like the one that got us into the Army. The doctors looked at us with the same bored expressions.

While we waited for the blood tests, one man paled visibly.

"I've only been back from Paris ten days," he said. "Tell the truth, I'm a little worried."

"You got a bad cavity there," the dentist said to me.

"I know."

"We'd just as soon fix it, free," he continued

"No," I answered, very politely. "No, thank you very much." The dentist merely shrugged.

After lunch, we turned in our bed clothes and sat down on our empty bunks to wait. The man who could not prove he had left Casablanca was trying to read a book.

"I'll probably have to go back there and then come back here again," he said. "And I'm supposed to meet my girl in New York tonight." He was not even on a roster yet.

When we fell out in front of the barracks with our luggage, the man from Casablanca stood on the porch.

"So long," he said, sadly. "I may not see you again."

We tried to laugh to reassure him, but no one was very successful.

"I heard about a guy that was pulled out at the Finance Office," said the technical sergeant. "It's never too late."

We threw our luggage in a tent that was marked off into compartments, then waited in front of a building marked "Signature Section."

A man had fainted a few minutes before, and the medics had carried him away in a litter.

"They'll probably never let that poor bastard out," said the technical sergeant. He lighted a cigarette, and I was surprised to see that his hand was shaking.

When we got inside the Signature Section, we lined up against a wall and waited until two permanent-party men called off our names. As they reached each name, they placed a folder on a counter, and each man walked over to his own folder.

And then we signed our discharges. I blotted mine in two places. I was still blotting when someone mentioned the Enlisted Reserve again.

At the door we fingerprinted our discharge papers. The corporal in charge of that section was having an argument with a dischargee.

"I just asked you to do it the Army way," said the corporal.

The dischargee said an unprintable word, then added, "USO Commando."

The corporal did not answer, but when the dischargee had gone out the door he said, "I guess it doesn't matter, but I was with the 34th."

Then we walked back and picked up our luggage, waiting outside while a few men ran to another tent to salvage some equipment.

In a few minutes, our guide, a newly inducted private who was an apologetic 18, took us to a squat, unbeautiful building inside of which were rows of men at sewing machines. Each of us had discharge patches sewn over the right pocket of either one or two shirts.

As we put on our shirts again, I felt confident for the first time. But not for long.

"A guy in the barracks got yanked in the Finance Office," repeated the tech sergeant. "Last minute. Been here eight days."

We dropped our luggage in the compartmentalized tent again and walked to the Finance Office. The building was crowded, and our guide told us it would be 45 minutes, at least, before we got in, so we wandered to the PX.

We all ordered Cokes, but none of us drank a full bottle.

A corporal, who had loudly sworn off smoking

but then borrowed a cigarette, lighted it and said:

"You guys finish your Cokes. I think I'll go back."

We all drank a huge gulp of Coke, then set down the bottles and hurried back to the Finance Office. We had been gone exactly five minutes, and we still had almost an hour to wait.

Finally we got inside the building and sat on the same kind of hard benches as in "Incoming Personnel." After about 15 minutes more, they began calling our names, and we stepped up to the cashier's cage, where we were each given $50 in cash, the rest of our pay (minus allotments) in a check, plus the first instalment of our mustering-out pay. Also the small gold discharge button.

As we stepped out into the sunshine again, the tech sergeant smiled for the first time.

"Not a damn thing can happen now," he said. "Not a damn thing. I'm a damn civilian." His eyes were watering, not much, just enough to be noticeable.

When the last man came out of the Finance Office, we lined up quietly and started for the chapel. We knew what was going to happen there; we'd been told at least a dozen times by men who'd already been through it, but we were a little frightened anyway.

An organ was playing when we marched in, wearing our ties and silent, and we sat down in neat rows, while the organist ran through "The Old Grey Mare," "Glory, Glory Hallelujah" and some hymns I didn't recognize.

A chaplain said something. I don't remember what, and then a very old and very small lieutenant colonel stood up, smiling through what were obviously not his own teeth.

I looked out of the window and saw a handful of new arrivals walking with their barracks bags toward a company area, and I didn't want to pay any attention to what the old colonel was saying. It was corn, pure corn, about the Army appreciating what we had done and about how most of us hadn't gotten the breaks we deserved, but it was a big army and we knew how those things are, and finally about the war we'd won and what a great thing we'd accomplished for our great country.

It was obvious that it was a speech the old man had made many times, but I didn't care. I thought it was a fine speech.

When an enlisted man began calling off the names and men began stepping up to the colonel, saluting him, getting his store-teeth smile and a handshake and their discharge papers, I realized I was making a damned fool of myself. I needed a handkerchief and didn't have one. [Ed. Note: We feel obliged to point out that ex-Sgt. Miller is the type that also weeps at movies.]

After I had my own discharge paper and was waiting outside, the tech sergeant came up, grinned at me and said, "I think I could kiss you, but I think I won't." Instead, he just patted me on the back, like a football coach congratulating a player after a winning game.

We walked to where we had left our luggage.

"I was planning to knock the block off that bastard captain we saw when we got here—" said the sergeant. Then he paused.

"—but I don't know why the hell I should bother," he concluded.

As we drove out of the gate a few minutes later, a bus load of men who were obviously potential dischargees was just coming in.

"Hiya, soldiers," I said, and waved. "Soldiers," I repeated.

None of them heard what I said, and it really didn't matter. After all, I was a civilian again.

★

THE ARMY WEEKLY

5¢ DEC. 28, 1945
VOL. 4, NO. 28

By and for men in the service

Army of the United States

Honorable Discharge

This is to certify that

Army of the United States

is hereby Honorably Discharged from the military service of the United States of America.

This certificate is awarded as a testimonial of Honest and Faithful Service to this country.

Given at Washington, D.C.

Date 31 December 1945

Dwight D. Eisenhower

CHIEF OF STAFF

THE GI

—Sgt. DEBS MYERS
Various Editions, 1945

THE CIVILIAN went before the Army doctors, took off his clothes, feeling silly; jigged, stooped, squatted, wet into a bottle; became a soldier.

He learned how to sleep in the mud, tie a knot, kill a man.

He learned the ache of loneliness, the ache of exhaustion, the kinship of misery. From the beginning he wanted to go home. He learned that men make the same queasy noises in the morning, feel the same longings at night; that every man is alike and that each man is different.

Maybe he was white or black or yellow or red, and if he was on the line it didn't make much difference, because a soldier on the line was so dirty you couldn't tell his color anyway.

Maybe he huddled at night in a hole dug in jagged coral or clammy sand and prayed: "God, let me get hit tomorrow but not bad, so I can get out of this." Maybe he didn't fight at all. Maybe he built latrines in Mississippi or cranked a mimeograph machine in Manila, taking chicken, knowing that you can't kill the enemy with a shovel or book at more than ten paces, still wanting to go home.

He was often bored; he wasn't always brave; most times he was scared.

Maybe he was young, like 20-year-old Ed Halpin, who landed at Normandy, H-Hour, D-Day, crawled on his belly up the beach and said: "Goddammit, no matter what place the Army picks to put soldiers, it always picks a place that looks like Oklahoma." Or maybe he wasn't so young, like Jack Privett, a 37-year-old pfc., who was killed in the Battle of Luxembourg and left a wife and five kids back in Blytheville, Arkansas.

Maybe he's just a memory in a photo album now, or a dogtag stuck on a cross of wood near a tiny town whose name you can't pronounce. Or maybe half his face was torn away and he's ashamed to walk down the streets any more because other people are whole and he's not. Maybe he broke his neck slipping on an orange peel in front of a whorehouse in Algiers.

Or maybe he made it. Maybe he came through all right. Maybe no one ever shot at him. Maybe he wonders why he was in the Army—what he did. There was John Padgett, a rifleman from the blue hills behind Chattanooga, who squirted tobacco juice on a bunker of the Siegfried Line and said: "Beats hell out of me what I'm doing here except I always did kinda have an itch to pat my behind at that feller Hitler."

Maybe he didn't know what fascism was—maybe he did. The GI did not destroy fascism. But he helped defeat the fascists and he took away their guns.

He was part of an army that left its bootprints on three continents, a hundred islands—deep in history. With his allies he saved the world; and hoped to God he'd never have to do it again.

He had learned the ache of loneliness, the ache of exhaustion, the kinship of misery. He had learned how to sleep in the mud, tie a knot, kill a man.

And having learned all this, if he got through all right, the soldier came home and took off his clothes, feeling silly; jigged, stooped, squatted, wet into a bottle; became a civilian.

The scribbled names of American soldiers are big and black on the walls of the fortress of Verdun. One of them says:

Austin White—Chicago, Ill.—1918.
Austin White—Chicago, Ill.—1945.
This is the last time
I want to write my name here.

ROLL CALL:
YANK CONTRIBUTORS

Many of *Yank*'s staffers went on to establish themselves as professional writers and artists after the war. Though several of them, inevitably, have since passed away, *Yank*'s influence on contemporary American literature and journalism nevertheless remains unmistakable.

Page(s)	Author	Footnote
14	Jonathan Kilbourn	Jonathan Kilbourn, a Yale graduate, continued his journalistic career as chief editor of *Medical World News*, as Sunday editor of the *Chicago Sun-Times*, and as drama and book review editor for the Sunday *New York Times*. He was 60 when he died in 1976.
37	Ralph Stein	A native of New York City's Yorkville district, Ralph Stein continued his career as a cartoonist/illustrator for various national periodicals during the years following the war, contributing a regular page to *Hearst* weekly magazine. While employed by *Hearst*, he was asked to take over the daily "Popeye" comic strip, which he wrote and drew for a number of years. Eventually giving in to his passion for antique and foreign cars, he authored a number of coffee table books on the history of the automobile, providing both the text and the photography. Mr. Stein presently lives with his wife in Westbrook, Connecticut, and devotes most of his time to his grandchildren.
38	J. Denton Scott	Jack Denton Scott went on to write a number of novels, nonfiction works, and children's books, as well as cookbooks. His 1976 volume *Discovering the American Stork* won for him an American Institute of Graphic Arts Book Show award. Mr. Scott was also a regular contributor to periodicals such as *Collier's, Saturday Evening Post, Cosmopolitan, Holiday*, and *Smithsonian*.
48, 338	Georg Meyers	Georg Meyers, a native of Kansas City, Missouri, had been a reporter for several California and Alaska newspapers before enlisting in the Army Air Corps in May 1942. After his discharge in 1946, he served for a brief time as sports information director for College of the Pacific's football program, under the direction of Coach Amos Stagg, and shortly thereafter became an editor for the *Seattle Times*. He retired in 1984 after covering the Los Angeles Olympic Games for that paper, and continues to author occasional sports and travel pieces from his home in Seattle. Mr. Meyers was awarded both the Bronze Star and the National Headliners' Club Medals in 1944—the former for bravery in battle, and the latter for writing about it.

53	E. J. Kahn, Jr.	Ely Jacques Kahn had been a staffer at the *New Yorker* since 1937, when he was 21. After the war, he wrote a number of nonfiction books, including *Staffs of Life*, *The Problem Solvers*, and *Years of Change*. He also published two volumes on racial rights in South Africa, *The First Decade* and *The Separated People*.

52, 86, 112, 157, 164, 200, 299   George Baker

In 1937, George Baker was faced with a choice between playing minor-league baseball or becoming an animator for Walt Disney. He chose the latter and subsequently worked on such classics as *Dumbo*, *Pinnochio*, *Bambi*, and *Fantasia*. When war broke out, he joined the Army and immediately became an original member of the *Yank* staff. His principal contribution was a droopy, put-upon private whose woeful experience in the service became *Yank*'s first regular feature. Outside of Bill Mauldin's Willie and Joe, the Sad Sack grew to be the most recognizable figure of the war. After his discharge, and for the rest of his life, Baker continued his association with the Sack in comic books and newspapers. George Baker died in Los Angeles in 1975, three weeks before his sixtieth birthday.

64, 247   Ed Cunningham

Ed Cunningham continued writing journalistic pieces after the war, and eventually turned his abilities toward publicity and public relations. He was a PR director for the Celanese Corporation in New York City at the time of his death.

73, 159   Burgess H. Scott

Burgess H. Scott joined the *Ford Times* editorial staff in Dearborn, Michigan, near his home in Detroit, and later published a book entitled *Ford Guide to Outdoor Living*.

80, 115   Dave Richardson

Dave Richardson was a copy boy on the *New York Herald Tribune* when he was drafted in 1941. He received his long-awaited journalistic break when *Yank* made him its first correspondent to the Pacific in 1942. There he obtained the Legion of Merit from Douglas MacArthur for his front-line coverage of New Guinea's jungle combat, and for such exploits as serving as a gunner in a bomber assaulted by Zeros, and as a crew member on a PT boat attacking enemy shipping.

He was transferred to the China-Burma-India theater, where he received the Bronze Star for jumping into battle with Gurkha paratroopers in Burma, manning a machine gun in a bomber detonating enemy bridges, working with a tribal guerilla force, and trooping 700 miles behind Nipponese lines with Merrill's Marauders on a mission to cut off Japanese supplies. For these efforts, he was subsequently awarded the National Headliners Club's Valor Medal.

After the war, Mr. Richardson stayed abroad as a foreign correspondent for many notable newsmagazines; joining *Time*, he covered such events as Gandhi's ascension to power, the Nuremberg trials, the Berlin airlift, the ouster of King Farouk, and the flight to Russia of the British diplomat-spies, Burgess and Maclean. With *U.S. News and*

World Report, he was similarly occupied with the early Cape Canaveral rocket shots, the military takeovers in South America, and Kennedy's Alliance for Progress. Mr. Richardson eventually began directing domestic news bureaus across the country for *U.S. News*, then shifted to Rome as the magazine's chief European correspondent. He retired in 1982 and now lives in Washington, D.C., as a free-lance writer and university lecturer on journalistic ethics.

84, 96 — William Saroyan

William Saroyan, already the author of such classics as *The Time of Your Life* and *The Human Comedy*, went on to write such memorable works as *My Name is Aram* and *I Used to Believe I Had Forever*. He died at the age of 73 in 1981.

155, 229, 235 — Mack Morriss

Mack Morriss, one of the foremost American correspondents during the Second World War, scored his biggest success as one of the first journalists to report from Berlin in 1945, a coup that caused some consternation to the Supreme Allied Command, as Berlin was yet strictly off-limits to the U.S. Army. After 1945, he became a reporter and staff writer for *Life* magazine before returning to his native Tennessee to write a novel, *The Proving Ground*, about his experiences as a Tennessee youth during the war. At the time of his death in 1976, Mr. Morriss was managing radio station WBEJ in his hometown of Elizabethton. He was 56.

99, 110 — Irwin Shaw

Irwin Shaw, already a noted playwright at the time of his enlistment in the United States Army and a regular contributor to the Mediterranean edition of *Stars and Stripes* as well as *Yank*, later became one of the foremost authors in contemporary American literature. His most enduring works include *The Young Lions, Two Weeks in Another Town, Lust for Life* (all three adapted for the motion-picture screen), *Lucy Crown*, and *Rich Man, Poor Man* (the basis for television's first miniseries). Mr. Shaw died in 1984 at the age of 71.

101, 179, 215, 234, 238 — Ralph G. Martin

Ralph G. Martin clearly became the most prolific of *Yank* alumni, turning out over two dozen books between VJ-Day and the present, most of them histories. In addition to a number of titles he coauthored with *Yank* alumnus Richard Harrity, he also wrote *Ballots and Bandwagons, World War II: A Photographic Record of the War in the Pacific, The GI War, Charles and Diana, Golda: The Life of Golda Meir, Jennie: Lady Randolph Churchill*, and *JFK: A Hero for Our Time*.

133 — Walter Peters

Walter Peters was a correspondent for ABC News until the time of his death.

234 — Walter Bernstein

Walter Bernstein developed his craft as a screenwriter and was subsequently blacklisted as a Communist by the House Un-American Activities Committee in the late 1940s. After surviving the era, he went on to write the screenplays for *Fail Safe, A Breath of Scandal, Paris*

Blues, The Molly Maguires, Semi-Tough, and (perhaps not ironically) *The Front*—a comedy-drama about blacklisted television writers.

139	John Bushemi	John Bushemi was killed in action.

142, 165, 342 — Merle Miller

Merle Miller began his professional career with his *Yank* reportage in 1942. At the time of his death four decades later, and at the age of 67, he was known for a number of varied and controversial books, including *Lyndon: A Biography of Lyndon Baines Johnson, Plain Speaking,* a similar volume on Harry S. Truman, *The Judges and the Judged, The Sure Thing,* and *On Being Different,* a frank exploration of his own homosexuality.

148, 334 — Marion Hargrove

Marion Hargrove was already something of a military upstart at the time he began writing for *Yank*; his first book, a tongue-in-cheek volume entitled *See Here, Private Hargrove,* chronicled his experiences as an enlisted man during boot camp and was a runaway bestseller throughout the war—which did little to endear him to Army brass. After VJ-Day, he continued his career as a somewhat irreverent author, and turned out such works as *Something's Got To Give, Marion Hargrove* and *The Girl He Left Behind.*

168, 208 — Saul Levitt

Clearly affected by the politics of war, Saul Levitt continued writing after the Japanese surrender, and was subsequently responsible for the hard-hitting dramas *The Andersonville Trial* and *Trial of the Catons-ville Nine.* He was also a noted film and television writer throughout the 1950s and 1960s, a frequent contributor of articles and short stories to a number of national magazines, and a novelist whose first work, *The Sun is Silent,* was based on his experiences during World War II. Mr. Levitt was 66 when he died in 1977.

176 — Andrew A. Rooney

Like Merle Miller, Andy Rooney's career as an author began with his written works for the United States Army. Immediately after the war, he published a number of his experiences as a soldier and continued professionally with volumes such as *A Few Minutes With Andy Rooney, Not That You Asked, Pieces of My Mind,* and *Word for Word.*

190 — Barrett McGurn

Barrett McGurn, a graduate of Fordham University at the outbreak of war, later became a reporter for both *The New York Times* and the *Herald Tribune,* earning subsequent promotions as the *Trib*'s Rome, and then Paris, bureau chief. He won several awards for best American press coverage from abroad, and authored a number of books, including *Decade in Europe* and *A Reporter Looks at the Vatican.*

223 — Ozzie St. George

Ozzie St. George went into the newspaper business after the war, initially in his hometown of Rochester, Minnesota. He subsequently served, at various times, as a reporter, sports editor, columnist, and copy editor in San Diego and Philadelphia before settling down in St. Paul, Minnesota, where he now resides.

243	Hyman Goldberg	Hyman Goldberg went on to write a number of pieces for the *New Yorker*, *McCall's*, and *Cosmopolitan* before hitting his stride as the author of several hilariously offbeat cookbooks, among them *Man in the Kitchen* and *Beginner's Cookbook*. He wrote a regular cooking column for the New York *Journal-American* under the pseudonym Prudence Penny, which he continued until his death in 1970 at the age of 62. At the time Mr. Goldberg authored the *Yank* piece on Brooklyn, he was a resident of the Bronx.
5, 168, 276	Howard Brodie	Howard Brodie published his World War II experiences in 1963, under the title *War Drawings*. Subsequently, he became a noted newspaper artist, whose courtroom drawings have been seen around the world.
311	Evan Wylie	Evan Wylie, subsequently a reporter for the *Saturday Evening Post*, coauthored an autobiography with Mahalia Jackson entitled *Movin' On Up* after interviewing her for the magazine. He also went on to write a number of books on birth control.
xi, 235, 326, 330	Joe McCarthy	In addition to his reportage in *Yank*, Joe McCarthy was a war correspondent for a number of other news services as well, and later became a major contributor of articles and short stories to publications such as *Look*, *Life*, *Reader's Digest*, *Holiday*, and *McCall's*, in addition to his regular humor column for *American Weekly*. He wrote two travel books, *Ireland* and *New England*, and an early JFK volume entitled *The Remarkable Kennedys*. Mr. McCarthy died in 1980 at the age of 65.
235, 330	Dale Kramer	Unbeknownst to his buddies at *Yank*, Dale Kramer also happened to be a wartime undercover agent for Army Intelligence who subsequently located Iva Toguri (Tokyo Rose) and served as a witness at her trial for treason. He later became a contributor to the *Saturday Evening Post* and wrote a number of books, among them *Heywood Broun*, *Chicago Renaissance*, *The Heart of O. Henry*, *Ross and the New Yorker*, and *A Bull Is Loose*.
333	Knox Burger	Knox Burger, a former editor for *Collier's*, is presently a literary agent in New York City.
236, 349	Debs Myers	A lifetime journalist, Debs Myers was the managing editor of *Newsweek* during the years immediately following World War II, and later became a political advisor to former New York City mayor Robert Wagner, to Adlai Stevenson, and to Robert F. Kennedy. Mr. Meyers died in 1971 at the age of 59.

BIBLIOGRAPHY

Colby, Elbridge. *Army Talk*. Princeton, N.J.: Princeton University Press, 1942.

Cross, Robin. *2000 Movies of the 1940s*. New York: Arlington House, 1985.

Katz, Ephraim. *The Film Encyclopedia*. New York: Perigree Books, 1979.

Rosie the Riveter (Novelty Songs of World War II). Redmond, Wash.: Kilroy Cassettes, 1987.

Life, Editors of. *Life: The First 50 Years*. Boston: Little, Brown, 1986.

Life magazine, 1942–45.

Lingeman, Richard. *Don't You Know There's a War On?* New York: G. P. Putnam's Sons, 1970.

Manchester, William. *The Glory and the Dream*. Boston: Little, Brown, 1974.

Manchester, William. *Goodbye, Darkness*. Boston: Little, Brown, 1980.

Mauldin, Bill. *Back Home*. New York: William Sloane Associates, 1947.

Mauldin, Bill. *The Brass Ring*. New York: W. W. Norton, 1971.

Mauldin, Bill. *Up Front*. New York: World Publishing, 1945.

Music and Sound of World War II, The. Sandy Hook, Conn.: Sandy Hook Records, 1985.

Newcombe, Richard F. *Iwo Jima*. New York: Holt, Rinehart & Winston, 1965.

Newsweek, 1942–45.

Pyle, Ernie. *Here is Your War*. New York: Henry Holt, 1943.

Rhodes, Anthony. *Propaganda—The Art of Persuasion: World War II*. Secaucus: Wellfleet Press, 1987.

Sulzberger, C. L. *American Heritage Picture History of World War II*. New York: American Heritage, 1966.

Terkel, Studs. *The Good War*. New York: Pantheon Books, 1984.

Time magazine, 1942–45.

Troy, Jane Levy. *Holding Together: The World War II Correspondence of an American Family*. New York: (unpublished) 1985.